irene snow

beyond
the dream

iUniverse LLC
Bloomington

BEYOND THE DREAM

iUniverse books may be ordered through booksellers or by contacting:

iUniverse LLC
1663 Liberty Drive
Bloomington, IN 47403
www.iuniverse.com
1-800-Authors (1-800-288-4677)

ISBN: 978-1-4759-8254-1 (sc)
ISBN: 978-1-4759-8256-5 (hc)
ISBN: 978-1-4759-8255-8 (e)

Library of Congress Control Number: 2013905364

Printed in the United States of America

iUniverse rev. date: 08/30/2013

To my teachers, with love . . .
and in fond memory of my BFF, Louise, whose loving
presence I will deeply miss along my journey.

Table of Contents

Acknowledgments

A book is much like a blossom. It begins as a tiny seed which, if properly nurtured, eventually becomes a flower.

A special thank-you to my grade IX English teacher for originally planting the seed in the fertile soils of my young mind.

There are surely no words to sufficiently thank my mother whose abiding love, patience, and wisdom were amongst my life's most cherished gifts. I will always be grateful for her constant support, and her gentle nourishment of the fragile seed of my dream throughout the many years I was blessed with her care.

My profound gratitude to my long time psychiatrist, mentor and friend, whose comforting presence was a solace in my dark hours, and whose expert medical help released me from the throes of agoraphobia. Moreover, he unfailingly nurtured the original seed of this book, thus ensuring it would eventually flower.

Heartfelt appreciation to my naturopathic doctor for her expert care, and for wisely sustaining the seed.

Special kudos to my editor at iUniverse whose amazing editorial evaluation led me to developing a sturdier flower. I also convey my sincere thanks to Rebekka P., my check-in co-ordinator, and to George Nedeff, my editorial consultant–both from iUniverse–for their constant patience, encouragement and support.

A much-deserved note of acclaim to my online editor, Teresa, @ http://www.a-1editingservices.com/. Her great edits, helpful comments and excellent advice have helped me expand my former boundaries of literary growth. Any mistakes in transcribing her edits are chiefly my own.

Last, but not least, I thank my husband who tended the bud as it grew, ensuring it would flourish and blossom. Without his enduring love, support and patience it would have been hard-pressed to come to fruition.

To the above individuals who, for purposes of keeping this story confidential, have been unnamed, I hope you know who you are!

May God bless you all!

Irene

Author's Note

Dear friends:

I invite you, with love, to join me on my journey. Those of you who accompany me may find my path quite similar to your own: a dark, winding road interspersed with sporadic patches of much-welcome light. It is this light which joins my heart with yours. It is this light that is my story . . . and yours as well.

At the time of this writing I am in the winter of my years, a very ordinary person with no particular credentials. Most of my adult years were spent as a wife, homemaker, and stay-at-home mom. My formal education ends with the completion of high school; so I speak to you solely from the knowledge I've garnered from self-study, added to the years I have lived, the latter which touch upon the pain we have *jointly* suffered by collectively traversing life's road. In this sense, I speak to you from my heart.

The desire to understand my self-defeating behaviour led me first to the field of psychology which gradually provided me with a smattering of insight into the far-reaching consequences of the early wounds that eventually give birth to the ego's defense system. Intrigued, I began digging deeper, and eventually it became apparent that our buried sores do *not* heal; they merely scab over and continue to fester beneath the surface, pervading our future years with poisons from the past of which we are largely unaware.

I address these issues along with a sprinkling of beautiful spiritual truths from *A Course in Miracles*–all of which have lightened my burden and led me to a happier place. By relaying these disclosures periodically throughout my memoirs, in brief, italicized inserts, I'm of the hope you may gain a broader understanding of your own underlying "shadow"–whilst bearing in mind that the best one can strive for is to merely scratch the surface of self or soul.

As part of the One Soul, we share a path of evolvement that will eventually lead us back to the Love that we are . . . beyond the illusion of this lifetime.

My story does not involve an instantaneous, or miraculous, redemption. Moreover, it is about visualizing the healing light in the distance that lovingly invites us to fuse with it; for *we* are that light. *God's Light.*

Let us walk together in Love, within the immutable knowledge that His most profound blessings accompany us.

Yours in love and friendship,

Irene

PART I – the guest house

This being human is a guest house,
Every morning a new arrival.

A joy, a depression, a meanness,
Some momentary awareness comes
As an unexpected visitor.

Welcome and entertain them all!
Even if they're a crowd of sorrows,
Who violently sweep your house
Empty of the furniture,
Still, treat each guest honourably,
He may be clearing you out
For some new delight.

The dark thought, the shame, the malice,
Meet them at the door laughing,
And invite them in.

Be grateful, for whoever comes,
Because each has been sent....
As a guide from beyond.
—Rumi

Prologue

"Monsters are real, and ghosts are real too.
They live inside us, and sometimes, they win."
—Stephen King

APRIL 30, 2012, MONDAY

It is a month today since my husband and I have returned from our winter getaway in Florida. Spring has always been my favourite season; yet today, as I see the tender, breathtaking buds of new life all around me, a profound sorrow weighs heavily upon my heart.

My beloved grandson, Gary, has been recently diagnosed with stage three Hodgkin's lymphoma. He's only fourteen. He'll begin chemotherapy tomorrow. Such a long, scary journey ahead of him! Yet he's being so brave and positive.

I long to be proactive in some way, but it's just my daughter and her husband who will be with him during his treatments. It's as they wish, and it's perhaps as well. I know, in the past, I've been mentally fragile. I'm still trying to get beyond that; but of late, I have once again become unsure of my strength. And if there's anything Gary needs right now, it's for those around him to be strong.

I find myself weeping off and on, the tears flowing of their own accord. My heart constricts painfully in the knowledge that Gary's diagnosis has brought me full circle. Now, as the camera of my mind pitilessly and obsessively projects reruns of a bad film I once viewed a long time ago, my past cruelly melds into my present.

The familiar stirrings of fear and panic roil within me, and I am becoming deeply afraid that my inner monster—the one that has lain quiescent for years—will rear its ugly head again and toss me back into the murky, black abyss which was once my home.

How well I remember that home. The *House of Darkness* where light fails to shine. It seems that from the moment of birth, every day of my life was leading me to it. To that very moment when the abyss would encase me and the monster that dwelled therein would claim me as its own.

My mind drifts back over the years, to the beginning . . .

Chapter 1 – Queen of the Castle

"I'm the queen of the castle,
and you're the dirty rascals."
—Childhood rhyme

It's the first week of April in the year 1941. The world is at war. Mommy is in labour, and I am in the process of being born. My soldier daddy won't be here to greet me. He was shipped overseas from our home in Cassellman, Canada last autumn.

I'll be living with Mommy and my maternal grandparents until the war is over. It may be a long one. Nobody knows.

Years pass and I'm far from unhappy. Being an only child and sole grandchild to two sets of doting grandparents, and my uncle's only niece, I'm the apple of everyone's eye. I've grown quite accustomed to being queen of the castle, and am probably more than a little spoiled.

I've shared a bedroom with Mommy for as long as I can remember. I've also shared her big double bed. Curled up against her warm flesh every night, snug and secure, I have valued this arrangement; yet taken it for granted that her bed is my rightful place.

A cold dose of reality awaits me.

The year 1945 arrives and heralds the end of the Second World War.

"The war is over, honey," my mother says gently. "Your daddy's coming home soon, and he's most eager to meet you. It's high time you become used to sleeping in your own room now, like the big girl you are. Mommy's going to make you up a bed on the pull-out couch in the *little room* and you'll start sleeping there. You'll be just down the hall from Mommy, and you'll be absolutely fine."

I, for one, don't think so. I feel abandoned and afraid in that small, gloomy, windowless den which inherited its name *little room* in view of its size. It reminds me of those horrifying moments when I found myself all alone in a downtown department store just a few short weeks ago. It started with me begging Mommy for an ice cream cone which she absolutely refused to buy me. I pled and cajoled, hoping she'd change her mind. Finally, she told me to shut up, or else.

I vividly recall the scene that follows when, furious and in a last ditch effort to get my own way, I throw myself on the floor and begin shrieking and kicking my feet. The first traces of fear beset me when Mommy fails to respond. I become wary and slyly peek through my lashes, but fail to spot her anywhere. She's gone! Vanished! Waves of blinding terror flood over me. My mommy has left me. Frantic, I jump to my feet and start screaming hysterically. *"Mommy! MOMMY!"* I shout her name, over and over. Finally, she re-appears, seemingly out of nowhere. I throw my arms around her and cling to her skirts, sobbing my eyes out.

"If you ever, *ever* pull a tantrum like that again," she vows solemnly, "Mommy will leave you and *never* come back!"

At four years of age, two frightening events had coincided to diminish my security: the first being a taste of potential abandonment by my mother in a department store, followed by being cast out of her bed. In both cases it was as though the rug had been pulled out from under me.

I believe it is around that time that I became overly fearful of being separated from my mother. Future circumstances would not only contribute to increasing this fear, but to rooting it more firmly as well.

Secluded in my new sleeping quarters, I often awaken from nightmares and run to Mommy's room for comfort. At such times, she always relents and allows me back into her bed, enfolding me in her arms until I fall asleep and all is well in my world.

This privilege is soon to come to an end.

A week or two later my daddy appears in full khaki uniform. He's a big, boisterous man with a crop of auburn hair and twinkling blue eyes. After hugging and kissing Mommy for what seems like forever, he spies me beside her in the foyer.

"So, *this* is my little girl? I'm *delighted* to finally meet you!" he bellows in his rich, sonorous voice. He sweeps me up in his muscular arms and tosses me high above his head, then catches me with ease. Momentarily stunned, I yowl in fear. Nobody has ever played rough with me before. Unlike my gentle uncle and grandfather, even his voice is frightening.

Later, when he invites me to open a huge box of presents, I am far too overwhelmed to remain fearful. I wade through a myriad of interesting items: genuine wooden shoes from Holland, a silver necklace of English coins, dolls from various European countries, and much, much more. I can hardly contain my joy, and I'm feeling very well-disposed towards this strange man who has just entered my life and calls himself my daddy.

Bedtime arrives before long, but I've now become somewhat used to being relegated to the *little room*. I check the closet for monsters before bedding down and, for the very first time, my new daddy joins my mommy to kiss me goodnight.

Sometime later I awaken, frightened from a bad dream. I hasten to Mommy for the usual solace. I'm quite shocked when the small night lamp is switched on and I see Daddy in her bed. He glares at me angrily, and shouts, "Go back to your room this instant!"

As I stand there immobilized, he booms explosively, "*Did you not hear me, young lady?*"

I hear Mommy plead, "Joe, she's just a child, and she's afraid."

"Yes and a cheeky brat at that!" Like a flash of lightening, he bolts out of bed and strikes me forcefully across my buttocks. "*Now!*" he bellows.

Suddenly, my little legs are mobile again. And my little heart is broken. Nobody has ever struck me before and I'm devastated. I glare at him, with what he'll later contend is one of the dirtiest looks he's ever seen, and stomp off to my room.

Once back in my own bed, I await Mommy's comforting footsteps. In vain. Herewith, I have experienced my first actual taste of rejection. Mommy has chosen this stranger over me. It's *his* fault, and I'm consumed with a rage and jealousy heretofore alien to me. At age four, for the first time in my young life, I've learned the emotion of hate. He has stolen my most prized possession: my mother.

Many years later I realize my unexpected appearance undoubtedly put a damper on my parents' first moments together in five long years. In my child's mind, however, the occasion was destined to set an unhappy precedent that would linger throughout my growing-up years with my new and unwanted father. The damage done in those few moments, and similar ones to come, would be irreparable; its poison destined to seep into later affairs of the heart and to contaminate them as well.

A decade or so later, my chickens would be coming home to roost.

Chapter 2 – Dethroned by the King

"If the world didn't suck we'd all fly into space."
—<u>Anonymous</u>

D addy has seized my crown and become the new reigning monarch. He is the king of the castle and the lord and master of both me *and* Mommy. I am not exactly shouting "Long live the king!" from the hilltops.

Due to postwar food shortages, families are provided with monthly stamps to comply with rationing. Each family is allotted a specific food quota. I am soon to determine that the king consumes steak whilst the peasants eat sausages. This is to continue long after these stamps become redundant.

"Why does he always get the best of everything?" I question Mommy one day.

"He's the man of the house, and he works hard every day to support us. It's a wife's duty to take care her husband. If he were to become sick, how could he look after us?"

"I think you love *him* more than me," I reply haughtily.

"That is just not true, honey. You are my little girl, and if it came to a choice, as a mother I would always choose you first."

"I don't believe you. He *always* gets the best, and I *hate* him. And I hate you, too!" I cry, as I stomp off to my room.

In short order, I am to realize the problem of having a new daddy

9

is something I can't ignore. It won't be going away anytime soon. I am stuck with it, and will have to learn to deal.

Deal I do, from lack of choice. Deep down, I never fully accept it.

We are now living in a two-bedroom wartime house in the east end of the city which is in close proximity to the army base where Daddy is stationed. He plans to continue his career in the armed forces. He had never been happy at Granny's home. He believed she interfered with his discipline of me, the latter which he was gung-ho to take over himself. His pleasure at leaving my grandparents' home was in direct contrast to my dismay.

Momentarily, my mind drifts back to one of the incidents which especially displeased him. I was having breakfast with him at Granny's dining table and watching with interest as he poured some Worcestershire sauce on his eggs.

"May I have some of that sauce, too, Daddy?" I ask.

"Condiments are not good for children," he snaps.

I, of course, have no idea what condiments are, and I am longing to try this great looking stuff on my own eggs. I begin pleading. Finally, he pours out a spoonful.

"Okay," he complies, "but you'll want to taste it first. Now, remember, you begged for it!"

Elated, I swallow the lot. As fiery flames scorch my mouth, I cry out in anguish.

"Drink some water," he says drolly. "Perhaps next time you'll understand when I tell you something is not good for you."

I have to concede his point. I nevertheless run crying to Granny. Her horror is my usual balm. Appalled, she sternly reproaches him for being so unkind to a mere child. I will later sorely miss running to her, the one person who has *always* been my champion, even protecting me from Mommy's occasional wrath.

Daddy's resentment cannot be contained however, and within a relatively short interval he moves out and goes to live in the army barracks. "If you want to have a life with me," he warns Mommy, "it won't be with your mother. I suggest you find a place for us to live in your spare time."

For a long while, I will blame Daddy for tearing me away from my gentle grandparents in whose home I have been queen, and loved unconditionally.

Once adjusted to my new life, however, I actually begin to enjoy it in certain ways. At Granny's flat in the heart of the city, Mommy never let me play alone on the street, and I never knew the joy of having friends my own age. Here in the suburbs there are kids in droves and I soon have many pals.

On the positive side of my relationship with my dad, I recall many good times we shared. Mommy endures several miscarriages and is finally told it's dangerous to become pregnant again. I become the son he never had by default.

I learn at a very young age from Mommy that my daddy is an only child who lost his own father when he was only seven years old. His mom–desperately needing a job and having no marketable skills other than domestic ones–was eventually hired as a live-in cook and housekeeper to a well-heeled family who did not have the generosity of heart to take in her little boy as part of the package. Deprived of choice, she had to place him in a boys' home for the next seven years–a rough and tough place where one had to protect one's food or lose it, and where learning to fight was part of survival. One of Dad's earliest conclusions was: It's a dog-eat-dog world where only the fittest survive.

On becoming "his son" he aimed to pass this knowledge on to me.

Determined to make a man out of me, he begins to teach me "guy things". He starts with fishing, and together we dig up night crawlers for lure. He insists I bait my own hook on the small wooden rod he has carved for me, and I soon become dauntless at manoeuvring the

11

squiggly worms that originally made me cringe. He is proud of me, and I bask in his positive praise.

He also brings me on snake hunts. We set off into the fields with forked sticks and capture the reptiles we occasionally find hidden under large, flat rocks. At times, we tote a large one home and can barely contain our amusement when Mommy absolutely freaks out before we free it. On our many nature hikes, he teaches me the names of all the flowers and trees and how to survive in the wilds.

He insists that I fight my own battles outdoors. He does not want me to come snivelling to Mommy or him. He often says my grandparents have made a sissy of me, and I'm determined to prove him wrong. Much to his great satisfaction I become a regular street scrapper, fearlessly taking on even the toughest of my peers with no hesitation.

As an army brat, my fondest moments are spent at the Olympic-sized swimming pool and in the mess hall, both located on the base. Daddy acquires a swimming pass for my personal use, and as the pool is only a fifteen minute jaunt by foot from our home, I am eventually permitted to go on my own. I especially enjoy the mess hall where movies are shown tri-weekly, a great source of entertainment for the military parents and their kids alike.

Daddy, a champion swimmer in his youth, spends many hours in the army pool with me as my personal instructor. He draws upon every morsel of his patience, along with his wealth of aquatic knowledge, in order to ensure my particular success as a swimmer. I later become aware he has hopes of vicariously reliving his dream of becoming an Olympic swimmer, through me.

Meanwhile, the downside of our relationship continuously creeps in.

My parents are both quick to anger and have many arguments. Daddy occasionally spends time at the mess hall enjoying a few beers with his buddies after work. This habit does not sit well with my mommy, especially when she has our evening meal waiting for him and he fails to show. Sometimes she becomes so mad that she flings his food all over the floor.

They also do battle over me. Mommy believes his disciplinary measures are much too harsh. Their various arguments tend to get out of hand at times. Provoked by Mommy's verbal outbursts, Daddy sometimes loses it and backhands her across the face. Once when I intervene, shrieking, "Please, please, don't hit my mommy," he sends me flying across the room. In the aftermath of such fights, Mommy usually calls a taxi and we end up spending the night at my grandparents' home.

On these occasions, and similar ones which appear particularly auspicious to my cause, I beg her to divorce him. I understand that divorce means he will be gone from our lives, and I think, *Hallelujah!*

"Let's leave him, Mommy," I cajole. "I really hate him."

"I don't want to *ever* hear you say that again, Irene," she reprimands me. "It is not nice to say you hate *anyone*. He's your father and he loves you. I know it's not an ideal situation for you; but nor is it for him. Because of the war, you met too late and you're unable to acknowledge him as your rightful father. This causes *both* of you a lot of pain. Whether you like it or not, I do love your father and want to make a life with him. But even if that were not the case, I'm poorly equipped to enter the work force and look after you as a single parent, and your dad could not afford to support us in separate homes. I truly think it's for the best that we cast our lot in life together as a family."

I can*not* relate to her thinking. Unable to see beyond my green-eyed monster, I am sorely pissed.

There is no doubt I'm afraid of my father. He's irascible by nature, exceedingly strict and not averse to spanking me when he considers I need it. He has been brought up by the old adage that "Children should be seen and not heard" and he staunchly adheres to it. I soon learn not to talk back to him, even as an explanatory reason for something I've done. He has dubbed me a cheeky brat from day one, and he sees no relevance in my explanations. Nor has he any inkling to hear them. I soon learn to keep my lip buttoned which is preferable to enduring the pain of his big hands smacking my bare buttocks.

My feelings of helplessness lead to the constant suppression of anger and rage. Aside from our occasional lighthearted excursions together, we are too often at loggerheads to ever truly bond.

Evening meals are mainly a curse. Determined that I learn to eat like a well-bred lady Daddy constantly monitors my eating habits, which generally fall short of his standards. If I fail to hold my knife or fork in the proper manner, he whacks my knuckles with his dinner knife. Before the meal is halfway through I'm reduced to tears. In sympathy, Mom sometimes intervenes by pleading my case, "Joe, please try to be patient. She's just a child."

Her words only serve to further inflame him, and he angrily retorts something to the effect of: "I am sick and tired of your interference whenever I try to discipline her. She'll not learn anything from your attempts to constantly shield her. It's you and your parents that have made her into the spoiled brat she is. Just keep out of it!"

In order to keep peace, Mom generally obliges. She also fears his wrath.

The movies at the mess hall on Wednesday and Friday evenings, and Sunday afternoons are the highlight of my week. After the film is over, it's a special delight to play with the other army children. Before long however, Dad calls a halt to my play time.

"I will not have *my* daughter running around and disturbing everyone's peace like those other little hooligans. Once the movie is over, you will sit in your chair like a lady and *stay* there!" he commands.

Confined to my chair and enviously watching the other kids having fun, I am again overcome with hostility towards this stranger who has walked into my life and taken it over.

Sometimes, I see him as a very old man confined to a wheel chair. I visualize myself shoving his chair down a very steep incline, whilst reveling in the knowledge that I have finally subjected him to tasting the fear he all too often instills in *me*. For now, when sent to my room, the best I can do is to shake my little fists at the stupid toddler picture of him that Mommy has installed on my wall. I stick out my tongue at his image, and make other rude gestures of contempt.

Time moves inexorably on, and our differences are never fully reconciled. We both vie for Mommy's affections and I, for one, smugly gloat when it comes to light that my rival is in the doghouse.

At some point I become aware that my mother has dubbed me a nervous child. I occasionally hear her say to friends, "Irene's extremely high-strung and temperamental. She's often moody, and frankly I don't know what to do with her."

At times, she quips, "Is this the good Dr. Jekyll who just came in, or is it the evil Mr. Hyde?" This, I suspect, arises from either my moody ways or from the "cruel tongue" she often accuses me of having when I'm angry or upset.

One poem in particular, which I only learn much later was written by Longfellow, becomes a precept she devotes exclusively to me. She often quotes its expressive words: "There was a little girl, who had a little curl, right in the middle of her forehead; when she was good, she was very, very good, but when she was bad, she was horrid." I believe she did this in fun; yet I nevertheless interpreted a subtle, underlying message that would never really leave me: *You are not a particularly nice person, Irene.*

Not being a placid child, I have difficulty sitting still for any length of time, along with a short attention span—unless, of course, a topic completely captivates me. Often Mom yells at me, "That's *enough* running about! *Sit!* For God's sake, *SIT!*" Confined to a chair with nothing to do, my limbs begin to thresh and flail in a state of constant movement until she finally shouts, "*Stop it! Stop that fidgeting! What the hell's the matter with you? Do you have St. Vitus's Dance?*" I learn that this is some form of movement disorder. Had I been born in a future generation, I'm left to wonder if I'd have been drugged to the hilt with Ritalin.

Unable to have more children, Mom tends to worry about my health excessively. During the 1940's and early 1950's polio is rampant in kids and she's constantly stressed that I may succumb to it. Her concern is not limited to polio. She frets over my every ache and pain, and at an early age her fears become my own.

Apart from being a nervous child, I learn to be a fearful one as well.

I am also an extremely imaginative kid, and quite creative. I begin writing poetry at a very young age and I excel in composition. I also love to paint and draw. My vivid imagination invariably has its dark side. My childhood monsters become very real and fill me with dread. At night in bed, I'm often afraid. At such times, I long to be a grown-up. I'm convinced that big people have no fears, and I profoundly wish I were a big person myself.

I've never had much liking for school. I've learned early to resent authority. I'm neither enthralled with my teachers nor the school work itself. I'm often disciplined for daydreaming in class. A frequent remark on my report card reads to the effect: *Irene has the intelligence but lacks the initiative.* This does not sit well with either of my parents, especially my dad.

I could care less.

I start the first grade early, at age five, and am only thirteen by the time I reach ninth grade in 1955. For the first term, school proceeds in its usual fashion. I apply myself as little as possible, with one exception: my genuine love of writing requires I devote quality time constructing my compositions. As it happens, my homeroom teacher is also my English teacher, and she becomes impressed with my writing skills. In time she makes an icon of me. Without exception, she asks me to read my essays to the class. She seems to revere my work, and she sets me up as a prime example to the rest of the students. It's the first time I've ever been recognized or even much liked by a teacher and I bask in the glow.

Following my first-term report card, Miss Steel privately calls me aside. "Irene," she says kindly, "I've seen your I.Q. test results, and you're a brilliant young girl. What I can't understand is that your marks do not in the least reflect your intelligence. You could be at the top of the class, and you are not. I wonder why that is?"

Speechless, I shrug, then stammer, "Do you m-mean I could do

16

as well as *The Brain*, uh, I mean Barbara Weldon?" This particular student maintains averages in the 90's.

"Most definitely, my dear. It's just a matter of balance. If you could give your other subjects even *part* of the effort you devote to your compositions, you would be in your rightful place at the top of the class. And I would be so proud to see you where you belong," she adds pointedly.

How I love this lady who seems to truly care about me! Following our talk, I begin applying myself to all of my studies for the very first time. My most important goal is to live up to her expectations and make her proud of me. Proud, she will be. Along with my parents, who will reap their own benefits—all from the amazing efforts I'm about to display for my beloved teacher.

I make a complete turnabout. I even approach my dad, much to his surprise and pleasure, and cultivate his help with my math. When my second-term report card reveals a mark in the nineties in both algebra and geometry he's beside himself with pride. My parents' exaltation over the unexpected shift in my marks pleases me greatly, but pales in comparison to the joy I derive from my teacher's personal gratification. Within my adolescent mind I construe her concern as a beautiful and unconditional thing, and I am to carry a genuine love in my heart for that special lady for a lifetime.

Shortly after completing my June finals, I'm confronted with the news that Dad is being posted to Lone River in another province and will be leaving when school lets out for the summer. This is mighty *good* news. He's had a few brief postings in the past, and Mom and I have held the fort on our own until his return which has not led to any change in my lifestyle. Except perhaps for the better, because he's absent. No such luck this time. This posting is for two years and the *bad* news is that Mom is adamant about going with him.

"We'll be following him in late August, once our house is sold and he has obtained living quarters for us in Karlstown," she informs me. Karlstown is the closest town to the Lone River army base that harbours a high school.

I couldn't be more distraught. I'll be leaving Jane, my very best friend. She, too, is an only child, and we have grown up together like sisters. Ever since age five, we have practically lived in each other's homes.

I sorrowfully convey this news to Miss Steel and we promise to keep in touch with each other by letter. She takes this opportunity to congratulate me on my good work.

"I knew you could do it, Irene," she beams. "I understand you've surpassed yourself on your final exams as well. Always remember, you're a highly intelligent young woman, and I believe you will be a great writer someday."

This remarkable lady and her belief in me has always been an inspiring force in regard to my writing and I believe, beyond doubt, that her loving presence was no accident in my life.

Everything seems to move quickly thereafter. Our house sells and our furniture is temporarily put in storage and will be transported to our new residence when applicable. Meanwhile, we move into a furnished, studio apartment that rents by the month where we reside until Dad drives home in late August to deliver us to Karlstown. Once on the road to our new home, I sit in the back of the car weeping disconsolately until he's finally had enough.

"If you don't stop that damn blubbering, I'll give you something to really wail about," he warns.

I quell the flood of tears that I allowed to escape . . . from the dam of impotent rage that remains wisely suppressed.

Chapter 3 – A Kindred Spirit

"A single rose can be my garden . . .
a single friend, my world."
—<u>Leo Buscaglia</u>

Finally, we arrive in Karlstown. Our new residence is a small apartment designed to serve our needs for the next two years.

I'm feeling very alone and conspicuous as I climb the stairs of my new high school on the first day it re-opens in early September. I know nobody and I don't even have a sibling with whom I can share this ordeal.

Following a few days of being totally ignored by my peers, I'm trudging home rather gloomily one afternoon when a classmate who is walking in my direction initiates a conversation with me. We have at least a mile's walk ahead of us to my place and it's even further along the same route to hers. This gives us plenty of time to become acquainted. She tells me her name is Lou, and by the time we reach my apartment building we've become fast friends and I invite her in. Mom, pleased I have found a pal, welcomes her warmly and serves us homemade brownies and milk.

And so begins the Lou/Irene connection. From that day forward we're inseparable. She introduces me to other girls who share *with* us but are not a part *of* us. It's her and me above all others. We've become Siamese twins, joined at the hip.

Life takes on a whole new meaning. She's a fun person who Mom will later believe has "led me down the garden path". A willing follower, I am nevertheless quite capable of taking the reins myself. In hindsight, we were not bad kids. We both had little or no interest in school work, and even less in our teachers.

In September 1956, the beginning of our second year in Karlstown, Elvis Presley makes his first debut on the Ed Sullivan show. Lou and I watch him agog, absolutely star struck over this gorgeous hunk of a man with his alluring voice, come-hither looks, and seductive movements. We both fall madly in love with him, and when his first movie *Love Me Tender* hits the theatre we watch it at least three times, finally leaving to go home because we must. Just about every afternoon after school we roll up Mom's living room rug and learn to jive together to his up-tempo songs such as *Hound Dog*, *Teddy Bear*, and *Don't be Cruel*.

We also begin skipping classes whenever a propitious opportunity presents itself. We take up smoking cigarettes as well. We sometimes go out with the young soldiers from the Lone River army base, but–not liking to be separated–we usually double-date. Mainly, we are carefree, mischievous, and fun-loving, which becomes a cause of concern for our parents who often try to separate us, especially when they find out we're playing hooky from school. At such times we see each other on the sly, until finally our folks become aware of our clandestine meetings and realize they would have to lock us up indefinitely to ever accomplish the impossible feat of totally separating us.

I manage to pass my tenth grade, as does Lou, albeit barely. While confined to my room for "homework time" there is always a romance magazine nearby which can be quickly hidden beneath my quilt if I hear my door open. Consequently, I have to cram for exams.

My eleventh grade progresses in a similar manner. After being caught playing hooky and suffering the consequences the previous year, which amounted to 32 detentions each and a memorable beating for me from my dad, we nevertheless remain intrepid. We resume our old tricks, but in a more calculated manner, and do not get caught again.

We share everything, from clothing to our small, weekly allowance. Our friendship is devoid of the competitiveness or sibling rivalry that is usual in sisters or friends. Conversely, our relationship consists of a deep and genuine, egoless love heretofore unknown to us . . . a love that will shape both of our lives. A brief love we will take to the grave and beyond.

I expect it is not an exactly unhappy time for my parents when my eleventh grade is over and Dad's posting is finished.

For me, leaving Lou is my first actual brush with genuine grief. We were joined at the hip, but the parting has left us severed at the heart.

MAY 1, 2012, TUESDAY

Gary begins his first 21-day cycle of chemo today which will include four treatments in the first week followed by a two-week break. He will undergo a similar cycle prior to being re-accessed. His oncologist told Eve, his mother, that despite his cancer being in an advanced stage it's one of the more curable ones. His cure stats are 85%. This news is positive and I try not to think of the 15% who comprise the dark side.

I reflect upon my studies of *A Course in Miracles (ACIM)*, a beautiful book recognized today as one of the most profound spiritual teachings of all time. A book dictated over a seven year period in the 1970's to a renowned psychology professor, Helen Schucman, by an inner voice which identified itself as Jesus.

It has become my personal Bible and has given me a much clearer perspective of life. Now, as I question why this horror should befall such a good, loving, and amazingly gifted child such as Gary, I recall its teachings:

Jesus assures us that, as God's invulnerable Spirits, nothing can happen to any one of us that is outside, or apart from, our own personal choice.

While it's difficult to believe anyone would choose suffering as part of their Earth school curriculum, it's our higher self alone that is fully aware of the lessons most necessary for the growth of our souls—some which are karmic and others experiential. Our pre-birth choices are also geared to the needs of other souls—as were those of Jesus when he chose the cross. Thus, we become one another's helpmates and guides as we learn and grow collectively, with pain our greatest teacher.

ACIM also teaches us there is only "one reality": As part of God, we are "spirit", not "body"; and whatever is "not real" is "illusion". Since it's impossible to actually separate from God, we have "imagined" our illusory world and bodies. And we have projected these images onto the screen of time and space, that we may know ourselves as self-conscious beings. And this we have done, time and again—over many lifetimes.

It is comforting to know that—no matter how we err, or how many

22

lifetimes it takes—our reality as children of God cannot be threatened. ACIM sums this up quite simply in its powerful introductory words: "Nothing real can be threatened. Nothing unreal exists. Herein lies the peace of God."

ACIM also brings to mind the precept my maternal grandmother lived her life by: *All things work together for the good for those who love God.* I embrace her trust and pray—especially during this distressing time—that it may be my own.

Now, as I sit with my husband Len in the lobby of Toyota awaiting the oil change on our car, he suggests I write a poem for Gary. I finally come up with two verses which I hope will bring Gary good cheer and I sign the poem: *With love and blessings from Grandma. Never forget you are destined for great things!* He will know what I refer to, as he's an accomplished pianist.

GARY, THE BRAVE

Gary, the Brave, beware of his sword,
Winning Life's battles, he never gets bored;
Be near him, yet fear him, for one can't afford,
Not to be awed by the victories he's scored.

He slays mighty dragons whilst questing for good,
He's feared and revered as "the engine that could";
For eons ago, he knew that he would,
Grace Life's sacred byways where angels have stood.

Once home, I open my laptop and continue the journal I began writing yesterday. Being occupied, and not dwelling on things, helps keep my monster at bay.

Jen, my naturopathic doctor, has been a great help. When I e-mailed her about Gary's diagnosis yesterday, she fit me in for a speedy appointment this morning. It's she who rekindled my interest in poetry when she strongly urged me not to allow my creativity to wither from disuse.

"I've started a journal since learning of Gary's illness," I tell her.

"I'm so pleased to hear that," she replies. "I think writing is a wonderful tool to keep you centred just now. I hope you'll continue with it. You've made such great progress, Irene, and I assure you that your initial grief and fear are normal; not at all the overreaction you dread may lead you back into the darkness. Keep in mind: You will *not* go back there! You are beyond it."

She's a serene and caring person, and her tranquility has the usual effect of lifting my spirits and comforting me.

My daughter, Dana, first introduced me to naturopathy which led me to finding Jen on a random Internet search. Yet, is anything truly random? One set of events leads to another. Jen encouraged me to go back to writing and I began with poetry. And now, my beloved grandson, through the tragedy of his illness, has led me to beginning my journal . . . which is destined to become my memoirs.

May the gods smile upon Gary and guide him back to health and harmony.

Chapter 4 – The Puppeteer

Man stands in his own shadow and wonders why it is dark.
—<u>Zen Proverb</u>

Once back in Cassellman, I'm eager to enter the work force. I soon land a job as a clerk at a downtown company which is a three-hour return commute from my parents' new apartment located in the suburbs near the army base. After three years of tiresome travel, I find a similar position in a company much closer to home. During this time, the acute sadness over parting with Lou has finally ebbed, Jane and I have resumed our friendship, and I've made many new friends in the workplace. I date various guys but do not find one to truly connect with in the form of a more serious relationship. That is, until I have reached my twenty-first year in 1962 . . . when my newfound German friend, Karl, enters the picture.

My very married friend, Karl . . . destined to become my lover for seven years hence.

Karl and I become telephone friends before we actually meet. Jane is dating a guy named Ricky at the time, and I'm good friends with him. Occasionally, during his lunch break which coincides with my own but not Jane's, he calls me to pass the time.

It's on one of these interludes that he says, "Hey, would you like to chat with my boss? He's German."

He knows, of course, that is the clincher. For the past year I've been going to a German nightclub downtown with a few of my girlfriends for dancing and camaraderie on Friday and Saturday nights. Around this time, I've become interested in an Austrian fellow and think it may be fun to learn his language. Consequently, I'm about to start summer classes in German with Leila, one of my new friends from the work place.

"You're kidding?" I respond in surprise. "Does he actually want to talk with *me*?"

"Yeah, he says so. I told him you want to learn German and I think that piqued his interest. So, what do you say? Should I put him on?"

I hesitate a moment, then say, "Okay, why not?"

Karl's first words are, "*Wie gehts?*" I understand he's asking me how I am.

"*Sehr gut, danke,*" I respond. Very well thank you. "But I think I'd best continue in English. I know very little German as yet, unfortunately."

"I could teach you a little. At lunchtime over the phone, perhaps?" he suggests.

Nothing like rushing in, I think. He's got this amazing voice however, sexy and resonant–the effects of which have already beguiled me. I have no idea at this stage that my own voice is having the same impact on him.

"I think I would like that," I respond a little shyly.

By the time my lunch hour draws to an end, I've filled a page with German sentences, just general things one might say in light conversation–small talk I can share with him if he's sincere about calling me back. I've thoroughly enjoyed the lesson, but most of all I'm strangely hypnotized by *him.*

For some reason, I choose to ignore the cautionary voice that reminds me Ricky once said his boss is married with four kids. As days run into weeks and I fill a complete scribbler with German words, phrases and verbs, my former interest in my Austrian friend wanes, and he soon becomes passé.

One day, I suggest writing Karl a letter in German to send to his office. "It will help me a great deal in my studies if you could edit it, and send it back to me," I explain. "Especially now that Leila and I have started our summer course in German."

"That's a great idea," he replies, sounding pleased by my enthusiasm to learn his language. "Besides, I'll be more than interested to see what you write me," he adds on a somewhat flirtatious note.

That night in the privacy of my room, equipped with my German/English dictionary, I spend several hours composing my letter, so set am I on impressing him. I find myself complimenting him profusely on his teaching abilities and his charming personality. On the spur of the moment I sign it, *With love and good wishes, from your friend, Irene.*

Following this letter, I notice a definite shift in our relationship. It becomes decidedly more intimate, and our daily conversations pertain more to learning about one another as people.

It's perhaps not surprising that we soon become curious to meet one another. The idea is aired between us on the phone one Friday. He suggests we meet for coffee after work but I have to decline. My elderly grandfather lives with us and I have promised my parents to be home early in order to keep an eye on him while they're away for the weekend. I explain my predicament and, aware that Karl works half-days every Saturday, I come up with an alternate suggestion.

"If you'd like to visit me at home on Saturday, I'd be happy to meet you then. You're welcome to have dinner with me if you'd like. My granddad always takes his evening meal in his room while watching TV."

"It would be my pleasure to dine with you tomorrow," he replies, and we agree he'll arrive at 2:00 PM.

I'm both thrilled and terrified. What if we're physically repelled by each other and have to endure a whole afternoon and evening together? I curse my impetuosity. A coffee in a restaurant next week would have been much simpler. Well, too late for regrets now.

After work, deciding to keep an optimistic outlook, I make a quick trip to the liquor store to buy a bottle of *Liebfraumilch* wine for the coming meal with Karl. I also drop into a German market for a few choice cuts of meat and other delicacies. I tell Mom, who is curious about my bag of goodies, that I've invited a friend for dinner the following day.

Saturday arrives and I find myself hovering near the kitchen window. What I've begun to think of as the "witching hour" is drawing near. My prospective "warlock" doesn't own a car at the time, and my eyes are continuously drawn to the bus stop directly across the street.

Before long, I notice a bus pulling in. Heart in my mouth, I surreptitiously watch as the passengers debark. There is only one. *Oh, God, he's walking this way!* I gasp. *Whew! He looks fairly passable from a distance at least.* I hurry to answer the door.

Briefly, I assess his looks. He is definitely attractive, though in a primal sort of way that somewhat deviates from the type that has most appealed to me in the past. He has unusually thick, dark hair that he wears a few inches longer that the style of the times. He's large-boned, square and solid of structure, though trim, and his height, about 5'10", surpasses my own by just a few inches. His amazing green eyes set beneath bushy brows and long, thick lashes are surely his most mesmerizing feature. Add this to an attractive Grecian nose, a well-formed mouth with full sensuous lips, and a strong chin and jaw line, and–to say the least–he's impressive. I notice his shirt is unbuttoned a few inches exposing a thick mound of dark chest hair and my first coherent thought is that this ruggedly husky, hairy, yet beautiful creature, has just stepped out of the jungle and into my living room.

I thank him for the box of chocolates, and usher him into the living room.

"Please be comfortable while I get us a cold beer," I suggest.

I sure as hell need one, I think, as I place myself at the opposite end of the couch from where he's sitting. I sense the atmosphere is electrified, perhaps by the tension generated from two people sitting face-to-face for the very first time, each desperately trying to keep up a steady flow of small talk whilst wondering what the other is thinking in regard to first impressions. I, for one, am hoping I'm passable in his estimation. I'm tall and slender with blue eyes and long, reddish-brown hair. I'm not what you'd call beautiful but I've been told I'm attractive. Yet, who's to know another's tastes? I shed a silent sigh of relief when my grandfather enters the room and, after I've made the appropriate introductions, decides to chat awhile.

Much later, when Grandpa has repaired to his room, we're both feeling a little heady from the beer, along with the bottle of wine we consumed during dinner. The ice has long since been broken and we are talking as freely as we do over the phone. Mellow music flows from the stereo and as we link arms and clink our liqueur glasses in *ein prosit,* a toast to each other, I find myself gazing into his haunting green eyes and feeling slightly bewitched. At this precise moment, he leans forward and places a gentle kiss upon my lips.

"You are a very attractive woman," he murmurs huskily.

In the next moment his arms are wrapped around me and we are kissing each other as though there is no tomorrow. Until suddenly, I become aware that there is.

"Oh God, Karl," I gasp as I pull away. "I can't jump into this. I can't."

"Forgive, me, please?" he urges lightly, making the face of a naughty boy who has just been chastised. "I promise to behave myself for the rest of the evening." I laugh despite myself.

"I hope you'll consent to seeing me again sometime," he continues in his somewhat stilted, yet very sexy, English.

"I would love to see you again, but I'm not sure it's a good idea for us to become too involved. You're married and I suppose that's the rub." I smile.

"I have to understand that, and I do. I will respect your feelings on the issue. I care for you dearly as a friend and if you decide to see me again I promise I will do my damndest to keep away from you."

His eyes twinkle merrily and he raises his right hand in a boy scout's pledge of honour. We both laugh merrily.

Over the ensuing weeks our relationship begins to flourish and grow in depth. We occasionally meet for coffee or a walk after work, and we spend every free moment we can muster chatting on the phone. We become best friends, confiding all things to each other.

He begins to tell me about Inge, his wife. He says she was fun to be with and a good companion when he first met her and that she encouraged him in his adventurous dream of immigrating to Canada by telling him how much she'd love to do the same.

"I don't think I was ever really in love with her. I liked her as a companion, but had no intention of marrying her. I was only twenty-two, and she was just a girl to run around with. Next thing I knew, she was pregnant. I told her I wasn't ready for marriage and tried to persuade her to get an abortion, but she wouldn't hear of it. Finally, when she was five months along, I felt it was my duty to marry her, but I knew from the onset that something was deeply amiss."

"Are you happy in the marriage?" I question.

"Not particularly. Within months of getting married, I became involved with a married woman for three years, so that should tell you a lot. After that ended, I pursued my dream to immigrate to Canada and Inge agreed to join me. However, she's not an easy person to live with. She's prone to mood swings, and frequently flies into a rage at the slightest provocation. I never know what kind of mood she'll be in when I arrive home. If she's annoyed with the kids and I try to mollify her she gets hysterical and accuses me of taking their side against her. Later, she may go out in the yard and vent her frustration by whipping the dog. Sometimes, she can be particularly kind and loving. She's like two separate creatures: a pussy-cat or a tiger, and one can't predict which to expect at any given time. I particularly feel sorry for the kids.

"She's also obsessive about cleaning. If I tell her to take it easy she says nobody appreciates her efforts to make a nice home. I can't win. If I keep my mouth shut, I'm indifferent. I once suggested she see a therapist. That really set her off. She began shrieking that it's me who makes her crazy and there is not a shrink in the world that will change that. I give up. I hate confrontations."

"That must be difficult to cope with," I sympathize.

"Well, *ja*, but it helps to have you, *Schlange*," he quips, addressing me with the nickname, *snake*, which he dubbed me with the first time we made love when he whispered tenderly, "I love the way you wrap yourself around me–just like a snake. You are my *Schlange*."

It's probably not surprising that as we became more attached we drifted into an ardent love affair. Thirteen years my senior, he is an exceptionally skillful lover and I experience the height of ecstasy in his arms. Before long, I am deeply and hopelessly in love with him. He is my first really great love, and I love him passionately and idealistically with all the fire of my youth. I will follow him to the ends of the earth if he so much as beckons me. He returns my ardor and I guess I expect, or hope, he will one day leave his wife for me.

As I reflect back over the various guys I dated, a pattern emerges. I always seemed to sniff out the most unattainable ones. Only they could hold my interest for long. Not unlike a play, where each actor has a part, I seemed to aim for the role of victim in my romantic relationships, which of course reinforced my earliest belief that I could never win first place in love: i.e., by stealing Mom away from Dad . . . because deep down I did not believe I deserved it.

The early roots of the "fear of success" had been planted.

In hindsight, I also see how gravitating to the wrong men over the years–those whom I sensed would not commit and would therefore cast me in my pre-conceived role as "loser"–was to become a self-fulfilling prophesy. With Karl the longest player.

It's around this time I become plagued by the green monster, and I begin quizzing Karl.

"Why do you stay with Inge if you don't really love her?" I enquire bemused.

"She's in a strange country with limited knowledge of English, *Schlange*, and she has no working skills. She couldn't possibly manage on her own. Besides, if I were to leave there's no way I could afford to support her and the kids as well as myself. Then there's the question of leaving the children alone with her. It would not be a good idea. It's mainly a matter of duty, I expect. However, in some ways I am grateful to her. She left her country for me, and we were virtually penniless when we arrived here. She went without a lot and still does. There is so much to factor in. It's not that I wouldn't *prefer* to be with you. You must know that. But even if I could, it wouldn't be fair to you either. You could never stop working as most of my earnings would go to support my first family, and it's only normal you'd begin to resent it."

"I'd gladly work forever if I could be with you, Karl."

"That's easy for you to say now, *Schlange*."

These conversations usually end in a stalemate. As time goes by however, I become more insecure and unhinged, and thus more clingy and demanding. At times, our words become far less pleasant.

As our love affair progresses my jealousy over his wife increases exponentially. I begin to pry and ask personal questions. I become exceedingly upset that he continues to stay with her. I resent the fact that our time together is curtailed, and Saturday night get-togethers are out of the question.

"Why must you always probe and pry into things, *Schlange*?" he often sighs. "We've been over this countless times. If I'm making you so unhappy perhaps it's best we don't continue things. I feel I'm hurting your life which makes me very guilty."

"As long as you don't hurt *her* life and have to be guilty over *that*, you're saying you can simply walk out of mine, is that what I'm hearing?"

"You're playing with words. That is *not* what I mean, and you know it. Much as I'd love to be with you, and much as it would be my choice if I had met you first, I *can't* leave my marriage. Meanwhile, it's not easy for me to know I'm constantly hurting you."

At such times, we occasionally make up before things get out of hand. He takes me in his arms, and unaware of how long it will be before opportunity knocks again, I forget everything but the joy of being there.

Nevertheless, the less pleasant times creep up with undesirable frequency.

In the interim, life goes on. I, too, have a life without him. I have a job I like, and many good friends, and I'm not about to sit home and twiddle my thumbs. Leila and I spend most weekends at the German club, although I'm beyond the point of looking at another man with any real interest other than a few hours of dancing and camaraderie.

I continue to immerse myself in my German studies and I'm beginning to converse with some measure of fluency. Karl is duly impressed. This, of course, is my main objective. Far be it that Inge is the only one to speak with him in his native tongue.

My relationship with my father during this time progressively worsens. He often screams at me to turn off my German music.

"This is my house, and I refuse to listen to that *Kraut* shit. If you don't like it, move out. I'll even help you pack," he roars.

My obsessive interest in German creates a great deal of turbulence with my dad. "I fought those bastards during the war so you could enjoy the freedom you have now," he claims hotly, and often. By now, however, I am a tad too grown-up for him to dictate my friendships and mainly, I relish his displeasure.

Every so often we enter a cold war for weeks on end. The jealousy still exists between us with Mom in the middle. When Mom and I chat quietly in the kitchen to avoid disturbing him while he watches TV in the next room, he often bursts in on us, erupting in anger and falsely accusing us of telling secrets.

I often contemplate leaving the nest. On one side, it would be great to have my own place where Karl could visit at will and it would spare us from renting a room to share our passion. Yet, my insecurities always well up and although I occasionally go apartment hunting, I end up backing down, then hating myself for my reticence. After all, the old man worships guts. My coming of age card from him several months ago–with its cash enclosure–attested to that: "*Today you are 21 and a man. Buy yourself a big fat cigar!*" it read.

In his eyes, cowards are the lowest form of vermin. Sometimes I feel such shame at having *any* fears that bitter bile rises in my gorge and I wonder if I could actually choke on resentment.

I'm beginning to feel torn in all directions and the insecurity I feel in my relationship with Karl leads me into pressuring him to leave his wife. I occasionally fly into jealous rages. If he really loves me, he should prove it, I argue. Detesting confrontation, he tends to walk away at times, insisting we simply can't continue this way. I then suffer the torments of hell until I'm able to contact him at work the next day. Contrite, I beg his forgiveness.

"*Schlange*," he says, "It can't go on like this. I'm on a constant guilt trip over you. I can't change things and I can't keep enduring the pressure you put on me. You're still young and I'm unfairly taking up your time with nothing concrete to offer you. I know it's up to me to be the strong one and end things, mainly for your sake."

I beg him not to leave me, while inwardly fuming that he finds me expendable. Mainly I'm furious with *myself* . . . for believing I can't live without him. As I blindly assure him that he really does make me happy, I simultaneously swallow my venom, as there is little doubt I deplore my weakness and would rather be telling him to go straight to hell. He always relents, but these episodes scare and oppress me, further destabilizing my already shaky mental structure.

I find myself becoming more and more ambivalent towards him, resenting his power to pull my strings and manipulate me at will. While contemplating these disturbing thoughts, I compose a poem which seems to encompass my newly-assumed status as a puppet:

The Puppeteer

He flicks a string to make me smile,
He tugs a cord to make me frown;
His crafty wiles, my heart beguiles,
And hence my life turns upside down.

34

Aware I hang upon a string,
Subjected to the beck and call
Of he whose fingers make me swing,
How can I have no will at all?

Since when did strings become life's chains
And feelings surge from love to hate?
How can I not just cut the reins
Which bind my soul, and seal my fate?

It was established early in my life that love was equated with jealousy,
anger and a rival, and it seemed that this powerful thought had taken on
a reality of its own, in all matters of the heart.

In hindsight, it appears I was re-enacting my earliest rejection and
abandonment issues, which in all likelihood reinforced an old pattern of
clinging behaviour. Inge represented the necessary rival (Father). Conversely,
Karl played a dual role: he depicted Father in his innate ability to thwart
my needs; but mostly, he represented Mother, subjectively determined as
my one ticket to survival.

Around this time I become haunted by two recurring nightmares,
both similar in theme. In the first, I lose my mother through death
and suddenly perceive I'm the last person on Earth. My body becomes
strangely weightless, and I know at any given moment I'll float away
or disintegrate. The second dream is a perfect sequel to the first in
that I've actually floated *off* the face of planet Earth and have become
entrapped in a black vacuum of nothingness.

In both versions, my fear is absolute.

How clever our dreams! Not only in their teachings, but in their veiled
prophesies as well. My fear of losing Karl undoubtedly rekindled my
childhood abandonment issues. He had become subjectively transposed with
Mother, and to lose him was to perish . . . as determined by the horrifying
sensation in my dream of having nothing left to cling to.

In further contemplating the message within such dreams, one might wonder: What could transpire if subjective fear were ever to become powerful enough to consciously manifest? Could one become overwhelmed by their most terrifying suppressions?

Did anyone ever say dreams don't *come true? . . .*

Just lately, I seem to be constantly obsessing over my dead-end relationship with Karl. It's wrenching me apart to contemplate the knowledge that we'll never be together. Moreover, his hidden message—*be a good little puppet or I'll clip your strings and release you*—galls me to no end. Not so, for wifey dear. *She* is in the driver's seat and can do what she will.

Lord, how I hate the bitch!

Sensing something amiss, Mom encourages me to open up to her. "You're moping about all the time, honey. What's wrong?" she queries.

I assure her all is fine, and ignore her look of disbelief. This is definitely not a topic I can share with her in hopes of gaining empathy.

In short order, I will find that out beyond a doubt.

A few days later I come home to an empty apartment. My diary lies open on my bed. My first thought is, *Oh, crap!*

I'm immediately hit with a plethora of emotions ranging from rage and shame that she has read my innermost feelings, to actual dread regarding her reaction which I know will not be good. I only hope she'll not share this revelation with my father. God only knows the shit that will hit the fan if *that* happens!

Upon hearing a key in the lock, I brace myself for the deluge to come.

Her eyes are red and puffy and I realize she's been crying. "My daughter, a cheap tramp! I can't believe it!" she spews. "Sleeping with a married man! Have you no conscience at all?"

I decide the least said, the best mended, and remain silent whilst she riles herself into a tempest of fury. Finally the accusations cease and it seems her tirade has waned.

Instead, the worst is to come. She stumbles and gasps for air.

Grimacing painfully, she grips her chest and leans on the wall for support.

"Mom, I'm *so* sorry to have upset you. Are you all right? Do you need a doctor? What can I do?" I ask, panicked.

"Just get out of my sight!" she mutters hoarsely. "You're responsible for making me ill. You'll be the death of me yet. Wait until you have children one day. I hope they hurt you like you've hurt me."

"Please, Mom, let me help you."

"Just leave me alone," she croaks, as she hobbles to her bedroom and closes the door.

End of discussion. I am more traumatized than she.

This particular form of emotional blackmail, intended to modify my behaviour to suit her needs, was part of my mother's repertoire over the years. It never ceased to terrify me, despite the lack of consequences to her health. And it undoubtedly played an unhealthy role in both my abandonment fears and my need for approval . . . especially in matters of the heart.

I am not blaming her. I, for one, can well understand the "sins of the fathers". Did I not bring the many onto the next generation of my own beloved children?

How unaware we are of the pain we cause others along our journey! Yet, such is the darkness we pass through, by way of error, in our search for light.

Despite her foibles, I will always know how much she loved me. She, like all of us, had her own dark road to trudge.

She does not reveal my secrets to my father, but she's incredibly hostile following the incident. She extracts a half-hearted promise from me that I'll end the relationship with Karl. I follow up the lie by attempting to get back in her good graces by my usual route: I propitiate her with a favoured item she has coveted. While she's delighted with my gift–which is more than I can comfortably afford–it does not detract from her doubts that I have ended it with Karl and she interrogates me relentlessly at times.

It seems I'm being forced to behave myself in all directions. Why don't I tell them all where to go? Let Mother have her damn heart attack. She seems intent on it. Then simply move out. And as for Karl, why not just toss his miserable crumbs in his face and end it once and for all? Surely I am worth more than that.

Or am I?

Fall finally blends into winter. The remainder of the sparse foliage of crimson and gold has long since swirled from the trees by the driving force of the bitter November winds. It's early December and the earth is covered with a dusting of snow. I hate the climate. I abhor the snow. And I detest the knowledge that I'll be freezing my butt off for the next several months. The "season to be jolly" is just around the corner and I am far from feeling merry.

I've had another run-in with Karl and my misery knows no bounds. It's been well over a week since I've seen him and he's handed me one excuse after the other. Today, on the phone, I broached the subject again. Now, as I flop on my bed whilst wallowing in self-pity, I replay the tacky scene in my mind.

"I've finally discovered in which place I fit in your life, Karl," I say coyly.

"And what place is that?" he inquires warily.

"Seventh. First is your wife, followed by the four kids and your dog. That totals six. I *think* I might be next. After the dog. Very flattering, Karl."

"I had no idea you were that good at math," he replies facetiously. Then, on a more serious vein: "You don't really feel it's that bad, do you, *Schlange*?"

"Well, you couldn't find a moment to see me this week due to taking your wife to the dentist, your kids to sports, and your mutt to the vet. However," I emphasize cloyingly, "I can forgive your neglect if you are free to see me tonight."

A deep silence ensues. My heart drops in a rush of disappointment.

"*Schlange*, I'd love to see you tonight. You must know how much

I miss you. It's just that tonight . . . uh . . . tonight is our twelfth anniversary and I'd be shot if I didn't show."

Overcome with bitter pain, I reply acidly, "Well, well, I sincerely hope your next twelve years are as blissfully happy as your last."

"That's extremely charitable of you," he says condescendingly, employing the tone one might use for a bratty child.

I slam the phone in his ear. *Damn him for being so unthreatened in the relationship that he can patronize me at will. Bastard.*

Now, alone in my room, I grimly entertain the familiar dread that I've been naughty again, and may be faced with another "perhaps-we-should-not-continue-things" spiel.

Escaping the feared abandonment once again, a lonely Christmas holiday ensues. We meet for a drink following our respective office parties, exchange gifts and share a few hours of unbridled passion in a rented room downtown. Somehow, it all seems tawdry and wrong. I blink back the tears that cloud my vision as we wave goodbye, each heading for our individual bus stops . . . and separate Christmases.

Once the holidays are over, some unsettling news awaits us at the office. Our current quarters are soon to become redundant and the dozen or so employees will be transferred to the main office downtown.

A few weeks later, the changeover incurs, and I find myself miserable in more ways than one. I no longer have a phone on my desk and, apart from lunch break when I call Karl from a pay phone, we have to speak on my boss's line which limits our conversation to a scant few minutes during which we're deprived of any privacy. To make matters worse, the main office—being faced with the dilemma of absorbing the extra employees from our suburban branch—has been forced to reduce my position to that of the office gopher.

Things are to get worse before getting better.

Sometime in January, the apprehension I've sporadically harboured over losing Karl becomes a reality. I have another jealous fit over Inge concerning something he carelessly mentions. Feeling spurned again, a dam bursts wide open inside of me.

"I hate her and I wish she were dead!" I shriek. "You cater to her every whim. She says jump and you ask how high because you're so afraid of upsetting her delicate mental balance. Well, how about mine? That's not important to you, is it Karl? Well, frankly, it is to me, and if it comes to which one of us will be in a strait jacket first, I opt for *her*." I then commit, for the first time, the mortal sin of threatening to call his wife and enlighten her.

He looks at me incredulously, as though he can't believe he has heard me right. His eyes harden and blotchy-red patches of colour appear on his cheeks.

"Only the lowest most despicable person would go out of their way to hurt five innocent people," he retorts in a frigid tone. "But do as you wish, if it gives you any satisfaction. Just never expect to see me again."

He turns on his heel and slams out the door as I simultaneously fling my glass of cherry brandy at his back. It misses its mark, and I watch the dark red liquid roll down the wall to unite with the broken glass on the floor. *It looks like blood,* I muse idly. *Undoubtedly mine, melding with the smashed fragments of my heart that are resting in a shattered heap upon the floor.*

I manage to clean up the mess before my parents arrive from their late outing with Grandpa, and spend the balance of the night sobbing into my pillow. Karl has called my bluff and in its wake I'm faced with the definite knowledge that Inge will always have first place in his life, if not his heart.

The following day—having spent a sleepless night following Karl's angry departure—I'm rife with nervous agitation. Subdued and apologetic, I call him at lunchtime.

"Karl, I just want you to know how sorry I am for the things I said yesterday. I didn't mean any of them. I was hurting and I wanted to hurt back. It did not amount to more than that. I would never willfully try to hurt your wife or children, no matter how upset I am."

"*Schlange*, we have to end it. I realize that now. You're constantly hurting. I'm constantly guilty. The strain and pressure of our arguments is too much for both of us."

"Surely, you can't be serious, Karl? I thought you loved me," I murmur sadly.

"It's not a question of love anymore. It's a question of maintaining our sanity."

Realizing he's adamant regarding his decision, I'm reduced to tears. I begin pleading with him to change his mind . . . to no avail.

My whole world is crumbling around me, and I make one last request. "Could we at least still be friends and speak on the phone?" I ask forlornly. A momentary silence ensues as I sense his indecision.

"Please, Karl?"

"Well, all right," he responds unhappily. "But just friends, Irene. It can't be more than that. Not anymore."

A glimmer of hope clings to my heart as I assure myself I'll do my utmost to beguile him again.

The days that follow are consumed with blinding pain as I entertain the uncertainty he may never go back on his decision. Unable to foresee a future without him, my whole life seems to be disintegrating. I have trouble trying to function at work. I'm a nervous wreck.

A few days later, the unthinkable happens. Alone in an elevator—delivering inter-office mail several floors up—I'm suddenly overcome with an all-encompassing dread, a fear more powerful and debilitating than anything I've ever known. The inner terror is so intense I feel I'm being divested of my last scrap of sanity and nanoseconds away from dissolving into a quivering mass of hysteria. My heart is pounding wildly in my chest cage, and seismic tremors of electrical shocks are vibrating spasmodically in both my arms. *Oh dear God, what's happening to me?* I cry silently. *Surely I'm either dying or going stark raving mad!*

I frantically stab the control panel. *Please,* I pray, *I have to get out of the lift. Now! I'm unraveling, totally losing control! Oh, thank God, the door is opening!* I blindly stumble out, momentarily leaning against

41

the outer wall. I spy two people in the distance. *I can't let anyone see me like this!* Fleeing in the opposite direction, I lunge into a ladies' restroom. Seeing nobody inside, I dart into a cubicle and flop on the toilet seat. My limbs are twitching convulsively, and I gasp for air whilst wave after wave of panic gushes over me. I have never known such horror. It is as though I am totally fragmenting.

After what seems an eternity, but is perhaps only a matter of minutes, the fear gradually subsides, leaving me drained and depleted in its wake. My gait is wobbly and unsteady as I timorously edge my way to the sink where I splash cold water on my face in hopes it may revive me.

As I gradually regain a sense of equilibrium and a modicum of composure, I try in vain to fathom the primordial savagery of the attack that momentarily possessed me, and which will leave obscure traces of its evil sediment forever in the recesses of my mind.

Fearful I may experience a recurrence of such unspeakable terror, I descend the many stairs by foot. *How will I ever manage to ascend multiple floors, over and over, on a daily basis? I simply can't get on an elevator—not ever again! Oh crap, I'll just have to own up to my boss about this mortifying episode,* I reflect piteously. *I can no longer continue delivering mail throughout the building—even if it means losing my job.*

Later, on the way home, I'm very much relieved. My boss was surprisingly compassionate when I humbly unburdened myself. I briefly mull over his words.

"I'm glad you've been forthcoming about this, Irene, and you mustn't feel ashamed of it. A friend of mine suffers from the same thing. It's called claustrophobia, which is a fear of being trapped. And especially in places with no escape. While the fear itself is irrational, it's nevertheless involuntary, and beyond conscience control."

This strikes me as weird. I've been in tight spaces before, but never experienced anything like *that*. Nonetheless, I accept his interpretation and gratefully embrace his kind suggestion of offering to switch my position with another person in a similar job classification, one who sits at a desk all day. It will mean a daily climb to our office on the fourth floor but that's the least of my worries. I thank him profusely.

Now, as my thoughts run to my father, I know he would consider me nothing more than a snivelling coward. This, I decide, will be my own shameful secret.

Before the close of the next day, I realize I've simply changed one uninspiring job for another. I'm now an envelope stuffer. Along with several other employees I sit at a large, round table cramming invoices into envelopes all day, non-stop. *Knights of the Round Table*, I observe drolly as I attest to the bored faces of those who share this monotony with me.

I'm surprised to notice one guy who's actually enjoying this horrid task. He's absolutely animated, and makes the weirdest facial contortions as he works. I wonder nastily if the lolling movements of his tongue are in any way vital to his job performance. I become sympathetic upon recognizing that he's intellectually handicapped, but this leads me to wonder how he managed to get hired in an office. I can't fail to notice that he stuffs envelopes faster than any of us, and with such *fervor*. Perhaps *that's* the employer's rationale? I recall a program on television explaining that the mentally challenged are generally well-suited to menial jobs and much more so than their more intelligent counterparts, the latter who have a difficult time adjusting to such tedium.

To relieve the monotony, I find myself trying to compete with him in speed. For awhile, I am winning. All too soon I begin day-dreaming and slacken off, only to realize he's ahead of me; his tray is almost full. It's not unlike the story of the tortoise and the hare. His steady pace wins the race.

With Karl no long seeing me, and losing out in an imaginary competition with a retarded person, I decide my self-esteem could not fall much lower.

A few weeks pass and Karl has still not suggested a meeting. Wisely, I don't bring up the subject. I'm far too down-trodden and depressed to weather another rejection. One evening, however, an idea strikes me. I clean out my bedroom closet and fill two large shopping bags with a stack of good clothes I rarely wear. Perhaps Karl's eldest daughter may be able to use them–or even his wife. I know his salary barely covers his living expenses. Deep-down I hope it may be an excuse to see him.

The next day I lightly broach the topic of the clothes over the phone. I hold my breath as he pauses. "That's a kind thought, *Schlange*," he finally replies. "The clothes may come in handy. I can always make an excuse as to where they came from. When did you want to give them to me?"

"Whenever, it suits you, Karl. Just let me know. I can meet you somewhere and drop them off."

"It's Friday tomorrow. That could work for me. If it's good for you, we could meet for coffee somewhere?"

My relief is palpable. *Oh, to just see him, even if nothing else! And maybe, just maybe . . .*

I arise early the next morning and take special pains with grooming. I don an expensive, clingy wool dress that especially flatters me. After carefully applying my make-up, I take extra time arranging my hair. Toting the two large bags–and telling my ever-curious mother they're out-of-style clothes for charity–I'm on my way.

The day drags endlessly. I can't think of anything but the evening to come. I'm praying that once Karl sees me, he'll want me even half as much as I want him.

Finally we meet in the designated restaurant. He sits directly across from me as we chat over coffee. Not only am I incredibly attracted to this man, I realize I am addicted to him as well. Just his nearness and the unique scent of him inflame me. I momentarily wonder if he releases some sort of pheromones that send me this crazy with lust.

As I regard him intently and with unconcealed need, I become aware that his eyes mirror the smouldering desire that's undoubtedly reflected in my own. Emboldened, I dare to inquire, "Are you expected home early tonight, Karl?"

"Not particularly. I said I had work to do. Why?" His small smile conveys the next move is mine. I will not ignore the green light.

"I was thinking that perhaps we could spend some time together elsewhere, but of course that's up to you."

"I think I could manage that, *Schlange*. So, what are we hanging around here for?"

Upon entering our usual little haven, our rented room downtown, we can't shed our garments quickly enough. It's a heavenly night. We are mutually eager and unrestrained in our need for each other and we passionately make love–over and over, until we are finally satiated.

I will later wonder whether his acceptance of the clothes had more to do with his own need to see me than an actual desire for the clothing itself.

And so it begins again. Yet I'm acutely aware of how careful I must be. I'm on the edge of a precipice and the situation is precarious. I can fall off at the slightest provocation.

Weeks slide by with Karl in a like fashion. My fear of reverting to another attack of jealousy and being dumped again is now added to the tedium of daily envelope stuffing. The strain is taking its toll and I'm in a quandary of indecision.

Feeling particularly despondent one evening, I rebelliously decide to move as far away as possible, thus permanently ending my dead-end relationship with Karl and the mental agony that accompanies it. Impulsively, I type a letter–containing a brief résumé of my qualifications–to a branch of the company in the Pacific Northwest. I inquire as to whether they have any job openings.

Within the week, I receive a reply in the affirmative. There's an opening within a two-week period which will be held for me if I confirm immediately.

I doubt I'm entirely aware, when I approach both Karl and my mother with my decision, that the whole thing is likely an ego strategy designed to make them sorry for causing me so much grief. A cry to be heard . . . not unlike a person who threatens to kill herself.

For scared little me, it's suicidal.

"Maybe it's for the best, *Schlange*," Karl says kindly. "I'll miss you, but it wouldn't be fair of me to ask you to stay. I have nothing concrete to offer you." *Oh please, Karl, just ask!* I cry inwardly.

Mother's reaction is similar. "Maybe it's for the best, Irene. At least that German bastard will be out of your life. You'll not have a hope in hell of a decent future while he's around. I must admit, I believe you're still seeing him. I know you wouldn't tell me if you were. In any case, my instincts tell me that you're making a wise decision and because I love you, I know I need to let you go."

So you're happy to be rid of me, too, Mom? I think miserably. *How flattering. Well screw the whole lot of you! I'm on my way. Who the hell needs any of you?*

Despite my flash of bravado, there's no doubt I'm inordinately distressed . . . and wishing fruitlessly that Mom will put her arms around me and beg me to stay.

A fortnight later finds me at the central train station, with my parents beside me on the platform as I board the train. My dad removes a bill from his wallet which he hands to the black porter who helps me alight. "Take care of my daughter," I hear him say as I sadly wave goodbye.

It's a long trip and I'm more than a little frightened. Once secluded in my tiny room, I remove the bottle of gin that's stashed in my tote bag, and–noticing a glass on the small sink–I pour myself a stiff shot and add a touch of water. As I toss down the contents in big gulps, I wonder why the hell I've chosen to move hundreds of miles across the country. There are branches of the company a lot closer to Cassellman. My head is reeling with the enormity of it, and for the umpteenth time I curse my impetuosity.

A few gins latter my nerves are more settled, and I decide to join the passengers in the lounge car. Amongst this lively crowd, my earlier manifestations of homesickness seem to dissipate. Following the evening meal, a few of us get together for cocktails in the club car.

On the last leg of the journey, as the train travels through a narrow, mountainous pass, I'm overwhelmed by the immensity of the Rocky Mountains. Their vast, towering peaks render me miniscule by comparison, and a shiver of fear races through me as–wedged between these grotesquely imposing mounds of solid rock–I perceive myself as small and insignificant. A speck of dust in the universe. The relief is intense when we begin to descend to sea level.

I am unaware of what awaits me.

Debarking from the train in a strange and seemingly inhospitable region, I become engulfed with the surreal sensation that I am a nomad who has been magically transported to an alien, faraway land. An ambiguous no man's land which will imprison me forever without exit. I perceive I'm the last person on earth, isolated and starkly alone.

I've no sooner boarded a cab and requested that the driver deliver me to the YWCA when the irrational fear I experienced in the company elevator overpowers me once again. As my conscious control fades, I descend into the most horrendous nightmare of my childhood . . . and become seemingly locked in it.

From some remote corner of my mind, where a sliver of sanity yet lingers–somewhere beyond the deluge of terror that's threatening to submerge me in a bottomless pit of no return–I manage to pay the driver and obtain a room at the YWCA. Aware that this *thing* is overcoming me, consuming me, gobbling me up in entirety, I'm blinded with panic. Soon, I will *be* no more.

Once removed from the prying eyes of strangers, I fling myself on the small cot in my rented room and hug the pillow in terror. My limbs begin jerking involuntarily, and–caught in this timeless horror from which I perceive there is no escape–I'm certain I'll die or go mad at any given moment. In a last-ditch effort to survive, I race to a pay telephone and urgently request the operator to dial my mother collect.

"I'm coming home," I gasp. "Something terrible is happening to me. I think I'm losing my mind and I only know I desperately need help."

Once I hang up the phone, all fear seems to drain out of me. I repair to my small room, swill down a few gulps of gin straight from the bottle, then find my way to a train station and purchase a ticket back to Cassellman. I'm told there will be a two-day waiting period before I can head home. Undaunted, I spend the remaining time happily touring the city. It's as though I had a bad dream which is conveniently over.

The journey home is similarly enjoyable. I'm back to my spontaneous, convivial self, fully enjoying the company of my fellow travellers. *What on earth came over me? What evil shadow possessed me?* I wonder.

There are no answers forthcoming.

I know only one thing for certain: It's *not* a phobia of elevators I'm afflicted with. It's something far worse.

But for now, at least, the monster has been mollified.

Nothing could have prepared me for the humiliation I face once home. I've seriously embarrassed my parents. What on earth can they tell their friends?

My father is downright furious with me. "You just *gave in* to your fears instead of *facing* them? What kind of horseshit is that? Have you no pride at all? Even if you'd forced yourself to stay at least a month you wouldn't look like such a coward. I'm very disappointed in you. I would have expected better from a daughter of mine."

A few of my less tactful friends mock me endlessly when I try to explain the horrendous attack which sent me scurrying back. "Yeah, we understand," they jeer, "You got chicken, right?" Undoubtedly, the more sensitive ones are harbouring similar thoughts as well. If I'm to discount the attack in the elevator, it's the most logical explanation I can come up with myself.

Never have I felt such a deep sense of bewilderment and shame.

It appears I'm destined to feel mortified for a few months to come. Word gets around and some unkind remarks are made about the failure of my trip. Being high-strung and nervous by nature, I wonder if I'm plagued with some sort of mental disorder. I discuss the problem with our family physician. He attributes the attacks to an anxiety condition and prescribes me some mild tranquilizers.

On the day of my twenty-second birthday, I land a new job. A home typing course has allowed me to put envelope stuffing behind me and to become a Dictaphone secretary to the financial manager of a large company. My new office is located several floors up and, hoping to regain some of my lost self-esteem, I force myself to tackle the elevators again. Despite preliminary feelings of intense edginess, I'm surprised and delighted to realize I do not experience the feared attack and I soon become desensitized. To elevators, at least.

As the weeks pass, I begin to feel more secure. The monster of fear does not raise its ugly head and it appears it may have been put to rest. I'm seeing Karl again, but I've managed to adapt more of an attitude I equate with the song, *Que Sera Sera*. Whatever will be, will be. I'm not obsessing over outcomes as much as I did in the past. I continue to go out dancing on weekends with Leila or one of my other girlfriends. I occasionally accept dates as well, though no one seems to measure up to Karl. Disconsolate as I feel at times, I cling to the hope that somewhere on this planet a person exists who holds the key to unlock my mind and body from Karl's thrall.

Meanwhile, the gossip about my fanciful flight home from the West coast is no longer novel and has ebbed in potency. I, however, have not forgotten my dismal failure, and I seek a way to redeem myself.

Opportunity knocks the following year in 1964 by way of an inexpensive return flight to Frankfurt from May to August; the former being sponsored by the German government for students of the academy where I'm currently studying. As the only student in their history to have achieved a mark of 100% to date, the director urges me to take advantage of this splendid opportunity to become immersed in the German language and culture. He goes on to say that an intensive tutorial in all levels of German is being offered at the *Goethe Universität* in Frankfurt for the month of August, and if I'm interested the cost is minimal and will include lodging in the girls' dormitory.

I'm twenty-three years old and have something to prove to myself . . . and everyone else. Come hell or high water, I'll stay there the three months. And preferably die of panic before I crawl home any sooner. This, I promise myself as I resign from my job and pay for the flight from my savings.

Bidding Karl farewell is nowhere near as heart-wrenching this time round. There's nothing final, or forever, about it. We've been seeing each other for two years now, and I promise to send him brief snippets of news while I'm away. Obviously the necessary precautions will be observed: the postcards will be sent to his office; the messages will be impersonal and written in German; and lastly, they'll be signed with a masculine moniker.

I'm nervous, yet excited. I'll soon be boarding a Boeing 707 Lufthansa and jetting for Europe.

Jane and Ricky–who have since married and are expecting their first child–drive me to the airport. As we sit in the airport bar, Ricky teases me mercilessly about the "very likely" possibility of my plane crashing. He's definitely succeeding in making me more than a little antsy as I recall my holiday flight with Leila a few years back when the plane was forced to make an emergency landing. Aware of this, Ricky is sadistically enjoying himself as he pantomimes the plane's engines conking out and the aircraft hurtling through space–all with appropriate sound effects. I'm glad to be swilling down my third pre-flight drink.

At the last moment, I suddenly remember my parents. Even though my dad is thoroughly pissed about my coming sojourn in a country inhabited by his most hated people, he has nevertheless promised to drive Mom to the airport to bid me farewell. He has merely refused to be there the required few hours in advance.

"Oh, God!" I cry. "My parents have not arrived and I have to board the plane! Suppose they've had an accident? I can't just leave. Oh shit, oh shit, oh shit!"

"Irene, you're damn well *going!*" Jane shrieks. "I'm positive there's *nothing* wrong with your parents. They're probably just delayed in traffic and you'll have wasted not only your money, but a once-in-a-lifetime trip as well. You may never have another opportunity like this again. Now *move it!*"

Momentarily, I'm torn between two poles, until a small voice reminds me of what I'll be hearing if I stay: *So, you chickened out of this trip, too, eh?* A wave of hostility overcomes me regarding my parents. They *would* have to spoil my trip.

"You're damn right I'm going!" I give both friends a big hug, and then pat Jane's tummy. "Take care of my godchild, okay?"

Her answer is drowned out by the surrounding din as I race off to board my plane.

Once aboard, I spot the young guy seated beside me. He tells me he's twenty and it's his first flight. "I'm petrified," he confides.

"No kidding? Me, too. But never mind, I've brought my bottle of courage along." I retrieve my medicinal flask from my tote bag, being fully prepared for the dry student flight. "Tada!" I sing. "Here, have a slug."

He grasps the flask as though it's a lifeline, which it probably is. Within a half hour of being airborne we're eagerly drinking from the same fountain, no longer strangers. Eventually, his continuous chatter begins to grate on my nerves and I open my novel, a hint he acknowledges by picking up his own paperback.

Whilst staring unseeingly at the pages before me, I visualize the image of my father's livid face when I first revealed I would be going to Germany for three months.

I announced this little tidbit almost directly on the tail of gloating over the 100% I'd achieved in my exams, knowing full well that–in view of this new revelation, which is tantamount to treason–his previous displeasure would pale by comparison.

Not surprisingly, but unexpectedly, he kicks me out. This is a ploy to make me sweat it financially and be forced to forego my coveted trip. But his move backfires. A friend is leaving for Ireland the following evening and will be gone for a month. I call him straightaway and offer to take care of his apartment, along with giving him a token donation towards his rent, if he'll let me crash there for the next few weeks. He promises to furnish me with a key.

I delight in telling my father I'll be out by morning.

I visit my mother when Dad is not around. She's beside herself about my prospective trip. "You haven't a clue as to what could happen to you alone in Europe," she admonishes. "A young girl by yourself, you could get raped or murdered. And how will you manage the exchange on the foreign currency?"

"Gee, thanks for the vote of confidence, Mom," I sigh. "Did it ever occur to you I could get raped or murdered right here? And as for the money, I'm not exactly an idiot, you know?"

"Well, you'll be in a foreign country all alone and I can't help but worry about you."

She finally concedes to the knowledge I won't be dissuaded. Prior to leaving, she wishes me well and extracts a promise of a telegram announcing my arrival.

Emerging from my reverie, I notice it's close to midnight. I've drained my flask and I welcome the terrific buzz that has gripped me in its wake. Much to my delight, the first-class passengers who are still awake are offered to visit the cockpit, a few at a time. I haven't a clue as to why I've been privileged to be placed in this section, but will later discover the seating was arranged according to marks.

This brief interruption is truly the highlight of the trip. We are introduced to the pilot and the crew of three other men, and we are entertained with a condensed, but witty, synopsis of aeronautics. *Have no fear of gravity, the plane* will *stay up.* An incredibly large window drapes around the entire cockpit, and from this vantage point the whole of the star-filled universe stretches gloriously before us, a vision to behold. Between the joviality of the crew and my own tipsy state, all fear has left me.

After four hours of inebriated sleep, I awaken to the most beautiful sunrise I've ever seen. From the vantage point of my first class seat, it's as though I'm actually enveloped *in* it, rather than viewing it from afar. And the brilliant rainbow of striking colour leaves me virtually spellbound and in awe of the incomparable artistry of nature's own exquisite palette.

We arrive in Frankfurt in the early morning hours, and we board a bus for another long haul–to Berlin. The flight package includes a tour of the capital city. It's evening before we reach our destination, grubby and dead-tired. Our bus pulls up in front of an ominous-looking antiquated building comprised of weathered gray stone. It's situated on vast grounds surrounded by a high, wired fence which brings to mind the somewhat unwelcome vision of a concentration camp. Once inside, we're given a buffet-style meal followed by some welcoming speeches which drag on interminably. At long last we retire to our sleeping quarters, the latter which are confined to a few large chambers we'll be sharing as a group–each room containing several three-tier bunk-beds. *Definitely a five-star guest house*, I muse facetiously.

The next day, after skipping the proffered early morning bus tour of the city in favour of a prolonged but well-needed sleep, I find a pay telephone and call Ulrich, my German pen-pal of the past several months. Neither he nor his parents speak a word of English, and I'm a total stranger to them; nevertheless, they welcome me into their home with open arms as a guest for the five days I spend in Berlin. We tour the city, visit its renowned zoo, art galleries and museums, and spend sunny, idyllic hours bathing and lounging on the sandy shores of the glorious *Wannsee*. Evenings, we dance, drink and make merry at some of the local *biergartens*, and I enjoy my first taste of *Berliner Champagner*, a delicious, heady mixture of beer and champagne.

It's a delightful five days which end too quickly. We bid each other farewell at the station where I board a train for a pro bono week with two separate German families in Hameln, courtesy of the director of the German academy back home who hails from this lovely village from whence the legend of the *Pied Piper* derives.

I'm awed by the warmth and hospitality of the German people I meet. Fun-loving and family-oriented, I wonder how one can choose wartime as a yardstick for judgment of a nation or its people. I'm to learn how unaware the average German families were of Hitler's atrocities and how–if acts they disagreed with came to light–they were forced to ignore them at the risk of their own mortal safety. Hitler's regime was absolutely totalitarian.

I'm overjoyed to find a letter awaiting me from my mother in Hameln. The worry that something untoward may have happened to my parents has been haunting me. Calling long distance to foreign countries in the 1960's is extremely costly and mostly unheard of in middle-class families, so it's fortunate I've been able to supply my mother with an address in advance.

She writes that Dad missed the exit for the airport and had to continue along the freeway to the next cut-off, then hightail it back. They linked up with Jane and Ricky in time to see my plane taking off. *I couldn't stop crying as I watched your plane spiriting you so far away. I couldn't sleep all night, and finally called the airport to ascertain the student flight to Frankfurt had arrived safely,* she writes.

I'm so relieved my parents are okay; yet sad that Mom and I missed our chance for a well-needed departure hug.

I'll always be grateful to have made that remarkable trip. Although I experience some pangs of homesickness during the first month, not once do I suffer a repeat of the horrendous anxiety that assailed me on my journey out West. I tour seven different countries and feel vibrant and free. For the first time, it's as though the umbilical cord has finally been severed and I can conquer the world on my own. I delight in being me, rather than an extension of my parents and I especially revel in the thrill of my newfound independence. I indulge in simple pleasures along the way: sipping *apfelwein* on a boat tour along the *Rhein* whilst viewing the thickly-wooded mountains on either side of the river, each dotted with castles and fairy-tale gingerbread houses that bring to mind the Grimm brothers' tale of Hansel and Gretel; bike-riding in Amsterdam; swimming in the North Sea; touring art galleries, castles, and ancient cathedrals; and last but not least, visiting relatives in England. Mainly I recall the wonderful new friends and acquaintances awaiting me every step of the way. I was alone, but never alone.

By the end of July, I arrive back in Frankfurt for my scheduled month of intensive German study at the *Goethe Universität*. After completing a tour of the student residence itself, I'm brought to a clean, yet fairly Spartan room, which I'll be sharing with a French girl from France. I'll soon meet students from many corners of the world and our sole means of communication will be German—an asset for all of us.

Europe is a summer full of fun, mirth and jolly times. I am a vagabond, a happy wanderer. Young and free, and meeting travelling companions around every bend in the road. Filled with wanderlust, I eat, drink and make merry. I have never felt so merry, or so young.

Europe is my unadulterated, unrestricted, magnificent, carefree youth . . . the beginning and the end of it.

Once home, Dad seems okay with me moving back in. I acquire a secretarial position in a company within a short bus ride from home, and Karl and I resume our previous relationship. All too soon I find myself back where I left off. Insecure in my love affair but far too addicted to call it quits and intensely annoyed with my mother's continuous scrutiny at home, to say nothing of the frequent battles with my dad.

By my twenty-fourth birthday the following year, my friend Leila is also married and no longer a part of the single scene we shared. I find myself frequently ruminating over my own future. Most of all, I yearn for a sweet baby to love.

Sometimes I dream I am pregnant . . .

Eve calls me this morning from the hospital around noon.

How's he doing?" I ask.

"Well, the first of the four treatments consist of a more potent array of drugs, so he had to stay overnight for IV hydration and observation. He's extremely nauseous and vomiting a lot. He's also running a fever. Blood work has been done and, barring anything unforeseen, he'll have another round of chemo later today, followed by a treatment on Thursday. If he begins to eat and drink, he'll be permitted to go home tonight and return as an outpatient."

"Poor, Gary. How's he taking it?"

"Very bravely. He's resolved to do whatever it takes to get better. I hope he'll be discharged today though. Last night, I slept beside him on a very uncomfortable chair and I ache all over."

Eve is surely God's gift to Gary. He could not have a more loving, caring and courageous mom, and I know her support and devotion will play a big role in helping him through the battles ahead. Eve is not a physically-well person herself, and I can't help but contemplate the tremendous strain this will place on her own uncertain health.

She calls back a little later.

"Gary's home and we're all about to have supper. His second treatment was much less aggressive and went well. He began to eat and drink, so here we are, and very glad of it."

As we end the call, I think: *That's good news! I'll sleep more easily tonight, the result of a grateful heart.*

I've become more contemplative on what's been happening in my life: the good and the not-so-good alike. If I could see the whole picture, I know I'd discern that *all* is *good*—all sacred lessons in the grand scheme of things.

While soaking in a warm tub, I perceive that everything is proceeding exactly as it should in my life and that until I'm completely shorn of my arrogance, I'll continue to experience reruns of painful occurrences in this, or future lifetimes.

In these quiet moments, I discern this current ordeal is not Gary's alone; but rather, a collective experience that will determine the personal growth of both Gary and his kindred spirits alike. For it is only by giving up ego's need for control and surrendering to "what is" with trust in the outcome, whatever it may be, that we can ever hope to perceive the deeper meaning within these experiences as foretold by the ancient spiritual master, Rumi, who describes them as "guides from beyond".

That is not to say we cannot pray for Gary to surmount his current trial, nor that we must repress emotions as they arise. Moreover, it is time to "let go, and let God".

For now, I pray to find my lion's heart, where my courage has been hiding; for while I comprehend my soul's path on an intellectual level, my emotions remain in turmoil. Curiously though, I feel stronger in this moment and am hoping that—for one of the rare times—I have perhaps gone beyond my intellect and fleetingly touched my core.

Chapter 5 – Star Light, Star Bright

Star light, star bright,
First star I see tonight,
I wish I may, I wish I might,
Have the wish I wish tonight.
—English nursery rhyme

It's a balmy night in June 1966. The trees, now proudly adorned in their new growth of foliage, rustle softly in the gentle winds. It's the season of rebirth, and the fresh breath of springtime delicately perfumes the air. I, too, feel profoundly aware of my own new life: the infinitesimal blossom of spring that is growing inside of me.

I recall the evening before Karl's birthday last March and our celebration which culminated in the passion that led to this moment. Wrapped contentedly in his arms in the tender aftermath, I somehow knew: I was impregnated with the child of our love. All the doctor had done tonight was to confirm it.

Eager to share my good news, I call my friend, Jane, from a pay phone before going home.

"Surely, you can't be serious about keeping this baby, Irene?" she declares in astonishment. "You'll mess up your whole life. I know of a good doctor a friend went to that I can—"

"Don't even *think* about it, Jane," I cut in. "I *definitely* plan to keep my baby, no matter what."

"Have you told Karl about it?"

"It's Friday evening. I can't very well call him at home. It will have to wait until Monday."

"How do you think he's going to take it? You gotta know it'll scare the holy crap out of him."

"Well, he'll just have to get over it, won't he? It's not as though I'm looking for child support, or anything *else* for that matter."

"I think you're making a big mistake, Irene. It won't be an easy run for you and as your friend, I care about you."

"Good. Then, why not try to share my happiness over this pregnancy? I'll consider that a *great* show of friendship."

Upon ending the call, I can't help but harbour some resentment. She continued to push the abortion issue no matter what I said. Why could she not simply be glad for me?

While waiting for my bus, I gaze upon the brightest star in the night sky, and whisper the ancient words of *Star light, Star bright.* I then wish on this, the first of many stars, for a strong, healthy baby. It's perhaps not surprising that I decide, if it's a girl, I'll name her Star.

Despite my longing for a part of Karl to treasure–along with being convinced I'll never marry because there'll be no one to replace him–I have not planned this pregnancy. Perhaps Nature has heard my unconscious plea. Obtuse as I tend to be regarding Karl, I retain a glimmer of hope the baby may prod him into leaving his unhappy marriage and we'll be together permanently.

It seems that, a few decades later, I am still looking for the happy-ever-after ending of my most-loved fairy tales.

Karl's explosive reaction comes as a shock when I relay the news of my pregnancy over the phone the following Monday. I have suddenly become a threat to his survival. I recall only the highlights of our conversation.

"Obviously you are going to have an abortion?" he enjoins.

"No, Karl, I want this baby and I intend to keep it."

"*Mein Gott!* I can't believe you are serious." he spews.

He finally plays his ace. "If you *are* serious about having this baby, I have no choice but to end the relationship," he declares harshly.

We've reached an impasse. Resentment and retaliation flare within me. He has now become my foe.

"Whether or not I ever see your face again, Karl, I'm keeping this baby. You've made your choice. I've made mine."

A few days pass with no word from him. I call to see if he's cooled down. It appears he hasn't.

"I can't believe you hate me so much for wanting your child that you no longer even consider me a friend," I say dejectedly. "It's not as though I'm planning to hurt your life or your family if that's what you're in such a knot about. I only want our baby; yet, you find my desire to keep this part of us so detestable you no longer even wish to have news of me over the telephone."

"Irene, I don't feel it wise we even remain telephone friends under the circumstances. However, if it gives you some comfort during this time, I'll make this one exception–for the duration of your pregnancy only," he adds firmly. "However, I cannot see you, not ever again. I've made one mistake and I don't wish to compound the error. My conscience is under enough strain."

How utterly magnanimous and noble of you! I think angrily. *Such a pious conscience you suddenly possess, you sanctimonious bastard!* I keep these thoughts to myself. I have this sick need to cling to him, and now more than ever.

I soon realize the punishment for keeping my child is to bear the burden of my pregnancy alone, devoid of Karl's goodwill along the journey I've chosen. His telephone friendship will be the one small crumb of emotional security he deigns to give me. At times, I'll miss him desperately as a lover, and wonder if my body can withstand the pain of such longing. There is nobody else and deep within my soul I know there never will be.

I only want Karl.

Daily, my life spreads out like a jigsaw puzzle with countless pieces to put together. I've yet to tell my parents. What about my job? What about money? What about a suitable place for baby and me to live? I decide to assemble a few pieces at a time to not stress myself unduly with the long range picture which hopefully will fall into place as time progresses.

I take a day off work and register myself at the maternity clinic in one of the downtown hospitals. Medicare is yet a thing of the future, and I can't afford a personal obstetrician. Without a family insurance plan at work, I'm reduced to the medical dregs which service the welfare cases and those who can't afford a specialist.

The lady at the desk throws the first stone. "You are Mrs. Irene . . . ?" I timidly correct her. "It's Miss."

From the sanctity of her glass house, she crosses off the Mrs. with a flourish, flashing her gold wedding band in front of my face in the process. Recoiling, as though from a lowlife, she snaps in a patronizing tone, "It's our procedure at this hospital to send unwed mothers to be interviewed by a social worker prior to being medically examined."

This is the first of many encounters in which I will court humility. I learn to eat my humble pie without giving the hypocritically pious society of the times the pleasure of seeing me choke on it. I soon come to realize it is not *how much* one has sinned that matters; it's being caught with one's knickers down that attract the vultures. And one mustn't discount the proverbial *scarlet letter* that's tacked on one's chest: the sign of shame.

It's a pleasant surprise to find the social worker is a kindly, personable lady. After listening to my story, she encourages me to ponder the alternative route of adoption.

"You'll find it very difficult as an unwed mother in today's society. Have you considered the impact this child can have on your future in regard to employment, marriage, lodgings, etc.? Some landlords, feeling unsure of a guaranteed rental income, will not consider renting to a single mother. You'll be coping with overwhelming responsibility, all by yourself in a mainly hostile world. It will not be easy for you–neither physically nor emotionally." Her voice conveys a gentle concern.

"I appreciate all you're telling me," I assure her truthfully. "I've carefully considered every alternative, even abortion. And I'm prepared to face whatever I must and pray for the strength to get through. You see, I *want* this baby. More than anything else in the world."

"Well," she says warmly. "I see you've made your decision. Since you believe there is no way you can continue living at home–in view of your father's strong feelings about Germans in particular–and you doubt you'll be able to retain your job while pregnant, I can arrange for you to live in a home in the west end of the city where you're not known. In exchange for your room and board and twelve dollars a week pocket money, you would be required to do some light housework. After giving birth, I can furnish you with a four month period of free care for your child in a suitable foster home. It will give you adequate time to get on your feet again, if needed. During this time frame, if you decide to alter your present plans, adoption will still be a viable option. How does this sound?"

"Wonderful!" I respond. "You have just resolved my greatest concern."

She hands me her business card suggesting I feel free to call her with any future issues I may encounter, after which I directly depart for the maternity clinic.

Following a prolonged wait, my name is finally called. The young doctor who examines me internally seems to be taking an awfully long time.

"Please excuse me a moment," he pronounces, and exits the cubicle.

Meanwhile I remain prone on the table with my legs still in stirrups. He returns shortly with an older physician.

"I'd like you to take a look at this," the junior doctor states respectfully. "I think I've found something here." I detect a hint of elation in his voice.

The senior doctor peers at my innards, and begins questioning me as to whether I've been bleeding between periods. I inform him I've spotted occasionally.

"You have a growth on your cervix and we'll have to do an

immediate biopsy," he emphasizes. "Due to your condition, I'll put a twenty-four hour rush on this with the people in lab."

He inserts a shiny instrument inside of me that resembles a pair of pliers. I feel a searing flash of pain, and jerk spasmodically.

"All over now," he confirms. "I'm afraid you'll have to be admitted right away as there's a slight danger of hemorrhage, and we can't afford to take any chances.

"All yours," he announces to his younger colleague before swiftly departing.

"I can't possibly come into the hospital before tomorrow morning," I stress. "I need to inform my parents of my pregnancy. I don't want to expose them to the shock of hearing about it from the medical staff. On top of all that, do you think I could have cancer?" I ask despairingly.

"Seems to me you girls never think of such problems prior to getting into these messes, do you?" he questions mockingly. "As to cancer, I expect it could go either way. Fifty-fifty."

Noticing my impromptu tears, he remarks dispassionately, "You did say you were twenty-five, did you not? Kind of a big girl to carry on like such a baby I would think."

I wonder how you'd feel if you'd just been told you may have cancer, you pompous, ignorant son of a bitch? I think bitterly, far too disconsolate to make a response.

Leaving the hospital at my own risk until the morrow, I ring Karl from the nearest pay telephone. In view of the thunder cloud threatening to open its flood gates and swirl me into a vortex of horror, I only know I need a kind word.

It appears I have come to the wrong person.

After explaining my day from hell and the growth that may be malignant, a small silence elapses before Karl replies.

"Irene," he begins in a tone that conveys subdued excitement and relief, "It's possible this thing is going to come out for the best for both of us."

"Whatever do you mean?" I interject in astonishment, knowing *exactly* what he means.

"Well," he continues, slowly but emphatically, "If the growth *were* to be malignant, the fetus would probably have to be removed and we would have no more worries."

"Except the case of cancer I'd have to concern myself with, right Karl?" I explode. "Better Irene die of cancer than Karl have a fetus to worry about, is that what I hear? I thought you were a bigger person than that, Karl."

I'm sniffling now, and quite audibly so. I hear him droning on in the background, trying to convince me I'm taking him wrong. Surely he's too blinded by his own tortured mind to be self-centered enough to keep affirming how advantageous it could be if the fetus were surgically removed? He needn't *say* it'll be great if I have a hysterectomy. He's bright enough to know he's *implying* it. In which case, I'll *never* be able to have a child of my own. As long as this little life can be disposed of, that's his only concern. *Just chuck baby and uterus out in a Glad bag, Doctor. Right, Irene? Why yes, Karl, of course. Anything you say, you miserable fucking bastard!"*

"I have to go now," I say coldly.

"Well, good luck," he ventures. "Let me know what they do about the flute."

I've never heard such an expression but I expect he's crudely referring to the fetus, obsessed as he is with its removal. He couldn't care less what *I* have to confront as long as it eliminates any future possibility of shit on *his* doorstep.

The black cloud that dogged me to the telephone booth has doubled in size.

Once homeward-bound on the bus, Karl recedes into the background as the imminent confrontation with my parents looms ahead. My thoughts are running rampant. Between the dread of my parents' wrath—especially my father's—and the fear of cancer, I feel consumed with anxiety.

"What's all this about you going into hospital?" my mother blurts out as I enter the door. "The admitting office called to advise they have a bed and expect you by 11:00 AM tomorrow morning."

Oh, shit. "Sit down, Mom. Please. There's something I have to tell the both of you." My glance includes my father who's hidden behind his newspaper on the living room couch.

Nervously I begin my story. I watch their facial expressions go through a series of changes: disbelief; shock; horror. Closely followed by my father's blind fury.

"Who's the son of a bitch who did this to you?" he roars.

"Oh, dear God, surely it's not that married German?" my mother cries.

"Yes," I mumble, lowering my eyes.

"*What fucking German?*" Dad bellows, as he hurtles out of his chair to face me in a head-on encounter. His face has turned a ghastly shade of reddish-purple and a massive, pulsating vein bulges from his forehead. His nostrils are distended, tiny bubbles of saliva appear at the corners of his lips, and his teeth are bared in rage.

"I'll *kill* the bastard who did this to you!" he snarls. "Where can I get my hands on him? I want to know his name and where he lives this instant! If he thinks he can fuck around with my daughter and get away with it, he's mistaken. When I get through with him, he'll never touch a woman again. *Tell me!*" he shouts furiously, further inflamed by my silence.

"*Joe, your blood pressure!*" Mom cries out, tears streaming from her eyes.

Ignoring her, Dad's enormous fingers dig savagely into my shoulder blades and he begins shaking me in a demented fashion.

"Please, you're hurting me," I wince.

"I'll more than fucking hurt you if you refuse to tell me where I can find that German bastard. Why are you protecting him? That goddamn *Kraut* has just been using you as his plaything. And *you!* You're nothing but a cheap tramp to be fucking around with him!" he rants.

"*Dad!* Will you please just *listen* for a minute?" I scream out blindly, the shrillness of my voice reverberating through the room and momentarily startling him into silence. "You can't do *anything!* He has a wife and four kids who are completely innocent of the whole affair. I went into this with my eyes open. *I* am at fault, as is *he*; but you can't condemn five other people who have hurt nobody." I square my shoulders defiantly. "I will not give you his name or his whereabouts—even if you choose to kill me. Along with my child," I add resolutely.

My heart thuds wildly as I stand helplessly before this formidable savage. His fists are tightly clenched and I'm quaking involuntarily. Nevertheless, I force myself to remain focused and return his stare unwaveringly.

"You're scum. Trash!" he hisses. I stand frozen, rooted to the spot while he yet faces me in the white heat of anger. Will he attack me pregnant? I have no idea. The last time he struck me was just a few years ago when I had come home from a weekend party at 6:00 AM. I was over twenty-one years of age at the time.

Shoulders slumping, he seems to reach a decision. "Get out of my sight, you worthless bitch," he spews.

I need not be told twice. I turn on my heel and head for my room. I hear him stomp down the hallway to his own bedroom, followed by my mother's footsteps. "Oh Joe," she sobs, "Our baby, our baby!" He does not respond.

I am paying a heavy price for my decision. Amongst other things, I am breaking my mother's heart.

Much later when night has fallen and the lion sleeps, and I lie quietly in my darkened room, Mom taps on my door.

"Come in."

"You must be hungry. Come and join me for a sandwich," she suggests.

Whilst sitting together at the kitchen table, I tell her about the growth on my cervix as we finish our small supper. "That's the reason the admitting office called," I explain. "I have to tell you, I'm more than a little scared."

"I'm sure the chances of it being anything serious are very unlikely, Irene. To me, that young doctor was being terribly unkind. You must try not to worry yourself unnecessarily. I feel certain all will go well tomorrow.

"In view of all that's happened today however, I think we can both use a little nightcap to help us sleep, don't you?" As I nod affirmatively, she pours us each a shot of gin, adds water, and then continues. "I want you to know that despite the fact I'm not happy about your pregnancy, I have accepted it and I will support you in whatever way I can. *You* are *my* baby, after all, and the most important thing right now is your future."

Later in bed as I recollect my father's fury, I recall Mom's personal take on his character. "He's had a hard life, Irene. He's a sensitive person deep-down, but feels it's a sign of weakness to show sentimentality on the surface. Ergo, the funny cards he buys us and his many other light-hearted gestures of affection. He does love us, but he has a hard time expressing his sentiments. I try to make allowances for him."

I reflect on standing up to him over Karl. He wanted to defend my honour, and my loyalty to Karl must have hurt him. Meanwhile, *I* know in my heart of hearts that I'm definitely *not* being charitable about Karl's family. I couldn't give a damn whether Dad tells them or not, vindictive as I feel over Karl's earlier attitude. Why the hell should I give a rat's behind about *his* precious family? He sure as hell doesn't care about *mine*. And perhaps his family *deserves* to know. If I were his wife, *I'd* want to know what my husband was up to on the side.

The truth in a nutshell: I can't bear to lose him entirely, despite his lousy attitude; especially not now, when I need whatever scrap of emotional support he deigns to give me.

I awaken to the hazy, gray light of pre-dawn. During these fleeting moments of quiet serenity—when even the songbirds yet sleep—I sit on the balcony with my coffee and drink in the peace of the morning prior to allowing myself to dwell on what lays ahead.

All too soon, my mind begins to churn. How can I bear to deal with that obnoxious ass of an intern again today? Bad enough, I have the growth to worry about. I don't need a dose of his nastiness on top of it. As I ponder this depressing thought, I suddenly recall that— although I don't have the family insurance plan with my company which includes pregnancy—I *do* have the single plan which would cover surgery for the removal of a growth if necessary. With that in mind, I reach for the telephone directory.

Sometime after breakfast, I have the good fortune of reaching the hospital's chief obstetrician personally. Upon explaining my plight, he agrees to take me as a patient if needs be, and promises to drop in to see me in the hospital later that morning when he does his rounds.

"Keep in mind, though, you are only twenty-five and your chances of the growth being benign exceed 90%. So, please don't be distressed over what the young doctor told you. That was very unkind. Unfortunately, some of them like to play God."

A punishing, vindictive God, I think bitterly.

It turns out the growth *is* benign. I'm discharged from the hospital later that day.

It appears my parents have been discussing my situation while I've been in hospital because my father lays down the law the moment I arrive.

"This is what's going to happen," he states. "I've decided to allow you to live here for the duration of your pregnancy rather than see you cheated by some fat cats in the west side of town who'll pay a pregnant woman the paltry sum of $12.00 a week for slave labour. I, for one, don't condone such outrageous discrimination, which is rooted in intolerance and greed.

"That being said, I'm advising you to start seeking accommodation for yourself and your child in time for its birth, unless you decide to give it up for adoption. I refuse to support something I don't condone. If you're old enough to fuck around, you're old enough to accept the consequences of your actions. Frankly, you're lucky I'm not tossing you out on your ass now."

Although my hackles are up over this last bit and part of me longs to tell him where to shove his goodwill, I remain silent. He has a valid point about well-to-do people who selfishly take advantage of the less fortunate and I can't help but take pride in his altruistic ideals. I was not exactly relishing the idea of being so deplorably exploited.

By the fourth month of pregnancy I approach my boss in regard to leaving the company. I'm already wearing looser clothing which won't hide my budding abdomen much longer. I'd far rather leave of my own accord than end up in the embarrassing position of being asked to resign. This is a sad moment, and more so because I liken my boss to my grade nine school teacher, Miss Steel–a fair and kind person; someone I've gladly striven to please over the past three years of my service. When I explain I'm leaving for personal reasons, he appears to be stunned.

"Irene," he says, with a great deal of concern, "You must know how valuable your services are to me, and how very much I'll regret losing you–not just as an employee but as a person as well. While I don't mean to pry into your private life, I nevertheless want to make it absolutely clear that if your reasons for leaving involve some sort of personal grievance with another individual within the company, I'd be very hurt if you were not forthcoming about it. I hope you know I'd do everything in my power to resolve any kind of inter-office dispute between yourself and another employee as quickly as possible, and hopefully to your entire satisfaction.

My eyes begin to tear. He's been so fair and square with me. I have to honour him with the truth, even though it could mean losing his high regard and respect.

Lowering my eyes, I begin haltingly, "You can't imagine how painful it is for me to be totally honest with you, but I realize it's the least you deserve. I've been seeing a married man for the past four years. It began as a simple friendship that in time became much more. I know it's wrong but I love this man with all my heart, and I've become pregnant with his child. I plan to keep my baby as a part of us I'll always treasure, no matter what the future holds. I'll work very hard as a single mother to support my child as best I possibly can. What it may lack materially, it will hopefully gain in love. Under the circumstances, I know I can't expect to keep my secretarial position and, for that reason above all, I feel it best to resign."

Upon concluding my tale, I look up into the most compassionate eyes imaginable and deep within myself I know I am not surprised. I've always known that Mr. Rivers has a heart of gold.

"What you've just revealed has taken a lot of courage, Irene, and I know you did this solely for me," he says gently. "I can't tell you how much I appreciate your honesty. I also want you to know how much I admire your intentions for yourself and your child. You're a very brave woman, and"–he regards me sincerely–"a *good* woman. I want you to know that your revelation does not alter my high opinion of you one iota and nor should it diminish the regard of anyone else who is worth their salt.

"All of this brings me to the bottom line: I'd like you to stay with us for the duration of your pregnancy, and to return after your baby's birth. Surely an uninterrupted income will be beneficial to your continued welfare. I hope you'll accept my offer and if you do, I want you to know that if anyone says an unkind word to you while in this office, it will not be tolerated by me."

"How can I ever thank you?" I sniffle, helping myself to Kleenex tissues from a box on his desk. "Of course, I accept . . . and with such a glad heart!"

As my abdomen becomes more distended, it's a welcome relief to observe that the behaviour of my co-workers remains irreproachable. Subjected to more than my share of leers and offensive remarks beyond these doors, it's a breath of fresh air to arrive at the office. Several of my female co-workers have even become the bearers of gifts: maternity clothes, hand-knit baby items, and even a five-tier child's dresser from my friend Jan, who has asked to be godmother.

Time marches on, and October sets in with a cool breath that heralds another winter. By mid-month, I'm seven months pregnant and beginning to resemble a massive elephant. One morning my boss calls me into his office to advise me that his strait-laced superior– the superintendant of the company–is beginning to feel reluctant about retaining an unmarried, pregnant secretary of such gigantic proportions in his employ.

"I strongly disagree with his thinking, Irene, but I'm afraid I have no personal say-so in the matter. I'm really very sorry, but I can at least assure you that Mr. Wood will be happy to have you back once the baby is born."

"I'm only grateful the company has been supportive enough to keep me this long. Financially, it's helped me a great deal. I especially thank *you*."

A few days later during lunch break, my co-workers present me with a lovely card containing a generous cash enclosure as a parting gift.

"We're having a get-together for you after work this afternoon, so don't plan on going anywhere," one of the girls admonishes me.

"Does anyone have a tissue?" I beg, teary-eyed with love and gratitude.

I call Karl at his office a little later that afternoon. Unable to resist provoking him a little, I say, "It's heartwarming to realize how wonderfully kind *some* people can be." I rave on about the gift from my co-workers and the dinner they've planned in my honour. "And to think that most of these people are merely fellow employees–not even close friends," I continue meaningfully.

The ensuing silence alerts me Karl has grasped the intended innuendo. *Touché.* "I'm only a little sad my good friend Karl has not offered to treat me to a farewell drink."

"*Schlange*, you're hitting below the belt," he rebukes me gently. I hold my breath. He inhales deeply before continuing. "However, you've made your point. How long is this party and where would you like us to meet?"

I'm ecstatic. I try to keep my emotions in check and respond normally. "These farewell dinners rarely go beyond 7:30 PM; but I can politely excuse myself by then if tonight happens to be an exception."

We settle on a place within walking distance from where I'll be dining with my co-workers. This will be easier for me and not a problem for him as he now owns a car. Since he's not overly familiar with the east end of the city, I choose the place. Little does he know the restaurant/bar I've chosen is attached to a motel.

I return to my desk euphoric. I can think of little else but Karl. *Finally*, I'll see him. I've hungered so painfully for him. It's been way too long. I know tonight will end the famine. His own desire revealed itself in the husky tenderness of his voice.

I find myself wondering how it's possible to be so bonded to a person–mind, body and soul. I recall his words, "*Schlange*, you'll never find a man to please you the way I do." How sad that I believe him so implicitly, and all others repel me. There's no doubt he's an expert lover who has stirred music in my soul, and molded me into the sensuous creature that belongs to him. I've asked him how he can delay his own passion to please me . . . over and over. And he's responded tenderly, "*Schlange*, I love to watch you. You have the face of an angel in your joy. You become transformed. It's my life's greatest pleasure to please you."

The poems I've composed for him over the years have misted his eyes. When he cradles me in his arms, I *feel* his love. It becomes a live entity which I fuse and become one with. I know he feels it, too.

How can he choose to leave me?

I know the outcome of tonight. I need only look at him with naked eyes, the mirrors that so aptly portray my love and desire for him. He's often said, "*Schlange*, when you look at me like that, if I had made love to you a dozen times already, I would crawl back to you on my eyelashes." I'm well aware of his Achilles heel: the eyes he hides from when we're at a distance, but become irresistible when I'm near.

Perhaps if I, too, were married, it might be different. He would not be as consumed with guilt and fear. Yet, I am single and cannot compartmentalize my life as he can. I have only one compartment: him.

An interminably long day finally draws to an end. Following the office party which I enjoyed as much as possible, being only half-there in spirit–with the other half in bed with Karl–I sit in the nearby bar at a table facing the door, eagerly awaiting his arrival. My heart somersaults when he enters. He looks so handsome with his rosy cheeks, and his dark tousled hair besprinkled with snow. He removes his damp jacket and lightly pecks my cheek.

"*So, Schlange, wie geht es dir?*"

"I'm just fine . . . now that you're here."

"Well, that's nice to hear." He smiles warmly, and sits directly across from me at the small, round table which I've chosen.

We chat casually as we sip our drinks. The atmosphere is subdued and a candle, encased in a translucent, red and gold container, flickers softly between us. As his knees touch mine, I'm overcome with the strange sensation that I'm part of the candle's flame. Gazing into his sea-green eyes–with my heart in my own–I regard him intently. His pupils darken, and his eyes become almost black . . . heavy with a passion that I know must mirror my own. He, too, becomes part of the all-consuming flame, and I'm grateful to not be alone in my need.

"I've missed you, Karl," I say guilelessly, from the depths of my heart.

"*Ja, Schlange.* Unfortunately I, too, have very much missed you. I must say I'm impressed with your choice of a meeting place." He grins, and covers my hand with his own. "Would you like another drink, or would you prefer that we leave?"

Oh, God, I think, *I've waited forever for these words. How can I delay another moment?* "Let's go," I respond breathlessly.

Once inside our motel room, we can't shed our clothes quickly enough.

"I'm as big as a house, Karl. I guess I'm not much of a turn-on," I murmur shyly.

"Are you kidding? There has never in my life been a woman to turn me on as you do, *Schlange.*"

His lips cover mine and his arms surround me as he gently lowers me onto the bed. There is no need for foreplay. There is only the need to become one as quickly as possible.

Our moments together have never been more exquisite. How

many times do we join together before we are appeased? Finally, within the soft afterglow that ensues, he cradles me gently in his arms. His large hands embrace my abdomen as our child does its own happy dance beneath his fingers, and I feel his heart speaking to me with love.

"I know, you still love me, *mein Schatz*," I whisper sadly. "Even if you would deny it, it is something my heart feels."

"*Ja, Schlange*, I do. Unfortunately, for both of us. I wish I could have met you first; that I could give you the life you deserve. I was wrong to let our relationship become this deep. Whether you believe it or not, I also pay the price in pain. I have to be strong and not see you again, especially once the baby is born. It's the only chance you'll have to remold your life."

"Do you not even want to see our baby, Karl?"

"Irene, have you not understood what I said?" he asks brokenly.

He is sitting on the edge of the bed now, and I slide down to his feet, embracing his calves, my head on his lap as I drench his skin with my tears. Softly, he strokes my hair and caresses the nape of my neck. He then takes my head lovingly within his palms and raises my face to meet his own. He is, for the first time, completely baring his soul to me, permitting me to see the tears that are coursing down his own cheeks. Profoundly moved, I begin lapping his tears. He kisses me with infinite gentleness. A kiss of love. And my heart stirs painfully in my chest as he whispers hoarsely, and for the very first time, "You are the only woman I have ever truly loved, Irene."

The following morning I awaken at home with my eyes glued together from the tears of the previous night. *Oh God, will I never have more of Karl than yesterday's beautiful memory to cherish amidst my broken dreams?* How I had yearned to halt time within those exquisitely tender moments. Yet, in their customary fashion, they had disappeared in a twinkling, leaving in their wake a hollow, searing, emptiness in my heart.

My baby reminds me of its presence by kicking vigourlessly. *I'm here, Mom, remember me?* Touched with ineffable devotion for this tiny entity, I'm temporarily lifted from my gloom. I watch in fascination as my abdomen roils about with each robust movement of the tiny dweller within. This joyous interval is yet another heartbeat in time—a flash of eternity one cannot cling to—its brevity making it all the more sacred. I become aware I'm unconsciously humming a few lines from one of my favourite childhood hymns: *All things bright and beautiful, all creatures great and small; all things wise and wonderful, the Lord, God, made them all.*

My eyes mist again as I recall that God is missing in my life. Unwilling to repent my wicked ways, I've relinquished my right to pray to Him. I've broken one of His commandments. Consistently. And I will continue to do so, if the opportunity should arise again. Nothing can keep me away from Karl. Not even God. If only I'd not felt forced into this parting of the ways with God. And now, quite likely, Karl as well.

I reflect on my early years in Sunday school. I loved to learn about Jesus, and all the wondrous things he did and I especially enjoyed the stories of how much he loved the little children. He was always my childhood hero, as far back as my early, formative years when I listened to my grandparents' most cherished tales of him. They were deeply religious and their views were bound to rub off on me.

I contemplate as to whether God could love me now. And once again, I try to fathom the reality of such a punishing force. I'd not dream of subjecting my worst enemy to the fires of hell for eternity. Yet, my church has told me this happens, that God *does* mete out hell and damnation to the sinful. I often wonder how a vindictive deity that dispenses such vengeance can expect to be loved. My own deeply-rooted fear has driven me away from both Him *and* His Church. Nevertheless, there are the times I miss His presence in my life . . . perhaps because my own heart perceives He cannot be anything *but* Love.

Such were my religious beliefs as a young adult, bequeathed me by my church.

Shortly after lunch the phone rings. It's my childhood friend Jeff. We've been seeing each other every Saturday and Sunday. How fortunate I am to have this kind, sunny-natured friend! He moved with his parents to the west end of the city prior to our return from Karlstown and during the ensuing years we rarely saw each other. Until he called me several months ago to say hello. A conversation that led to one of many dates.

Jeff is tow-haired with clear blue eyes and a pleasant face. Large-boned and heavy-set, he's a few inches taller than me. He's still the shy, rather laid-back boy he was back then and I know I can never regard him as more than the good friend he is, and always has been. Strangely enough, even when his elaborate gifts appear, I fail to see beyond my own self-centred pleasure at having such a dear friend. Or perhaps it's not so strange and I simply don't wish to confront my own selfishness. Ending the relationship would leave me feeling alone and in the cold again.

At least I've been honest with him, I remind myself. I justify my behaviour once again as I recall my conversation with him a few months earlier when I could no longer delay revealing the news of my pregnancy. My words were quite blunt in regard to my feelings. Once again, I reflect upon the evening when I came clean about my situation.

We were sitting together in a small bar near my home, and I was nervously nursing my second glass of wine when I finally blurted out, "Jeff, there's something I have to tell you."

I vividly recall the flash of fear in his eyes.

"You want to break things off," he says dejectedly. "I think I've always known it wouldn't last between us."

"No, no; not at all. But I'm afraid it may be the other way around once you've heard what I have to tell you."

He sits attentively, his eyes questioning. He's so naive and guileless, never expecting more than a chaste good-night kiss at my door. I feel a deep sadness that his innocence and purity of soul may soon be sullied by my own lack of such qualities. I'm his first steady girlfriend. This quiet, timid guy with a heart as big as the sky deserves so much more. I take a deep breath and begin falteringly.

"Well, before we started seeing each other, I was . . . um . . . seeing a married man for four years. I . . . um . . . knew from the beginning it was wrong to become involved with him but I think sometimes love chooses us, rather than the other way around. In any event, one thing led to another, and . . . well, I'm now pregnant with his child. But we're no longer seeing each other," I babble, not mentioning the phone calls or any other details.

Meeting his eyes fully, I witness the pain and quandary therein.

"Jeff," I say sincerely, touching his hand, "I'm so sorry. I know I should have told you sooner. It was just such a painful subject to broach. Please feel free to leave if you wish. I'll definitely understand."

"I need to think this through, Irene. I don't want to say anything rash. It has definitely come as a shock to me. If you don't mind, I do need to leave now, but I promise I'll call you tomorrow."

Sure enough, he rings me early the next day. "Irene, I want to marry you straight away. I love you and I want you both: you *and* the baby. I promise I'll love your child as my own. Please say you'll marry me."

I don't know what I had expected but it was not a proposal. *If only Karl was making this offer,* I ponder sadly. I try to let Jeff down as gently as possible.

"Oh, Jeff, I can't marry you or anyone just now. I'm terribly mixed up. I was deeply in love with Karl, and–although I'm no longer seeing him–I think I still am. I love you dearly . . . but as a friend. I'm not *in love* with you. Although I wish with all my heart that I was. You deserve so much more than I can give you. I know I'd be cheating you to accept your proposal at this juncture. I really can't do that to you, Jeff." *Or myself,* I think sadly. *I'm not attracted to you in that way. I could never happily share a bed with you.*

78

He tries to dissuade me, telling me that love can grow on a person. I wonder how that can be right when the chemistry is so wrong.

Selfishly I continue to see him, because I need a friend.

Now, as I take his call, I find my morale picking up at the sound of his cheery voice.

"Yes, I'd love to go to dinner and a movie this evening," I happily respond to his query.

He arranges a time to pick me up and I'm temporarily distracted from my blue funk over Karl. *Perhaps,* I think optimistically, *Karl will change his mind once the baby is born. How can he resist the temptation to view his own flesh and blood child?*

During the months I'm home and unemployed, I enjoy a much-improved relationship with Mom. She's content in the knowledge I'm not seeing Karl, as apart from the times Jeff or a girlfriend drop in for a visit, I spend all my free time at home. I insist upon continuing to pay room and board, although she deems it not necessary. In exchange, she uses the extra income for entertainment for the two of us. A movie buff at heart, she insists we go to the cinema a few times a week. I'm to look back on those days as a very happy time with my mother.

Apartment hunting is a discouraging ordeal. Officious landlords inquire as to why a young, pregnant woman wants to rent an apartment alone. After doling out the usual excuse–I'm separated from my husband but financially solvent and will be returning to my job after my baby's birth–their hesitation is palpable. They generally hedge by handing me the "don't-call-us-we'll-call-you" line, before whisking me out of the door with asperity. One building owner goes as far as asking boldly, "Is this baby your husband's then, or what?"

My due date is December 13, 1966, so it's a little close for comfort when I finally acquire lodgings on the third day of that month, thanks to my mother. She discusses my predicament with the rental agent in charge of the large apartment project in which we dwell, and vouches for my reliability and financial solvency. He calls her a few days later to say that a young couple would like to break their lease. "If your daughter's still interested, it's a one-bedroom apartment and she's welcome to it within the week."

I'm ecstatic, and I adore my new little home located two streets west of my parents' apartment. It's also in close proximity to my workplace—a definite plus. Utilizing a child's coaster that I've borrowed, I cart over clothing, books and other sundries daily. I scrub and clean, wash all the cupboards, and awkwardly polish the hardwood floors. I notice the apartment has recently been painted. *Great!* All the walls are white, but they are clean and fresh, and that is fine with me.

A friend's brother delivers my bedroom furniture in his truck and the same friend loans me a pull-out couch and a few chairs for as long as I need them. These items, along with an old television and small TV stand belonging to my mother, temporarily complete my living room. One of Mom's friends donates a small basket-weave table with two matching chairs for my kitchen, and others donate used curtains for my barren windows. My married friend, Lily, gives me a crib and carriage she has stored in her attic to add to my growing collection of baby needs.

Several of these donations arrive unexpectedly while I'm in hospital. During my absence, curtains are hung on windows and freshly-cut flowers are on the kitchen table to herald my arrival. The baby and I will return to a ready-made home, cozy and livable, and in its own way unique.

Less than a fortnight later—following a brief but intensive labour—I'm presented with an adorable baby girl, weighing in at eight pounds, one ounce. As I gaze upon my child for the very first time, my breath catches in awe to behold life's tiny miracle snuggled trustingly in my arms. She's such a breathtakingly beautiful child . . . all pink and white with wispy, dark locks and large cornflower blues eyes framed with sooty, black eyelashes so long that, with lids in repose, they cast deep shadows upon her cheeks.

Surely there's nothing more magical than the first greeting between mother and child. I'm overcome with a surge of indescribable love and tenderness such as I've never known before. Holding her to my breast, I want to protect her with my life . . . that no harm may befall her, not ever in this world. I have instantaneously bonded with this little girl and am inextricably entwined in the throes of mother love.

My heart has never been so full.

Proud as any new mother, I call my own mom as soon as I have access to a telephone. She answers on the first ring.

"Hi there, Grandma," I chirp gaily. "It's a girl! We're both fine."

"Oh my God, that was fast! It was almost 2:00 AM when I dropped you off at the hospital. I guess I should have hung around instead of going back home in the cab, but first babies usually take forever. I'm so glad you're both fine. I've been lying here on the couch beside the phone the whole night. I haven't slept a wink."

"She was born at 5:20 AM. Oh Mom, she's absolutely gorgeous! I've never been happier or so completely awed. The act or birth itself, being finally presented with my sweet baby . . . it's all been such a profound experience. I can't wait for you to see her."

"Me, neither. I'll have your father drive me up to see you both at visiting hours this afternoon. Try to get some rest between now and then."

"You too, Mom. By the way, do you think Dad may change his mind and see the baby?" I interject dubiously. "If only he'd see her, just the once. I know she'd win him over. She's such an irresistible little creature."

"Why don't you swallow your pride and try to get around him nicely?" she ventures. "I, too, am hoping he'll come around. She *is* his granddaughter, after all."

I promise to do my utmost best. It's of major consequence that my father accepts my child. Of far greater import than it ever was in regard to his acceptance of me. Just contemplating the fact that both my baby's father *and* grandfather have refused to see her has caused me immense sadness.

By the time my parents arrive, the congratulatory bouquet of flowers Mom sent is already sitting on my night table and a light floral scent permeates the room. After chatting for about fifteen minutes during which time Dad has been regarding his watch impatiently–he hates hanging around hospitals almost as much as funeral homes–he finally looks at my mother.

"Well Sourpuss," he says, using his pet name for her, "Are you about ready?"

"Are you guys going to see the baby in the nursery before you leave?" I inquire hopefully.

"Of course," Mom says cheerfully. "That will be the highlight of my day."

"I'll just wait here for your mother," Dad announces.

Ever the implacable military man, I think sadly. How fiercely proud he is! Surely, he must be curious to see his own granddaughter? I have never begged my father for anything; yet now, through moist eyes, I lay my pride aside.

"Please, Dad," I plead. "Please see her. Just this once. It's not *her* fault she's here." I begin to gasp and am unable to continue. A few errant tears trickle down my cheeks and I doubt my father has ever seen me express such need.

"All right, Brat, but just this once," he says gruffly, but his eyes are compassionate.

"Oh, thank you, Dad!" I glance at my mother, and her grin is triumphant. She gives me a surreptitious thumbs-up as she bids me farewell and they depart for the nursery.

Later, when Dad is taking a nap–he's currently retired from the army and working shifts as a guard at a plant–Mom calls, as I knew she would . . . if only to appease my curiosity.

"Such a beautiful child!" she utters. "Your dad was very impressed as well. He couldn't conceal his grandfatherly pride. You should have heard him raving on. 'Just look at her!' he exclaimed. 'She's the biggest kid in there! And strong too! Look how she's squirmed out of those tight blankets! A chip off the old block. She's a real beaut, isn't she, Sourpuss? The others look like bald, red-faced, wrinkled-up little apes by comparison.' He could hardly contain himself.

"I think he felt embarrassed afterwards. When I mentioned how pleased I am that he likes the baby, he quickly informed me that it didn't alter his original decision about not having any part of her. That's pride talking. I know darn well that little Star has won the big lug over, though he hates to admit it. We just need to give him a little time, Irene."

Unbeknownst to me then, this small child would bring love to all she touched. To my father, her great gift would be the adoring and unconditional love of the daughter I never could be. Innately understanding his outer gruffness and not fearing it, she'd instinctively see beyond his rough exterior to his inner sensitivity . . . in a way I never had, or could. He, in turn, would become putty in her little hands.

Severe bleeding, accompanied by anemia, has kept me in hospital longer than expected and I'm eager to get home. It's not enough to hold my baby sporadically. I want her with me constantly. Sometimes, at feeding time, she's the last baby to be brought into the ward I share with five other girls, and I always feel panicky. A cataclysmic sense of doom overtakes me and I dash to the nursery, plagued by an exaggerated fear that something terrible has happened to her.

From the outset, I'm never to get over the fear of losing her.

I call Karl to wish him a happy holiday. We've chatted regularly on his lunch break since I've been hospitalized, but it's now Friday, the last working day before the holidays. Christmas is on Sunday.

"Listen, *Schlange*, I can't dawdle or I'll be late for the office party," he declares. "We're having a big bash at the club across the street, and most of the crowd has split already. You take it easy. Don't run away, okay?" he quips. "Oh . . . by the way . . . a Merry Christmas!"

Well, a holly, jolly Christmas to you too, Karl! I grimace as I hang up the phone. *Thanks for your glorious contribution to making things merry. Ten minutes less at your damn party wouldn't exactly have killed you, you miserable ass!*

The next morning I awaken to the disappointing news I'll be

here another day. "All being well, you can go home for Christmas tomorrow," I'm told. I'm yet to learn a major blizzard will keep me snowbound on Christmas Day as well. Meanwhile, as I try not to brood about Karl's brief parting shot, I re-read the poems Mom gave me: one, which she wrote for the new baby and, beneath it, the words of the lullaby she composed so many years ago for me, *Hush-a-bye*.

Jane and Ricky arrive that evening bearing gifts: a small, plastic, table-top pine tree with slots cut out for the real candles that accompany it, along with a Dr. Spock baby and child care book, and a volume of nursery rhymes for "Baby Star." Jeff drops in later and presents me with an elegant new woolen coat. It's a lovely shade of burgundy, topped with a lustrous lynx collar.

"You need a new winter coat, Irene," he stresses, when I balk at such an extravagance.

By the time my visitors depart, my spirits have soared. I'm feeling pampered and loved by my friends, I've been blessed with a beautiful, healthy baby, and my dad just may be having a change of heart regarding her. I have so much to be thankful for.

Why not infuse this drab room with some holiday spirit? I think gaily.

"Hey, girls, what say I light up this little tree?" I suggest jovially. Everyone agrees enthusiastically. Once the candles are lit, I turn off the overhead lights. The whole room becomes magically transformed with an iridescent glow of real yuletide warmth.

"Wow, that's spectacular!" someone exclaims.

Turning my back a moment as I grope for my cigarettes on the bed, I hear a piercing shriek.

"Holy shit! It's on fire!"

Momentarily frozen, I view my little tree going up in flames. *Oh God! That's all I need . . . to burn the damn hospital down!* Sparks of charred plastic begin flying towards me. I suddenly react. With a quick backhanded swipe I flip the small tree into the nearby waste paper basket. Tossing my blanket over the roaring flames, I quickly smother them. Then, like a thief in the night, I furtively slink down the hallway, disposing of the blackened blanket in a laundry hamper

I spy along the way. I find a fresh cover for my bed and dart back to my room, nobody being the wiser.

Upon entering the ward, I'm engulfed in a miasma of thick, gray smoke. The atmosphere reeks from the acrid fumes, and I'm thankful the babies are in the nursery overnight. Conversely, I'm in deep doo-doo if a nurse comes round. I pry open a few windows and allow the cold, biting air to permeate the room.

"Good grief," I jest, "You girls might want to cut down on your smoking!"

Feeling safe once again, we all begin laughing at the tragic-comedy we have just witnessed.

And this is my most exciting recollection of the memorable Christmas Eve of 1966. . .

MAY 10, 2012, THURSDAY

Gary completed his fourth treatment two days ago. Thankfully, this is the last of the poison to be administered in his first 21-day cycle, and he'll now have a break for two weeks. He's not permitted to go to school as the toxic effects of the chemo lower his immune system. Fortunately, the school has supplied him with a tutor for several hours a week at home. He'll need this help to complete his ninth grade successfully.

His morale remains positive, a good sign. Recently, when he and Eve discussed his illness as they often do, she asked him, "Do you ever think, 'Why me'?" His response amazed her and me as well, when she later shared it. "Actually no," he replied. "That would be kind of arrogant, don't you think, Mom? After all, why *not* me?"

Such a profound and egoless thought for one so young! How proud I am of this loving boy with his wise and loving heart.

Gary's sixteen-year-old brother, Jim, is showing his own beautiful, bold colours. Upon hearing that Gary is becoming anemic and may need a blood transfusion, he actually volunteered to donate his own blood if it proved a good match, despite his phobia of needles. Such dear, brave boys—both our grandsons!

Eve went on to say she's extremely rundown from lack of sleep. Not surprisingly, she's contracted a severe head cold. Due to her mitochondrial illness, she's more susceptible to infection, and has to be extra careful. An ordinary cold can lapse into something far more serious. Since becoming ill, she is no longer able to work and has lost her driver's license. Her husband, Phil, has become the family's sole chauffeur. He's been driving back and forth to the hospital whilst ducking into work in between. This, along with worry about Gary, has been a tremendous strain on him as well. I'm grateful the next few weeks will provide them all with a needed rest.

In the midst of all this, our youngest daughter Dana, who is almost eight months pregnant with her second child, has been recently diagnosed with gestational diabetes. She'll be working until three weeks before the baby is due. She's extremely fatigued and somewhat anemic. She is under close medical observation.

I will not obsess, I will not obsess.

At this moment the phone rings. It's Eve, presenting me with some more unsettling news.

"I don't think I mentioned the lump Jim discovered behind his ear a few months ago."

As my heart skips a beat, she continues. "I didn't want to worry you needlessly. His pediatrician told me it was just a lymph gland. I think she regarded me as the typical anxious mother. In view of Gary's diagnosis and the fact Jim's lump is still there, I mentioned it to the oncologist. She said it should have gone down by now if it's just a swollen gland, and I'd do well to have it re-checked. So, I've made him another appointment to see his pediatrician this Monday. Of course, I'm assuring myself the odds are against both my kids having Hodgkin's disease, right?"

Rhetorical question or no, it requires a response. "Don't even go there. The odds are probably a million to one," I assure her.

Well, shit, I surely hope one can count on the odds being against it, I speculate wordlessly before ending the call.

No, no, no. I will not obsess.

Chapter 6 – Guides from Beyond

Wherever you go,
go with all your heart."
—<u>Confucius</u>

The first week alone with my child is rather unsettling. I know nothing about babies. I have no idea how to properly change a diaper, let alone bathe an infant. I had some brief instruction in the hospital which is all I have to rely on.

So, we learn together, my little one and me, and I eventually become quite adept. Despite feeling scared and incompetent at first, I'm otherwise enjoying this time alone with my child. I decide to postpone going back to work for at least a few months, or until my funds begin to dwindle.

I love the freedom of my own apartment and the independence of being solely my own boss. It's not at all the scary venture I once thought it to be.

Karl and I still speak daily on his lunch hour. I've sent him a few of the nicer pictures that Jeff took of Star in the hospital, and I'm encouraged by his reaction.

"She's very enchanting, but what do you expect when she has such an attractive old man?" he jests. "She should make Miss Canada of 1986."

"Perhaps you might like to meet her in person one day?"

"I don't know if that's advisable, Irene. I'm consumed with guilt over what our relationship has done to you. Even your friend, Jane, blames me. She said if I truly cared about you, I'd set you free to have the life you deserve. She called me as soon as she learned you were pregnant. She said if I ended things you'd definitely get an abortion. I know she's right, despite your decision to keep the baby. I'm the older one, and the married one, and I'm being unfair to keep you tied to me."

I can't believe Jane has done this. I tell him he mustn't feel guilty, that I'm a big girl; that I entered the relationship with my eyes wide open. I go on and on, to no avail.

Later, I call Jane.

"You had no right to meddle in my life," I berate her. "You wrenched Karl away from me at a time I needed his support more than ever. As it so happens I did *not* get the abortion you were hoping for, and Karl is *still* in my life, although hesitant to be more than friends with me, thanks to the massive guilt trip you've given him. You have no idea the grief your interference has caused me. Frankly, I doubt I will ever forgive you."

She's quick to defend herself, telling me it was done out of love for me. I end up telling her if love can be that evil I never want to see her face again, that our friendship is over, and I slam down the phone.

I've been feeling more kindly to Karl since he confided this to me. I can only sit tight now and hope in some way I can subdue his guilt. Or that his need of me will eventually override his conscience.

By the end of January, I go to the family physician and ask for a prescription for the birth control pill. The post-natal bleeding has finally ceased and I have every intention of luring Karl back into my life. And the life of our child.

The next time he calls I casually announce, "I've started the Pill. I'm determined I'll not get pregnant again. At least not as a single mom. I need to be straight with you, however, so I'm telling you now: Like most people, I have my needs. I can only hope you choose to be the one to fulfill them."

Silence; but this is okay. I change the subject. I've made my point, and I don't think he has seen through my bluff.

The ten weeks that Star and I are continuously together pass much too quickly. There's nothing that would please me more than being her fulltime mom; but sadly, that's not possible. I've staved off returning to my job for as long as I can. Finally, it's not just the money that's running low; my boss has been pressing me to return to work as well.

Tomorrow, Star goes to her day-sitter for the very first time, at just over ten weeks old. As I sing lullabies and lull her to sleep in the rocker I've bought for that purpose, my heart aches with regret. The subdued glow of the amber lamp plays shadows on her lovely face. "Where did your dark hair go?" I whisper softly. "Without me noticing, your hair has turned to burnished gold. I'm going to miss you in the coming days, my darling."

The first week at work is difficult. I miss Star desperately. Each day, at noon break, I call her sitter to confirm all is well. I'll eventually get used to leaving her during the day, but I'll never happily accept it.

The nagging worry still plagues me: what if something should happen to her?

A recurring nightmare begins when she's only a few months old. I dream I find her lying dead in her crib. Shaken into wakefulness, I rush to my sleeping child and place my finger beneath her little nostrils until I feel the warmth of her exhaled breaths. Fearful and disoriented, I have trouble getting back to sleep after such episodes.

In general, the time with my child as a single, working mom, although rewarding, is also fraught with stress. She's prone to both ear and bronchial infections. Not infrequently, we spend half the night at the emergency clinic of the St. Ann's Children's Hospital. The next day, I bundle her warmly and tromp through snow-laden streets to the sitter's home, juggling her in my arms along with my purse and a heavy tote bag filled with her daily needs: diapers, formulas, and strained baby food. At work, my nerves are stretched like taut wires from the uncertainty that plagues me whenever she's ill. Fearing she may become worse, I worry that the sitter may forget to administer her antibiotics, amongst other important things.

I yearn to take care of her myself at these times, especially when she's running a fever; but this leads to static at work. Mr. Rivers was transferred to another city shortly after my return, and Mr. Lebeau, my new boss, is not nearly as empathetic. He's already reproached me for the rare absence when Star has been ill. I'm not without covert resentment. The married ladies take countless days off to tend to their sick children without being chastised. In the knowledge that I'm single and in need of my salary far more than they, I become an easy target for his frustrations over absenteeism in general.

At barely four months old, Star is hospitalized with bronchial pneumonia. I'm beside myself with worry. She's placed in a cooling tent to reduce her high fever and I yearn to be constantly beside her, but I can't afford to lose my job. There's no welfare for the single mother in the 1960's and if I can't support my child, she'll be placed in a foster home until I'm gainfully employed. Not so for single moms who are separated or divorced, without paternal support. *They* are given government aid in similar straits, and there's no way their children are removed from the home. I seethe at such bias based solely on the sanctimonious prejudices of the time.

Star recovers from her bout of pneumonia, but as time goes by, I'm becoming overwhelmed by the vast weight of responsibility I have for this tiny life I adore. This is compounded with the guilt of waking her after a sickly night, and lugging her to the sitter's home. A sunny child, she always wakes up smiling and chirping, and goes to sleep at night without a fuss. She's a happy, loving little girl and my heart longs to give her more of myself. Yet it seems there are never enough hours in the day. Between sterilizing formulas, doing laundry, cooking, cleaning, and my job, our personal time together is limited. Most evenings, about an hour before her bedtime, I cradle her in my arms in the big rocking chair and sing her songs. During this time, we become as one in our mutual love and need of each other.

The months go by, and as the constant stress begins to take its toll and my own health begins to suffer, I'm faced with a greater concern. What if I lose my job? Prone to bronchitis, I often drag myself to work when I'm feverish and ill. I eventually end up confined to my bed with pneumonia. Being too wiped out to look after Star and fearing she'll come down with my illness, I pay a co-worker's young daughter to bring her daily to her sitter's home and back. Fortunately, we get over that hurdle but my boss calls me into his office when I return.

"You're a very good worker, Irene," he begins. "That is, of course, when you're here. I regret to have to tell you that if your absences continue I'll be unable to carry you on the payroll indefinitely."

Following his chilling pronouncement, my terror is paramount. How can I avoid being ill? Fear unites with guilt, taunting my waking hours and adding its own funereal march of terror to my dreams at night. Dreams of my baby's death become more frequent. Following them, I sometimes awaken her and embrace her tightly, kissing and hugging her in an outpouring of love. These moments delight her and she easily goes back to asleep. Whilst I recoil in my bed in fear of unknown horrors that are beyond my control.

I begin ruminating more frequently on my relationship with Karl and wishing the three of us could be together as a family. We've been lovers again since Star turned six weeks old. How well I remember that first night and how it came about. Shortly after giving him that little jibe about having "needs of my own" I broached the subject again on the phone. My mind drifts back to that Friday afternoon.

"Star is getting better-looking every day," I confide. "Seems she takes after her daddy."

"How can I argue when you present me with such great truths?" he replies amicably.

"Well, surely you can't just take *my* word for it. Besides, she's been begging to see her handsome dad, and it's becoming monotonous."

"Has she now? Are you saying she might like me to drop by this evening?"

I can't believe my ears at this turn of events, and I'm not about to look a gift horse in the mouth.

"Well, actually, yes, but she says any day is okay with her. She's not a pushy child."

"Not at all like her mom, eh?"

"No, she's a lot more patient and laid-back. A lot more like her dad."

"Well, well, I think you just might find yourself in the background once I meet her, *Schlange*."

"I'll always be willing to take second place to her, Karl."

As yet a fulltime mom at home, I'm able to feed her earlier that evening. Karl will arrive around 4:45 PM, and I want to be ready. Once she's finished her bottle, I place her safely in her crib while I take a quick shower. I let my long auburn hair flow freely down my back the way he likes it and subtly apply a little colour to my face. Twirling about before the full-length mirror, I appraise my image. I look even thinner that my 117 lbs. in this ankle-length, green-velvet hostess skirt and silky aqua blouse. I've lost all the weight I gained during my pregnancy plus a few extra pounds, thanks to my very active lifestyle. *Great!*

Just then the doorbell rings and I hasten to answer it.

"You look ravishing, *Schlange*," he smiles. He nevertheless keeps his distance, as do I. A mutual reticence seems to prevail, but that's okay. His favourite liqueur will loosen us up before long, especially since neither of us has had any supper.

He sits on my new davenport. It folds into a double bed which I consider an apt choice, and not solely in view of Karl. Jeff often spends Saturday nights at the apartment to avoid the long drive home, and it gives him—or even a girlfriend—a place to crash.

I bring us each a cherry brandy over ice which I set on the coffee table, another new addition to our rather quaint little abode. I then slip into my bedroom where Star is resting quietly in her crib. I've dressed her up for the occasion and she looks adorable in her green organdy dress. Reaching out for her I'm greeted with her angelic smile, and my heart does its usual flip-flop. How lucky I am to have this lovely child!

Karl's expression is infinitely tender as he holds his daughter for the first time. She beams her special smile upon him and his whole face lights up.

"You were not exaggerating, Irene. I have never seen a more beautiful child."

"A toast to our beautiful love child," I say glibly, and we link arms and click glasses in our usual *prosit.*

Sometime later, I bed Star down for the night. After replenishing Karl's drink and my own, I place some of our favourite German records on the gramophone and sit beside him on the couch. I'm feeling a little heady from the brandy, and my desire for him at this moment is an acutely painful thing. As one who is parched craves water, so I yearn for the elixir of his love.

I silently beg him to touch me but he remains frozen in place. I wonder if he's waiting for me to make the first move; yet, I hesitate to reach out for fear he may reject me. Recalling his words on arrival– that I looked ravishing–I edge closer to him, somewhat encouraged. I place my hand upon his knee, lightly caressing him while we talk. Still no response; yet unbridled desire flares in his eyes. *Damn you,* I think. *You're waiting for me to come to you. Well, so be it.*

Emboldened by the liquor, I arise and begin swaying to the music while gradually removing my clothing. Entranced, he watches me as I dance for him. Finally, adorned solely in my lacy black underwear, I halt abruptly.

"I refuse to remove another garment," I tease lightly, but with an edge of seriousness. "If you're not fully impressed with the show, it's over."

In a flash he crushes me in his arms. "I was longing for you to seduce me, *Schlange*," he whispers excitedly in my ear. "*Yes, yes, yes,* I'm impressed!"

I murmur an expletive as his mouth covers mine, and from that moment on I am lost.

Within seconds, we are joined together on the couch.

"Be still, *Schlange*," he utters hoarsely. "I don't want this over before it starts."

"Oh God, Karl, it's been so long. How can I . . . ?"

"*Ja*, way too long. Hush, now. Just relax and don't move. Feel the pleasure."

As my body stills, I allow myself to feel the exquisite tenderness of being wrapped in his love. Tears fill my eyes, the joy is so intense.

"You're crying," he says, his voice concerned.

"My heart is so full. In your arms, I *become* . . . all things beautiful. Love. Joy. In these moments I know the ecstasy of heaven on Earth."

"*Ja. Ich, auch*," he murmurs raggedly. I, too.

I wonder how I can feel such profound bliss when there's scarcely any movement between us. He kisses my lips gently. We drown in each other's eyes. Minutes pass. The rapture continues to build until I can hardly contain it. I'm a mass of quivering sensation.

"*Now. Please*," I whimper.

"Look at me," he says with infinite tenderness, and as I gaze upon his beautiful face and we begin to dance together in the blissful harmony of our love, I cry out his name.

"*Ich liebe Dich*," he says later, as my head rests on his chest and he cradles me gently in his arms.

"*Ich liebe Dich, auch, mein Schatz*," I murmur softly. I love you too, my sweetheart.

It's midnight before we're finally sated and he reluctantly leaves. I make a fast tidy-up, then collapse contentedly on the couch in my nightgown where I choose to remain for awhile as I reflect upon our time together. The only trace remaining of our night of love is the musky scent of our union still clinging to the air, and the half-empty liqueur bottle and two glasses that still stand on the coffee table.

That and the footprints he has left in my heart . . . which assure me he has finally returned.

Since, there has been no turning back. We see each other regularly on Friday evenings. I've given him a key and, for the most part, he drops in at will. On occasion, he awakens me with an early morning kiss before work, and I slip out of bed to join him on the davenport. Later, after making love and showering together, he waits for me to wake Star up, and proceeds to coo to her fondly whilst she eats breakfast and we have a cup of coffee together.

Our relationship undergoes a subtle change. We've both mellowed in many ways. I try not to ask for more than he's able to give. He, in turn, is more understanding and compassionate, even when I occasionally lapse. He has become very protective toward both Star and me, and I no longer feel wracked with uncertainty that the slightest provocation will send him out of my life forever. We share many tender moments with our daughter, and although I am not his wife, I know in my heart that I am definitely his woman: his very special and much adored woman.

At times I consider Star's future, and wonder what torments she may be exposed to as an illegitimate child once she starts school. Distressed, I discuss this with Karl one day.

"She's never been christened," I say in conclusion. "I only registered her birth with the city. If she's baptized in your name, I can always claim to be a divorced, single mother—even if it requires I move once she's school age. It could spare her a lot of shame. And your family would never have to know."

"I would never want her to suffer," he says immediately. "I know you're not out to intentionally hurt me, and if you think it will help our daughter just make the necessary arrangements and I'll go along with you."

He soars in my estimation at this point and I share my latest brainstorm with my mother who becomes immediately distraught.

"I thought you were no longer keeping company with that man. Good Lord, Irene, won't you ever smarten up? You'll be the death of me yet, you know? You put me through so much worry."

"I am *not* keeping company with him. I merely contacted him as I thought it may benefit Star," I equivocate. "Surely you don't want to see your granddaughter going through the stigma of being illegitimate once she starts school?"

"I still think you're making a foolish move. What if you meet someone else and decide to get married *before* she starts school? In that case, you could christen her in the name of your new husband. That would be much more ideal, don't you think? At least tell me you'll hold off on this hare-brained move for a few more years."

"All right," I agree. "You win. For now."

Despite Star's frequent illnesses she's developing normally and growing up into a happy, carefree little girl. Strangers often stop to stare at her, becoming instantly captivated. Her wide-set, impelling, sky-blue eyes, the exact shade of her grandfather's own, literally sparkle as she graces them with her radiant smiles. She's inherited Karl's classic high cheek bones and finely-sculpted facial structure. This, combined with a delicate nose, primrose cheeks, bow-shaped lips and golden tresses, bequeaths her with an ethereal quality. People naturally gravitate to her.

She begins to talk early and at eighteen months we're able to engage in brief conversations together. Her personality is as winning as her outer exterior. She's almost *too* beautiful to be real, possessing the celestial immanence of an angel. I often find myself gazing upon her in awe, wondering if she is naught but a fragment of a dream. At such times, I feel a shiver of apprehension.

I am so afraid of losing her.

She has become my dearest little friend, the one who greets me happily each night, my little chatterbox. I enjoy taking her for evening and weekend walks in her stroller when the weather is fair, outings she loves. I allow her to bathe with me in the "mommy tub" as she dubs it. She loves playing the mother role and insists upon taking her turn to wash *me*. Weekends, after locking our bedroom door to keep her out of mischief, I sometimes serve her breakfast in her crib in order to catch a little more rest. She never whines or complains and has a wonderful knack of amusing herself when I am sleeping, or busy at home. One morning I awaken to find my buttocks slippery with Vaseline. Once I recover from my fright, I chuckle to realize she's played the "mommy role" again. She has performed the same task I do after changing her diapers.

Despite her sunny nature, pressures mount in other areas. In her first two years, she has four different babysitters. It saddens me to see her shifted about this way, to say nothing of losing a sitter on short notice and needing to find another, like yesterday. None of this can be helped any more than the worry of bringing her to a different home and hoping I've made a wise choice. I feel wracked with guilt despite the fact she adjusts remarkably well wherever she goes, and is lovingly accepted. And especially adored by the sitters' children, one of whom referred to her as "a star that fell from heaven."

The day arrives when Mom informs me of Dad's conversation with a group of men on the topic of how they would define "a real man." Dad says simply: "My daughter. I doubt any one of you would have her guts." This is the supreme compliment coming from my father, and although I can't hope to receive it directly, I'm gladdened by the second-hand knowledge that he's proud of me.

In retrospect, I guess I may have made it, Dad . . . had not life, and fear, so cruelly blocked my path.

During this time I'm extremely grateful for Jeff's friendship. What would I do without his constant help and patience? During Star's hospitalization with pneumonia, he drove miles out of his way to collect me from work and bring me to her bedside every evening. Later, he'd drive me home prior to making the long trek back to his own residence on the opposite side of the city which is closer to where he works.

Apart from Friday night which is discreetly reserved for Karl, Jeff insists on engaging a babysitter on Saturday evenings. He insists it's our date night and refuses to hear my pleas of exhaustion by insisting that all work and no play makes Renie a dull girl which is definitely not good for her. Sundays, the three of us enjoy a picnic in summer or a crisp drive in winter, always stopping along the way with a special treat for Star in mind. These outings culminate in our Sunday evening ritual: dinner at my parents' home. They are fond of Jeff, and perhaps retain the hope our frequent outings will lead to something more serious.

I will not forget his kindness, or the fact I have been unworthy of it.

Jeff's marriage proposals continue, and as my morale gradually lowers from the stress I'm encountering, his offer becomes infinitely more tempting, especially with the fear of losing my job hovering over me. I also yearn to give my daughter the security of a stable home life and a more relaxed and less harried mom. For this, I'm aware, she needs a permanent dad. At times, I come dangerously close to accepting his proposal; but then the image of Karl and my love for him overtakes me and I hear myself saying automatically, "Please, Jeff, don't keep harping on that. I'm just not ready for marriage yet. Besides, you know I love you as a friend, and that's really not enough."

"Irene," he remonstrates for the umpteenth time, "That kind of love comes with togetherness."

"Perhaps, but so does contempt."

We always end up in a stalemate.

Momentarily, I recall my last birthday. A week before, Jeff told me he had something special planned and he stuffed some cash in my handbag.

"That's for the sitter and the hairdresser. Get yourself all dolled up next Saturday."

When he arrived at my door the following week, he pinned a corsage of beautiful orchids on my best dress.

"You look stunning," he beamed.

Soon afterwards we headed downtown, destination unknown to me prior to arriving at one of our most posh hotels.

How can he possibly afford this place? I wonder. Yet, he's single with a good job and living at home with his parents, which surely must help him expense wise.

We ride the elevator to the top floor where the view of the city is absolutely breathtaking.

Over cocktails, we chat amicably. "Remember the flowers I sent you for your birthday when you were living with your folks?" he reminisces. We both crack up.

"Yeah, the ones I never received, because I was out at the time?"

"Right, your old man was so annoyed to be interrupted during the hockey game on TV that he assumed the delivery boy was *peddling* flowers, and sent him on his not-so-merry way.

"Yes, and quite rudely at that. To think it was my first bouquet!"

After a scrumptious dinner with a mellow wine, we relax over coffee and liqueurs. Violins play melodiously in the background, and from our table by the floor-to-ceiling glass windows that surround this enchanting room we have an extensive and spectacular view of our hometown. The city–elegantly bejewelled by sparkling neon lights that blend intrinsically into the stardust of the black-velvet sky–is so exciting at night. Jeff chooses this singularly bewitching moment to present me with a small, elegantly wrapped package.

"For you, the one I love. Go ahead, please open it," he urges.

My heart takes a nose dive as I instantly suspect the contents. What on earth can I do now? If I refuse to open it, he'll be dreadfully hurt. Delaying the inevitable, I unpeel the ribbon and silver paper at a snail's pace, all the while wondering how on earth I can extricate myself from what's to come. Time runs out, and I'm forced to raise the lid of the blue velvet box. There, sparkling radiantly is an exquisite solitaire diamond set in a band of gold.

"Oh Jeff," I cry. "It's absolutely beautiful. But surely you know I can't accept it. I—"

"Please hush, Renie. Don't say another word." He puts a finger to his lips for emphasis. "It's bought, it's paid for, and it's yours. If we *never* get married, it is still my gift to you as a friend. It's your birthstone, even if you never consider it as more. Meanwhile, it would make me so happy if you'd just wear it with pleasure. We won't set any dates. Please don't say no." His voice is the saddest I've ever heard.

How can I not relent? "All right, Jeff, I'll wear it. I'll try it your way. We'll be engaged. But please, don't take this as a promise. I'm terribly mixed up in my life and very unsure. I know I care for you dearly as a person, but I'm not where I should be."

"No promises, I promise. Thank you, Irene. Thank you. You've made me so happy."

As he places the ring on the third finger of my left hand, I sense myself sinking deeper into a quagmire, and I wonder if I can ever fumble my way out. I'm grateful when he asks me to dance.

Caught up in the sheer delight of the picturesque setting and the ambiance of the evening, I can't help but feel a little like Cinderella at the ball as we waltz together. Yet, from somewhere, a voice taunts me that I'm in the arms of the wrong prince. My eyes blur as I sway to the dreamy strains of the orchestra for there is one thing I know. Jeff *is* a prince, and in *his* castle–which offers all the privileges of reigning feminine monarch that I've hopelessly coveted from Karl–there is not a fraction of a doubt: I *would* be queen.

Almost a year later I'm still wearing Jeff's ring and still seeing Karl and loving him even more than before if that can be possible. Guilt is added to guilt, and I feel I'm being pushed along by the tides of fate with no actual say in my destiny.

In retrospect I know I was operating on automatic pilot. Seemingly deprived of taking command on a conscious level, my subconscious mind began subtly guiding me. There is no doubt my soul knew exactly where it was going . . . and that it was ever moving forward to meet its destiny.

Friday night arrives and we hear Karl's key in the lock. Star races to meet him.

"Hi, Daddy!" she greets him affectionately, kissing him on the lips as he swoops her up into his arms.

"How's my favourite little girl?"

"My fine, Daddy. Did you bring Star chocolate?"

"Do I ever forget?" He whisks a few bars of German chocolate from his pocket. "You have to promise to share it with your mommy."

"Star will, Daddy. Promise."

She perches happily on his lap, and whilst they chatter, I pour a drink for Karl and myself. Nuzzled against her father, she munches happily on the chocolate. He regards her with a world of tenderness, but an almost imperceptible sadness lingers in his eyes.

This is not easy for him, I muse. I recall the many presents he has bought her—stuffed animals, dolls, and a silver locket in the shape of a heart. He never arrives empty-handed. Yet I know he longs to do more. My eyes begin to mist, and I excuse myself to go to the bathroom. It always makes him feel guilty when I cry.

Later, we both tuck her in and kiss her goodnight. On the way to the living-room I pick up a double-sized fitted sheet from the linen closet which Karl helps me drape over the davenport. Meanwhile, we hear Star thumping merrily on the bars of her crib with the wooden hammer he recently gave her.

"*Das Zimmermann,*" he smiles fondly. The carpenter. "I told you she'd like those tools I bought her." He's actually preening.

"Men!" I snort incredulously, as he captures me in his muscular arms, clasping me in a bear hug that leaves me breathless.

It's our turn to love. . .

Early the next morning, Saturday, the door bell rings. Star knows she has another caller. Her beloved grandpa. Upon hearing his heavy tread on the outer staircase, she begins jumping up and down, unable to contain her elation.

"*Daddy! Daddy!*" she squeals joyously as she opens the door and raises her tiny arms to accept his embrace. He transports her high above his head as she giggles ecstatically.

"Well, well, well. How's my special girl today?" he booms, using almost the same words as her visitor last night.

"My fine, Daddy. We go for drive now, okay? Star all ready. See my pretty dress?" She twirls around and around.

"Oh, yes, I do. And what a pretty girl you are!"

Her small face glows as she wraps her arms around his legs, and then suddenly spots her grandma.

"You didn't say hello to *me* yet Star," Mom says, simulating petulance.

The large man grins smugly, unable to contain his exhilaration. In Star's eyes, he knows he's number one. From the start she's been magnetized by his gruff personality and there's an ocean of affinity between the man and the child who has so innocently penetrated his facade and discovered a treasure-trove of love therein. And the man has allowed himself to become vulnerable to the child by granting her, and her alone, the key to unlocking his soul.

How easily she won him over. Unlike me as a child, she has never been frightened by his gruffness. She relishes being tossed in the air or having a rowdy play-fight with him on the floor. Mom's words come to mind as I watch the two of them joyously unite in kinship.

"You know, Irene, I'm so glad for your dad. He missed all your early years, never knew what it was to hold you as a baby, rough-house with you as a toddler, or watch you grow from infancy onwards. He's sharing all of this with Star. Her devotion has made him very happy, you know. The war years did a lot of damage to father-child relationships. Your dad has found the little girl he always longed for: he has found *you* . . . in your daughter."

I recall my sincere response, which was not without a tinge of unbidden sadness for what should have been but wasn't; for what would not, or could not, ever be . . . because we had met too late. "Yes, Mom, I know. And he mightily deserves it."

They all leave for their outing, and I join them later at my parents' home. Star and Dad are playing their favourite game of "Cheers".

He pours a tiny bit of his beer into a shot glass for her, then they clink glasses and say, "Cheers!" She loves this game, but after a few rounds Dad tells her, as usual. "That's it for now, sweetheart. I don't want you growing up to be a boozer like Daddy. How about you get me another beer?"

She tears off to the fridge, his willing slave. Running back with a cold bottle of beer, she slams it down on the glass-topped coffee table, chirping proudly, "My got you beer, Daddy!"

A great smashing sound ensues as the glass spirals and crumbles into smithereens. Mom dashes out of the kitchen and begins yelling, "Just look what've you've done, Star! You need to be more careful. You've broken Granny's good table. Naughty, naughty girl!" Star's eyes moisten with tears.

Dad sweeps her up into his powerful arms and regards Mom furiously. "Don't you *dare* chastise the child for doing what she's told–and so happily at that. Which I daresay was seldom the case with her mother," he adds wryly as he looks my way. "It was an accident and my fault if anyone's," he continues.

"Now, don't you worry about Granny," he soothes. "You're a good girl for doing what you're told and bringing Daddy the beer. Daddy's very proud of you. And Granny's very sorry for yelling at you. Aren't you Granny?"

Mom, having cooled down, looks at Star and solemnly apologizes. I smile reflectively as I contemplate the entirely different outcome had I done the same as a child.

Star calls all the men in her life Daddy, which includes her grandfather, Jeff, her babysitter's husband, and her biological father as well. I decide it's in my best interest not to enlighten her. If she happens to tell my parents, "Daddy came to see me last night," I can always claim it was Jeff. I've told my parents she does this, perhaps mimicking the sitter's kids who call the male figure, Daddy. In any case, Dad is honoured and would be the last one to want me to correct her.

On a freezing Saturday in January 1968, in the early morning of Dad's fifty-eighth birthday, he receives a call while on the night shift.

"It's George here, Joe. Sorry to have to contact you at work but you need to know Eileen's in hospital. When Alison and I dropped her off early this morning she had a major fall. The pathway to your door is very icy. She's scheduled for surgery this morning."

My phone rings bright and early, awakening me from a sound sleep.

"Your mother's in hospital," Dad barks as a preliminary greeting.

"Oh my God, what happened? Is she all right?"

"She broke her fucking leg. Happy birthday to me! I've just worked a double and I'm dead-tired. Her timing's beautiful."

"How on earth did it happen?"

"She was at the Legion hall with Alison and George and she fell on her way home. Half-pissed, I expect. It's a multiple fracture and she's scheduled for surgery at 10:00 AM. If she'd been a horse, I would have shot her. I've given the hospital your number. I need some fucking sleep. I'm taking the phone off the hook. If there's an emergency, send the cops over," he concludes, and abruptly disconnects.

How damn self-centered can you get! I think incredulously. How about *my* stress and pressures and my own need for sleep? I call the hospital and speak with Mom prior to surgery. She's been given painkillers and is very groggy.

"We'll be up to see you after your surgery, later on today when Dad gets up," I promise. "I'll get a sitter for Star. Don't worry, Mom. You're going to be fine. We love you and we're rooting for you."

Later that evening, Dad and I drop in to see her. She's still heavily sedated and not making much sense. I hold her hand, assuring her everything will be okay. Dad stands to one side, saying very little. Finally, after a quarter of an hour, he regards me somewhat impatiently.

"Well, Brat, I think we should get the hell out of this joint and let your mother get some rest." *Yeah, right,* I think, knowing he's itching to leave the hospital.

Once home, my voluntary sitter–a friend of Mom's–greets me at the door.

"Star's running a fever," she says. "I don't know where you keep the thermometer but she's very fretful and burning up."

I thank her, and bid her a quick farewell. Alarmed, I rush to Star's crib and sure enough her forehead is like fire on my wrist. A journey to the hospital is in the offing. Wan and depleted, I wonder how I can possibly make it.

It's 3:00 AM when we finally arrive home. Star has a severe ear infection and I have a prescription for antibiotics for her. After settling her down I collapse on my bed fully clothed, only to be awakened at 7:30 AM by the shrill ringing of my alarm. Waves of exhaustion roll over me and I feel too weak and numb to move. Much later, I hear Star stirring. I jolt awake again, frantic to see it's after nine o'clock and I'm already late for work. Taking my chances, I call in sick and spend the day administering to my daughter and napping whenever she does, completely drained and utterly fatigued.

Jeff is currently in hospital as well. He passed out at work the day before Mom broke her leg and is undergoing tests. Much to his disappointment, recent events have prevented me from finding time to visit him.

One evening, after seeing Mom, I ask Dad if we can have a short visit with Jeff.

"You have to be kidding me, Brat. That hospital is way the hell out of my way, and I'm dead tired. You must be too, and we both have to work tomorrow. He'll just have to accept that the best you can do is talk to him on the phone while we have all this other shit to contend with. He's a big boy. I'm sure he'll understand."

It appears the "big boy" does *not* understand. After ten days in hospital and a battery of tests that have revealed high blood pressure as the main cause of his problem, he's finally discharged. And fails to call me. After a few days with no word, I assume he's still feeling miffed over my failure to visit him. Our last telephone conversation ended with him in a bit of a huff. I decide to call and defend my position again. It's not been my intention to hurt him. Circumstances, along with his hospital being four hours return by bus, left me with little choice.

"Don't apologize," Jeff says forlornly. "I've been doing a lot of thinking in hospital and I've finally opened my eyes. It just won't work out between us." He hesitates, awaiting my response.

How I wish, for his sake, that I can deny his words and assure him I truly love him. Instead, I hear myself reply solemnly, "Are you saying you want to break off our engagement, Jeff?"

"I think it's for the best, Irene; but I want you to keep the ring as my gift to you, and as a souvenir of our time together which I'll always cherish."

I later reflect upon what a dear person he is. He ended things in such a nice way. No recriminations. So unlike my own attitude with Karl.

When Mom is finally discharged from hospital she's unable to balance herself on crutches and ends up confined to a rented wheel chair until the cast is removed and she can get back on her feet. For the next five months, I drop in regularly with Star in the evenings and take care of the jobs she's unable to manage from her chair–chores Dad bitches royally about, such as sweeping and washing the floors, vacuuming, laundry, etc.

From day to day, I wonder how I'll ever get through the weeks to come as Mommy, Daddy, breadwinner, secretary, and housekeeper in two homes. Surely I must be drawing from some hidden reservoir of strength I do not realize I possess.

By July 1968–when summer rolls around and Mom's cast is off and she's finally able to hobble about with a cane–Star and I join my parents for a two-week beach holiday, each renting our own separate cabins on the lake. I've never been more in need of a break.

It's such a joy to just be a mother, and I bask in the pleasure of being with my little one 24/7. Nights, Star snuggles close to my flesh as we sleep together in an old brass bed. Days, she delights in the lake. She splashes in the shallow waves for hours on end, in between using her little red shovel to excavate mounds of sand to fill her matching pail. She then upends the pail and dumps the contents onto the ground to form a sand castle for us to decorate. She especially enjoys our jaunts on the lake in one of the boats supplied by the cabin owners.

Usually, in the afternoon, I wheel her to the village in her stroller, a mile's promenade. Together, we meander through the shops, and then stop off for an ice cream cone before heading back.

A stroll. Such a simple, everyday thing. Nothing to think twice about. If it had been portended that the time would arrive when I'd be too beset with fear to even walk a block beyond my door, surely I would have chortled at such an inane prediction.

Early in August, Star and I join my parents for a trip to the cemetery. Mom wants to visit her parents' graves before the cold weather sets in. It's one of those divine summer days, fair and warm with a gentle breeze in the air. As we drive through the winding tree-lined paths, I think how lovely this particular cemetery is. So unlike most graveyards.

As I watch Star scamper through its scenic grounds, chasing squirrels and picking handfuls of wildflowers for me, my heart swells with love for her. *She seems to gravitate to the tranquility of the surroundings as much as I do and she feels quite at home here*, I muse idly.

I am never to forget that idle thought.

The following month Karl announces his wife will be going into hospital for a hysterectomy. "They've found several tumours," he informs me. "It could be serious."

I find myself hoping she'll die. Though guilt besieges me over such an evil thought, I'm convinced I'm caving in from all the strain of the past months. Her death represents my life and, as such, my daughter's as well. Not more or less than that.

A week or so goes by before I see Karl again as he's solely responsible for his children's welfare while Inge is hospitalized. Now, as he sits beside me and gives me news of Inge—all positive—his words are a distinct blow. My last shred of hope has been clipped and I have nothing left to cling to. I begin sobbing uncontrollably.

"I'm s-so sorry, Karl," I blubber, "But I was h-hoping she would die. I think my nerves are shattered these days with all that's been h-happening in my life. I was hoping that if she died, we could f-finally be together. Please don't hate me."

"Of course, I don't hate you." He gathers me to him. "I understand more than you will ever know. I'm so sorry, *Schlange*. This is hurting you so much. Me, too. I wish with all my heart I could be with you."

He begins dabbing at my tears, then kissing me gently as he holds me tenderly. Finally, need takes over, and we become lost in the usual sea of passion.

Later that night after crying myself to sleep, I awaken from a horrible nightmare, drenched in sweat. In the dream, I'm walking aimlessly along the sidewalk when suddenly there is no more gravity. Weightless, I begin soaring with lightning speed through a vast, timeless space. Whirling through the darkness of the universe, I become aware this is a flight without end. I scream and scream until sheer terror awakens me.

My heart is pounding frantically and I'm gripped with fear. *Oh Jesus, how can I cope with this horror? I bemoan. I need something! Perhaps a drink? Yes, most definitely a drink!* I jump out of bed and dash to the fridge. Grabbing a cold beer, I guzzle at least half of it in eager gulps before bringing the remainder to my bed. I light a cigarette and fix my eyes on its fiery tip as I greedily inhale the smoke whilst swilling down the balance of the brew and wondering whether I am finally going mad.

I'm later to equate this dream with the similar ones I had of floating off into space during the time Karl briefly left me years ago. How perceptively these related dreams portrayed the loss of control that was taking place in my life within their vague forewarnings of impending doom.

The next morning, I've just completed the final touches on my makeup when I become light-headed. Grasping the bathroom sink,

I notice the floor tiles swirling wildly beneath my feet. Dizzy and disoriented, I flop down on the toilet seat and drop my head between my legs praying the insane spinning will cease. I sense the hand of death is upon me and stark terror grips me. I inhale deeply several times until the sensation finally lessens. Finally, the tiles stop moving and my head clears, but I'm badly shaken. Somehow, I manage to deliver Star to her sitter and catch my bus for work.

I'm unaware that this is to mark the first of many similar episodes to follow.

The following Saturday evening, Star's godmother drops in for a visit. She is adept at telling fortunes with the cards, and I persuade her to read mine. After glancing at the first sequence, she quickly sweeps the cards aside, demanding I reshuffle the deck.

"What did you see that was so terrible?" I inquire, somewhat alarmed.

"Uh, you got some bad cards. Probably a poor shuffle. We'll try again."

"Oh, no, not before you tell me what you saw," I insist. "C'mon Jan, you know I enjoy having my fortune told but I don't really believe in that crap, so you'll not upset me."

"Well, okay, if you insist. I foresaw a death in your family, towards the end of next year–1969. In December."

"Who?" I demand shrilly. Despite my acclamations of disbelief, an unearthly shiver courses through me.

"I really can't say. I removed the cards too fast. Hey, are you okay?"

"Yeah, sure. I think a goose just stepped over my grave."

Sometime later, it happens. The monster, which has been silent all these years, finally breaks loose and strikes with a vengeance.

Jan and I are reading an article about jealousy aloud and making the odd comment to one another when I'm suddenly stricken with such intense fear that I feel I'm being divested of all rational thought.

Hysteria wells inside of me, its powerful force threatening to burst forth in a mighty flood of half-crazed panic. Only one coherent thought remains: *The monster sleeps no more.* And I know I must terminate this visit before it fully breaks loose. For how can I bear the shame of unravelling in front of my friend?

I muster my last shred of control to devise an excuse to get rid of her. A migraine comes to mind. Something physical, and comprehensible . . . and acceptable. I tell her I have to lie down straight away.

Finally I'm alone . . . but not alone. *It* is with me. The *monster.* I feel as though I am fragmenting, losing my very self. Fleeing to my bedroom and frantically tearing off my clothes, I plunge into bed. My fingernails dig into my pillow like giant claws as I curl up in a fetal position and wait . . . praying the attack will subside. The waiting seems interminable but finally the ferocity slackens and the dread gradually seeps through my pores to unite with the atmosphere, leaving me drained and exhausted in its aftermath.

Eventually I sleep. I drift into the total blackness of unconsciousness, all senses numbed. I sleep the oblivious sleep of the dead.

Several days pass uneventfully, and I begin to relax. I assure myself it was just an isolated attack of nerves. After expending a great deal of mental energy trying to determine the root of it and getting no further ahead, it seems the only solution is to close the door in its face. And that I do. With pleasure.

The nervous illness that is to gradually monopolize my life creeps up so insidiously I'm unaware anything serious is happening to me.

An interesting event transpires the following month, October. I'm acting in an amateur show at the Legion, directed by my mother, and I've invited my friend Marla to attend.

Following the show's finale, a live orchestra begins playing music, and several couples get up to dance. While chatting with Marla, I happen to catch a glimmer of a familiar face. It suddenly connects that it belongs to the widower I met last year at my sitter's home. He had brought his motherless child to her for permanent care. I later learned he lived out of town and dropped in weekends to visit his infant son. I recall finding him attractive, and entertaining the hope I may meet him again one day. Yet, I've never laid eyes on him since. I'm unaware I'm blatantly staring at him until our eyes meet and he grins in recognition. Somewhat embarrassed I return his smile, and demurely lower my eyes.

Moments later, he approaches our table and asks me to dance.

He's a very attractive man with dark hair, brown eyes, a straight nose and a strong chin. There's a definite similarity between him and Karl in facial features and physical structure, although I'm not fully aware of it at the time. I learn his name is Len, and I introduce him to Marla when we return from our dance.

"I wonder if I might join you girls?" he asks shyly. "I'm with my sister but she's so busy chatting with her friends, I'm sure she won't miss me." We welcome him immediately.

"How's your little boy?" I ask with interest.

"He's doing okay. My daughter took care of him at home this past summer during school holidays. Apart from that, he's been staying with my sister-in-law, ever since our mutual sitter called it quits. I guess that gave you a problem as well?" He raises his eyebrows in a gesture of solidarity.

"Oh, yeah." I roll my eyes, and we both grin.

He asks about my daughter and we fall into relaxed conversation. I soon learn our little ones are only six weeks apart in age, Star being the elder. He tells us his wife died following a Caesarean section, and he was left with the baby and three older children, now fifteen, fourteen and twelve respectively. We discuss the ups and downs of single parenthood, with Marla inserting her own comments as a single, divorced mom. We also learn he's thirty-six, nine years older than we are.

He eventually asks Marla to dance, and later requests a second dance with me. It's a slow song, and for the first time in years I find a thrill of tension running through me as his strong arms enfold me. I'm strangely attracted to this dark-haired, husky man with his ruggedly handsome features and kind, brown eyes.

"Would it be okay if I call you sometime?" he asks while we dance.

"Yes. I would like that. I'll slip you my telephone number before we leave," I add.

Having noticed Marla seems attracted to him as well, I decide to go the surreptitious route. He seems to catch the drift and says that will be fine.

A few days later, Len calls and invites me to meet his children. "My fourteen year-old daughter, Meredith–she likes to be called Merry–says she'll be more than happy to babysit for you while you visit my home," he offers. "She did a great job of looking after little Keith last summer. She grew up fast after her mom died."

He brings me to the lovely three-bedroom bungalow that he has built single-handedly and he introduces me to his two older sons, Mark and Ken, both very friendly and welcoming kids. It's a very relaxed and homey evening which I enjoy, and he later drives me home around ten o'clock. He kisses me good night in the car, and I'm pleasantly surprised to perceive an alien flame flicker hotly within me. A flame heretofore reserved exclusively for Karl.

I look forward to seeing more of this man.

From that evening forward, we begin dating regularly. Len teaches gymnastics to kids on Monday, Wednesday and Friday evenings, so our time together never conflicts with my Friday night trysts with Karl. Saturday becomes our regular date night, reserved for the two of us. We spend Sunday with the children, often playing board games at his large dining table. At such times, Star–who is about six weeks shy of age two–attempts to draw Keith out of himself. He's extremely introverted and rarely speaks, but it appears she's determined to change that.

One Saturday evening, following a movie, Len and I stop off at the Greek restaurant near my apartment for pizza. He's no sooner ordered than I become aware that my monster, yet alive and well, has surfaced. Overcome by fear and the usual sensation of loss of control, I grab my coat and prepare to make a run for it.

"Cancel the order, please Len," I cry. "I have to get out of here. *Now!*"

Without further ado, he snatches his own coat and says, "Okay, let's go."

I race to his car. As he unlocks the door, he inquires with concern, "Are you okay?"

"No, I'm not. I have to go home."

Once inside my apartment, he says, "Irene's not well, Merry. I'll be along shortly. Can you wait in the car?"

Meanwhile, I lock myself in the bathroom as waves of dread tumble over me. My heart is thudding mercilessly, and I'm unable to draw a full breath. I gasp for air, afraid I may suffocate. This one's a doozy, and I writhe in terror as it goes on . . . and on . . . until at long last the panic subsides, and it's over as suddenly as it started.

I join Len at the kitchen table.

"I was becoming very worried about you," he says kindly. "Are you feeling any better?"

"Slightly. That was one god-awful attack. I think a beer may help. You're welcome to join me, but I know Merry's waiting for you." He thanks me, but declines. I grab one from the fridge and take a few very long swallows, then light a cigarette.

"I get these attacks from time to time. I don't know what causes them. The anxiety is so bad I feel as though I'll die or go crazy while they last." I fill him in as best I can. He's the only one I've discussed these episodes with to date. For the most part, I've felt too ashamed.

Easy-going and unassuming as he is, he accepts my attacks as part of the nervous illness that afflicts me. Without question or judgment. Admittedly he doesn't understand them; but nor do I.

I invite Len, his family, and my sitter's kids to Star's second birthday party on a Saturday in mid-December. Karl and I celebrated with her the previous evening. It's a fun afternoon for all of us and it's held at my parents' larger apartment. My dad, an accomplished cook and amateur baker, has made her cake himself. The frosting is white with the exception of the star he has designed in pink icing and placed in the centre. It's quite impressive.

The children enjoy a slew of party games and Star is thrilled with her presents which are mainly toys, except for a small, wooden rocking chair my Dad has picked out for her himself.

"Oh Daddy!" she squeals, as she sits in it and begins to rock. "My very own rocking chair! Thank you."

Only Keith is not enjoying the festivities. Introverted as he is, I've wondered if he may be autistic. He sits on the floor in a corner, holding his wee "blanky" with a thumb in his mouth, absolutely refusing to join us at the table for dessert. Perceiving this as a slight, Star boldly approaches him with a large slice of cake on a cardboard plate.

"It's *my* happy birthday Keith," she chastises him. "I want you to have some of my cake." She hands him the plate, sits down on the floor beside him and says sternly, "Eat!"

And eat, he does. Thrilled with his compliance, she absolutely glows. "You like my good cake, Keith?"

He nods, tentatively rewarding her with the ghost of a smile. It's the first time I've seen this little boy smile, and it's such a delight.

From here on in, with the advent of Star who takes him under her wing like a little mother hen and prods him out of his inner sanctum with both determination and love, he becomes a totally different child. In time, he becomes almost as outgoing as she.

The Christmas holidays follow close on the heels of Star's birthday, and for the first time in ages, I find myself enjoying the festivities. This year it's not just Karl who has a family to spend the holidays with while Star and I are pushed into the background. We'll be sharing the holidays with *our* new family: Len and his children. My parents have invited them for Christmas dinner and we'll be celebrating Christmas Eve at Len's home in the country.

Karl visits us on the last working day of the holidays. He arrives armed with gifts for Star, and once she's bedded down, he says, "Okay, *Schlange*, now for the operation. I'm all set with my surgical equipment, see?" He extends his hand to expose a large darning needle.

I admit I'm a little nervous, even though I know he's no novice in regard to piercing ears: he's done so for both his daughters.

"I always lose earrings," I mentioned last month. "Perhaps I can persuade you to pierce mine one day?"

Being close to the holidays he responded, "Okay. How about at Christmas, and my gift to you will be a pair of gold earrings?"

The time has come.

"Relax," he says, "This won't hurt a bit."

Later, he admires his handiwork. "Looks good, *Schlange*, and *I* didn't feel a thing, did you?"

"You damn near killed me, Karl," I tease. "You're a lousy doctor!"

"Bull!"

"No way. Screw you, Karl."

"Ha! Not *me, Schlange. You!*"

We begin play-fighting like children . . . until war turns to love.

Later, we share our usual hot bath, along with a final cherry brandy which we each balance on the edge of the tub. Once the water cools, we wash each other under the shower with a bar of pink Dove; the latter in deference to Inge's choice of soap, but mostly her bionic nose . . . an idiosyncrasy of Karl's which no longer bothers me.

As we joke around playfully, I reminisce fondly on our many good times which date back to Friday night double dates with my friends. He has met them all. He's such an intrinsic part of my life. Much as I'm attracted to Len and have grown to love and care for him, I know that I'm still emotionally bound to Karl . . . which does not play lightly with my conscience.

After Karl leaves, I spend some time in front of the mirror admiring my new earrings. They are beautiful golden hoops with intricate engravings. He has bought me many nice gifts over the years. And always, before he leaves, he puts some cash in Star's bank.

"A little something to help you look after my daughter's needs," he says, when I happen to catch him.

Later, he makes a game of it and hides money under cushions or pillows or what-have-you. I'm like a kid on an Easter egg hunt after he leaves, and he always wants to know if I have found any "eggs" the next time he calls. *It must be difficult for him,* I muse. *He doesn't have a large salary, yet he always does his best to supply us with these little extras, along with the many lovely gifts.* I regard the black onyx ring he gave me last Christmas. I wear it on my ring finger and dearly treasure it, having long since given Jeff's diamond to my mother. *You're a good man, Charlie Brown,* I murmur silently, *and oh, how I love you!*

My nervous attacks become more frequent in the New Year. They seem to happen spontaneously. From one moment to the next I never know when they'll rear their unsightly presence. I now live in constant fear of having one occur. They alternate between episodes of light-headedness and dizziness mixed with feelings of disconnection from reality, and just plain attacks of intense fear. One variety is not more bearable than the other. Both imply a total loss of control and are frightening as hell.

For a while now, I've been dropping Star off at Mom's when I do my food shopping, because these attacks have begun plaguing me in grocery stores. Lately, it seems that every time I enter one my reaction has become a conditioned response: *supermarket equals fear.* The acute terror hits almost instantaneously. Panicked and humiliated, I ditch my partially-filled food cart and make a beeline for the door.

All too soon, I stop setting foot in *any* supermarket. I order our groceries in entirety by phone and have them delivered to the door. I've now become too afraid to enter a store . . . *any* store.

The first time I'm hit with an attack at work, I realize I'm in big trouble. I've no idea how much time I've lost in the restroom, huddled in a cubicle in absolute fear. I wonder what I can tell my boss if he's been looking for me. I decide to blame it on a splitting headache. It sure as hell sounds more reasonable than saying I freaked out for no reason.

Many years later I'm to discover I've been suffering from panic disorder—an illness of the future; only to be recognized as a mental health condition by the American Psychiatric Association in the year 1980. Not exactly a prospect in any way conducive to obtaining adequate help; or, more importantly, a measure of compassion for anyone unfortunate enough to be ravaged by it.

A week later I submit to a complete physical examination by a physician I've been told is highly competent. I want to find out if there's a physical cause for the nervous attacks I've been having. After a thorough check-up, I return for a follow-up appointment.

"The results of your tests are all satisfactory," he says, as he peruses the papers in front of him.

"Then it must be my mental health. There has to be a reason for these spontaneous attacks of terror that beset me. I simply can't go on like this. My life has become an absolute hell. Surely, there's some help for me?" I beseech him.

"Look," he says condescendingly, "I've had patients come to me in a far worse nervous state than you. Some of them are crying and moaning in my office and unable to even sit still in a chair."

How do you think I react when I'm in the middle of an attack? I think. *How dare you patronize me!* Yet I wisely forego voicing my thoughts. I can't afford to alienate this doctor who may have a means of saving me, despite his shoddy bedside manner.

"The best I can do is to offer you a prescription for tranquilizers," he concludes.

"Oh, thank you," I murmur in relief. At last I have found some help!

I fill the prescription for Librium and take it faithfully for the next few weeks as directed, but during this time I am still plagued by the fearful episodes. Disheartened, I find myself facing the same physician, explaining that the tranquilizers have not helped at all.

"Even the increased dosage you suggested over the phone has not improved anything. I've had two subsequent attacks at the office and my boss is not exactly blind. He's already noticed one of my disappearances which I blamed on a physical cause. I don't know how long I can keep hiding this. I j-just can't lose my job. If t-that happens I'll lose my child as well," I babble miserably.

"You're taking this whole thing too seriously," he admonishes sternly. 'It's not as though your condition portends your being nailed in a coffin any time soon, my dear."

Oh, really? Well, I'd sure as hell like to see how you'd be reacting if faced with my condition, you pompous ass! How can you regard a person's affliction so nonchalantly when you have not walked in their shoes? Again, I wisely swallow these sentiments.

I accept the prescription he proffers for another brand of tranquilizers; along with his suggestion I discontinue the Pill which he says has been known to cause depression in some women.

I leave his office with two prescriptions in hand: the second is for a diaphragm.

Despite this new course of action the attacks continue to flourish, drawing ever closer together. Scarcely a day goes by that I'm spared from one. I continue to fight on, trying my utmost to keep my disreputable monster under wraps. By April 1969 I've entered the eighth month of this nervous disorder which has been steadily worsening with no help forthcoming. I'm worn-out, battle-fatigued, and a nervous wreck. I'm hanging onto a cliff by a thread.

A few days later I experience, for the first time, an unrelenting, non-stop attack. There's a settee in the ladies' restroom and one of my co-workers finds me curled upon it, panting in terror.

"Oh my God, Irene, are you all right?" she gasps. "You don't look well at all. Your boss wants some letters typed but I'll gladly do that. I think you should go home and haul your ass into bed."

"I think you're r-right, Carol," I stammer breathlessly.

Moments later, I approach my boss.

"I'm sorry about your l-letters, Mr. Lebeau. I'm feeling d-deathly ill. I t-think I may need a doctor. I'd like your permission to go home." Swaying back and forth, I grasp his desk for support.

"I'll call you a cab, Irene," he offers, not unkindly. "You're shaking, and your deathly pale. You really *should* see a doctor."

Even if his concern is based on the fear I may drop dead in the office, I'm grateful for this thread of human kindness. Once the hack arrives, I give the driver my mother's address.

I rush into her apartment and fling myself on the couch, sobbing in abject misery.

"Oh God, I don't know what's happening to me. I'm in absolute panic and it won't let go. I've been c-constantly fighting it, but this time *it's winning*," I cry, as Mom tries in vain to console me. "It's f-finally taken possession of me. *Oh God, oh God, whatever can I do?*" I pluck a magazine from the coffee table and find myself unable to concentrate enough to absorb the words of even one sentence.

Surely it's my inherent will to survive that prompts me to make my own distress call to a psychiatric institute in the downtown area.

My mother is wonderfully supportive. She drops everything and accompanies me to the emergency unit by cab. After assisting me with the registration, she sits patiently beside me. As visions of straitjackets dance in my head, I'm certain I've finally gone mad.

Whatever will become of my precious daughter if I'm locked up? I recall Dad once saying that no matter how much he loves Star, he's working shifts and would be unable to sleep with a young child running around the house.

I simply can't bear for her to be placed in a foster home, I despair. These unwelcome thoughts churn in my head, further inflaming my dread.

The shrink assigned to me is a tall, dark-haired youngish man–in no way the ominous person I had expected. Draining every power I possess, I valiantly try to achieve a degree of coherency in expressing my disjointed thoughts. My body portrays its distress in non-stop movement as my limbs shake and jerk involuntarily.

Finally, I come to a halt and fearfully await the doctor's assessment.

God be thanked! He's assuring me I'm definitely connected to reality and mustn't worry about going crazy.

"I believe you're suffering a severe nervous reaction based upon indecision and the inability to confront your situation which, admittedly, is a deeply distressful one. You're also troubled by a great deal of guilt. I believe some psychotherapy would help you immensely. We can carefully sort through all of your concerns together. In the interim I'll prescribe you some medication to lessen the severity of your symptoms. How about we see each other for an hour every Wednesday afternoon at 1:00 PM?"

My relief is palpable. I have *not* lost my mind! This is not just *any* doctor, this is a *shrink!* I eagerly agree.

I am embarrassed and distressed when I confront my boss and confess my nervous disorder, but I consider the Wednesday psychotherapy sessions vital to my well-being and, by association, my daughter's as well. He grants me permission, but is by no means pleased. "I sincerely hope this practice won't have to continue too long, Irene."

I sure as hell hope not, I sigh inwardly.

After meeting with the shrink for several weeks and not experiencing any further attacks, I begin to take heart in the assumption that I may be cured. It nevertheless comes as a blow to learn on my next appointment that he'll be leaving for permanent residence in Europe. I feel my lifeline has been clipped and I'll surely drown.

"What happens to me now?" I utter dismayed. "Obviously, I'm being dismissed."

"From me, yes," he declares. "However, if you feel it necessary, I can refer you to a colleague. Personally I think you can make it on your own from here on in. Once you make a decision as to exactly what you want to do with your life, I guarantee the attacks of anxiety you've been suffering in the past will likely become non-existent in the future."

An inner voice taunts me with the refrain that perhaps I've been okay thus far because I've had this doctor as a crutch and that

I should definitely ask for continued follow-up. Conversely, I feel childish and cowardly to plead further assistance. I decide to take his advice and summon the courage to traverse my shaky path alone.

Following my dismissal, I continue to take the Valium tablets and pursue my life as usual, but a decision continues to evade me. Aware I'm burning the candle at both ends–Len has also become my lover–my guilt has increased two-fold, especially since Len is so focused on marrying me. Marriage would allow me to become a full-time mother for both Star and his children and would be the ideal solution for both of us. Yet the very thought of parting from Karl is almost too painful to bear.

I reflect upon a recent conversation with the shrink along these lines.

"Well, since it appears you'd like the best of both worlds, why don't you simply take it?" he suggests.

"Surely, you're not insinuating I should marry Len and continue the affair with Karl?" I question, somewhat shocked. "You *can't* be serious? *Are* you?" Surely, he doesn't condone such indiscretions?

"Well, it would be an answer to your dilemma, would it not?" he replies cryptically.

His response alerts me that this could be a trick question designed to trap me. So be it. It's important to be completely honest, and I can't help but grin at the incongruity of his suggestion.

"Well, in all honesty, I can't say I haven't *considered* it," I venture.

"Oh? And what have you come up with?"

"A headache. A very *severe* headache. And that's precisely why I *remain* in this dilemma. I know I'm no saint, but I could not deal with the guilt of entering a marriage to a good man like Len with such an intention. It would be the ultimate betrayal. I can scarcely cope with the guilt I have now as a *single* person with two lovers. No, Doctor. Such an alternative is inconceivable."

"I see. Well I guess that narrows down the alternatives, doesn't it?"

What am I to do? I ponder desperately, as I've been doing time and again. How can I ever rid myself of my fatal addiction to Karl, the idealistic first love of my youth? While Len can ignite my body, Karl still possesses my soul. In a way, I'm betraying both men. Yet, most of all, I'm betraying myself and my daughter . . . by denying us both a better life.

I realize I am trapped within the painful vortex of indecision. A black, boundless void, though not an empty one. It's filled with the cackling demons of anger, guilt and fear.

A few days later, the monster awakens once more. I'm besieged with yet another brutal attack in the office. Turning to prayer for the first time in years, I solemnly invoke God's help.

On a psychological level, the panic attacks that resumed so violently over the past year paralleled the two I suffered years ago—all a surface manifestation of an inner perception that my survival was threatened. Marriage to Len was ultimately my wisest choice; yet Karl (Mother), represented my continued survival. Ravaged by indecision—not unlike the physical threat of being chased by a bear—my body was reacting in a similar fashion by sporadically releasing doses of adrenaline as it does in the fight or flight response. My state of continuous physiological arousal was affecting every system of my body to the point where the ensuing panic attacks were merely the tumultuous symptoms of the gradual splintering of my very core.

On a spiritual level, in full understanding of what ACIM reveals (that nothing can happen to us apart from our own personal choice), the subsequent attacks may well have been auspicious in their revival by propelling me ever more aggressively toward my destiny.

And when even they failed to fully sway me, my subjective mind sought another ploy: it aligned me with my higher power.

Whereby the decision would be made for me.

The following Saturday evening when Len and I arrive back at my apartment after our date, Merry offers to wait for her dad in the car to give us a few parting moments alone. Quite unintentionally our goodnight kiss leads us to my couch, and it's not before the following morning–when attempting to remove a diaphragm that's shockingly not there–that I realize I was unprotected. Horrified, I call Len.

"I hope you become pregnant," he says heatedly. "I know that's the only way you'll marry me." I feel deeply moved by his words and my heart is filled with a tender love for this man who, unlike Karl, always picks me up when I fall down . . . though perhaps, in all fairness, because he is able.

And from that fateful union, a child is conceived: our precious daughter, Eve.

Len and I set a date for our wedding, and proceed with the necessary arrangements which are few. Only a handful of family members will be invited.

A week or so later, I resign from my job. The deed is done.

Star led me to Len, which brought me to this very moment of honouring what I believe was my pre-birth contract. There are no accidents. I was meant to follow her lead.

My daughter Eve played her part as well–by signing the bottom line in indelible ink.

God's messengers appear to us in many guises: and by far the most beautiful . . . those of a child.

The most difficult task is informing Karl. He's aware I've been dating a widower but has likely assumed it's platonic, as it was with Jeff. *There's really no pressing need to fully clue him in,* I tell myself: *He's not exactly a stranger to burning the candle at both ends himself.*

The following Friday, I drop the proverbial bomb once Star is in bed.

"Karl," I begin haltingly, "I have something to tell you. I know you're aware of the anxiety I've been suffering over these past months. Well, it's finally reached a point where I feel I'm caving in. I doubt I'll be able to hang onto my job the way things are going. Len, the widower I've been seeing, has asked me to marry him. He's been proposing on and off, but I've always declined because of my deep love for you. I've come to care for him dearly over the past while;

although emotionally, my heart still belongs to *you. That* has not changed.

"My life circumstances, however, have been drastically altered, especially in view of my overwhelming stress. I'm also consumed with guilt that I'm not giving our daughter the life she deserves—a less stressful existence in a home with both a mother *and* a father. Please know that I understand how much you'd like to personally give her this gift. I also understand you feel it's your duty to honour your obligations to your first family and I don't fault you for it. However, much as I love you, Karl, I have decided to marry Len. I know you'll understand my reasoning and I only ask you to wish me well. You will never know the grief I've suffered in making this choice."

As the tears stream freely down his cheeks, in accord with my own, I put my arms around him. "It won't be over until it's over," I whisper. "We have another two weeks."

How can I ever forget Black Friday? It's the month of July and the day before my marriage to Len. Karl has come to say goodbye to both his daughter and myself. In a different era, perhaps a few decades hence, I may have been able to insist upon Karl having the privilege of remaining in his daughter's life—meeting with her on occasion—despite the fact that he was not my ex-husband. Not then. As his mistress, such a bold deed would have reduced me to a pariah.

We know this is the end of an era . . . for the three of us.

When Star's bedtime finally arrives, he falls to his knees and clasps her small body—now clad in colourful pyjamas—to his large one. Grief, stark and oppressive, registers in his eyes as he hugs and kisses her for the last time.

"My love you, Daddy," she lilts joyfully, not understanding the enormity of the occasion.

Emitting small, choking sounds, he crushes her to him, relying upon his heart to speak to her of his love. Somehow she conceives this is a highly-charged moment. Whenever she's held tightly, she generally squirms to be released. Yet, she remains silent now, and clings to her father in reciprocation of his love.

"Take her," he croaks.

I know he doesn't want her to see him cry. Anything untoward I may have felt he has done in the past is washed away in this moment of witnessing his personal agony. Quickly, I extricate her from his arms and deposit her in her crib.

"Why you cry?" she asks in her bell-like voice. "You sick, Mommy?"

"No, sweetheart, I'm not sick. Mommy had something in her eye, but it's all better now. Star got a big kiss for me before she goes to bed?"

She raises her lips to mine before I gently tuck her in and we exchange our nightly endearments.

I return to Karl who's seated in the large armchair in the living room. I've never seen him in such a state. His shoulders heave in spasmodic jerks as he weeps profusely.

"It's all right, Karl," I soothe. "Cry. You need to release it." I sit on his lap and enfold him in my arms as he sobs, wretchedly, unashamedly–allowing his torment to be wrenched from its depths. I'm aware that this tough German with his stoic pride is baring his very soul and it is painful to witness.

"I love you," I gasp. "I always will."

"And, me you," he gulps. He entangles his fingers in my hair; and as my own torrential storm breaks loose, we weep together as we share the incredible sadness within our hearts . . . for what can never be.

Later, at the front door, we face each other for the last time. We stand quietly, our eyes riveted, each with the mutual hope of indelibly imprinting each other's features forever in our minds . . . details that seconds later will blend into yesterday's memories.

"I guess this is goodbye, Karl," I murmur softly. Should I say more? Should I thank him for the multitude of things that were good and valuable? For all the love?

No words will come.

His eyes reveal his comprehension. In this poignant moment, he too is mute; but our eyes portray what a thousand words cannot. He opens the door, and then turns to me once more.

We do not kiss. He takes my hand and presses it tightly within his own.

"I cannot say goodbye to you, *Schlange*. It sounds too eternal. It's *auf Wiedersehen*."

Until we meet again, I silently translate.

I watch sadly as he descends the first flight of stairs. When he reaches the landing, he looks back. Our eyes lock for a moment, and then he is out of sight.

My mind is blank from that moment on.

There is no doubt that Karl, too, was a guide from beyond–another great teacher–and that his appearance was not random in my life. In hindsight, I learned from him that love is abstract and goes beyond a wedding band. He, too, had his own soul's lessons to learn, and duty kept him on his path. As part of Life's plan, he gave me Star, and through loving him I would later learn that all great truths of the heart are abstract . . . the latter a truth I have applied in regard to loving God Itself.

Len and I are married the next day. He is overjoyed. Although I care for him dearly, I'm a sad bride.

I have finally clipped my reins and I no longer belong to my puppeteer. It seems my life has never been *more* "upside down."

I enter my marriage in grief tone.

Chapter 7 – Destiny

"Your children are not your children.
They are the sons and daughters of Life's longing for itself.
They come through you but not from you,
and though they are with you yet they belong not to you."
—Khalil Gibran

Following a three-day honeymoon in the motel across the street from my parents' home—during which time Len's teenagers and the little ones crash in my apartment–Star and I make the trek with Len and his brood to our new home in the wilds of Cedar Dam. I am nursing a massive hangover. I've been drunk for most of the weekend.

Young and resilient, I gradually begin to adjust to my new life. Although I'm fond of the bungalow Len has built, I'm admittedly not enthralled with its location. I'm removed from my friends, no longer on a city bus line, and limited to the phone calls I can make, most of them involving long distance costs.

On the upside, I'm now a homemaker and stay-at-home mom and the previous pressures have lessened considerably. I apply myself to my new endeavour with zest. I experiment with different recipes and become more adept in the culinary arts. It's difficult to know just how much to prepare for such a large family, but Merry is a great teacher. I soon become very attached to her. She's always eager to assist me, and between us we paint rooms, hang drapes and re-decorate at a minimum of cost.

At times, it can be nerve-wracking to have three rambunctious teens home on summer holiday, but for the most part I enjoy it. Still a kid at heart myself, I take pleasure in doing things with them and having them underfoot helps distract me from brooding over Karl whom I still miss profoundly. Too young to be a mother replacement, I opt for the role of big sister and I insist Len do any disciplining of the older ones. Star and Keith are my jurisdiction. This seems to fare well, and as the weeks slip by I become more secure in my new skin.

All is not smooth sailing on the sea of matrimony, however. I begin to see a side of Len that was fully obscured during our courtship. I had previously marvelled at his relaxed, easy-going nature, so different from my own more volatile temperament. Upon becoming his wife, I soon witness his other face. He can be quite vocal and we soon begin having rows.

One day, while I am bent over tackling a stain on the floor, he approaches me from behind.

"Oh my, I can't resist!" he chuckles. He proceeds to boot me in the backside and I find myself sprawled on the floor on my tummy. Furious, I pull myself up.

"You damn idiot!" I sputter. "Don't you even care about the baby?" Without thinking I slap his face. He instantly retaliates with a backhanded slap of his own which sends my head reeling. Though stunned by the sting of his powerful welt, I'm far more wounded that he would actually hit me.

"You bastard!" I screech. "That does, it! I'm outta here. A gentleman would never strike a woman, let alone a pregnant one!"

Infuriated, I storm off and begin packing a bag. Meanwhile, I can't help but recall the one time I slapped Karl in a similar manner. He merely walked away.

I'm just about ready to leave when I hear the bedroom door slam and a key turn in the lock. Len has locked me in from the outside! At this point, I lose it. I begin kicking the door in fury, screaming at him to let me out. He won't budge. I canvass the window but, being pregnant, I'm afraid of the drop. Finally, I become hoarse from shouting. I'm aware the teenagers must hear me but are simply wise enough to lay low. Len doesn't appear to care. I finally stop hollering and simply wait. Eventually, he'll have to make a move.

An hour or so passes before he deigns to open the door. "Do you still want to leave?" he says. He appears subdued.

"What the hell do you think?" I retort. "And I *will* leave one way or the other. You can't keep me locked-up indefinitely."

All fight has left him. "You don't have to call a cab. Tell me where you and Star want to go, and I'll drive you there."

I'm not about to refuse. My personal funds are low and a cab will cost a fortune. "To my parents' home for now. After that, I'm not sure."

"It was a self-defense thing," he says, once we're ensconced in the car. "I hit back automatically. I didn't mean it."

"Yeah, like you didn't mean locking me up for a couple of hours, right? I don't want to hear it."

After he drops us off, I put Star down in the spare crib in my former bedroom. I later tell my parents what transpired and that I don't plan to stand for that crap.

"You undoubtedly set him off by slapping him," my father says.

"Yes. And you can have a cruel tongue as well," my mother chimes in.

"No matter what I may have said or done is no damn excuse for him to have retaliated with such force, and to lock me up afterwards," I sputter.

"Well, don't think we'll get involved in your quarrels and harbour you here. You probably deserved exactly what you got," my father claims.

"Star and I will be out of here first thing in the morning," I say quietly as I abruptly stalk off.

Stung, I get into bed and quietly sob. I should not be surprised by Dad's reaction. He has slapped my mother more than once, and she thinks she deserved it because he said she baited him with her angry words. If verbal provocation is an excuse for assault, why doesn't he belt his superior at work–or anyone else who has incensed him? Because *that* would entail consequences. He has hit both Mom and me simply because he can. *Thank God the times are beginning to change. Though painfully slow,* I muse. I momentarily reflect upon my growing-up years when it was *solely* a man's world, women and children being not more than chattel. It was okay for a man to "physically discipline" a wife or child to keep them in line. Mom has never raised a hand to him; but conditioned as she is by the sexist views of the times she believes he has the right to strike *her.*

Dismayed, I wonder if I've married my father.

The next day, Star and I go to her godmother's place. We stay for the next three days, but my friend lives with her widowed mother and I know we can't impose upon them indefinitely.

Mom calls me there to ask when I'm going home. Len has called her with his side of the story and he's sorry. "I think you should call him, Irene."

"Surely you're kidding? I know you've probably told him exactly where we are, and he hasn't been man enough to pick up the phone and call *me,* so why should I strain myself?" I argue.

"Well, um, that's probably because your dad told Len that he's the one in the driver's seat so he should just sit back and wait for *you* to call *him.* Your father said you'll eventually hang your tail between your legs and go home. You and Star have nowhere else to go. That's the truth, Irene. You can't just run away—"

"*What!*" I screech. "How could he betray me like that, his own daughter? What a miserable bastard he is! I *hate* him! And you, too, for siding with both him *and* my fucking husband!" I slam down the phone.

Thank you, Dad, for making things crystal-clear, especially to my husband. I address him silently, and bitterly. *I'm totally screwed. I have nowhere to go, I'm out of funds, out of a job, and pregnant with a toddler to look after. Besides all that, I'm still battling a nervous condition that leaves me too fearful to face the unknown, not that you're aware of the latter or you'd have thrown it in my résumé as well, you miserable ass!*

How is all that for unlimited choices, Irene? You just have to make the best of it.

I call Len and arrange for him to pick us up after work. Inwardly, I'm seething.

For a few days the atmosphere remains cool between us and I sleep on the couch. He eventually comes sniffing around and tells me how sorry he is; that he hit me back solely by reflex and that he locked me in the room hoping I'd quieten down and not leave him.

"If that *ever* happens again, I *will* leave you," I retort. "And you may as well know that I'm not at all happy being stuck in the middle of nowhere with only a couple of foreign farmers for neighbours. Unless you think of selling and moving to Cassellman, I intend to go back to work and leave this godforsaken hole as soon as the baby is born." I really don't know if I can do this based on the current state of my nerves. But he doesn't have to know that.

A few days later, he puts an ad in the local paper advertising the house, and a "for sale" sign on the front lawn. I have at least won a small victory, perhaps sufficient enough that I can stop dragging my tail along the sidewalk.

Our marriage has started off on a rocky road. He can be the kindest person there is but I'll often come face to face with the power of his male anger which inwardly frightens me. I'm now aware that I'm not the only one to harbour the inner company of a Jekyll and Hyde. I've met my match, and then some.

Things run smoothly for the next while, and the lazy days of summer drift quickly by. Once the teenagers return to school I find myself with more time to ruminate. When Star and Keith are fed and dressed I begin my day. Performing my household duties and keeping an eye on the children is an automatic function and I find Karl's presence haunting me. Daily I continue to mourn my loss as I pine the death of our seven years together. I continue taking the Valium tablets to help me cope as I still have a great deal of anxiety when alone all day with the little ones. I don't feel quite as frightened when the rest of the family are home.

My greatest happiness is on behalf of my daughter. She has a live-in companion in Keith, and although they sometimes bicker as little kids tend to do, they could not love each other more and they're inseparable. They share a bedroom on the main floor which previously belonged to Len's two teenage sons who now occupy a room of their own which Len built for each of them in the basement.

The little ones have their own crib, but likely as not they're curled up in one crib by morning. They share everything together, including their evening bath which they relish as play time. I let them splash in the tub for at least an hour. Loving the water as they do, Len takes the garden hose and fills up a large wooden vat on the lawn which becomes their private pool. During the warm summer afternoons they play in it contentedly for hours on end.

They also get into a lot of mischief together and we aptly name them the *Terrible Twins*. Hardly a morning goes by that they don't empty their dresser drawers in entirety, and I awaken to their clothing strewn all over the floor. Merry makes the fatal mistake of leaving a few of her favourite water colours from art class behind one of their bureaus which are discovered and ripped to shreds.

On another occasion, they decide to wash the basement floor and sneak downstairs where they ingeniously find a way to reach the high shelf that contains the laundry products. When a pungent odour of disinfectant reaches my nostrils, I dash downstairs. Spying a chair pushed up against the dryer, I immediately devise how the little culprits have accomplished their feat. The entire bottle of bleach has been emptied on the floor and my two busy beavers are diligently pushing a mop.

One day their mischief backfires, scaring the daylights out of them. After plugging in the electric floor polisher and turning on its switch, much to their dismay it begins moving of its own volition and speeding rapidly towards them. They race down the basement steps with the polisher literally hopping down after them. Upon hearing their terrified shrieks I'm astonished to see they are huddled together, trapped on the landing, with the electrical machine zooming around them as though it possesses a will of its own.

I'm not without frustration on such occasions, and soon learn the wisdom of never, ever trusting quiet children. When they're at their silent best, I can be assured the conniving little rascals are up to some preposterous act. Len and I often chuckle fondly over some of the devilment they create, Star usually being the instigator. They're nevertheless very special, lovable little creatures and their cute little sayings and antics rarely fail to amuse us.

They will bring a lot of joy into our lives . . . for such an infinitely short while.

Things begin to fall into place in my married life. In the hope the house will sell soon we have not yet arranged a room for the new baby. My pregnancy is going well. I get along famously with my step-children, and my parents drop in a few times a week and often take Star and Keith for an outing. Star is christened in Len's name and he becomes her legal father. Although I still have some generalized anxiety when home alone with the little ones, my monster has been mainly quiescent since quitting my job. I still experience intense fear upon entering supermarkets, so I simply avoid them and make a list for Len and Merry who take care of grocery shopping one evening a week. From time to time I make an effort to go into smaller shops; at first accompanied, then alone. I find I'm making some minor gains and reclaiming some self-esteem in the process.

The initial grief over Karl recedes somewhat as the days pass, and I find I'm beginning to reap some real joys in my new life. I'm beginning to relax . . . in my fool's paradise.

I'm completely unprepared for the tempest when it strikes.

In the late afternoon of Thursday, November 13, 1969–following my six month pre-natal check-up–I'm pleased and content. The obstetrician has assured us all is well with the baby and, feeling no urgency to rush home, we linger over a quiet meal in town.

We arrive home around eight o'clock and I'm still feeling the glow of pleasure from being able to dine out in comparative ease again, minus the constant dread of a potential anxiety attack hovering over me.

Star and Keith have been tucked-in for the night by Merry, and I slip quietly into their room to plant a goodnight kiss on their cheeks. Keith is fast asleep; yet Star is lying silently on her back, her eyes wide open. I smile at her fondly.

"So, my baby stayed awake to see her mommy, did she?" I tease.

"My feel sick, Mommy," she murmurs hoarsely.

"What's the matter, sweetie?" I inquire, concerned.

"My throat hurts lots."

Her forehead is burning. Alarmed, I take her temperature, which registers at 105 degrees rectally. Frightened such high fever may cause convulsions, I administer aspirin and place her in a cool bath of alcohol and water. I'm unable to sleep as I can't control her fever for long. I bathe her continuously throughout the night. It's the only way I can lower her body temperature temporarily.

By mid-morning the following day, her fever soars to 106 degrees and I call Len at work.

"Please, honey," I implore, "You have to come home. Star's seriously ill and I need to get her to hospital immediately."

Arriving at the St. Ann's Children's Hospital in downtown Cassellman not long afterwards, Star is examined by an intern.

"Nothing to worry about," he assures us. "It's a severe throat infection but some antibiotics will have her right as rain in no time."

That night, we move her crib into the master bedroom to be sure I'll awaken if she stirs. It's a wasted effort. The aspirin is doing little to control her high fever, and once again I spend most of the night bathing her. She completely refuses to eat which I determine is due to the soreness in her throat, but she's resisting any liquids as well. There's no way I can entice her into taking her medication. She simply refuses to open her mouth. Finally I'm forced to raise my voice to ensure she co-operates in swallowing her antibiotics and drinking a little water. Her mouth is parched and I worry she may become dehydrated.

By Saturday afternoon I'm frantic that despite my continuous ministrations her fever cannot be controlled. Once again, we rush her to the hospital only to be admonished that we must give the antibiotics a chance to take effect.

By Sunday, after another sleepless night, I'm totally disheartened. It's almost 48 hours since she began the antibiotics and there is still no sign of improvement. If anything, her condition appears to be worsening. Noticing a large swelling on one side of her neck which feels hard to the touch, I am gripped with the first stirrings of panic. I place a call to the hospital ER and am connected with one of the physicians on duty. I briefly explain what's transpired over the past few days, along with the new set of developments.

"Obviously, I'm unable to make a diagnosis over the phone," the doctor says, "but we've had a few cases of mumps lately. I suggest you continue the antibiotics and if she still shows no sign of improvement, bring her back in tomorrow."

Overwhelmed with the dread that such a high fever could lead to brain damage, I continue to bathe her. I have to practically force her medication down her throat as her rejection of it, along with all food or drink, is absolute.

Monday morning heralds the fourth day of Star's illness and the end of the fourth night that I have scarcely slept. Len has left for work and I find myself nodding off from time to time, constantly prodding myself to stay awake and alert. Her temperature continues to peak at 106 degrees and I sense her condition is critical.

Stricken with an unbidden flashback of my friend Jan's prediction when she read my cards over a year ago, I am overcome with the horrifying premonition that it was Star's death she foresaw. I call my mother in panic.

"Can you please come over?" I sob. "Star is no better. There's not an inkling of improvement. The hospital has refused her twice already and I'm afraid they may send her home again. I've got to get some medical help for her soon. *Someway! Somehow!* Otherwise she's going to die!"

"Calm down, honey. Your dad and I will drive right over and we'll see that something gets accomplished today."

I take my baby into my arms and begin rocking her. "Dear little Star, Mommy loves you so much," I croon.

"My love you too, Mommy," she replies in a hoarse whisper. Sick and flushed with fever though she is, she places a parched kiss upon my lips.

"My baby, my baby, my beloved little girl," I whisper, as I clasp her small body tightly to my own, maternally possessive of this little life, desiring only to protect it from all harm.

Silently I cry out to God, beseeching Him from the depths of my anguish to spare her; but there is no comfort forthcoming. I think a part of me already knows–and has perhaps known since the moment of her birth–that God wants her too, and that I am powerless in face of the Great Cosmic Force that is reaching out to claim her. Never have I felt more helpless and wretched. The loss of Karl is but a teardrop within the ocean of grief that currently engulfs me.

The jarring ring of the telephone interrupts my fearful reverie. It's my dear friend, Lily. Bursting into tears, I explain what's transpired.

"Irene, try to be calm for a moment. I want you to take down the number of Dr.Schmidt. He's our family pediatrician and one of the best in the city. Insist his receptionist put you through to him, and avoid a third-degree from her by saying it's a personal matter. Tell Dr. Schmidt I referred you, and let him know exactly what's happening. I assure you he's an extremely conscientious doctor and once he's heard Star's symptoms he *will* see her. I guarantee it."

"Oh, Lily, bless you a hundredfold. I'll call him right away."

Moments later, I'm wailing to the doctor in a half-demented fashion. Manic from fear and lack of sleep I try to explain Star's symptoms whilst constantly reiterating my belief that she is dying and I'm unable to obtain medical help. Somehow, he catches the drift of what I'm saying.

"Mrs. Snow," he replies gently. "I'm sure it's not as serious as you believe. Many children become exceeding ill; yet they are far more resilient than you may think. They generally respond rapidly to the right treatment. I'm leaving my office now, and I'll be doing some rounds at the hospital for the next hour." He advises me of its location in Cassellman. "If you can meet me there within that time frame, I'll examine your daughter. Just bring her to the ER and have me paged."

"Oh thank you, thank you! We'll be there within the hour," I acknowledge gratefully.

I've no sooner hung up the phone than my parents arrive. I relay the turn of events.

"We're so far away I'm afraid we won't make it in time if Dad drives us," I explain. "I can't face arriving too late and getting stuck with another idiot intern who will likely send us home again. Dr. Schmidt is a highly qualified pediatrician and it's imperative Star sees him. I'm calling an ambulance."

Trembling, I dial the number of a service within my vicinity. "It will cost you $30.00, payable on pick-up," a male voice decrees. "We don't accept cheques."

"No problem. You'll get your money. Just please hurry!"

"What money?" Dad quizzes.

I explain as I get Star into her snowsuit.

"Why those thieving bastards!" he roars. "What happens if someone is dying and a relative doesn't have the ready cash? Do they just take off and let the person die, for crisssake? I—"

Mother cuts him off. "I guess you can always get a police ambulance in that case. Please Joe, cool it. Now is not the time to go on the rampage, and for God's sake keep your big mouth shut when the ambulance arrives. Irene has enough on—"

Her voice trails off as I rush around attending to last minute details. I'm only relieved that Merry stayed home from school to help me today. She'll be there for Keith.

Mom accompanies me in the ambulance while Dad follows by car, and within the hour Star is being examined by Dr. Schmidt.

"The swelling on her neck is caused by a large mass of localized infection," he informs me. "Your daughter has a severe throat infection, but I've seen similar cases and I assure you they were all treatable. You have her in the right place. I'm admitting her in view of the severity of her condition and the dehydration that's incurred. We'll have her on I.V. immediately. Please try not to worry yourself unduly, Mrs. Snow. Your little girl will be fine within the next day or two."

Mom and I spend the balance of the afternoon at Star's bedside and Dad, who hates hospitals, leaves within the usual quarter hour. Len meets us after work.

"I have to stay in Cassellman with my parents for the next while," I tell him. "It's not possible for you to drive me to the hospital every morning, and then get back to work on time. And there's no bus service in Cedar Dam. Mom has offered to accompany me to the hospital each day for the duration of Star's confinement. I can use her support just now. I know how difficult it is for you to take time off without pay and I wouldn't expect it. I'm sure Merry can look after Keith for the next few days."

"Stay with your parents as long as necessary, honey. You mustn't worry about anyone or anything but Star right now."

I hug him gratefully as some of the tension begins to ease, and I try to make sense of my dread. Perhaps I'm making a mountain out of a molehill. I'm so overtired, after all. That's probably why I'm being foolish and jumping to false conclusions. I try to convince myself of this, but I'm unable to derive any real comfort thereby. If it is true that Star will be fine, why do my maternal instincts continue to transmit such waves of despair?

And why can I not subdue the intuitive voice from deep within that augurs a tragic loss?

MAY 21, 2012, MONDAY

Gary's second 21-day cycle of chemo begins today. He's begun to lose his hair and Eve endeavours to make it a more positive experience by explaining: "Hair cells, like cancer cells, are very fast-growing, and that's why chemo causes hair loss. Every chunk that falls out predicts the annihilation of tons of cancer cells as well. It's a good omen." Gary grins and accepts this.

No longer permitted to be in large groups while his immune system is compromised by the chemo, his oncologist relents and allows him to watch his Friday night team play floor hockey in the church basement providing he wears a medical mask. He goes weekly with his dad to encourage his mates.

Seeing Gary engaged in a lengthy chat with one of the parents last Friday, his father later asked him, "What was that all about?"

He replied nonchalantly, "Nothing much, Dad, Just the cancer."

Later, a friend said, "See you next week!"

"I sure hope so," Gary replied, then grinned at his stricken pal and quipped, "Just kidding."

I look forward to these tidbits of news from Eve and the knowledge that although Gary is aware of the gravity of his illness, he's not succumbing to dark thoughts. By being optimistic, he's attracting positive energy from the universe. Energy to help him through the coming days.

There's much we can learn from Gary. Brave, funny Gary. Our family musician, entertainer and clown. I recently congratulated him for using visualization as an aid to dissolve his tumours. He laughed. "Yeah, my mom said they're the only living things I'm allowed to kill."

Our Gary gives us so much pleasure. When his classical pieces bring tears to my eyes, he grins delightedly, knowing his music has spoken to my soul.

He's also our family magician, and recalling his talent in this venue, I write him another poem.

THE MAGIC MAN

Our Gary–known as Magic Man–
Slays dragons with no sword in hand;
He conjures up a potent spell,
That shifts them to the dens of hell.

Though smoke and mirror tricks imply
His hand's just quicker than the eye,
Some grasp the truth within the lie,
And know he's oft made monsters sigh.

As Christ, the Great Magician, said:
"Faith heals the sick, and wakes the dead;"
And Gary, too, will soon reveal–
ALL magic waits to be made real.

My dearest Gary, may you continue to know that your dragons are illusory and that your special magic can confine them forevermore to the dens of darkness from whence they came.

Chapter 8 – It's Not Goodbye

"The wound is the place where the Light enters you."
—<u>Rumi</u>

E arly the next morning, Tuesday, November 18th, Dr. Schmidt calls me at my parents' home. Prematurely in dread of what I may hear, I tense in apprehension as soon as he identifies himself.

"Mrs. Snow, I'm afraid it's more serious that I originally believed," he pronounces gravely. "We've discovered a malignancy."

My mind numbs at his words. As if from a great distance, I hear my voice falter pathetically. "You m-mean the lump on her neck?"

"No, the cancer is in the blood. We called in our top hematologist and he's been on the case most of the night. He's 80% certain it's leukemia. Of course, it will have to be confirmed with a bone marrow test and—"

His words are scathing arrows piercing my heart, and inwardly I'm recoiling in horror. *No! Stop it! It's not true! I don't want to HEAR anymore!*

"Please, can you explain to my father? N-nothing seems to be registering," I gasp. The receiver slips from my hand as my eyes appeal to my dad who's been listening intently.

Fleeing to the spare bedroom, I fling myself onto the bed. Writhing in anguish, I begin weeping in a half-crazed agony of despair. I bemoan her fate to God. *No! Please, please, don't let it be true!* I silently beseech Him. *It's so unfair. She's barely three! Please let her live. She's everything to me, my whole world!*

"Calm yourself, this instant!" a voice intrudes harshly. "You don't know that she'll die. Leukemia hasn't been confirmed yet. And if it *is* that, people *do* get remissions that sometimes last for several years. Medical science is constantly advancing and a cure may be around the corner. Meanwhile where will *you* be? In a nuthouse, that's where! And not a damn bit of use to your daughter. If you love her as much as I think you do, you'll not allow yourself to collapse–for *her* sake! She needs her mother. Now more than ever. Don't be so damn selfish!"

How can my mother be so cruel? I vent inwardly. Nevertheless, her dose of tough love causes my sobs to subside and the split pieces within me begin to join together as my thoughts turn to Star and the hell that faces her.

"Do you really believe it isn't hopeless?" I sniff, my eyes seeking my mother's, pleading for reassurance.

"Of course, I do. I love her, too. Now dry your eyes and blow your nose," she replies more gently. "I'm happy to hear you sound more like my daughter."

Sometime later, compelled to share this agonizing news, I surreptitiously call Karl. Our conversation is a blur in my mind, but I recall his shock.

"Would it be okay if I come to the hospital?" he inquires hopefully.

"Oh Karl, there's nothing I'd like more, but my mother will be with me constantly and I need her support. Your presence would only cause static just now. I hope you can understand and accept that. I'll call you every single day with news."

Dr. Schmidt rings back to say that Star has been transferred by ambulance to the St. Ann's Children's Hospital. Within the hour, Mom and I enter her room. She looks so small and pitiful lying there all alone with her little arms strapped to the sides of the bed to prevent her from tearing out her I.V.

My poor innocent baby! What must be going through her mind? Does she think I've abandoned her to this fate? How can I possibly explain anything to her? Momentarily I recall her shrieking like a wildcat the previous day when the I.V. was attached to her wrist.

"Mommy, take it *off! Take it off!*"

"Oh baby, I wish I could, but I can't. It's to make you better."

"My don't *want* to stay here! My want to go *HOME!*" she wails. "Please, please take me home! My love you." Her eyes appeal to me.

"I'm so sorry, sweetie," I reply helplessly. "I love you too, and I wish I could bring you home with me right now, but you need to stay here until the doctors make you better. It won't be for long, I promise."

"Mommy can always kiss Star better," she responds trustingly. Crushed, I turn my head to conceal the tears that gush forth.

"Please don't cry, Mommy. My sorry I make you cry."

Oh God, how can I ever get through this? *She* is trying to comfort *me*.

"Mommy's okay now, baby. Please understand that I love you and miss you and want you home with me always. But sometimes it takes more than Mommy's kisses. Try to be my good, brave Star and stay here for a little while. The doctors and nurses are very smart and they know just what to do for little girls when they're sick. And I'll help them make you better faster by giving you lots of my magic kisses. Like this, see?" I begin smothering her tiny face with kisses, then nuzzling my lips under her chin and nibbling her neck which tickles her and always makes her laugh.

Now it's a brand new day and I rush to her side, overjoyed to see her. We hug and kiss and she says gaily, "Mommy, Mommy, you're here! Star waited for you. My love you, Mommy."

She's such a loving little creature. How lucky I am to have her, I reflect fondly, suppressing the inner voice that cruelly taunts, *"For how much longer?"* I know I can't think that way. I have to stay positive. The very thought of losing her drives me to the edge of madness.

The first thing I do is release her free arm from its bondage. The doctors permitted me to do this yesterday, when I assured them I could prevent her from ripping out her IV.

"Now, you remember your promise to Mommy, right?" I point to the tube attached to her arm. "If you pull it out, the doctors won't let me unstrap you anymore. I can't undo the other arm because it's too dangerous, but at least you can move one arm about. You understand, sweetie?"

"Yes, Mommy. Thank you for taking it off."

I enfold her in my arms and begin singing softly, *Twinkle, Twinkle Little Star*. Her voice, still raspy from the soreness in her throat, joins me in the melody she knows is especially her own.

Len has taken the afternoon off to be with me during Star's pending bone marrow test. For now, both Len and my mother and I try to distract her thoughts from the hospital atmosphere by doing our utmost to amuse her. Len has brought the toys I requested and she squeals delightedly to see her favorite blue, furry pussy-cat that shares her crib each night.

"Pussy-cat was lonely for Star," I state solemnly. "He says he wants to sleep with his mommy."

"Oh, thank you for bringing him, Daddy!" she exclaims, hugging the stuffed toy fiercely with her free arm.

Soon after, she's taken for her bone marrow test and Mom leaves to go home. Len and I follow the gurney as Star is wheeled to her destination. I kiss her cheek before she enters the surgical unit.

"Mommy and Daddy will be back soon," I promise.

Trudging to the elevators, the tears run freely down my cheeks. It's been such an effort to hold them back over the past few hours. Now I no longer care. The whole damn hospital can stare at me. It matters not.

"Come to the coffee shop, hon," Len suggests. "A hot drink and a snack will do you good."

I have no appetite. Sipping my coffee, I watch Len bite into his hamburger enthusiastically and I'm aware of a flash of resentment that he can even eat at such a time, let alone reap such joy from his food. *She's not his real daughter, so why should he care?* I think balefully. Momentarily, I hope he will choke.

Sometime later, we're sitting in the office of the assistant chief of oncology, awaiting the verdict of her test. How can I bear to hear it? *No! Don't SAY it!* I scream silently. I wonder if I can bolt out of his office and pretend this horror has never touched my life. Yet this is a nightmare from which I'll never awaken.

I only hear disjointed sentences and fragments of the doctor's rather lengthy talk with us.

"I sincerely regret to tell you . . . acute leukemia . . . one of the worst types . . . odds of remission unfavourable."

"How unfavourable?"

"We don't like to venture such an opinion."

"Tell me, I have to know." *Oh my God, why am I persisting like this? Why am I demanding more punishment?*

Oh no, did he really say that . . . one chance in a million?

I must have blanked out. Is he still speaking? I try to tune in again.

". . . parents as important to patient's well-being as medical staff . . . imperative we all pull together . . . parents supply the love and encouragement. . . doctors, the necessary medical treatments . . . rest is up to God . . . must not give up . . . where there's life, there's hope."

My heart is breaking, yet my eyes are dry. I sit dormant, as though suspended in an alternate reality. I clench my husband's hand, almost crushing it from the strength of my pain.

I will hold together for Star. I will not let her down.

I call the minister, Dave, the one who married us. Next, I call my mother.

"I know'" she says. "Dr. Schmidt called here as soon as word reached his office. I rang the hospital right away. I begged them not to tell you. Why couldn't they just leave you in peace for the balance of your pregnancy? I don't want you getting all upset and losing your baby." She's weeping, and it's my turn to comfort her.

"It's okay, Mom. I'm all right. I'd have been so angry not to have been told. They did the right thing. Star's my baby, after all. I have to know what I'm up against. The minister will be coming. We'll all pray she gets a remission. Everything's possible with God.

"And listen up," I banter. "My pregnancy will be a cinch. My uterus is a hell of a lot stronger than my brain. Just be thankful I'm carrying the baby in the right place, okay?"

Oh God! I despair later, *one chance in a million! A hope in hell!* Momentarily, I wish I had the faith of my maternal grandmother. Perhaps then I could hope to get through this ordeal. I begin to reel as the ground swirls beneath me. Len reaches out to prevent me from falling. He guides me to a chair and I dig into my purse for my jar of smelling salts. I'm feeling so faint lately.

"Take a Valium before we go back to Star's room," Len advises.

We walk to the water fountain and I swallow one of the small, yellow tablets, grateful that my obstetrician has allowed me to up my dosage to 45 mg. per day. "You're fortunate you're taking Valium," I recall him mentioning. "It's the only tranquilizer that's completely safe during pregnancy."

We approach the elevators in silence, Len's arm protectively around me. *What would I do without him?* I wonder. There's no end to his help and support.

Star has been moved to a private room for isolation cases. We're told it's hazardous to her well-being to be inadvertently exposed to bacteria and we're given instructions regarding the ritual we're to perform before entering her room. We must scrub our hands with a disinfectant soap, cover our clothing with a sterile hospital coat, and make sure to don a facial mask. Upon leaving, all garments are to be disposed of in a hamper and fresh ones utilized upon return.

I peek through the small window in the wooden door of her room. She's laying quietly, her eyes wide open, raptly gazing at a long, narrow shelf that covers one side of the wall. It contains a variety of toys supplied by the hospital. At the very centre, there stands an enchanting little angel adorned in silvery gossamer. The walls are decorated in an array of holly, pine and mistletoe, and other Christmas mementos.

"Oh Len," I sigh sadly, "She may be here on Christmas Day."

"In that case, we'll bring her presents to the hospital and spend the day with her," he assures me. "I'll celebrate with the others when I get home on Christmas Eve. They'll understand."

"Hi, Mommy! Hi, Daddy!" Star exclaims, her eyes lighting up as we enter. "See pretty angel there?"

"She's lovely, sweetie. Would you like to hold her?"

She nods, and I place the tiny figurine in her free hand. Gazing upon it in fascination, her eyes take on a magical glow. Momentarily, a mystical aura seems to enshrine her and I become aware of a transient recognition of timelessness that seems to emanate from her intrinsic identification with the heavenly little oracle. I perceive she has descended from another plane of life and is foreseeing a joyous glimpse of the dimension from whence she has come. *No!* I cry silently, as I visualize her rising, and the pre-determined certainly of her destiny becomes cruelly apparent.

An icy finger of terror penetrates my being as my frightening perception gradually fades.

She is never to lose her affinity for the elfin-like, silvery angel. Even when unable to touch it, her eyes fix upon it hypnotically and I sense a kindly spirit has chosen this inanimate little entity in which to abide, and dwell ever close to its own. I'm compelled to leave it close to her side.

She's been placed on a cooling mattress which is frigid to the touch. Her fever seems to have reduced somewhat and her eyes appear brighter. We entertain her until the minister arrives, and we join with him in prayer as he beseeches God, in His infinite mercy, to preserve her life.

Such a kind man, this minister. He rarely misses a day's visit during Star's confinement, and he becomes a well of strength and comfort to both my mother and me during our time of sadness.

Apart from the odd break, my mother and I remain by Star's side. The security of Mom's constant presence helps sustain me until Len arrives after work.

I'm in a state of constant distress and I juggle the amount of Valium I'm permitted in order to get me through the day. Nights, I drink the few pints of beer my obstetrician has allowed me in the hope I can relax enough to sleep. I generally fall into a hazy oblivion somewhere around midnight which rarely lasts more than five or six hours. I'm clinging to a narrow ledge and desperately trying to hang on.

The insensitivity of the young interns worsens my already shaky state. "Do you think she'll pass safely through the night?" I ask tremulously, prior to departure around 9:00 PM.

"It can't be predicted," is the general answer. "She could hemorrhage internally and go at any time." I become desperately afraid to leave, fearing she may die in my absence.

On one occasion, when I'm sitting alone on one of the chairs outside Star's room, an intern flops down next to me, and says callously, "You know of course, that your daughter's condition is fatal and that it's just a matter of time. I strongly suggest you allow an autopsy to be done. I'm certain you'll gain a measure of comfort from the knowledge that, through her, you'll have made a small contribution to the advancement of medical science."

I flee to the restroom in tears.

Over the weeks, I become Star's main nurse. I bathe her, feed her the bird-like amounts she deigns to eat, change her, and attend to all her needs that fall within the realm a parent can handle. I daily apply hot compresses to the mass on her neck, feeling elated when the swelling gradually diminishes entirely. It pains me to see she's lost her last shred of dignity when she's forced to regress into diapers. So often attached to bottles and tubes, it's seldom feasible to allow her up to use the potty chair. In the beginning, she cries with shame to have soiled herself.

"It's okay, sweetie," I console her. "It's not your fault you're not able to get up. You'll only have to wear the diapers for a little while. Soon you'll be up and around and wearing your pretty panties again." She's too young to understand she's going to die soon, and I will wield any white lie if it will lift her morale.

The nurses are captivated with her, and take great pleasure in grooming her during the intervals she's spared extensive treatments.

I often arrive to see her adorned in a feminine little frock, her golden locks arranged in a most becoming style. Briefly, I forget how ill she is. "Oh my, you look so pretty!" I enthuse. She smiles coquettishly–as pleased to be complimented as any female, young or old.

Towards the middle of the second week, I notice a change in her. She's always possessed such a strong will, and from the onset she bitterly fought the medical staff who administered her uncomfortable treatments. It now appears her beautiful and indomitable free spirit has been broken. She lays quiescent, without a murmur, no matter what is being medically done to her. She seems to have given up and her pathos stabs at my heart.

Her tiny arms and legs are black and blue from the incessant flow of needles that have injected blood platelets, glucose, and antibiotics into her veins. I'm a helpless onlooker as she daily draws closer to death. Her small bottom is a mass of raw flesh, a side-effect of the antibiotics, I've been told. Applying salve to this appalling wound, I feel her pain as my own. *Oh, God,* I cry. *Please, please, make her well. I don't want my baby to die!*

During the second week of her confinement, there's another notable change in her behaviour. She no longer wants her grandmother in her room. "Go away, Granny!" she cries distressfully. "They Mommy's chairs! *Get off!* My don't *want* you here. My only want Mommy!"

My mother's eyes mist, and I plead with my sick child to let her granny stay, but she only becomes more agitated. "My only want *you* here, Mommy! Send her *away!*"

Unable to understand Star's sudden rejection of the grandmother she's always loved, I'm beside myself, especially in view of my mother's sadness.

"It's all right, Irene," Mom consoles me, "Don't be upset. When you were a child, you became cantankerous when you were ill and only wanted your mother with you as well. Don't force her. She's very distressed. I know it's not because she no longer loves me."

Despite Mom's explanation, when I see her gazing wistfully through the window of Star's room, it seems there's no end to our pain.

irene snow

Dad speaks little during this time. He comes to the hospital on only two occasions and will not enter Star's room. He looks at his beloved granddaughter through the small window before quickly turning away, his face a marble carving. He'll not permit his grief to be seen. It's locked within his soul, the one place no living being has ever fully penetrated, except his little Star who holds the key . . . his parting gift, which belongs to her alone.

One of the nurses shows me how I can rock my baby without disturbing the various bottles attached to her veins, and it's glorious to have her nestle in my arms again. She loves being rocked. At such times we become one entity in our love. Mother and child. Flesh of each other's flesh, and joined together by the powerful symbiotic need we have for one another.

As I lift her onto my lap, a look of concern crosses her small countenance. "My don't want to hurt the baby in Mommy's tummy," she pronounces gravely.

Ill as she is, she yet worries about the new life she eagerly awaits, as she recalls my earlier admonitions when she'd bound joyfully into my arms. Tears sting my eyes. Nothing seems to matter anymore. Only Star.

"Please don't worry about the baby. It's really very strong, and you won't hurt it. Besides," I add brokenly, "I only love *you*. All I ever want is *you*. More than anything in this world."

I can't identify with the new life I have not yet come to know. Not the way I can relate to little Star, who plants sweet, moist kisses on my lips and says, "My love you, Mommy."

Holding her close, I vividly recall the morning when she and Keith came tearing into my bedroom to join me under the covers–their usual ritual upon awakening.

Keith calls me Mommy for the first time.

"She's *my* mommy, Keith. Not *yours*!" Star declares possessively, while trying to shove him away from me.

"I'm Keith's mommy now, too," I explain as gently as possible. At first, she's not too happy with this; yet in no time at all, her big, loving heart accepts me being his Mommy as well.

152

I later explain to them both that there's a baby growing in my tummy. Her delight is uncontainable.

"Star going to push baby in carriage, okay Mommy? My help you take care of baby, too." I assure her she can do all of these things.

"Can Star feel baby in Mommy's tummy?" she often asks. I let her place her hand on my abdomen when I feel it moving. "Oh, Mommy! My feel the baby!" she exclaims in wonderment. "When does it come out? Star can't wait to hold the baby."

I wonder now, if she will even live long enough to *see* the baby she so yearns to hold?

On a cold winter's night in early December, I feel I'm caving in from the distress of watching my baby painfully struggle for life. I've raised and cared for her alone. She's the castle I worked so hard to build, all by myself. Now, that castle is falling apart . . . stone by stone. And I can only stand by and watch it crumble. My entire soul has been wrapped in the one package: my Star. How often I thought of her as the *jewels in my crown*. These words almost seem blasphemous now. I wonder briefly if God has found my idolatry offensive and will punish me for it. Yet, how can He fault me for adoring this angelic little child He has blessed me with, this little one who has always brought me so much sunshine? In my darkest hours, she has brought me light. It was *she* I'd come home to from work each night. And *she*, who greeted me happily at the door.

In these painful, yet precious last moments with my child, I'm stricken with the knowledge that there was only us and I would willingly trade my life for hers, that she may be spared.

As I dress her wounds, I notice how they've worsened. As I allow myself to fully *see* her bruised, raw flesh, I know I love her far too much to cling and hang on, and that there is one last gift I can give her: her freedom to die.

Kneeling beside her bed, I pray silently: *Dear God, You know how much I love Star and want to keep her, but I can no longer bear to witness her suffering. If it's Thy will that she recover, I beg you, restore her soon to health; but if it's Thy will to take her, please don't let her linger like this any longer. In Your infinite mercy, I beseech you to relieve my child of her pain . . . in whatever way may be Your Divine Plan.*

Star is unusually tired tonight, and she drifts off to sleep as I softly sing her favourite songs: *Edelweiss* (for she truly is my blossom of snow); *Somewhere My Love; Twinkle, Twinkle Little Star;* and *Hush-a-bye,* the lullaby her grandma composed for me as a child which has since become Star's own.

"Mommy will be back in the morning. I love you, baby," I whisper, and quietly slip out of the room.

Before leaving with Len, I recall Star's raw flesh and approach one of her doctors, insisting that all antibiotics be removed from her I.V. "The side-effects of the medication are causing her more pain than the illness," I say. "I want her life to be in God's hands now."

I don't know if the doctor did as I asked, but I do know I honoured a prayer. In that moment, I relinquished my child—the one thing I loved and wanted more than anything in the world—to God.

We arrive at the hospital a little late the next day. I check my watch in the elevator and it reads 11:15 AM. I feel a sense of urgency, and as I toss my coat over a rack I ask Mom to meet me at Star's room. I race to her bedside and notice she seems to be in deep repose. Urging her to awaken, I nudge her gently, then more firmly. Her eyes remain closed.

"Mommy's here. Mommy loves you. Wake up, sweetie!" I grasp her hand firmly, reassuring her of my presence. I feel the pressure of her tiny hand as it reciprocates by clasping my own. Yet her lids remain closed.

My eyes link with the tiny angel. It is strangely translucent and emits a mysterious glow. It seems to be smiling.

It knows! This is my only coherent thought. Spotting Mom's face in the window, I rush to the door. "She won't wake up," I gasp. "Please go in and hold her hand so she'll know she's not alone while I find a doctor!"

I spy a white coat as I tear down the hallway. "You must come quickly, please! My daughter won't wake up," I implore him.

I need not say more. He races back to her room with me, raises one of her eyelids and listens to her heart as Mom and I stand anxiously by.

"Both of you are to wait in the lobby until further advised," he says brusquely.

"No, please. I want to be with my daughter."

A nurse enters the room and he barks at her, "Get them out of here!"

The next thing I know, we are ushered into a waiting room full of people. The nurse says something and the crowd suddenly begins to disperse. *Why?* I wonder. *Nothing is making sense.* I'm feeling so numb. The nurse sits beside me and takes my hand.

"Your little girl was awake just before you arrived. She was asking for you on and off all morning. I'm so glad you were able to get here."

"*Oh no, no!*" I sob. "I couldn't awaken her. I felt her grip my hand when I called her name, but she wouldn't wake up. *Oh God, I was too late, too late!*"

"No dear," she assures me. "She knew you were there. She waited for you to come to her and that was her way of telling you. I'm absolutely certain of that."

There's a great deal of commotion in the hallway. People are running down the hall with a gigantic cart that I've never seen before. Somehow, I know they're headed for my baby's room.

"Why won't they let me be with my baby? I promise I won't disturb the doctors. She needs me. Please," I beg the nurse.

"She won't know you're there, my dear. When the heart stops beating one is unconscious."

I know it doesn't register that when the heart stops beating one is also dead. I simply sit there, desperately unhappy that my presence is barred from Star's room.

I'm vaguely aware the nurse is tending to me, urging me to

swallow some water, placing a cool cloth on my forehead. *Why?* I wonder. She clasps my cold hand in her warm one.

"What's your husband's number at work? I'll call him."

"No, please. I'm okay, and the doctors will make Star better."

She leaves, and returns shortly thereafter. Suddenly, I have a lucid moment.

"Is she going to die?" I ask desolately. I am very subdued. I am frozen, like a statue.

"It's in God's hands now," she replies compassionately, but her eyes are sad.

"God will do what's best and let her live," I whimper pathetically.

She places both her hands upon mine, regarding me gravely. "He'll do what is best, but He may feel, in His wisdom, that it's better to take her." She is very placid and her serenity is a solid wall I can momentarily lean against.

I have no recollection of my mother's whereabouts at this time. Two of her friends had dropped in earlier. Maybe they are comforting her somewhere while this nurse takes care of me.

I momentarily raise my eyes and see the large cart being slowly wheeled down the corridor by downcast figures but I refuse to give up my last shred of hope. Not until I am told.

A doctor appears at my side. "I called your obstetrician. I'm permitted to give you an injection of Valium," he says kindly. It seems so strange. Why would they want to do this? I'm not making a fuss. I'm totally inert.

I refuse the injection. They would have to put me to sleep forever to ease the pain that will come if my daughter is dead. And that is not their intention.

My father has materialized out of nowhere. So has my husband. Someone must have called them. A young nurse is beside them. I rise to my feet and ask the heartbreaking question. "How is my daughter?" My husband grips my arm to support me.

"She is dead," I am told. Simply. Bluntly. Yet is there really a way one can sugar-coat such a statement? *She's dead!* It rings harshly in my ears. Yet, I'm not hysterical. I'm strangely removed and detached.

The waiting is over.

I enter her room and request to be alone with her. I want no one with me—not my husband, my mother, or any of the staff. This is a private, personal moment. We were together at birth and will be together at death. It was only ever us.

I stretch out beside her on the tiny bed and cradle her small, lifeless body in my arms. Such a special gift, this little girl who gave of herself to the all. She bequeathed my dad with the adoring love of a child, denied by his only daughter. And she provided Keith—the introverted little boy locked in his own world of darkness—with the courage to risk his first brave, tentative steps into the sunshine of *her* world. And she indirectly led me to my marriage. She accomplished so much in so short a time.

How can this beautiful, bright, happy little girl who has brought so much joy be gone? I reflect on her joie de vivre, and how she delighted in each day, each new discovery. Life, to her, was a challenge and a wonder. She'll not see her third birthday two weeks from today, or another Christmas. Without her, the sun has gone from my life. I gaze upon her, endeavouring to etch her lovely features forever in my mind. Her tiny face is at peace. For this much, I am thankful. A nurse enters the room and I ask for scissors. I clip a lock of her burnished-gold hair to keep as a cherished souvenir. I embrace her again, whispering tender words of love that I beseech her spirit to hear. I gently kiss her lips, knowing I will never be able to hold her again. I don't want to leave. I want to cling to her tiny form forever.

It takes all my will to extricate myself from my child. I notice the two head ocologists lingering outside of her room. I thank them for their efforts to save my little girl's life, and witness their increased sadness at my pathetic display of gratitude. *It's not easy for them either,* I think sadly. I give my consent for an autopsy. How can I deny the help this gesture may give to another child someday? Star loved all people and all life . . . all creatures great and small.

On my way to the elevators with Len, I suddenly remember Karl. *Oh God, I must tell him!* I run blindly to the pay phone I've been using daily to keep him informed. "She's dead," I announce hollowly. I only recall the gist of his response. He wishes he could do something, at least attend her funeral, but understands my family won't want him there. As I notice my mother glaring at me from outside the pay booth, suspecting the purpose of my call, I quickly say goodbye.

We're to be denied the need to share our grief.

Driving home with Len, the magic of Christmas is all around us. Snow is falling gently. The city is festively decorated and gaily lit with coloured lights. People bustle along the streets, laden with cheerfully-wrapped packages. It's a winter wonderland. Not unlike the morning of Star's birth.

But now she is dead.

Mein schöner Engel. My beautiful angel.

Carols lilt in the air, ringing out the spirit of the season. I've never been more aware of Christmas than I am now. Nor have I ever felt so empty.

I whisper Karl's words, imploring Star's spirit to hear: *It's not goodbye, little one. As your daddy once said, it's auf Wiedersehen.*

Chapter 9 –
Auf Wiedersehen, Mein Engel

"Ever has it been that love
knows not its own depth until the hour of separation.
—Khalil Gibran

The events of the past few hours have been dreamlike in nature, as though I am outside of my body, watching a film. The external part of me that removed itself from the stinging inner core deluded me. It merely delayed my grief by providing me with an outer coat of armour. Not unlike the tortoise, I retreated therein, secure in the knowledge that despite the boulder that just struck my shell, it had not been broken. Now, within a span of seconds, my outer shield magically dissolves leaving me naked and defenceless. In this appalling moment of stark awareness, it crystallizes that my child is really gone. *Forever.* And I'm helpless to change things.

Flooded with raw grief and blind, savage rage over an agony too great to endure, a violence explodes within me, overpowering me with murderous madness. I yearn to avenge this atrocity, to strike back and kill. Claw, ravage, mutilate. Nothing short of the most treacherous retaliation will appease this wild storm of passion within me. But I need something to maim. Some *thing.* And there is nothing. No *thing.* And this is one of the greatest ironies of all: being threatened by *nothing*. For God is the perpetrator of this heinous deed, and I'm powerless to strike back and hurt Him as He has hurt me. My former prayer is forgotten. I want my child back, and it's an insufferable yearning inside me. My loss is irretrievable.

Unable to redirect such distress, I plummet into the torments of hell.

A storm descends. In a torrent of sobs, I howl out my pain in a deranged, unceasing lament. The sounds emitting from the recesses of my being are foreign to my ears. Wild, bestial, primordial cries that emanate from life's hunger for life from the dawn of time. I have lost my young and have instinctively reverted to a crazed, wounded animal. Lost in the depths of my ancestral heritage, I unite with the sense of having known this anguish before, of reliving some far distant past where I keened in the same demented fashion as now. A past where similarly oppressive tortures initiated me to life by attuning me to my absolute powerlessness, leaving me with the comprehension that there are things much greater than I. Cosmic forces which my savage anger cannot combat.

Forces from which one inevitably gleans one's first real taste of helplessness.

I cannot estimate the minutes, or hours, that pass in this black hell of despair. It's a timeless dimension in which I am caught in an interminable nightmare. Writhing in pain, I wail in desolation. Curled upon my mother's couch, my body rocks incessantly to the rhythm of my cries.

Drained and depleted, I eventually surface and become dimly aware of my surroundings; yet I blindly reject Len's or my mother's efforts to comfort me. I am inconsolable.

Much later, I become aware of my father. His face is a frozen mask as he sits quietly in the armchair across the room. Our eyes meet, and his suffering mirrors my own. Star has been his world as well. In this moment of comprehension, I reach out to him, seeking the comfort of a kindred soul. Climbing onto his lap I cry, "Oh Daddy, my baby, *my BA-BY! She's GONE!* I'm hurting so much, I'm broken in pieces."

"Yes, Brat, I know you hurt," he soothes. "It won't always be this painful. I know that's hard for you to believe just now when your grief is so intense. But it will get better in time, I promise."

"Oh God, I wish I could believe that. I never knew such pain was possible. It's inconceivable to think my heart will ever heal."

By the following morning, the hysteria has passed; yet I remain immersed in a private hell of my own. I really don't want to live anymore, for how can I go on without my precious Star? I know I must survive for the sake of my unborn child. Yet how do I know the new life in my womb is not just another one of God's sadistic jokes? He may just be waiting for me to love my new baby in order to zap it and further destroy me. He'll not get that chance. I'll be wiser this time.

I will *never* let myself love again. Not *ever.*

I'm staying with my parents until the funeral is over. Outwardly, I'm civil and polite, though I only speak when spoken to. I resent the idle chit-chat of my husband and my mother, designed to divert me from my grief. Can't they see I don't want to be distracted? It's my time to mourn, and I have to find my own way of coping with this ordeal. Unlike the others, Dad makes no attempt to smile or chatter and within our quiet sadness we share a bond of understanding.

A few days later, I prepare to see my child. I'm glad I've insisted on no outside visitation. I don't want any intrusions upon these last moments with my little girl. I take special pains with my appearance, and wear a blue, floral-print maternity dress. I know Star would not like to see me in black, looking drab and pale. Whenever I'm dressed-up she always says, "Pretty Mommy." I must honour her today by being her *pretty mother.*

"You should not be going to the funeral parlour," Mom pleads. "You should remember her alive. You're not well enough to stand more pain."

Yet, how can I let my baby down by not appearing? Surely her soul would know if I were not there.

Pale and subdued, I enter the mortuary. The first thing I notice is Star's name—glaringly apparent—on the sign above her viewing room. *"Oh God,"* I murmur as I grasp my husband's arm, certain I will crumble.

"Are you sure you want to go in?" he asks concerned.

"I have to."

Upon entering the room, I behold a stunning array of flowers. In the midst of these glorious blossoms is a tiny pink casket which houses a small golden-haired angel. All thoughts vanish as I slowly approach my daughter. I gaze upon her tenderly. She is not less breathtakingly lovely in death than in life. There, beneath a trellis of perfumed roses, her small face radiates the peaceful bliss of having reached out and touched heaven.

My eyes mist with tears as I speak to her silently from my heart: *Sweet, sweet baby, if there is one thing I can be grateful for, it's that your pain is over. I may never understand why this terrible illness befell you, but I do know you gave so much to life in the few years you were with us . . . and to my life in particular. I hope you know how grateful I am that you came to me. I'll never forget you, my precious one. You'll live forever in my heart.*

Momentarily I notice the unusual way her hair has been arranged, all swept back off her face. I begin to re-arrange it in the long flowing style that so becomes her.

"Good Lord, what are you doing?" the funeral director gasps as he enters the room. "Your daughter has had an autopsy. You must be extremely careful about touching her head, and you must not pick her up. Do you understand what I'm saying?"

"Y-yes," I falter, exhaling a breath of gratitude. Although I've strayed from God, He has not deserted me.

There, you look like my pretty Star again. I whisper silently. *I know you wouldn't have liked your hair like that. I'm going to miss you so much, little one . . . your hugs and kisses, your playful antics, your smiles and cheers. And oh, yes, your tender empathy when I cry.*

Stricken, I place a small stuffed-animal beneath her hands, a gift from Karl. "Your daddy would want you to take this with you, my darling . . . so you won't be lonely."

For the first time, I notice the exquisite floral star atop her casket. It's entwined with clusters of pink and red baby rosebuds. *Star's very own star,* I muse. Its ethereal beauty complements her own. I recall Len and my dad making all her arrangements.

"Who chose that?" I ask, turning to Len.

"I did," he says solemnly. "I hope you like it. I thought it would suit her."

"Oh, thank you, thank you!" I am too choked to say more.

I behold my little one again–a celestial being lying peaceful and sublime–and I reflect on the precious child she was: loving, bright, and intelligent beyond her years. Her death seems such a monstrous loss and it's tearing me apart to see her this way . . . lifeless, and asleep. I kiss her tiny cheeks and delicate rosebud lips, and stroke her silken hair. There's a fathomless depth of love in my touch. It's that of a mother speaking silently to her cherished lamb. A gentle maternal caress which tactilely awakens a child to its first glimpse of love . . . from hands the child will always know as Mother's.

"I'll never stop loving you, but I must say goodbye now, darling," I breathe silently.

I know I cannot come back. Not ever again.

My eyes, blurred from tears, can no longer see her.

I do not return, neither to the funeral the following day, nor the cemetery thereafter. I know my heart cannot bear to see the tiny pink casket–which holds the child I love more than anything in the world–being lowered into the earth for the rest of time.

The day of her burial, December 5th, a friend of my mother's stays with me while the family goes to the funeral. Apart from being grateful for her company–and frequently replenishing my drink in a futile effort to blot out the horror besetting me–I recall little else.

My aunt and uncle return to my parents' apartment later with Len and my mother and dad. Mom is gaunt and pale. I'm told she collapsed in a heap by Star's graveside. Dad pours her a stiff one and remains mute while the rest of the group chatter aimlessly in an effort to avoid the true issue. The idle chit-chat conveys the message that Star's beneath the ground now and as such, confined to the past. Yet I long to speak of her, and I really don't want to hear their superfluous drivel. Unable to abide it any longer–they're discussing dental problems! Christ, who the hell cares?–I retire to the kitchen where Dad has since escaped. He's sitting alone, nursing a beer.

"I can't bear it," I mutter tonelessly, my eyes darting in the direction of the living-room.

"Nor can I," he says bluntly. "I wish the hell they'd all shut up and fuck off."

That's my dad, forthright and straight to the point. For the first time in days, my lips form the ghost of a smile, knowing his thoughts duplicate my own. He's taking this whole thing very badly himself.

"Do you believe she's in a happier place?" I ask sadly.

"Yes Brat, I do. During the war, I saw many men die. Some were my buddies. I recall the joy on their faces prior to crossing over–as though they were glimpsing something truly beautiful on the other side. So yes, I do believe Star is in a happier place–and much more so than we are."

In that moment, I feel very close to my dad.

The days that follow are a blur of agony, filled with poignant memories. I find myself wondering if my baby is cold beneath all the ice and snow, and as winter's blizzards rage, I ache with the need to swathe her in warm, woolen blankets. She remains alive within me, and I become very reflective.

I recall the day of her baptism when she stands so solemnly in the church, a vision in her blue-lace dress. Her face is filled with awe and I sense she's innately aware of the significance of this spiritual moment.

"I'm honoured and proud to have Star for my daughter," Len says later.

How dearly she's come to love him during the short time he's been her new dad! Daily, when they roughhouse together, her tinkling bell-like voice rings with delight as he tosses her in the air. And she's enthralled to be the guest of honour at her christening party. Her pleasure is perhaps only topped by seeing the large cake with her name on it, and the beautiful gift from her godmother she proudly wears: a genuine pearl on a gold chain. Bubbly and effervescent, she blithely swings her curls and charms the entire group, including the minister himself.

My precious memories will have to last me a lifetime. From this time forward the craving of all my senses for this little girl will be denied me.

She is *me*, a part of my flesh. Yet so much more. Perhaps she's my heart? But, no, my heart still beats against my chest, a cruel tune of unspeakable grief. She must be an indefinable part of me. Something more than the genes and chromosomes she inherited. She must be my spirit . . . for surely, my spirit is gone.

After spending several days in hiding, neither wanting nor caring to return to life as it was, I know I can no longer postpone confronting the commitments that await me. Unable to delay the inevitable, I cling tightly to my mother before leaving for the home which can no longer *be* home with Star not in it. How can I even bear to sit at the table and see her empty chair?

Len, sensing my trepidation, brings me for a long, tranquil drive through the countryside prior to our return. I feel myself merge with the vast snow-swept hills, becoming one with the desolation of the season.

A daughter of winter.

All too soon, I see the faces of my step-children, waiting at the door to welcome me home. My eyes catch sight of little Keith, who stands excitedly beside his older siblings. In that heart-wrenching moment, only one thought prevails: there is only one-half of the *Terrible Twins* left. I run sobbing to my bedroom.

My castle has fallen to pieces. I wonder if I will ever find the strength to rebuild it. Too desolate and bereft to think of the many blessings I have left in my life, I can only think I have no desire to try . . . that all is lost: Karl, Star, my very soul.

I only know I have failed.

For the longest time, my precept will be a child's nursery rhyme: *Humpty Dumpty*. How well I will identify with its expressive words.

Because *I* am *Humpty Dumpty*.

And the *king's horses* and *king's men* are my doctors and psychiatrists.

Chapter 10 - Humpty Dumpty

Humpty Dumpty sat on a wall,
Humpty Dumpty had a great fall;
And all the king's horses, and all the king's men,
Couldn't put Humpty together again.
—English nursery rhyme

As one snowy day drifts into another–each as bleak and joyless as the last–I merely exist, with no real purpose or aim. Without Star's happy smiles to lighten my life, the lustre has vanished and I find myself wishing we had died together. The coldness of winter has suffused my heart with its icy breath and I'm entrapped in a desolate tomb where time has frozen. I cannot visualize this as a time of transition; nor can I contemplate another spring. Hurt, broken and disillusioned, I've entered a season of timeless mourning.

Daily, I dwell on an introspective island of my own fabrication. It is surrounded by a moat, and a draw-bridge that I refuse to let down. I do not welcome intruders. It is necessary I brood and serve penance alone. I selfishly brought Star into the world. She deserved so much more than I was able to give her. I have forfeited my right to be happy.

Outwardly, I simulate a facade of superficial cordiality. My mask is multifaceted and conceals a host of negative emotions. Inwardly I'm furious to be left with a ready-made family. Initially, what appeared a fair trade–I take on Len's four children to ensure the well-being of my one–has become a travesty. By a cruel twist of fate, *he* has won the jackpot by inheriting a live-in maid and baby-sitter, whilst *I* am left saddled with the proverbial bag. How unfair that one of his children was not taken instead. After all, he has plenty. Wallowing in grief and self-pity, I vow to never love again and pay so dearly in pain.

It seems that somewhere within my sick self there dwells a glimmer of certitude that hate will sustain me and thereby protect me from the underlying abyss of fear and horror from whence there is no return. Evenings, as I'm forced to watch Len and the older kids play-fight with Keith, I'm haunted with memories of Star taking part in these rituals and I wonder how Len can be so insensitive. I retreat to our bedroom unnoticed, a scalding bile curdling sourly in my gorge as their merry sounds resound faintly in my ears. How *dare* they be happy when my daughter lies cold in the ground. How I hate them all!

On the plus side, we won't be living in this godforsaken town much longer. Our house sold while Star was in hospital, and Len took care of the details. Prior to Star becoming ill we went house-hunting in Cassellman and found a one and one-half-story cottage we liked which the owner–aware our house was on the market–promised to hold for us. Moving day is December 24th, which is fine with me; I prefer to spend the holidays in my new home. Once out of here, I'll no longer have to visualize Star and Keith tearing around this *House of Tears* together and sitting side by side at the dining table. I'll buy a completely different dining-room set and a child-size table and chairs for Keith, which he can share with the new baby once it's out of a high chair.

The upcoming move has the advantage of keeping me ultra-busy with the daily packing which gives me less time to think . . . with the exception of Keith's haunting image. His presence is a splinter that nettles irritatingly beneath my skin, a constant reminder of my deprivation of Star. As I daily tend to his needs I taste the caustic pain of my own adversity. I see my *Terrible Twins* playing joyfully together and I feel the corrosion in my soul that only one remains.

At not quite three years of age, Keith is too young to understand why his playmate and friend is not coming back. He inquires about her daily. And often.

"Where Star gone, Mommy?" he continuously asks.

"To heaven," I constantly reiterate.

"Where heaven?"

"Way up in the sky. Far, far away."

"Can we go there and see her?"

"No, Keith. Perhaps someday, but not now."

"When will she come back to see us?"

Oh, God, how can I bear this every day of my life? I inwardly chafe. "She won't be back anymore. Heaven's a place where people go when they're very sick and the doctors can't make them well. They get better there but they can't leave anymore."

"Didn't she like us, Mommy? Is that why she not coming back?"

That *does* it! I feel myself going berserk. *"Of course, she liked us!"* I snap. "But people *can't* come back from heaven! Now, listen up. I'm telling you one last time and don't *ever* ask me again. Star is *not* coming back. *NEVER, NEVER, NEVER! Got it?"* I shriek. "Now go to your room this instant!"

His limpid hazel eyes glaze with tears as he regards me forlornly. Sadly, I'm too wrapped up in my own grief to realize this small child shares it. He too has suffered a tragic loss: his beloved best friend.

"GO, damn it!" I raise my hand menacingly. I know I'll not strike him. Star's death is not his fault. Yet, I have to keep him out of my way as much as possible. I'm too fragile to cope with his grief while mine is still so acute.

It's a relief when the teenagers arrive home from school and absolve me of all responsibility for Keith. They amuse him elsewhere while I do my chores and prepare the evening meal. How I relish those glorious moments of relief from the dagger which consistently pierces my damaged heart.

Only Len will, to some extent, become aware of the depth of my rancour. One day, I let it all hang loose.

"Do you have any idea of how it tears me apart to even look at Keith?" I confess. "I know it's not his fault that Star is gone, but each time I see him I see only half of the *Terrible Twins*. He's a *constant* reminder of my loss. Furthermore, do you even have a clue how it wrenches my heart when you and the teenagers start jostling with him on the floor . . . *right in front of me*? You're all laughing and having fun, minus little Star who loved these activities. Can you imagine for a second how desolate that makes me feel? I have the urge to kill the whole damn lot of you! Feeling the way I do, I will soon not be much good to any of you. I seriously think that I need to get away somewhere . . . until I heal."

"Oh, my God, honey, I had no idea what you've been going through. I'm so sorry. I want to do everything in my power to help you heal–right here, with us. Please let me try. I'll explain things to the teenagers. It's important we *all* realize how this hurts you and rubs salt in your wounds. We'll no longer play with Keith in the living room right under your nose, I promise. We all need you, you know. Even in your grief you're doing a great job for us. I don't know what I'd do without you. Please say you'll stay with us. Whenever something upsets you, you only need to discuss it with me and I'll do everything in my power to make things right, you must know that?"

"It's no life for Keith. He'd be better off with someone else looking after him, at least temporarily. I just can't seem to accept him right now. He's become a sore reminder of my loss and his constant questions about Star tear me apart. My heart seems to have frozen in her absence, and I feel empty and devoid of love."

"You'll love again in time, honey. As you begin to heal. Keith is not exactly without love. His brothers and sisters adore him as their very own baby. You've done the right thing to let them take over as soon as they come home. It's good for both you *and* Keith.

"I want you to know that I loved Star, too, very much. And her death has not been easy for me either. I miss her deeply. I never know whether I should talk about her to you or not. I'm always afraid I may upset you, so I try to hide my feelings."

"Oh Len, thank you for being so understanding. Perhaps the move will help me heal. Meanwhile, I'll try my best to continue with things as they are. And please, please, feel free to speak of her. It's awful to feel that because she's dead all is over and done with, and I can no longer mention her name. It is *not* over, Len. I don't know when it ever *will* be over, God help me."

Things tend to improve after our talk. Nobody makes overt displays of attention to Keith directly in front of me. Evenings, Len and the teens watch TV in the playroom downstairs. I expect they play with Keith then. As long as I no longer have to bear witness to their antics, it matters not. I generally retire to our bedroom. I prefer to be alone than in the company of happy people. Alone with Star . . . encapsulated in my bereavement . . . steeped in an intense, unending sorrow.

Shortly after serving Keith his noonday lunch, I send him upstairs to his room for a nap. Unable to cope any longer, I tell him he must rest until his brothers and sisters come home. Aware that this is an extensively long nap period for a three-year-old, I'm not without guilt. The tale of the little princess locked in a tower comes to mind, and I make the association. At such times I truly wish there *was* some place else I could go in order to heal.

One day, Keith approaches me again about Star.

"Mommy, Mommy, guess what? Star's back!" he confides happily.

"What are you talking about?" I gasp.

"She visits me. Every day in my room. She says she loves me and we play together."

My hand grasps the edge of the table as I begin to sway. *As if it's not enough that I'm feeling dizzy and faint again* most *of the time!* Surely this latest development is a figment of his imagination? Whatever. I simply can't handle my own painful memories, let alone Keith's paranormal conjectures!

"Play with her all you want, but I'm telling you one thing: I don't want to hear you mention Star. *EVER AGAIN! DO YOU HEAR ME, KEITH?"*

"Yes, Mommy. Sorry, Mommy."

"Well, I'm sorry too, Keith," I add more gently. "But it hurts Mommy when you talk about Star. Do you understand?"

"Yes, Mommy."

Of course he doesn't understand, poor child. I run this by my mother on her next visit. She seems to think Star may actually be appearing to Keith.

"Oh for pity's sake, Mom! *You*, of all people, saying something like *that*! I can't even *speak* to you about psychic phenomena. You turn me off like a bad channel. Since when did *you* start believing in ghosts?"

"It's just a feeling I have, Irene. I know it sounds strange, but I'm inclined to take the child seriously. I'd like to speak to him about it."

"Be my guest, but just don't involve me with that rubbish. I don't want to hear about it! I *can't!*"

Consequently, I never did hear about it, and would live to deeply regret it. Keith no longer recalls the experience and Mom is no longer with us. Had my mind been open to all possibilities, as it is today, I would have known beyond doubt that it was Star who came to Keith. Loving him as she did, that is exactly what she would do. She would never have left him alone in his sadness.

Or me, in mine.

Sometime after our move, and a sad Christmas, is behind us, Mom drops over for tea one day.

"You know, Irene," she says gently, "you're no longer the person you used to be and it hurts me to see you like this, so drawn into yourself. I understand how much you miss Star, but we can't bring her back no matter how much we brood or grieve. She loved you too much to want you to suffer like this. There are so many others that love and need you, and you have a new baby on the way. I know it's difficult for you, losing Star so recently, but if only you could try and give a little more of yourself, I know it would help you. You have a good family and they all care about you. Surely you remember how much Star loved them all?"

"How can you even *suggest* I'm not trying?" I cry. "The day after an exhausting move–just three weeks after losing Star–I made a big Christmas dinner for the whole damn lot of you: Len and his four kids, you, Dad, and my godmother! And I stayed up half the night moving furniture and unloading boxes to accomplish it. Even Dad congratulated me on my guts when he noticed my tears salting the carrots I was chopping. I tried very hard to make Christmas a happy occasion for everyone. Just how much do you expect from me, damn it?"

"I know. I know. You're making a good outward show of things, but you do it by rote. There's no longer any enthusiasm in what you do. You walk about like a zombie, one of the walking dead: alive, but not alive. You seem to be devoid of emotion. You're *my* baby and it hurts me to see you like this."

Oh, mother, devoid of emotion, I'm not," I reflect silently after she leaves. *You can't imagine the fear and horror that stalks me, and threatens to split me apart. A monster is my constant companion, and its cold, chilly breath brings goose bumps to my skin.*

My one comfort is Star's furry, blue pussy-cat. I carry it with me during the day and sleep with it at night, feeling that a part of her is with me. Len wisely refrains from commenting on this practice.

My new baby is in no hurry to arrive, and can I blame it? Perhaps it senses its security is intact within the womb, and it prefers to remain there. Smart child. My obstetrician disagrees, and by the time I'm three weeks overdue he arranges to have my labour induced.

I'm admitted to hospital on a crisp wintery morning in February. Len takes the day off to be with me. At 1:00 PM, my obstetrician breaks my water.

"That will probably do the trick," he smiles. "Your labour will likely start within the hour. If not, there are other ways to skin a cat."

As predicted, my labour begins at exactly 2:00 PM. True to form, it's once again swift and violent and my new baby is born three hours later. I'm ecstatic to learn my child is a girl.

Later, as my little one nestles in my arms at feeding time, I see beyond her crossed eye and outstanding ears–small flaws that can be surgically repaired at a future date. I've dealt with so much worse. I gaze with awe upon her lovely face. Thank God her blood tests are normal. I've been so worried that she, too, may have leukemia. She's healthy and I could not be more grateful.

Dr. Schmidt, who I've chosen as the pediatrician for my new baby, drops by latter for a chat and to inform me that the head doctors at the children's cancer ward are delighted to hear I've delivered a healthy baby. "They send you their congratulations and very best wishes," he smiles. I'm touched to learn they cared enough to keep tabs on me.

I only wish I was not feeling so panicky inside. My trusty cache of Valium tablets is in my purse and I sneak one as necessary. I'm still relying on the 45 mg. dosage to get me through the day; yet somehow, it's no longer succeeding to calm me. I must need a higher dosage. The anxiety is getting out of hand.

Once home with Eve, my baby, I sense I'm on a downward spiral. I'm no longer having the isolated attacks of excruciating panic I suffered in the past, but my present condition encompasses a chronic and more generalized fear which is increasing exponentially and I'm finding it almost impossible to cope.

I begin relying on the odd drink to subdue the terror that constantly threatens to pounce. Daily, as the fear intensifies, I increase my intake of booze to offset the tranquilizers. I'm unaware of my folly. I simply perceive something terrible befalling me and am unable to deal with it. I fear I'm going insane and I can't think beyond the possibility of being institutionalized. I only know I must get Eve on a schedule. Perhaps she may then have a hope of being taken care of at home by someone . . . while I'm away. This becomes my first priority.

I add cereal to her formula from almost day one, and within her first few weeks of life I introduce strained foods to her diet as well.

She adjusts well to this rigorous regime and at only six weeks old she's accomplished the remarkable feat of eating three meals daily with no ill effects. Along with sleeping through the entire night. It's as though she's aware her mommy's not well, and she's doing her part to facilitate her own survival.

Daily I pick her up to change her, bathe her; or simply hold her. In my frenzied state, I seem to be dropping nearly everything I touch, but never my child. I try my best to look after her during these early days that we're alone together. Although my heart is still frozen—afraid to really love again—the maternal instinct is there, and I don't want any harm to come to my precious little girl.

I believe beyond doubt that God was watching over the both of us during this trying time.

My drinking increases with my anxiety. Too frightened to leave the house on my own, I induce various family members to pick me up a bottle from the liquor store. Nobody is actually aware of just how much alcohol I'm consuming—including me. I hide a bottle of vodka under my bed—cagey enough to realize it will be confiscated if discovered. I can't let this happen as I desperately need it to get through the day. I drink it straight and as I gulp a few mouthfuls I welcome the burning sensation in my throat which denotes almost instant anesthesia . . . though the comfort's short-lived.

One afternoon when Eve and Keith are resting and I indulge in a nap myself, I have the most unsettling experience. I awaken to find my eyes frozen, riveted to a spot directly in front of me. I can no longer move them from side to side. I have no peripheral vision. My limbs, too, are paralyzed, and I'm totally unable to move. Electrified with fear, I cry out; yet only the minutest flicker of sound emanates from my throat. I'm unsure how long it takes before I snap into full awareness, but I do know I'm scared out of my mind. I vow this is my last afternoon nap.

Horror heaps upon horror as similar anomalies begin assailing me at night. I become aware I'm caught in a dream and, desperate as

I am to awaken, escape is futile. It's akin to being trapped in a coma. At some level I'm lucid, but unable to rouse myself to an awakened state. Occasionally, I'm able to open my eyes, only to find them as frozen as the rest of my limbs.

I seem to be hanging onto the edge of a cliff by my finger nails and I just don't know what to do about it. Despite the love that's been blocked within me, there's one thing I'm sure of: I do not want to be separated from Eve.

The day arrives when I actually fall off the cliff. While Eve and Keith are napping one afternoon, I pick up the novel I've been reading. It's a tale of a Caucasian man who gets lost in the wilds of Australia and is befriended by an Aboriginal. One day, the white man removes a looking glass from his knapsack and shows it to his native friend. The latter, upon seeing his face in a mirror for the very first time, becomes horrified. He believes he's seeing his soul, and that it has deserted his body. His absolute belief that death is imminent leads him to a grassy knoll beneath a nearby tree where he sits quietly and languishes. Within three days he actually wills himself to die by the power of his faith.

At this exact moment, my mind makes a powerful association. It occurs to me that I, too, am willing myself to die and that my subjective mind has taken over and I have no hope of halting the frightening chain of events that have been set in motion.

Overwhelmed by this powerful illumination, I become consumed with terror. Wildly agitated and unable to sit still, I race to the bathroom and begin splashing cold water on my face. Inadvertently catching sight of my reflection in the vanity mirror, I'm appalled to see a pair of blue-rimmed obsidian eyes staring back at me. Unable to comprehend that my pupils are dilated from fear, I recoil in horror from the demented face of this frenzied, black-eyed creature before me. Only one thing is clear: I have to save myself from this *thing* that has disrupted my equanimity and desires to overtake me. Like an unwanted tenant housed in my mind—which not only defies eviction but seeks first place as the landlord—it benumbs my flesh with the chilling thought that one of us will have to go. *It* appears to have no intention of abdicating control and I feel powerless before it.

Somehow I manage to reach Len at work and implore him to come home.

As I fearfully await his arrival, sheer desperation provides me the wherewithal to place yet another call: this one, to my obstetrician.

"I had hoped your new baby would be good for you and that by caring for it your emotional health would improve," he says. "Childbirth, however, can sometimes react adversely by inducing depression or further deterioration of a chronic nervous condition, which seems to be your case at present. I'll refer you to Dr. Garret. He's a good friend of mine and a nerve specialist. Do call him right away. You can't continue like this alone. I know he'll be able to help you," he adds compassionately.

The incredible will to survive has somehow given me the fortitude to hold my demons at bay long enough to make my final SOS plea of the day . . . to the nerve specialist my obstetrician prefers not to label a shrink. I'm connected immediately and given an appointment for Saturday, the following day. It's the first week of April, and tomorrow is my mother's birthday.

Happy Birthday, Mom! Your daughter has just blown her mind.

I know I've hit the bottom of the pit and that I'm faced with two choices: I either remain in it forever . . . or find the means to claw my way out.

Chapter 11 – Descent into Hell

Breakdowns can create breakthroughs.
Things fall apart so things can fall together.
—Unknown

I run sobbing into Len's arms the moment he arrives home. Trembling convulsively, I try to articulate my plight. Surely death or irrevocable insanity is a hairsbreadth away. "I'm s-so terribly scared," I quake. "I'm in constant terror and it won't let up. It's relentless. I can't make any sense of it. *Oh God, I'm f-fighting as hard as I c-can, but I'm disintegrating inside. I've lost all control!"*

"It's going to be okay. I promise. I love you too much to let anything happen to you. We're going to beat this thing together."

That night I fall into another sleep trap. Obscured once again in a terrifying nether world of nothingness where sleep is a death from which I'm unable to resurrect myself, it seems an eternity before I escape the morass of horror that engulfs me. I finally jolt into full awareness, stricken with the chilling thought that I'm losing all contact with reality. As Len's arms reach out to enfold me, I heave a sigh of gratitude to notice the first faint glimmer of dawn penetrating the window shades.

I'm petrified to leave the room and Len brings me coffee and some toast in bed. The food seems to clog in the back of my throat and refuses to go down. Afraid I may choke, I eventually give up.

Enshrouded with dread, I gaze helplessly ahead only to notice the whole room has rotated. Furniture, windows and door have altered in sequence and appear in different locations. Everything is totally surreal. I jump out of bed and grasp for the door knob only to find my grip is lifeless.

"*Len,*" I scream, "*Help me!*"

He rushes into the bedroom and embraces me. "The whole r-room is rotating," I gulp. *"I'm going absolutely m-mad, Len!"*

"It's okay, try to calm down. We're going to the psychiatrist later. I know he'll help you. Try to keep positive. Get back into bed for now," he soothes.

He tucks the blankets around my shaking form and gently administers to me. I've regressed to a terrified child, and Len is the trusted parent who represents my only security. I surrender my wavering trust to him, and cling to his belief in me which represents an assumed lifeline between reality and the depths of insanity.

That which I feared had finally come upon me. My unsettling dreams of the past had finally manifested in the flesh, and I was painfully stuck in the reality of having become one with my most terrifying suppressions . . . in an almost continuous dose of adrenaline.

On a spiritual level, I question how I could have chosen such darkness. Perhaps there are those of us who must touch hell in order to actively seek heaven. I only know that God did not leave me comfortless. Len and my mother were there to walk me through the night.

By mid-day, I'm en route with Len to Dr. Garret's private office downtown. My wet brunch of several beers–which I somehow managed to swallow with ease–has done pathetically little in helping me muster the courage to leave the relative security of my home and face the terrifying outdoors. Alcohol seems to have lost all potency in face of the power of *It*–the monster that is ruling my psyche. I fear there is no safety in the vast open spaces where I'm reduced to a mere speck of dust that can rapidly be sucked into orbit. Nevertheless, this doctor is my only hope of salvation, and it's vital I reach him.

Images of Europe filter through my mind. I momentarily see myself as I was then, the happy wanderer, proud and free. Sleeping on a park bench in London, alone and undaunted, when arriving too late to obtain hostel accommodations, there is no other affordable place to rest my head. With my baggage safely checked in at the train station and my purse tucked under my head as a pillow, I haven't an ounce of trepidation. Of course, it doesn't hurt to be confronted by the kindly bobby who–hearing my tale of woe– offers to keep an eye on me overnight while patrolling the park.

How can life suddenly reduce me to a snivelling infant, robbing me of my last shred of dignity? Shuddering, I know I have to escape this inner realm where my monster now reigns supreme–this dark hole in which I've only one concern: my immediate survival. Anything *but* survival is merely an undesirable distraction. I no longer see the flowers or the trees; nor do I glimpse the melodic bluebird on the wing. Surely I'd gladly shoot it, if I spotted it. More than anything, I despise that miserable little bird of happiness who deigns to wilfully shit on my mother's birthday cake today.

And *my* birthday cake tomorrow.

My first impressions of Dr. Harvey Garret are lasting ones. He's a slender, middle-aged man with a thin, hawkish face and hard grayish-blue eyes. His dark-brown hair is graying at the temples and thinning at the crown. He observes me in a cold, detached fashion from half-moon spectacles perched on the end of his beaklike nose, and I immediately pick up unfavourable vibes. My primary appraisal will not be lacking in insight, as he will soon prove to be a self-centered, insolent man, totally devoid of empathy.

"Well?" he begins tonelessly, "What seems to be troubling you?"

I gulp nervously, momentarily tongue-tied as my fear begins to escalate. He's so remote and expressionless. If only he could smile or radiate some human warmth to put me at ease. Surely he's perceptive enough to recognize the external signs that are a dead-giveaway of my inner turbulence? And he can't be oblivious to the horror that contorts my face–the crazed image in the looking glass I bolted from once again this morning?

"Well? I assume you're here for a reason, are you not?" he asks impatiently. "Or," he interjects mockingly, "could you perhaps be suffering from a speech impediment?"

I visibly flinch. How can he be so unkind as to sneer at my illness? My eyes, burning from suppressed tears, beseech him to be merciful. Falteringly, I try to elucidate my dread.

"I-I'm in a state of constant panic. I f-fear everything, and perhaps most of all m-myself. I'm afraid to s-see or talk to people . . . even on the telephone . . . friends included. I f-feel disoriented, and strangely detached from my b-body. Everything seems surreal. I've never taken street drugs but have r-read about bad trips and how they are nightmarish, and often p-people think they can fly. I-I feel able to fly too, but in the sense that I'm no longer aware of having any real substance. These sensations terrify me. It's like I too am on a really bad t-trip, but I can't escape it . . . b-because it's become my reality."

A mighty dyke opens, letting loose its waters in one convulsive flood. I outline the gruesome contents of my dreams, my episodes of bodily paralysis, and the implacable monster of dread that I can no longer sanely co-exist with, ad infinitum. Ad nauseam.

"P-please," I inquire tremulously, needing to know, yet dreading to hear, "A-am I insane?"

"When did this anxiety condition begin?" he asks pointedly, ignoring the question which has taken such pluck to put forth.

"W-when my daughter first became ill. It g-gradually snowballed after her d-death this past December. But it dates back f-further than that. It's flared up before . . . intermittently, and in varied intensity and duration . . . but n-never this bad. S-seems stressful situations precipitate it and . . ."

"What kind of stressful situations? Please clarify the existing conditions preceding some of your previous anxiety states."

I try to dredge up past catalysts, whilst gradually becoming depleted from the strain. Savage panic screams to gush forth and I dare not permit its escape. Surely it's my sheer dread of confinement that's providing me the tenacity to attain this deadlock with the monster without splitting wide open.

Concluding my tale at long last, I disclose my heavy indulgence in booze and tranquilizers. Whatever the outcome, I want my case assessed as accurately as possible.

"Are you aware of the dangers involved in drinking?" he reproaches me. "You're leaving yourself prone to forming a lasting dependency upon alcohol."

"I only know I have to do *something*. I can't exist in this mental agony without *some* form of aid!" I exclaim defensively. "Anyway, I think I've developed a tolerance to both Valium and liquor. Neither seems to ease the constant terror."

"Mrs. Snow," he intervenes, "I have one thing to make clear." He is livid. "Either you stop drinking *at once*–and that includes *any* form of alcoholic beverage–or I refuse to treat you. If you don't wish to adhere to this condition, then I must insist you leave my office directly."

Imbued with guilt and shame, I slither lower in my chair. His inflexibility forewarns me of drastic consequences if I should ever overstep my boundaries. God forbid. Unmoved by my suffering, he'll forsake me in a flash.

Direly shaken, I reply meekly, "Dr. Garret, I-I'm sick and I n-need help. It required stupendous courage for me t-to get here today. I apologize if I've said anything misleading that may imply I'll not do everything in my power to get well. I'll do anything you say. I've no intention of jeopardizing my well-being by disregarding any of your medical orders, w-which, of course, includes ceasing to drink."

"Good. I'm glad we understand each other." His jaw remains like granite. His stony, marble eyes consult his watch. "Well, I expect that about covers everything for now."

"May I just ask you two brief questions that concern me deeply?"

"Go ahead, but be quick. I'm afraid our time has almost run out."

"Thank you. Deathly as I feel, I worry I could unwittingly misuse the power of autosuggestion and will myself to die as the Aboriginal man did in the book I was telling you about. Could this actually happen?"

"It's highly unlikely such a thing could occur today. This particular ability is primarily confined to man in his primitive state. Civilized man has evolved far beyond this stage."

"Well, that's a relief," I breathe gratefully. "My next question is in regard to what's happening to me—*now*."

Observing me coolly, in the condescending manner I'm to familiarize myself with in the future, he sucks reflectively on the stem of his pipe. Wringing my hands together, I tensely await his diagnosis, my consternation increasing with his prolonged silence.

"Please . . . am I crazy?" I blurt out.

The corners of his lips rise slightly in a sardonic half-smile. "No, you are not crazy. You're very much *in* reality as a matter-of-fact and it *is* a nightmare for you. You've personally described it well: a bad trip. You're unable to deal with a situation you find too painful to bear, and you're suffering from severe emotional shock. However, in view of all you've been through, I'd be inclined to be *more* concerned about your sanity if you *didn't* have a rather profound reaction."

"Will this panic *ever* go away?"

"The worst should probably be over within two or three weeks," he comments drily. "Now, I must consider the next move regarding your case."

He summons Len into his office and briefly recaps our discussion. He then passes his verdict without further preamble.

"Mr. Snow, I must emphasize that your wife is suffering from a disabling anxiety condition and is currently incapable of looking after herself, let alone the home and children. As I see it, you have one of two choices: either you hire a homemaker, or I hospitalize her which is the only viable alternative. Frankly, I prefer the former. In my opinion, she'll recover more rapidly in a loving home environment."

"We thought of an alternative solution," I interject.

"Oh, and what might that be?"

"Well, my husband knows how desperately afraid I am to be alone right now–with *anyone* other than him. I-I'd be terrified to stay with a stranger. As it turns out, Len's had a lot of back pain lately which is not exactly facilitated by his physically taxing job at the plant, so we were thinking he could perhaps take some time off using his back pain as a justifiable reason which could serve as a mutually beneficial—"

"I thoroughly disagree with such fraudulent practices," he expostulates. "Besides, such a ploy would only add to your burden of guilt." He graces me with a contemptuous stare. "I want you to adhere to my original suggestion. Understood?"

I nod. Nevertheless, anger flares hotly within me, temporarily lowering the temperature of my terror by a few notches. *What the hell does* he *know about my guilt?* I fume silently. *Prior to his censure, I felt no sense of impropriety whatsoever, and I surely don't need the guilt he's projecting on me now!* I think of the mortgage payments we have to meet, and the children we have to feed, and bills to pay which will now include his fee. A hired sitter is out of the question, even if I had no fear of strangers. Unlike Mr. God here, sitting piously on his throne in his English tweeds whilst passing his holier-than-thou judgement upon us, we have to concern ourselves with survival in its most basic form. *Can he even vaguely relate to such mundane problems?* I ask myself. *Pompous ass! If I were not so mercilessly wracked with panic and utterly dependent upon this sanctimonious son of a bitch, I'd high-tail it out of his office!*

Sadly, I'm not the Irene of before. The best I can do is silently voice her thoughts.

I do not respond to his attack; nor does my husband. Being in no condition to shop around for another doctor I'm in a position of subservience, as is Len on my behalf. This won't be the first time I'm subjected to this doctor's rude, caustic tongue, and I'll continue to hold my peace, ever fearful of being dumped.

"I'll write you a prescription for some major tranquilizers, Mrs. Snow. Apart from that, I'll see you twice a week for starters. My usual fee is $20.00 per session. However, in view of your circumstances,

I'll reduce the price of my services by $5.00," he declares flatly before dismissing us.

This humane gesture surprises me. Perhaps I've misjudged the man. "Why, thank you, Dr. Garret. That's extremely kind. You know," I banter lightly, fighting my inner havoc in an effort to extract a smile from this impassive individual who yet faces us so sullenly, "I've always thought a psychiatrist was a rich man's luxury."

Unstable as I am, the last thing I want to do is evoke his wrath, and I'm totally unprepared for his vitriolic response.

"I find your remark objectionable and offensive, Mrs Snow. Perhaps you might use your own case as a prime example of my help being a necessity rather than a luxury."

Reduced to tears on the homeward journey, a black cloud of despair unites with the fear that has ballooned upon leaving his office. I meant no harm, yet somehow I insulted him. Stung by his outrage and dreading it may bring unwelcome repercussions, I shrink into a quivering blob of frightened humanity.

In retrospect, I believe his wrath was unwarranted, and Dr. Garret was not without his own hang-ups and underlying guilt.

In bed that evening, I stare into the semi-blackness of the night. Obsessed with the pitfalls of sleep, I struggle to ward off the cascades of drowsiness that tumble over me. All is still, save for the rhythmic sounds of Len's breathing . . . soothing me . . . hypnotically beckoning: *Come hither to the land of dreams.* Mesmerized, I blindly yield to the compelling call.

Lulled by a pleasant floating sensation, I'm unaware of the hazards awaiting me—until a final coherent thought interrupts my hazy flight: the sudden awareness that I'm falling asleep! I struggle in vain to surface but I'm plummeting downward—swirling into the lower levels of consciousness and beyond. Surpassing the limits of voluntary control where I can jar myself awake at will.

For the first time, I'm fully cognisant of an actual demarcation line which separates wakefulness from sleep, and I'm helplessly transported from one dimension of consciousness to another. The crossing is horrendous–comparable to a swift downward tumble through space. I know it's too late now. There's no turning back. I've crossed over the line . . . into a nightmarish sleep-world of insanity and death. A world equated with total loss of control.

Locked within the subterranean depths of an endless, gray emptiness, I'm gripped with the urgency to escape this labyrinth of horrors. Darting frantically through a maze of dim, endless passages in search of an exit, I become pitifully aware there is none. I'm eternally trapped in the bowels of hell.

Yowling in despair as I impotently strive to awaken, I watch helplessly as my body detaches from my mind and is sucked into a swirling black vortex which instantly swallows it up.

"NO, NO, come back! Come BACK!" I screech, devastated to realize my body is gone. As my last shred of control deserts me, I sense that my mind–all that remains of me–is rapidly disappearing as well . . . sinking into an abysmal black void, the momentum increasing with the speed of light. I realize I'm losing my *self* . . . in totality. I know that my flight is eternal and that I'll never hit bottom.

Because there is none.

Possessed by intense, all-consuming panic, I hear myself screaming, *"NO! NO! NO! HELP ME, PLEASE, GOD!"*

Eons seem to elapse before I ascend to reality. Awake and saturated with dread, I wonder how I can continue living this way. Day and night–hounded, plagued and tormented. As I change my sweat-soaked nightgown, I vow I'll never sleep again. Sometime later, I realize my pledge was pointless. Sleep overpowered me once more–this time completely unnoticed and uneventful.

My sleep patterns don't alter in the weeks ahead. They begin with me entering a lucid, inescapable horror; yet once I awaken, I'm never aware of sleep overtaking me the second time round, at which time my slumber is dreamless.

My mother drops in early the following morning. "Happy Birthday, dear!" she smiles, yet her eyes are sad. "Well, I guess it's not really a happy occasion for you, is it?" she amends. "You mustn't worry, honey . . . about the way you are just now." She sits on the edge of my bed. "You've had a rough time since Star became ill. You're probably going through some sort of delayed shock. Len tells me the doctor says it will only be temporary. You're going to come out of this thing and get better. I know you are."

"Oh, Mom, do you really think so? Promise me I'll get better." I plead, like the distraught child that I am.

"Of course you will." She puts her arms around me until I've drained myself of tears. "I love you dearly, Renie," she murmurs soothingly, using her pet name for me. "I won't leave you alone in this. You'll not have to be hospitalized. I'll take care of you, I promise."

"Oh, thank you, thank you! What would I do without you? I've been so scared. But what about Dad? Surely he won't approve of you coming here every day to look after me?"

"I haven't discussed it with him yet, but I will," she says, her eyes revealing an almost imperceptible flicker of concern.

"Oh, no! He'll be absolutely furious! He'll *forbid* it!"

"Now don't concern yourself about your father. *I'll* handle *him*. I plan to stay with you, and *this* time he won't prevent me from taking a stand on what I believe is right!

"I wanted to look after Star while you were working, Irene—at least by the time she reached age two. I could have kept her amused and fairly quiet every third week while your dad slept days. I was always so concerned about her being shifted from one sitter to another. And I worried about you. I know what a rough time you had, especially with that boss of yours who was such an unyielding person and treated you so unfairly. A rest would have done you the world of good. If it weren't for your father to contend with, I'd have insisted you quit that damn job. I could have helped you financially until you got back on your feet. I'm going to make it up to you, Irene. I feel I'm partially responsible for what's happened to you." Her eyes glisten tearfully.

"Please don't cry, Mom. Things happened. They were not your fault. Just knowing you'll be with me now is a godsend."

True to her word, Mom begins looking after me. In retrospect, her strenuous ordeal surely equated with toiling daily in a psych ward–with two strikes against her: not only was she untrained, she was also deprived of even a minute degree of detachment. Her daughter was her private patient.

One day runs into another and the hand of death touches both my waking and sleeping hours. Daily, my body seems to defy the force of gravity and whenever I stand, I feel as though I'll ascend into space; conversely, my nightly adventures depict my descent. Both states are equally menacing in their threat to totally dissociate me: to separate my inner self from my outer exterior.

Fear remains my constant companion. It refuses to be appeased by the tablets of 50 mg. Nozinan I ingest five times a day, the latter which seem to exacerbate my feelings of unreality, while introducing even more nasty side-effects to the cavernous repertoire of unpleasant sensations I already have. No matter. I persevere. Is there any other choice?

From a mighty will to get well, I summon the motivation to appear at Dr. Garret's office two evenings a week. I retain only fragments of our conversations which have dimmed over the years. To his credit, he involved himself with the issues at hand rather than wasting time delving into my childhood, and from time to time he actually offered the rare constructive comment. My most lucid memories, however, embrace his hurtful, biting sarcasm, and I endeavour unsuccessfully to retrieve any recollections of real kindnesses.

"I fight the terrors of hell just to come here," I divulge during one of our sessions. "Almost three weeks have passed and it's not getting any easier." *Could I be some sort of enigma–the only person in psychiatric history to be fastened in this unspeakable fate forever?* Such conceptions prey on me, further enervating me and intensifying my toxic fear of dissolution.

"I consider the fact that you have the *will* to manage it a good sign," he replies. "Perhaps you're not as sick as you *think* you are." He sucks on his pipe reflectively, scrutinizing me closely.

"Don't you *believe* I'm ill?" *Can he possibly think I'm malingering? Will he drop me as a patient?* I wonder fretfully.

"I did not say you *aren't* ill. I merely said that perhaps you are not as ill as you *think* you are. Which reminds me, are you still in your jail?"

"Pardon me?"

"Your bedroom's your jail, is it not? I expect you enjoy your prison. Why else would you stay there?" he says wryly.

Why does he continuously goad me? I ponder sadly. *What is the challenge in playing cat and mouse with a disabled opponent? Make that a disabled mouse.*

"You've no idea the terror I face to leave that room," I reply defensively.

"Hmmm. You do manage to get yourself here," he smirks.

I do not reply. I've already mentioned the hell I go through to get to his office. Surely, he could not do better were our positions reversed.

Mom and Len are my security blankets during these fear-stricken weeks. Mom arrives before Len leaves for work, and departs upon his return. Len spends the balance of the day by my side; and the teenagers prepare the evening meal to insure he needn't leave me. Imperilled to leave my room, yet equally endangered to remain in it by myself, each party has a protracted taste of the bedroom shift. Barring my trips to the shrink, I eat, live and sleep in these four walls. It's my virtual abode.

Soaking in the bathroom tub just several yards from my bedroom provides me with a modicum of comfort. Immersed in its liquid warmth, a measure of sensation permeates my benumbed flesh and my body no longer feels as frighteningly weightless.

Dr. Garret introduces a variation of the jail theme at our next session.

"Have you perchance felt motivated enough to step out of your prison since our last visit, Mrs. Snow?"

"I tried several times, but couldn't get much further than the door," I confess miserably. "Everything began reeling. I felt dizzy, faint, and numb–as though I were fading out or dying. The usual. I don't know how I can continue going through this torture. I know I come here, but the trip is a hell on earth. I'm clinging to Len the whole time. I'm unable to attempt anything that equates with even a fraction of such magnitude for days afterward. Is there nothing you can give me for even *partial* relief from this dread . . . some medication that may make it a little more bearable for me?"

"Well, well. I don't recall ever telling you it would be easy. Much of your recovery depends upon *you*."

His piercing granite eyes are inscrutable as he nonchalantly sucks on his pipe. My fingers cling to the small plastic container of water that never leaves my hand, and I sip the liquid in fluttery jerks. The silence in the room is overpowering. If only he would *say* something. He continues to suck his pipe as I sip my water.

Sip-sip-sip.

Suck-suck-suck.

The tension mounts.

"You must be very thirsty," he comments abstractly, digressing from my earlier entreaty.

"Uh, yes I am," I gibber, gripping my cup. *Shit. He's detected that I have to hold onto something. Anything. It's symbolic of holding onto reality, for nothing seems real anymore, least of all me.*

"Well," he continues, "Don't let your excessive thirst concern you. Dryness of the mouth is a common side effect of your meds."

Have I actually heard him correctly? Is that the actual extent of his observational abilities? I wonder incredulously.

I re-direct the conversation to the original issue.

"Is there nothing that will help me? What about hypnosis?" I inquire hopefully.

"It would be useless in your particular case."

"How about shock treatment?" Only later would I realize how far I had fallen to even suggest such a drastic alternative.

"Why, that's absurd! You are *not* psychotic," he states emphatically.

"I doubt my suffering is any less than if I were. Surely, there is *something* then? *Some* way of sedating the fear that constantly crawls within me?"

A prolonged silence ensues while he hedges, perhaps weighing alternatives. Finally, he reaches into his desk drawer and removes a vial of blue tablets.

"You may ingest one of these prior to any new venture that particularly frightens you," he states. "They are fast-acting and you'll notice a rapid decline of anxiety. I propose that between now and our next meeting you supplement your Nozinan with them, and implement the goal of moving out of your jail. Begin this therapy for short periods, increasing the time element in gradients."

"Oh thank you, Dr. Garret. You can't imagine my relief!"

"Good. I expect our next encounter will disclose you've become far less reclusive, and that your progress has exceeded a tub bath. It's time you moved beyond your cell which is symbolic of the grave you've buried yourself in with your daughter. Since you're so fond of ruminating, I suggest you think about that between now and our next session."

"Oh my God, that allusion definitely bears thought!"

I firmly clasp the small vial of *survival* tablets as I depart.

Dad drops in a few days later with Mom, and I overhear him talking to Len.

"If I were you, I'd stick her in the hospital," he advises. "Once she's woven enough fucking baskets and become fed-up with finger-painting, she'll *want* to make some effort—if only to get her ass out of there. Don't expect her to do *anything* while she's being coddled at home. She's been seeing that shrink for weeks and she's not any better. Everyone's getting worn down with this shit: my wife; your family. And where does it all end? You sure as hell don't need this crap after a day's work either. It's a job for a fucking hospital!"

Angry and hurt by my father's total lack of empathy, and terrified he may have influenced my husband, I confront Len as soon as Dad leaves.

"Please, don't put me away. I understand my dad's thinking. His nose is out of joint because Mom's here every day. I maintained two households when she fractured her leg, while he did sweet bugger-all, except benefit from my maid service. He figured his outside job should absolve him of all else. Ergo, his sworn sentiments: 'If your mother had been a horse I would have shot her'. What a mean, selfish bastard he is!"

"Don't worry about what *he* says. *I'm* responsible for you now, and regardless of what *anyone* says, I want you here with me, no matter how long your recovery takes. Your father just can't grasp the fact that people don't recover from a nervous breakdown overnight."

To my mother's undying credit, she did not give up on me either. Intent on rescuing me, she perpetually scourged her memory for any past ruse that succeeded in deleting the contortions of fear from her little girl's brow. In retrospect, love was the glue that held me together through those fear-wracked days: the love and support of my mother and husband. Dr. Garret's harsh, belittling manner was offset by their constant, gentle support, and both were instrumental as buffers in assuaging the bite of his jibes. In my darkest hours, their constructive aid provided me with a wavering faith in recovery.

Not long after this incident, Mom informs me we need to have a serious talk. Alarm bells go off as I prepare for the worst.

"You know, Renie," she begins hesitantly; "It's been six weeks since we've been confined to this bedroom together. Apart from Len or me, you won't allow anyone else to sit in here with you. Much as I love you, it's taking its toll and beginning to wear me down. You're going to have to get used to staying with other members of your family at some point."

"But Mom," I wail abjectly, "I need *you* with me! At least give me a chance to improve *a little* before you desert me! You know how terrified I am to be with anyone other than you or Len."

"I'm getting up at 5:00 AM every morning and not sleeping well most nights. If I get sick, you won't have me at all."

"Please don't *say* that! I don't ever want to lose you. How can I survive without you?"

"Don't upset yourself, Irene. I can't afford to be ill because I *want* to help you. That's why I've decided that once school closes for the summer–which will give you close to six more weeks with me beside you all day–I'll begin to drop over at noon. But if you'd gradually spend a little time in your room with one of the others *now*, you'd find it much easier to adjust later." My heart pounds wildly and a corrosive onslaught of dread seeps through me as she continues.

"Merry's been out of school for over a month now, simply because you can't be alone in your room. It's not exactly fair to her, Irene. If you could gradually adapt to staying by yourself for a short time, I could handle lunch and the baby's needs and Merry could go back to school."

"First you want me to accustom myself to staying with the others in my room. Now you want me to stay *alone* in my room as well. How can you keep upsetting me this way?" I ask tremulously.

"You wouldn't be alone, Irene. I'd be within calling distance. In any case, I'm not asking you to make any of these changes immediately. We have plenty of time and we can begin in very small doses. I would only like to see the urge for self-help begin to stir in *you*."

"You think I'm not trying too, I suppose? I'm not trying when I can't even hold my own baby without feeling she's totally unreal? She's in my arms; yet, they feel empty. Can you even mildly relate to the desire of wanting to feel close to your child, yet being as dissociated from her as everything else? Simply because every iota of your energy is sapped in the mere act of surviving? Of holding your disconnecting self together? Well, it's a living hell and I don't need any additional guilt trips because I'm guilty enough as it is that I've been unable to move forward. How could God do this to me? He won't help me, and nobody else can. God sees every sparrow that falls. So says the Bible. What does He do about it? *LAUGH?* Is He Dr. Garret's twin fucking brother?" I rant. I begin sobbing in great gulps as my heart rips to shreds.

"Go ahead and cry, Renie. Let your pain surface." She puts her arms around me. "I've tried to communicate with you, to draw you out of yourself–into *my* world, where I can relate to your feelings. You'd be surprised how many things I *do* understand; though perhaps not all. But I *do* know what it's like to yearn to be close to your child, to really want to *feel* her there. I have a little girl too, and *she's* detached from me." My mother looks sadly upon me, her eyes brimming with tears, her voice choked with emotion.

"I'm so sorry to put you through this hell with me, Mom," I murmur.

Together, we cling to one another. And in that poignant moment, a low roar of rage stirs inside me. Rage against *It* . . . for hurting everyone around me. Never have I longed to fight harder to get well than in those brief, loving moments within my mother's arms.

When Len arrives home, I relay my plans for the next day.

"I'm going to sit with Mom in the living-room for at least five minutes. I promised her. Just contemplating it leaves me absolutely petrified."

"You'll be taking a giant step forward by doing this, hon. If you can manage to not retreat–no matter how deathly you feel–you'll have won a small victory over the fear. It's a hell of a battle but I know you can do it. I believe in you."

Upon awakening the next morning, I'm stabbed with the realization that this is a momentous occasion. Apart from my visits to Dr. Garret, it's my first serious retaliation against *It*. Directly evolving from this perception is the monster itself, running rampantly within me, eagerly prepared to do battle. Surely the anticipation of meeting my opponent head-on is as great in its distress quotient as the actual act itself.

Mom arrives shortly thereafter, and for the first time I toss down one of the blue pills Dr. Garret as given me in the hopes of gaining some courage. Half an hour later Mom is still waiting for me to make a move. The "fast-acting" pill has failed to deliver the promised results. I momentarily wonder if the good doctor has tried to placate me with a sugar pill.

"The pills don't work!" I gasp in dismay.

"The others do nothing for you either, Irene. I know it's hell to face this ordeal unaided, but we have to start somewhere," she rationalizes.

"Yeah, cold turkey all the way. Well, I-I just can't, Mom. I'm sorry."

"Well then, I'll sit in the living-room on my own for the next five minutes–unless, of course, you decide to join me."

"No, please. I'm terrified to be alone! How can you *do* this if you love me? How can you be so heartless?"

"I have to be cruel to be kind," she declares firmly. "I just learned about the daughter of an acquaintance of mine. Like you, she suffers from crippling anxiety, to the extent she's been confined to her bedroom for ten long years. *SO!* You'll either get the hell out of yours, or you'll stay there and rot. By *yourself!* I will *not* be a party to it. It's essential to your eventual cure to face this thing. That's why I'm forcing your hand. It won't vanish automatically. You've got the guts, damn it!"

I'm trapped and I know it. Damned if I do, and damned if I don't. At least if I do, I won't be left alone in my bedroom. It's the lesser of two great evils.

My mother's ruse to extract me from the bedroom was indeed a kindness. By taking a stand, she forced me to begin my ascent from the pit.

Avoidance behaviour had become firmly established within me. Believing I had a greater level of control over my fear whilst hiding out in my bedroom, I was averse to leaving it. And who's to know if I might not still be there if not for my untrained mom who–in a courageous act of tough love—employed her own drastic measure by using a technique I later learned had a medical label: flooding.

"I-I'll go with you," I whimper. "Just don't leave me."

"That's my girl. I'll be with you every step of the way, I promise."

Engulfed with terror, I have no recollection of reaching my destination. Dimly aware of sitting beside my mother on the living room couch, I am estranged from the world. I clench the cushion beneath me in a mighty effort to prevent myself from ascending into the atmosphere. The deathly feeling that plagues me elevates to its highest pitch as my conscious control once again fades out, allowing my subconscious mind to call all the shots. The latter offers me the usual two grim choices: death or insanity.

"You're turning white, Mother." I perceive Merry's voice from across the room.

Oh God, I *am* dying! My limbs begin to jerk involuntarily. My heart is a staccato drum, beating wildly against my chest. Consumed by waves of dizziness, I sense the lights growing dim. I'm approaching the finish line, and I'm obsessed with terror. I will *not* "go softly" into the night. *I DON'T WANT TO DIE!* I try to speak but my vocal cords are frozen. My nails pierce the flesh of my arms and my teeth grind into my lower lip as I grapple tenaciously to arouse life into my deadened flesh. I need to *feel* in order to know I *exist.*

Merry speaks again, as if from a tremendous distance. "Yeah, Mother. You should see all your white hair. You're going to have to dye it."

Oh, God, so that's what she meant! Perhaps I'm not dying after all? The deliverance of the moment is nothing short of spectacular. I'm overcome with relief that I've once again been spared from the hand of death.

Tortured as my life is, I desperately want to keep it.

My most anguished thoughts of rage, grief and fear, sustained and emotionalized, had eventually become powerful enough to surface and lead me straight to this hell: a black empty abyss where I gnashed my teeth in dread and there was no door in sight. Losing Star–which paralleled with losing "self"–had brought me face to face with my most terrifying nightmares.

On a psychological level, my sleep traps aptly revealed "loss of self" by depicting the dissolution of both my mind and body.

On a spiritual level, where fear is the opposite of love, I was a lost, broken thing, experiencing the illusion of being irrevocably separated from Love (my Source), and the result was separation anxiety in totality: blind terror.

I would later understand the true meaning of hell. It is a state of total fear. It is being removed from Light and Love.

I had to move forward.

In order to regain enough confidence to desensitize myself to the fear, I had no other choice than to walk right into it; allowing it to overpower me and do its worst. Until it finally became self-evident that I would survive the worst.

It was imperative my subjective mind accept this truth. Only then would things change.

My sojourn in the living-room lasts all of five minutes but it marks my first real turning point. Time still tortuously creeps but no longer stands still as I gradually emerge from the darkness.

While wedged in the creeping stage of desensitizing myself to the fear, it seems my every endeavour to face it is ineffective. Daily, I sit for short intervals in the living-room with my mother before gradually progressing to the kitchen and dining room. The mental upheaval involved in taking each baby step forward is nothing short of tripping out in horror. Regardless, I keep on keeping on. And Mom and Len praise and encourage me every step of the way.

Finally, the monumental day arrives when I actually expand my territory from the interior to the exterior of my home. I sit outdoors in the sunshine for short intervals with my mother. This is another triumphant milestone. Finally I've become saturated with enough success-oriented behaviour that I'm able to function with only moderate anxiety, both inside my home and on the grounds surrounding it.

Mid-June marks a full month since I've taken my first tentative steps to rise from the flight to fight stage of my illness. While there are many giant steps ahead, I'm no longer regressing. The teenagers are writing exams and most days at least one of them is home. I've finally adjusted to being alone with them, a well-needed break for my mom. Best of all, I've at last surfaced from the prison of my bedroom–aka my grave–and resumed most of my duties as wife, mother and homemaker again.

During this time of transition, even sleep has become more a friend than a foe. The sleep traps have ceased, along with the inner conflict that accompanied them. Ironically, a calming effect from the Nozinan ensued *after* I'd subdued my fear by my *own* efforts; at which time I began sleeping up to sixteen hours a day. Since then, having lowered the dosage of my meds, I feel more connected to reality as well.

There's yet another mighty river to ford–the movement from home-base into the main stream of life: stores, travel, and people. At first accompanied, then finally alone. One baby step at a time. When I enter a store, the old symptoms rush back and I'm overcome with panic, dizziness and sensations of unreality and there looms the additional horror of either collapsing or flipping out before the prying eyes of strangers. Trapped in shops, my world again becomes totally unsafe. Gravity seems to vanish and, despite Len's steadying support, I perceive I have nothing to cling to.

Somehow, I manage to stay in the fight, because consciously I opt for life. Nevertheless, I'm exhausted from the dread that accompanies these excursions and leaves me weakened, heartsick, and drained. I often shed tears of frustration when my mother or Len–unwilling to see me regress–oppose my pleas for relief. They nag me unceasingly if my progress wanes; yet, to their inestimable credit, they grant me the freedom of moving ahead at my own particular pace. Providing I *keep* moving. By extolling my gains and minimizing my losses, they reinforce positive behaviour and I thrive on their praise.

Consequently, my confidence rallies sufficiently to regularly take a headlong plunge into the black pool of uncertainty which threatens to submerge me, again and again.

I know I'm one of the lucky ones. I could not have made it alone.

Dr. Garret's eyes remain closed to my progress. He treats my illness as a satire and continues to bait me unmercifully. Itemizing each small victory, I keep hoping he may recognize the sheer gut force that goes into every new rung I mount on the ladder. Not once do I hear the encouraging words I so avidly seek. Hurt and bewildered by his constant invalidations, I feel bitter and hostile towards him. Yet, concealed beneath the anger is an aggrieved child, unwilling to recognize the saddest of truths: her doctor's approval is vital.

One Saturday afternoon when Len and I arrive downtown too early for my session with Dr. Garret, I bravely suggest we walk through one of the city's largest department stores. For me, this is a first and the moment we set foot in the door, the floor tiles begin to whirl before my eyes and my surroundings begin fading in a blur of horror. Innately aware of the dense crowds around me, stifling and suffocating me, I struggle to draw a full breath and feel perilously close to blacking out. I'm compelled to tear out of the store, save for the voice in my head and its monotonous refrain of, *You have to do it; you have to do it*. I force myself to plod on . . . and on . . . until finally our pre-determined time of fifteen minutes is up. I'm back on the street. Alive! And, oh so elated in view of my first victory over stores!

I'm eager to share my win with Dr. Garret who has been needling me about my lack of progress in stores. Perhaps I can finally absolve myself of the shame that's been haunting me prior to this gain.

Later in his office, I blurt out my success story.

"My husband walked me around a large department store prior to seeing you," I exclaim delightedly. "There were *throngs* of people and I was absolutely terrified; yet I actually managed to hold my ground and—"

I pause upon hearing his derisive chuckle. His wide grin could put a Cheshire cat to shame. Suddenly, to my absolute chagrin, he tosses his head back and laughs aloud.

"I see," he guffaws. "Your husband's walking you around now, is he? Congratulations! You've progressed to a dog on a leash!"

Stung, I wonder if he's just a hateful person or I have done something to merit his antipathy. Burning with shame, I do not reply. Such a flagrantly cruel retort truly does not merit one.

But most deflating of all is the knowledge that I haven't one to give.

By the end of June, I've definitely made strides. My confidence has progressed to that of a toddler. I'm able to go almost anywhere without fear, if accompanied by a trusted person. I daily take small walks on my own as well; albeit still needing to glance over my shoulder to ascertain I'm being watched from my home lest something dire may happen to me, the likes of which I can't define. Many weeks will elapse before I gain enough confidence to give up my vigil and tackle a full circle around the block on my own; yet I'm encouraged by my gains.

The decrease in my ghastly symptoms somewhat relieves my fear of dying. I recall asking Dr. Garret, "How do I get over my fear of dying?" His somewhat flippant, yet enigmatic response was: "By living." Such was the limit of his feedback. I now wonder why I didn't think of asking how I could get over my fear of *living*. I never realized the intensity of one was equivalent to that of the other.

I've sometimes wondered if it is as well that was the case: It meant that suicide was never a viable option.

One evening in early July Len and my mother persuade me to go with them to the Legion, a social club for veterans and their families and friends where, for years, I played darts on a league and attended most of their functions. I've not been back since my breakdown as I'm still prone to flurries of apprehension when mixing with people outside of the family circle and I've not gotten over my fear of having an unexpected panic attack, a combination which keeps me a social recluse.

After considerable prompting, I find myself crossing the threshold of the Legion's front entrance. Sheer terror clutches my breast and the familiar sense of deathliness steals over me. *Oh, God, what if I have an attack inside and am forced to take wing and fly? I'll feel like a social disgrace.* Upon spotting the swarm of faces beyond the door, I know I have to make an escape before I'm seen. *RUN!* I command myself. *NOW! Oh no, my feet our rooted to the floor! And someone has spotted me. Oh Crap! Now, they've all seen me!* My mind races with the knowledge that they've undoubtedly all learned about my breakdown and are curious. News travels fast in a small suburban community. *Please God, help me get through this without making a total fool of myself!* I paste a smile on my face. *How will they react to my presence?* That's my last coherent thought before they are all literally *upon* me!

Old friends and acquaintances flock around me, greeting me enthusiastically with a flurry of hugs and kisses, expressing genuine delight at having me back amongst them. Perhaps they can never understand where I've been on a personal level, but on a human level they are aware I have suffered and they are embracing me in their warmth and acceptance.

In the midst of such affection my previous fears ebb and I hug them all in return. I sense I've "come home" and within this wondrous advent I recapture the childlike belief that the melodic little bluebird really *does* bring happiness.

At least every once in a while.

Perhaps, I think ruefully, *I may even find it in my heart to forgive it for the times it has shit on my cake.*

Music throbs in the air, and it's announced that a dance contest is about to begin. The best couple in an all-round set of various dances will win a prize. Bob, one of the Legion's best dancers, approaches me.

"Hey there, Irene, let's show them how it's done. With you as my partner, it's a cinch to win."

I stiffen, and prepare to make an excuse.

"Go on, Irene. It'll do you good," my mother urges. Len backs her up. A barrage of negative thoughts cross my mind. *I'm so nervous! What if I trip and make an ass of myself? Or panic and have to escape?* Meanwhile, Bob's hand grips mine and, before I'm fully aware, I find myself being propelled onto the dance floor.

We've always excelled together in a multitude of dances, and as it happens a polka is the first to be played. Twirling together on the floor, I merge unbidden with the gay, frolicsome strains of the lively music. As the rhythmic rhapsody of the music begins to permeate me, mind, body and spirit, my former qualms and uneasiness diffuse within the stimulating crescendo of sound. Caught up in the joyous movement of the dance itself, I'm aware of becoming reintegrated into a state of wholeness and harmony. For the first time in months, I feel in tune and gloriously alive.

"*Good GIRL!* I *knew* we could do it!" Bob beams. Holding my arm and proud as a peacock he struts off the floor with me after the set . . . waving the cash we have won as first prize.

From somewhere deep within, I decipher the answer to my age-old question: How do I get over the fear of dying?

By living, Dr. Garret decreed.

In the preceding moments, I have truly *lived*; and within those joyous moments of living I have lost all fear of death . . . and of *living* as well.

This discovery marks another beginning.

An immense climb yet lies ahead, but I will not lose sight of the faint shaft of light at the mouth of the pit.

JUNE 15, 2012, FRIDAY

Gary has now completed his second cycle of chemo, and is concluding a two week respite.

It was originally determined that he had some small tumours in his neck and spleen and a massive one in the chest. The enormity of the latter was unknown to Eve prior to the completion of Gary's first cycle of treatment when he awakened one morning with chest pain. His father dropped both Gary and Eve off at the hospital where Gary was immediately sent for a chest x-ray. Later, the oncologist assured them both that the pain, which had currently dissipated, was likely a strain from a recent bout of vomiting and nothing serious to worry about.

"In regard to the x-ray," the doctor went on to say, "I have some good news for you. The small tumours are no longer visible and the large one has significantly reduced."

Intrigued, Gary asked to see the film, and with Eve's consent, the doctor obliged.

Eve later told me, "Thank God, I didn't see the damn thing in the beginning! I almost freaked to see the size of it *now!* I'm only glad to learn it has shrunk and the others appear to be gone. That's the hope I'm hanging onto!"

Now, as I hear the tuneful ringtone I have set particularly for Eve on my portable phone, I take a deep breath. She and Phil had an appointment today to find out the results of both the CT and PET scan Gary recently underwent following his second cycle of chemo in order to determine his progress to date.

"Good news," Eve declares. "The scans also show that the small tumours have disappeared; and the large one has shrunk about 60% . . . *and* . . . *the PET scan reveals no more malignant cells!*"

"Wow!" Is that the end of the chemo?" I ask hopefully.

"No. He'll have two more cycles to be on the safe side. It's important they shrink the large tumour as much as possible to be sure the remaining network of cells is not rekindled. However, the oncologist is extremely pleased and believes that will be the last of the chemo. At the most, he may need some radiation if a small section of the existing tumour remains."

"That sounds promising–especially considering he's a stage three."

"Yes, that's the doctor's stance as well. He'll start his third cycle on June 18th, so his birthday will fall on his two week break which he's pleased about. He'll be able to dine out."

"Great. We look forward to celebrating his fifteenth birthday with him."

"There's more good news. Jim's test results regarding the lymph node on his head were negative."

"Oh, thank you, Eve. You've just made my day!'

Once we disconnect I e-mail my youngest daughter, Dana. She's due to deliver in three days and because of her gestational diabetes, she's been under close observation. I'm concerned about her.

She e-mails me back with the following message: *Still hanging in. My obstetrician is concerned the baby may be getting too big. If she doesn't arrive by due date Monday, they'll induce me the week after. Can't wait to have it over with. Don't worry, all well so far. Will let you know when on my way to hospital. Love to you and Dad.*

And that is the news of my day.

Chapter 12 – The Monster's New Mask

*"We don't see things the way they are.
We see them the way WE are."*
—Talmud

July arrives, along with Len's holidays. On the day we are to depart for a week's retreat on the lake, a brilliant sun plays hide-and-seek amongst the wispy clouds. Watching it dance hither and thither beneath their wispy white veils, bejewelling the atmosphere with a lustrous sheen of mother-of-pearl, I could not wish for fairer weather to accommodate a family about to set forth on their first holiday together.

The teenagers are a string of eager beavers as they pack into the back seat of the unsightly eye-sore that stands in the driveway of our home: our antiquated relic of a car. Since our old station wagon died, we are now the not-so-proud owners of an extremely ill Impala. Its engine sputters and coughs consumptively, its body has rusted from the ravages of too many winters, and portions of its floor have eroded and occasionally spark into small flames. At such times, much to my amazement and chagrin alike, Len merely pulls over, grasps a hunk of burning floor and tosses it out the window. That being said, the Impala has not disappointed us. It seldom fails to get us to our destination.

Len, Keith and I sit on the bench seat in front, and five-month-old Eve is perched on my lap. As the winding ribbon of highway rolls by, the voices in the rear ring out in song. I remain quiet and incognito behind the dark shades which camouflage eyes that remain tired and puffy from little sleep. This ninety-mile journey marks a noteworthy endeavour on my part. *Surely it will induct me into the hall of fame,* I muse facetiously. Ever since I so rashly committed myself, I've yearned to duck out. Yet in view of everyone being so pleased that I finally acquiesced to their pleas, I could hardly renege on my promise–in spite of the horror of slipping back into panic at a point so far removed from home.

At long last, the highway branches off onto a winding, dirt road which eventually leads us through a densely wooded area to a welcome clearing where the exterior view of a quaint log cabin, nestled between tall, stately fir trees, cheerfully greets us. Beyond the cottage lies the lake–an infinite mirror of molten silver–its waves lapping gently against a sandy shore. My senses awaken to the quiet beauty of the surroundings and I perceive the first tender buds of renewed confidence stirring within me, their petals yielding submissively to the whimsical caress of the pine-scented winds which hold the hidden promise of sweeping my anxiety into the distant horizon.

Once inside the cottage, the kids quickly unpack their belongings. "We're going swimming now. You coming, Mother?" Mark, the eldest, hollers.

"I have to warm a bottle for Eve. Go ahead and have fun! You too, Len. I'll join you all later."

I'm still adapting to this new form of address. Len presented the teenagers with the option of calling me "Mother" or "Irene" when we first married, and they all decided to adopt the former, much to my pleasure.

I momentarily recall my own mother's words shortly before Eve was born. "You know, Irene, I was often concerned about you being an only child, and perhaps all alone in life one day. You're fortunate to be part of this large family. You'll not want for friendship later in life. I know Keith tends to be a painful reminder of your loss because he and Star were so close, but your heart *will* heal in time."

Although seven months have elapsed since Star's death, the wound is still raw. I look at Keith and as yet only tend to see the portion of him that's been severed . . . for Star was surely his other half. Still unhealed, I'm unable to comfort this little boy who shares my grief. I can only hope my mother is right, and I'll come to see him as the separate person he is, rather than a sore reminder of what life has stolen from me.

I am not without regret for being unable to deal with my loss more charitably . . . and for the pain it undoubtedly caused others.

As I retrieve Eve from the high chair provided by the cottage owners who have also supplied a crib, I enfold her in my arms where she contentedly begins to drink her warm milk. I reflect upon a previous conversation with Dr. Garret. "I feel so guilty that I'm unable to fully open my heart to my new baby. It's as though I'm *afraid* to love her," I confess.

On this rare occasion, he's much less flippant. "It's not abnormal in relation to the sequence of events that have transpired in your life. You've erected a wall as a barrier to prevent you from further pain. You've been irrevocably hurt and love represents pain to you. Consequently, you *have* become afraid to love. Yet, it's only by learning to love again that you'll achieve a healing."

I gaze tenderly upon Eve and speak to her softly. "I don't know how or when it happened, sweet baby, but you have completely entwined your heartstrings within my own . . . as Star did before you. I love you as much as I loved her and if I were given the choice between your life and hers right now, I could not make it. You're a special gift, dear one—a *healing* gift. You have awakened my dead heart by showing me how to love again."

Within this tender moment I recognize the fundamental truth of Dr. Garret's words, and become aware of a perception which heretofore eluded me: *it is love, not time, that heals all wounds.*

After kissing my little girl and setting her down for her nap, I join the others.

"Hey, Mother, wanna play water ball? You and Dad can play against us."

"Later, okay? After my swim."

I've inherited my dad's great love of the water, and now as I propel myself effortlessly through the waves I recall his boyhood dream of swimming in the Olympics. His aquatic proficiency as a young lad was first noticed by an eminent swimming instructor who donated pro bono time to underprivileged youngsters at the boys' home. This renowned man, aware that the proper training could elevate my father to Olympic material, invited Dad to be his protégé. Dad was overjoyed, and under his instructor's guidance, he went on to win countless medals. Sadly, however, Dad's elation at eventually being chosen to swim in the Olympics for Canada was to be short-lived. The participants had to personally absorb all costs and his mother couldn't afford the expenditure. Not only was his dream ground to dust by default, but an opponent he'd out swum in an international competition went on to win a medal for his country.

My parents visit us a few days later and we all enjoy a hearty lunch on the picnic table outdoors. My stepchildren have really taken to Mom and Dad and call them Granny and Grandpa, much to my parents' delight. I've recently stopped taking Nozinan, and am enjoying the two pints of beer Dr. Garret has permitted me on social occasions.

A short while later, Dad dons his bathing trunks and says, "C'mon Brat, have a swim with your old man!"

"You're on!" I squeal, pleased.

Gliding across the lake, we soon leave the shoreline in the distance.

"Let's relax awhile," he proposes.

As we tread water and amicably converse, yesteryear blends into the present yielding a kaleidoscope of memories.

I'm a child again, alone with my dad in the middle of the lake. Water nymphs that we are, we're having such fun as we tirelessly engage in our games. Diving underwater, we exchange a kiss, along with some words beneath the surface, the latter which we try to decipher upon emerging for air. But it is not all fun and games. For countless hours, he patiently instructs me on becoming a professional swimmer. Momentarily, I taste the remembered joy of his words.

"I believe you're ready to tackle the English Channel now, Brat. Marilyn Bell is the youngest to have succeeded to date at age sixteen. At thirteen, you can beat her by a few years, no problem."

Why did I let him down? I ask myself. *Above all, why did I let myself down?*

As we swim back to shore, he mentions with an edge of sadness. "I'm pleased to see you've not lost your style or grace in the Australian crawl. You know, Brat, you could have come a long way with your talent."

There were times I wondered if my refusal to accept my father's offer of a professional swimming trainer was a rebellious means of thwarting him from living his own unfulfilled dream vicariously through me. I now believe it was more likely due to my "fear of success", the subconscious belief that ignited in my child's mind when I first arrived at the assumed conclusion that I could not retain first place because I did not deserve such an honour. Consequently, as the fires became too hot, anxiety arose . . . along with the need to duck out.

Taking that thought to another level, my attraction towards unattainable men also supplied me with a safe haven. Subjectively perceiving that their inability to commit complied with my inner script of fearing success, they provided the perfect means of copping out.

As you would say, Dad, I really fucked up. But you did give me something very special, you know? Climbing out of that pit I fell into was the bravest fight I fought in my life.

You gave me a piece of your courage.

His voice penetrates my reveries. "How about that ten buck race you're always chickening out of, Brat? I'll give you a several yard handicap?"

"Conceited, aren't you? Well, for ten bucks you can forget it. I know I can't beat you!"

"I've had that bet on the table for well over a decade. When the hell do you plan to take me up on it?"

"When you're very, *very* old," I retort. He grins and joins the teens for a swim and some water-play before going ashore.

I've no way of knowing we've shared our last swim; and that our bet will never come to pass.

Our week's holiday soon draws to an end. Once home, we collect our camping gear and set off for the final week of Len's vacation, this time at a campground on a lake closer to home. Things couldn't be more primitive, especially with a baby on board. I wash diapers by hand, sterilize bottles on a Coleman burner and prepare formula, all performed in a tent. To top it off, Keith suffers a forty-eight hour intestinal infection and–between him and Eve–my hands are rarely out of soiled undergarments. Keith's are the worst. He's become a three-year old cesspool. At one point, I ask Merry to help by rinsing out a pair of his underpants under the communal tap. She blanches. "I'm sorry Mother, I can't. The stench makes me want to vomit." Len laughs uproariously.

"Pipe down or *you* can damn well do it!" I shout at Len. He smirks. I hurl the sodden garment at the bark of a nearby tree. "From now on, *you* either do it, or he goes bare-assed!"

There's no way his tender tummy can handle changing diapers under *any* circumstances, or so he says. Of course, that was chiefly woman's work back then.

I later laugh at the irony of wanting to be well enough to be a wife and mother again.

We return home in early August and as I count down the dwindling days of summer my mind goes into overdrive. *What if I'm unable to adapt to staying home alone when the teens are back at school? Will I have to be institutionalized? What will happen to Eve and Keith?* Once again, it boils down to the lesser of two evils, and another nightmare of therapy looms ahead.

My initial attempt takes place when the teenagers are visiting their maternal grandmother.

"Hon," I suggest to Len impulsively, "how about picking up the kids and leaving me alone in the house? I have to start this god-awful thing somewhere."

"Do you think you'll be okay on your own?" He regards me with concern.

"Frankly, no. But we know I've no other choice than to get used to it. Besides, it's only a quarter hour return by car, providing you don't stand around and shoot the breeze."

"I'll call the kids and specify they meet me outside," he assures me.

My heart is pounding wildly and I pray he leaves quickly before I give in to this powerful urge to beg him to stay. Finally he departs, promising he'll be back as soon as possible.

I dart to the window and frantically watch his car leave the driveway. He waves and offers me a thumbs-up prior to disappearing from view. The monster chooses this timely moment to surface with a vengeance—and my last shred of confidence dissolves. Cackling with pleasure, *It* hastens to subdue me. My grip on reality begins to slip, and I sense that I'll float away or disintegrate at any given moment. *Oh God, there's nothing left to cling to!* Blinded with terror, I stagger across the floor, unsure as to where I am going. My last coherent thought as panic overtakes me is that I'm about to black out.

Sometime later—I've lost all sense of time—Len finds me huddled in a corner, cowering like a rat and frozen with dread.

"Oh, my God, are you okay?" He grips my face with both hands. *"Answer me, honey!"*

As I edge back into reality, I become aware Len is home. And I'm *alive!* Bad as it was, I have *lived* through this horror. *I have DONE it!!*

Again, only time and practice will eventually reprogram me to the awareness that I *can* do it; the operative word being *eventually*. Meanwhile, the nightmare of relearning seems to drag on forever.

By early September, I'm coping alone in the home with Keith and

Eve while the teenagers are in school and Len is at work. This has been one of my greatest accomplishments to date.

A few weeks later, Dr. Garret and I part company. He wastes no time in addressing the matter at our final meeting.

"Mrs. Snow, do you think your husband would like being obliged to work evenings and Saturdays?" he states acrimoniously. He scowls darkly as he sucks his pipe.

Aware of where this may be going, I merely shrug my shoulders in an "it beats me" kind of gesture.

Taking this as a form of tacit agreement, he continues, "I'm glad we see eye-to-eye. In the future, if you're still incapable of travelling alone and unable to take weekday appointments, I'll no longer be able to work with you. However, you've come a long way since last April, and with continued practice and confrontation, you should be able to attain your former state of well-being without my continued services. Think it over and advise me of your decision."

I nod in agreement, though I know I'll not be returning. As yet, I can't contemplate a long bus trip downtown on my own and I refuse to impose upon my mother for company. She's done more than her share.

Once home, I write Dr. Garret a courteous note advising him day appointments are out of the question. I thank him for his help in the event I may need it at some future point, though I sincerely hope *not*. In any event, perhaps he has done me a favour. His rude manner has served rather well in therapeutic value. It has rekindled the flame of wrath within my spirit, thus significantly raising my tone level from flight to fight. He's helped me *feel* again, if only by harvesting a crop of contempt within my craw. As I post the letter, I believe beyond doubt that I definitely *don't* need this Neanderthal to survive. Good riddance! As I turn my back on the mailbox it symbolizes a two-way gesture. Humming, I saunter the half block back to my door.

It is over. I have no regrets.

I continue my daily therapies of taking walks and going into small, nearby shops unaccompanied. Each new venture calls forth a hideous confrontation with fear. Taut from the strain of perpetual battle, I'm desperately in need of peace. I now suspect I'll *never* be able to take a new step without overwhelming anxiety. I'm still unable to enter supermarkets, a dentist's or doctor's office, a school building, or any place similar, barring the company of a family member or trusted friend. However, I *am* able to function alone at home, albeit with mild-to-moderate anxiety. And I *am* able to enjoy a mutual social life with my husband, and to do a handful of things on my own. Far simpler to retreat, if able.

By now, I am able.

I've clawed my way to the mouth of the pit only to see a mountain arising before me. A seemingly insurmountable ascent heralds the peak that marks my freedom. Meanwhile, the monster and demons lay dormant. If not incited, they do not attack. But not unlike mischievous children, they are shrewd in their silence. They cackle derisively as they wilfully scheme to dupe me with a change of venue and a different disguise.

My journey is far from complete but I've attained ground level. For now, that will have to suffice.

Chapter 13 – Ghost in My Bed

"Sins, like chickens, come home to roost."
—<u>Charles M. Chesnutt</u>

A tentative acceptance of Star's passing is not less elusive than the passage of the seasons. Its dawn is a subtle perception of movement and change, undetermined by temporal means. Even as summer has become fall, it too has imperceptibly *become*.

Her presence–like the magnificent canvas of nature surrounding me, which splashes a bold blaze of prismatic autumn colour on all that it touches–remains in my memory. I haven't stopped missing her; yet I've undergone a comparative healing. The quality of my grief is no longer as raw, and is distinctly more tolerable. In surfacing from my inner world where time stood motionless and still, a transformation has taken place. I can now nurse my pain from *without*; hence, I'm able to deal with it more lucidly. And I'm distinctly more involved with living than dying.

My transition may well be noteworthy, with one exception: I've merely risen on the emotional scale from the level of fear to anger; whereby I've substituted one unhealthy obsession for another. Since fear is the taproot of anger, I'm simply in touch with another facet of fear itself.

I'm entirely unprepared for the new and unexpected battle ahead.

My breakdown has shown me how genuinely Len cares for me. Unlike Karl who, at best, would have wept while I perished, Len has loyally and unselfishly stood by me and I've grown to love him deeply and romantically.

Being in love is not without its drawbacks: my self-confidence is still at par with that of a child and I cannot maturely, or rationally, handle such a high-charged emotion. I'm defenceless and susceptible. Insecure and afraid. A sitting duck for the unholy blast of subjective anger that arises from the roots of my earliest rejections.

Ironically, the effects Len formerly desired to induce at the start of our marriage–by way of baiting me with fuzzy love stories of Brenda, his first wife–have finally become a reality. A year overdue. Back then, I'd been virtually invincible, my emotions still wrapped up in Karl. Now, a whole battalion of angry demons rise to the fore and, within their grisly dance, a host of past insecurities are reawakened.

In the customary style I employed with Karl, I begin interrogating Len frequently about his former stories that currently awaken old ghosts. Depending upon his attitude or response, I can be a tiger or a lamb.

Unaware that my heightened fervor for Len has re-ignited my age-old fear of rejection, I'm currently handling it with anger–the selfsame wrath I often suppressed over the years because it had no viable outlet. I finally begin to let the sleeping tiger loose. Because I can. And at times it has the bestial savagery of its namesake.

I resort to my usual method of remedying past grievances–by picking players via association. Brenda–no matter that she's dead–has become the rival (Father), with whom I'll vie for first place. Len performs the customary dual role. He, too, plays Father, who represents Karl and all those self-same bit-players–"bastard men" in between–who've thwarted me from attaining the glorious pedestal I once held and lost; but, like Karl, he also has the role of Mother, in that he represents my security and continued survival.

I have no idea that this is a subjective game whereby I'll blindly and compulsively follow the dictates of my subconscious mind without a clue that the outcome will be a self-fulfilling prophecy, and I'll consistently defeat my purpose of attaining the success I consciously seek . . . because I've long since subjectively concluded I don't deserve it.

Brenda has become the silent phantom who walks by my side and sleeps in our bed. Perversely, she represents the challenge of a live rival, and before long I become ambivalent towards Len for having married her. Our arguments begin that autumn, sometime after my sessions with Dr. Garret have concluded. When a flashback of one of Len's earlier revelations annoyingly strikes, I'm on tenterhooks until I can question him about it.

I'm not always happy with his answers.

Meanwhile, I'm oblivious to the knowledge that Len's own insecurities prompted him to bombard me with such cozy–and mostly untrue–tales in the first place. My long-standing relationship with Karl left him uncertain about being first in *my* life. At last, assured of my green monster's existence, Len's able to flash the jealousy card at will and enjoy some delayed satisfaction . . . with nary an inkling that my half-crazed reactions reveal the insecurities that have deepened since my breakdown. How can he be attuned to a facet of *me* that even *I* am unaware of?

As nightmares of Star's death diminish, others arise. Hurtful ones depicting my relationship with Len. His face begins to morph into Karl's, and I'm startled into wakefulness. My first thought is: *Bastard men! They're all the same. Len. Karl. My father. All cut from the same cloth!*

The dreams recur. Karl and Len have somehow melded together in my mind and the association is not a good one. Our arguments increase and I again become privy to Len's own inner rage which is not pretty when unleashed.

In the worst of my fear when I clung to Len for my very survival, he was never more kind. Relishing his role of protector, he seemed to prefer me clingy and afraid. As I regained a fleeting control of my life his own power diminished, leaving him fearful and threatened. In hindsight, he mourned the special place he'd held in my life during my breakdown. He, too, nursed insecurities and his deepest fear was losing me. He, too, fought his fear with the fury of a tiger.

Like me, he only wanted love. How can we know—before we truly learn—that beyond our ego, LOVE is what we are?

At times our battles get out of hand and our home is virtually ransacked. Our fights are costly. And it doesn't stop there. We become prone to physically assaulting each other.

I begin adding booze to my diet again.

It's anger that prompts my first trip alone to my parents' home about three miles away. Len takes the car and leaves, as is par for the course during our various rows.

Rather than give him the satisfaction of leaving me stuck at home again because I'm afraid to leave, I impulsively call a cab. An act which insures I no longer have a means of retreat.

As I watch for the taxi, an electric finger of panic charges through my flesh, warning me that untold horrors loom ahead. I force myself to concentrate on my anger and the thrill of revenge that will be mine when he comes home to face the unexpected: his fearful, timid wife has actually flown the coop.

Once in the cab, I pray I can contain the anticipatory anxiety that is menacingly flooding my senses. *Please, God, just help me hang on until I reach my destination!*

Mom and Dad are far from overjoyed to see me. "I expect you've had another fight," Mom accuses.

"Look at the bright side," I say. "I've *achieved*! This is the first time I've been able to leave home on my own. Until now, I've not managed more than walking a few blocks away from the house."

"It goes to show your fear is all in your head, doesn't it?" my mother retorts crossly. "If you can do this in temper, you should be able to do it any time. The trouble is, you won't push yourself. I know what fear is, Irene. I've always been an anxious person, and I know what it is to have to push myself to do things in the face of anxiety."

My joy of victory is immediately squashed. *Damn her!* I bristle silently. *She can't imagine the horrors I go through to get from point A to point B. Or the guts it took to get here—even with the aid of temper and a few beers.*

"I don't have an *ordinary* case of nerves!" I shout back. "There are *levels* of anxiety, and since you've not walked in my shoes you're not in a position to parallel my fears with your own! I'm virtually *terrorized* to do things alone. I'm gripped with panic and unreality so acute that it overwhelms me. If I won a million dollar lotto and was forced to make a solitary trip downtown to collect it, I'd simply have to forego it. And that's the God's honest truth!"

'Don't hand me such horseshit!" my father barks. "You'd pick up your million like anyone else. You've proven you can move your ass *this* far on your own. Simply kick it a little harder—and *further*—in the future?"

It's useless to try and explain things. If my own parents can't understand my fear, nobody else ever will. At least they're teaching me the value of keeping it obscured.

Unbeknownst to me at the time, anger will befriend me: if only in the sense that it *will* force me—beyond all else—to move forward from time to time. My fears have endowed Len with predator rights. He often walks out, secure in the knowledge I'm trapped and unable to move. The thought crystallizes that it's imperative I conceal my fear. And most of all, from *him*.

The doorbell rings. It's Len. "I thought I'd find you here," he says.

"Go home with your husband!" my father commands.

Len and I drive off in silence. Once home, he locks himself in the bedroom. I take a pint of beer from the fridge and bed down on the living room couch. *At least he knows I can bugger off now too,* I contemplate, prior to drifting off into sleep.

In the future I'll often be the first to leave home in a fight. Once I begin driving locally on my own, I'll sometimes manage to grab the family car before he can reach it. There's always a teenager at home to keep an eye on the children, so no worry there. In sniffing out *his* insecurity—that he becomes direly upset when I leave him, and

221

will always come in search of me—I begin having my long-awaited turn in the driver's seat. Payback. I've spent too many months as a passenger.

Such silly games we sometimes play! Not unlike robots we become programmed to re-enact our misperceptions of the past in the present, thus perpetuating them throughout our lives by ensuring that the thoughts we've suppressed—both favourable and not so favourable—become the driving force behind our self-fulfilling prophecies.

For Len and me, it would seem one of our favourite defense mechanisms was regression. There's no doubt that, above all else, we were notorious for reverting to childish behaviour.

I serve the family a delicious supper the evening following our argument. The house is sparkling. I've baked a cake for dessert and I've taken pains with my grooming. I welcome Len home with open arms and he happily returns my embrace. Another truce has been affected.

Later, as we get ready for bed, Len asks, "Are you still mad at me?"

Unable to control the unruly demons that are creating such inner dissonance, I'm compelled to unleash them in the desperate need of having my insecurities assuaged.

"Unhappy would be more accurate. You're so much like Karl. Here's a news flash. Inge and Brenda were born on the exact same day of the exact same month. Interesting, isn't it? You and Karl both had a lot in common: a wife, four kids, and the same breed of dog. Except in your case the wife and the hound are currently missing."

"The wife isn't missing, Mrs. Snow," he says tenderly. "*You're* my wife."

"Please, Len. Don't *ever* call me that." He looks hurt. Good. That makes two of us. "*She* was the *first* Mrs. Snow. The inference leaves a bad taste in my mouth. It reminds me I'm a second-hand rose—you know, like in the song. You'll have to buy me that record for Christmas."

Scrutinizing Len closely, I'm momentarily transfixed. *What an incredible likeness there is between him and Karl!*

"Honey, I'm *not* Karl," Len uncannily cuts into my thoughts. "*I* wanted you, and *I* married you, remember?

"Only because your precious first loved died. Big deal. Karl would have done as much if Inge had croaked. If dear Brenda were alive, you'd not have left her for *me*!"

"That's where you're so wrong. I was a twenty-year-old kid when we married. You're the only woman I've ever truly loved. Believe it or not, I would have definitely left my marriage for you."

"That's easy to say. You'll never have to prove it, will you?"

"I was out seven nights a week back then, involved in every sport imaginable. It was my escape. Doesn't that tell you anything?"

"Yeah. You loved sports."

"Well then, why don't I run out and play sports every night now? C'mon hon, use your head. You would have been my incentive to leave the marriage. It was no great love match for either of us. She was unhappy at home and I was her way-out. My dad and I were on the outs and I was living with my brother–not exactly a win-win situation for me either. I married her because she said she was pregnant which turned out to be a false alarm. End of story. Neither one of us moved on to a happily-ever-after. I represented security to her and little else. If we'd divorced, I'd have been thrown out of my home whilst she lived there with the children. I would have had to support the lot of them with hardly a cent left over. I'd rather kill than give away the house that I worked so hard to build."

"Why didn't you kill her then? That would have proved you didn't love her." I keep a straight face although I'm smiling inside. I like what he just said. It will definitely tide my demons over for a while.

He looks at me strangely. "Are you out of your mind, Irene? I couldn't just *kill* her!"

"I know. I'm joking," I grin.

Apparently relieved not to haggle over a murder he failed to commit, he begins kissing me. Appeased by the apparent sincerity of his words, I eagerly receive him.

We amend our quarrel without further words.

Harsh November winds, together with occasional snow flurries, herald the usual end: the arrival of winter, and the closing of the year. I detest November with a passion. It's the reminder of sad tidings, carrying a backlog of pain on its winds; it's the day-to-day countdown of the decline that led to Star's final fall.

As Christmas 1970 draws near, I cringe. It's a revival of Christmas past.

I place a memoriam in the newspaper in early December in commemoration of the first anniversary of her death. I painstakingly cut it out and place it in her photo album: It reads: "The brightest star to ever shine, God's Star you were, not really mine; when night-time falls and my day's through, I pray you'll light my way to you."

I whisper softly: *I hope you know how deeply you are engrained in my heart, little one.*

Christmas is not exactly the sorry occasion I would have anticipated. Shopping with Len for the children actually gladdens my heart as I anticipate them eagerly opening their gifts. Len takes Keith and the teens for a hike in the woods where they choose the "perfect tree" which we all decorate as a family. My parents join us for the Christmas Day festivities and although I slip away occasionally to mop up the errant tears arising from memories of Star, the day goes by without a hitch and I derive some real yuletide pleasure from the love and good will surrounding me.

Later, when my parents have departed and Len and the kids are watching TV downstairs, I seek some quiet time alone. Thankful the day is over and I no longer have to keep up appearances, I remove my mask and privately release the river of tears I've held back–a well of raw grief that remains in my heart for the beautiful child who is no longer here to share this special day with us. I still miss her so. I often stop to look twice when I see a little girl on the street with features like hers. Now, as I dry my tears, I release my emotions once again in poetry as I begin writing yet another poem in memory of my Star.

Despite the good moments, I am glad to have this Christmas behind me.

If there's a positive aspect of suppressed anger rising from its subjective zone of fear, it can only be that "fight" is a major catalyst in leading one out of the dregs of despair. The anger I direct at Len keeps me less centred on Star.

As a New Year begins and my demons accompany me into it of their own volition, they continue to whisper their tale that bastard men are all the same and need to be punished. I remain unmindful that Len and Karl are symbolic of my mother; but also my father. And that I long ago determined that my dad—in the act of rudely dethroning me—committed the most grievous sin of all: robbing me of first place in my mother's heart.

JUNE 20, 2012, WEDNESDAY

I'm mulling over last night's dream about a rather large pet fish, the approximate size of a small perch. I keep it in an enormous bowl which Len, in a clumsy moment, knocks over. The glass shatters into myriads of shards, and the fish flounders wildly on the floor as I search for a suitable receptacle for it. Finally, to prevent its certain death, I'm obliged to place it in a container which is too small to adequately accommodate its ungainly proportions. I watch sadly as it consistently pelts the sides of its restricted enclosure, yearning to find a degree of comfort in its inadequate space.

Upon awakening, I suddenly become aware of two things: *I am the fish*; and *I, too,* am longing to expand my own particular space . . . or consciousness. This particular illumination immediately brings to mind the autobiography I began over thirty years ago and I'm suddenly overcome with the desire to finish it.

I seek out the weathered, yellowed pages I've saved, and decide to gradually edit and re-type them and eventually incorporate the contents of my daily journal into the manuscript itself.

On some level, I have realized it's time to tackle my fear of success. . .

In order to complete my book, I know I'll have to deal with the negative subjective prompters that, even now, are smirking somewhere within the dark caverns of my mind, whilst shrieking gleefully, "You are not a good girl and you do not deserve to succeed!"

PART II – the prisoner

I sit within my prison walls
As daylight breaks, then twilight falls.
I watch the shadows eve' has cast
Upon these walls and held there fast;
I dream that one's a ship's large mast
That I have seen in times long past,
When once I too could sail the sea,
So long ago . . . when I was free.

Oh, to be free! To sail the sea!
To shed this bondage chaining me!
To raise my eyes and see the sky,
And gulls therein, that ever fly,
Quite near my ship as I drift by;
Yet in this cell I'm doomed to die.
I can no longer even weep,
With eyes long dry I welcome sleep.
—Irene Snow

Chapter 14 – Cell Without Bars

One may understand the cosmos, but never the ego;
the self is more distant than any star.
—G. K. Chesterton

Len and I relish the respites between our quarrels. We rejoice in our love, whilst indulging gratefully in the priceless moments it offers. We fervently try to compensate for our lapses, and cannot do enough to please one another.

My demons nudge me excessively and I struggle to keep them in check. Finally, some powerful inner force compels me to heed their call. Depleted from battle fatigue I no longer desire another round with my husband, yet I feel powerless to bear my torture alone. Eventually, I swallow my pride and approach him—often trading hostility for feminine allure—in order to obtain the relief I seek. Meanwhile the voices shriek raucously: *He's a bastard. Accuse him!* They abhor the gentler tactics which are generally irresistible to Len, and hence they lose out. At least temporarily.

Like Karl before him, Len does not possess a silver tongue, and inevitably his best intentions are defeated with a fateful faux pas. The demons then burst forth with alacrity.

No one is aware of the baggage of fear I still haul about. When the teenagers accompany me somewhere, they've no idea that their presence—while always a pleasure—is also an oblique cover to mask the anxiety that assails me when travelling about on my own. I've been reduced to a thirty year-old toddler, and I feel deeply invalidated to tote a nanny nearly everywhere I go. I chose to bear this shame alone, and I become deviously adept at inventing excuses to avoid any situation that may arouse my inner monster. Although I've learned to live with this strange illness, I've never fully accepted it.

Winter dwindles into spring and my friend, Jane, drops over occasionally. I've long since overcome the bitterness I felt when she intruded upon my personal life by telling Karl he should leave me. Not one to hold grudges, that particular grievance is passé. Our long-standing friendship was too valuable to set aside.

Jane is now divorced, and one day while we're sitting on my front porch, she says, "Renie, I really don't blame you for not wanting to travel on buses with the kids. What a nuisance! So, can I possibly induce you to come and see my new apartment if I collect you and the children in my car for a visit, then drive you back home?"

"I have something to confess to you," I say tentatively. She regards me curiously as I continue. "You know the phobia you have of birds?" She nods. "Well, I have something similar, but far more crippling. I may as well be honest and clue you in, mortified as I am."

She listens attentively as I explain my fear of going places either alone or with the little ones. Concluding my narrative, I'm imbued with a sense of relief for having confided in her.

"It sounds like some form of phobia to me," she offers. "Especially with the symptoms you mention of overwhelming panic, and even the surreal feelings. Your reactions equate with my own whenever a bird comes anywhere near me. Perhaps it's a fear of the unknown?

"I was in a pet shop recently and some idiot left the door of the budgie cage open. Despite the scores of people in the store, would you believe the birds flew directly at *me*? I think they sensed my fear. I was absolutely frozen to the spot, screaming like a banshee. Finally a group of salespeople ran over and caught the little varmints in nets. I know I made a complete ass of myself but I simply lost all rational control. Consciously, I know the birds won't hurt me but I'm simply petrified when they come anywhere near me. I walk blocks out of my way to pass those city parks with their miserable collection of pigeons."

We grin over our foibles and I feel silly that I withheld my fear from her. We've always had the freedom of unmasking ourselves to one another, and the act of disclosing our heartaches and humiliations has welded our friendship and allowed us to laugh at ourselves in the process.

We enjoy the balance of her visit playing "Psychiatrist", our favourite game, as we each try to analyze the other's hang-ups. We finally agree I definitely have a phobia of some sort.

"And to think my shrink was not shrewd enough to come up with your diagnosis, Dr. Jane," I quip.

"Truer words were never spoken," she beams. Then dropping her voice conspiratorially she adds with a grin, "Of course, it may help that I happen to be phobic."

After Jane departs I sit idly for a while, basking in the fresh air of spring. My demons are quiet as well, and a welcome sense of peace settles over me. Perhaps there's a name for my problem? Or a remedy? Somehow, I must learn more. That's definitely on my "to do" list for the immediate future.

Keith is pedalling his small car along the sidewalk and Eve sits happily in her playpen under the shade of the tall tree on our front lawn, amusing herself with her toys. *Despite its difficulties, life is good,* I decide.

Len and I buy a used boat and motor which we bring to the lake on our camping holiday in July. The teens and I take turns joining Len on the boat for fishing excursions and sometimes we just go for a joy ride where we rapidly skim over the waves, feeling their spray as the wind hits our faces. Keith and Eve squeal with delight on these outings, which are the ones they enjoy most of all. Evenings, after scaling our catch of the day, we wrap the fish in aluminum foil with butter and herbs and bake it with potatoes in the open fire. Later, once the little ones are bedded down in the tent, Len and I join the teens around the campfire where we often have a sing-along. Late at night Len and I occasionally slip down to the beach in our swimsuits, and if it's completely deserted, skinny-dip under the stars.

Bringing up young ones provides its share of frustrations. I'm soon to learn Keith has bathroom mania. A few times a week a disaster hits. He awakens early and soundlessly commits havoc in the upstairs john. On one occasion, he washes his hair in the toilet bowl creating a minor flood on the floor. Another time, he shreds an entire roll of toilet paper, applying Vick's ointment to each tiny piece, which he individually glues to the walls. His bathroom creativity is unsurpassed, and I'm regularly treated to new delights. Finally, I implore Len to install a catch on the outside of the door, high enough that Keith can't reach it, and I resort to giving him a potty at night. Undeterred, he sneaks a chair from his older brother's bedroom and worms his way back into his own special fun room. Keith has assumed Star's pride of place as the instigator of mischief in the home.

My memories of Christmas 1971 are not particularly pleasant; nor am I proud of them. They nevertheless accurately reflect where Len and I were at that point of our journey.

We are sitting at the kitchen table, enjoying a Black Russian–a powerful mixture of vodka and Tia Maria–on Christmas Eve. It's almost midnight and Ken, who has still not retired for the night, has joined us and is drinking a Coke. Fondly recalling Keith's latest comedy, I relate it to both of them.

"You won't believe this," I begin. "Before Keith went to bed, he asked me if we'd turned the furnace off. He said, 'I don't want Santa to burn his ass when he comes down the chimney'."

We all crack up. Then suddenly Len becomes serious. "You know, hon, you're really going to have to watch your mouth around the children. Keith will be going to school soon, and the next thing you know he'll be swearing like a trooper."

Abruptly my happy mood dissolves. "Keith sleeps *upstairs*,

remember? So do his big brothers who can teach *me* a thing of two in that department." I look at Ken who grins sheepishly.

"The boys never swore until you came along," he persists. I, of course, have no idea that he's baiting me.

"That's a lot of bullshit. If you believe that, you've never washed your ears. I heard them swearing long before I ever swore in front of them. In any case, they're not babies and they know where to refrain from using bad language. Free speech is encouraged these days . . . even in writing class. Perhaps it's *you* who should haul your sanctimonious ass out of the dark ages and stop being such a fucking hypocrite. Besides, it's not as though *you* have such a pious mouth!"

"Ask Ken if he ever heard me swear before *you* lived with us? Their mother never swore in front of them either. They didn't hear *any* foul language in the house before *you* came along."

"Well, why the hell swear now? I'm not twisting your arm."

He actually smirks. "*You'd* drive anyone to swear!"

That does it! The demons can no longer be contained. "I'm pleased that Brenda didn't drive you to swear. I'm impressed that her speech was so impeccable. Such a fine lady! She must have worn a halo. I wonder what *her* bad habit was," I add nastily, hoping he catches my veiled innuendo. I leave the table and stomp off.

I get as far as the bedroom only to realize I've forgotten my drink. I hear Len and Ken whispering together as I re-enter the kitchen. I'm now totally pissed and itching for a fight. "If you don't mind, Ken," I say acidly, "I'd like to speak with your father alone." Sniffing the animosity around him, he clears out quickly.

I pour myself another drink.

"I suppose you're going to get drunk," Len mutters disgustedly.

"You don't smoke, you rarely drink, you didn't swear until I came along. Wow, lucky me! I married God!"

He smirks again, and momentarily preens. The SOB is actually gloating which is definitely my green light to lose it.

"It must be tough on you being married to a mere human when Brenda was a saint like you–neither drinking, nor smoking, nor swearing—"

"Yeah, well, it is kind of rough. And Brenda quit smoking when we got married. For me, actually. Which is more than *you* would ever do," he says mockingly.

At this juncture, I literally *lose* it! I no longer care *what* I say, or *who* hears it! My fury runneth over.

"Well, well, I wonder why she didn't quit eating for you, too," I remark bitterly. "Or do you not consider gluttony a vice as well? At over 200 lbs., she must have stuffed like a pig! I was told she once ate ten chocolate bars in a day. At that rate, it cost you more to keep her in sugar than me in tobacco. No wonder your old double bed sagged so much on one side before we replaced it. Was it fun to sleep with a gorilla?" I choose this moment to smirk right back at him.

I see I've hit home. Out and out warfare is about to ensue. Who threw what first? I no longer recall. He pitches the head-set I've given him as an early Christmas present across the room with such force he dents the wall and my gift along with it. I throw my empty glass against the opposite wall and it shatters on the floor. All hell breaks loose as we hurl invectives at one another and damages mount up to the tune of our tempers. Inflamed, he overturns the large wooden stereo and heaves his foot into the back of it. I pitch his tape recorder onto the floor. It goes on and on, until we are both physically drained. He then snatches my purse and rips the telephone wire from the wall to ensure I can't make a call. As I try to grab my handbag from him, he shoves me aside and strides out the door.

No words can describe my rage. I'm livid. He's leaving me trapped here while he's gone. *Again!* No purse, no phone. *Damn him,* I fume, *he does it every time. I'll fix the bastard!* I prepare another Black Russian which I drink while reconnecting the phone. He has no idea that Jane showed me how to do this on her last visit. Ricky played the same game until she learned how to reconnect the wires. I leave him a childish note specifying: *I've reconnected the phone. In case you think you're so bright, any stupid ass can do that. Sorry, Einstein. I've effed-off in a cab (must refrain from using the F word in deference to your delicate breeding). And, by the way, in view of how trustworthy you are, surely you*

don't think I keep all my money in my purse anymore, do you? IDIOT!
F.U.

I'm still shaking in fury. I've not punished him enough. I grab the small TV that sits on his dresser in the master bedroom. He loves to watch it in bed. *Well, not for awhile, buddy!* I open the front door and march to the edge of the road where I hurl his prized possession onto the hard macadam. Satisfied as I see it explode before my eyes, I add a postscript to my fond little note: *P.S. If you're looking for your small TV, it's in the middle of the road. But perhaps you've already run over its remains???*

I grab a warm coat, shove a pack of cigs and a lighter into one of the pockets, and pour a fresh drink before vacating the premises.

I slip into the detached garage at the back of the house. Having neglected to shovel the mountain of snow in front of it, we're unable to use it just now. I fibbed about having money; but he needn't know that. Besides, at this late hour, where could I go?

I perch on an old table underneath the side window and begin my vigil. Consulting my watch, I see it's well after midnight. *"Cheers, and a Merry Christmas, Irene!"* I hiccup drunkenly. I swill down the rest of my drink. I've scarcely finished my first cigarette when I hear a screech of tires as a car swerves wildly in front of our house. *It's him. God.* I scrutinize his movements as he slams out of the car and begins hauling the final vestiges of his TV to the side of the road. *Mighty neighbourly of you,* I snort. By this time I'm totally smashed, yet I can still grasp how thoroughly pissed he is. *Oh, yeah, just look at his stance. He's bristling like a cat: back up, walking stiffly into the house now. At any moment he'll spit. Oh crap, I hope he doesn't think of checking out the garage when he sees that I've gone!* A wave of panic momentarily clears my fuzzy head, and I wonder if the morgue wagon makes pickups on Christmas Day. Too late to worry about that, he's discovered my absence. The back door slams as he stomps out of the house. *He's getting back in the car, thank God!*

Within an hour or so he returns home. I wait patiently for the indoor lights to go out before I stealthily ease myself through the back door of the house and walk into the kitchen, half-frozen. My ears are keenly attuned for the slightest movement as I slink quietly down the hallway. I stop abruptly when I hear Len's angry voice from beyond our bedroom door.

"Do you know what time it is? It's after five o'clock," he declares brusquely as I dare to open the bedroom door. "The kids will soon be awake for their presents and I think you might want to help me clean up the mess downstairs. The tree is on the floor."

My heart lurches. Oh no, not the playroom, too! I silently follow him downstairs. The tree is lying on its side with shattered decorations all around it. "Smart!" I mutter caustically. Before he can reply, I hear the patter of little feet on the stairs.

It's Keith. Just what we need! "What happened to the tree, Mommy?" he inquires in dismay.

"Well, sweetie," I ad-lib, "Santa accidentally knocked it over. He left a lot of presents for all of you and he had many more to deliver to other children, so Mommy and Daddy said we'd clean up the mess. Anyway, it's far too early for you to be up so I want you to go back to your room until we call you. Meanwhile, you can take your Christmas stocking upstairs to see what Santa put in it, okay?" He grabs it happily and charges back up the stairs.

It's well after seven by the time the basement is half-way presentable and I can hear Eve stirring. Exhausted, I make my way upstairs to her room. She's nearly two now, and this will be the first Christmas that holds any meaning for her. Like Star, she talks extremely well for her age and chatters excitedly while Keith and I watch her extracting the tiny toys, trinkets, fruit, and sweet treats from her stocking.

Once the older ones have arisen and everyone's had breakfast and opened their gifts, I leave them in the playroom and make my way upstairs, filled with foreboding. Everything is in a total shambles. Furniture is overturned, windows are bared, and broken objects are strewn all over the floor. Drapes and curtains have been ripped from their moorings, and plants, soil, muck and shards of clay pots are scattered everywhere. Our bedroom is a similar disaster. *This can never be allowed to happen again,* I tell myself in dismay . . . futilely . . . for the umpteenth time.

Suddenly, the grim thought hits me: What will I do about my parents? They're scheduled to arrive at noon. There's no way I can allow them to see *this* mess, and I'll never have time to clean it up. Besides, I have the daddy of all hangovers. My head is throbbing painfully and I'm shaking like a leaf inside. I have to cancel them. *Oh, shit.*

Having cooked the turkey and stuffing weeks earlier to save time on Christmas day, I take the frozen packages, along with all my pre-chopped veggies and special goodies, and stuff the lot into a humongous shopping bag. The least I can do is ship my parents a meal. As an after-thought, I toss their gifts in the bag as well.

"Take the bus over to your grandparents," I advise the teenagers as I hand them the large bag. "Tell them your dad and I have had a really big argument and we're not on speaking terms. No need to mention the condition of the house. I'll call them later. I'm sure they'll be glad of your company. Tell them I'll make it up to them in a day or two. I honestly don't think I can survive just now, I feel so sick."

Sometime later, after I've swallowed more aspirin and am lying prone on the couch, the phone rings. It's my mother. She's furious. Never again will she accept another invitation to our home. She and Dad have had their fights at Christmas but never have *they* been rotten enough to let *their* parents down at the last minute and cancel everything. How can I be so selfish?

"Don't tell me you've had another fight over the dead?" she continues to vent. "You should be ashamed of yourself! And what a bloody nerve you have, shipping all the food over here for *us* to prepare for everyone! Not that we don't love the teenagers, but just because *you're* upset you think it's okay to plunk everything on your father and me! I don't want to see your face again!" I try to apologize. She continues ranting. *Slam!* I hear the phone bang down and am left with the buzz of the dial tone ringing in my ear.

"You needn't look so smug," I tell Len as I look up and see him standing by the door. "You're always pleased when I'm on my parents' shit list, aren't you?" I grab a beer from the fridge.

"If you're going to drink all day, so am I!"

"Your prerogative," I shrug carelessly.

Unused to drinking, Len is snoring within a few hours. Sometime later, after the little ones have been fed and put down for their nap, I flake out on the couch. Christmas dinner is a cold bologna sandwich for the kids and me. Len can damn well take care of himself.

The next morning I awake frozen. The thermostat registers an all-time low. I turn the dial but the furnace won't start. Len's resting on the living-room sofa under a mountain of blankets.

"There seems to be something wrong with the furnace," I announce coolly.

"Oh, you've noticed," he replies icily. "Well, I decided it's too hot in here so I shut it off. Incidentally, it's staying off."

"You're an ace bastard," I declare, aware that he knows I have no idea how to turn it back on at its source. I leave the room and hasten upstairs to check on the children. They're still sleeping–with extra blankets over them. *At least he has* some *decency*, I think caustically.

I hear the doorbell ring. Mark hollers, "It's the minister! I see his car out front."

"*Shit!* I don't want him to see the house like this. Don't answer!"

"He'll know you guys are home. The car's in front of the door."

"Next time I see him, I'll say some friends picked us up. Whatever. *Just don't answer!*"

That evening Len puts the heat back on. He's either cold, or has had a change of heart. It matters not. After freezing all day and having to bundle the children in winter clothing, the ice-cold fury within me is far more frigid that he can hope to induce by merely turning off the furnace.

When I awaken the next day, I notice Len has tidied the house. I realize he's trying to make amends, but I doubt my heart will ever thaw.

"If you'd like to choose some new drapes and plants, I'll take you to the shops," he offers.

"Why? We have so much anger we'll only wreck them eventually. Why don't we just put newspapers on the windows? They're less costly to replace if we rip them apart."

"I've never done things like this before. You seem to have the key to riling me beyond control."

"Likewise," I answer truthfully. "I've never been hell-bent on destruction either. Perhaps we should get a divorce while we're still ahead. Quite frankly, I'm not ready to die just yet anyway, and I'll eventually be in the morgue if I stay in this marriage. Sometimes you get physical with *me*. And before you say anything, I know *I'm* no better. I'm the village idiot that will fight you tooth and nail until the bell rings and the referee says I'm out, but you're many times stronger than me and I always get the worst of it."

"I didn't touch you when you broke my TV. Do you think I ever *want* to hurt you? Why do you keep goading me when you see I'm losing my temper? You're not happy until I see red and am totally enraged. I had time to cool down the other night, even though I was still angry about the TV. Look, I'm sorry for my part of it, honey. Sometimes, I can't help myself. I say things to get back at you that I don't mean. I feel annoyed I've given you the satisfaction of telling you I didn't love Brenda because I think it gives you the upper hand. Then I say something to make you doubt me. I no sooner open my mouth than I'm sorry; but it's too late.

"You're the only woman I've ever loved besides my mother," he continues. "I never fought with Brenda. I was indifferent. Besides, if she'd see I was pissed about something, she'd keep quiet. She'd not dare fly back at me the way you do. On the other hand, I run after you. I search the streets for you. I worry about you. I come to you and apologize. I give you anything you really want and you know it. I sold the house I built myself because you were not happy there. I've never been like that with anyone in my whole life. Nobody could love you more than I do."

I begin to soften. He holds me tenderly while I shed the tears of despair that my anger and hatred masks. I'm a little girl who is hurting. He's bandaging my wounds and kissing me better, and I respond with love.

At least, for the moment, I've emerged victorious over Father, my true rival, and I'm safely ensconced in my rightful first place . . . within my mother's arms.

The New Year heralds Eve's first surgery–at barely two years of age–to correct her crossed eye. Shortly after she's admitted to hospital I learn I won't be able to visit her during her three-day stay. Due to some contagious disease that has penetrated the hospital doors, it will be closed to visitors. Surely she'll feel abandoned! I ponder hauling her out of there, but conversely she needs the surgery which has been arranged for the following day. Len thinks we should go ahead with it and I comply; yet not without serious trepidation.

The day we arrive to bring her home she's sitting with another small child in the corridor in front of her ward. Her small head is partially concealed by the profuse bandaging that covers her right eye. My heart goes out to her, and I can hardly wait to embrace her.

"Mommy! Mommy!" she yelps joyfully, as she spots me and begins racing forward in a frenzy of excitement. In her eagerness, she trips and falls headlong onto the tiled floor. A few bounding leaps have me beside her, cradling her in my arms and soothing her as she cries, only thankful she has not been harmed. The past few days have been a nightmare of pacing the floor and calling the hospital. Deprived of visiting my baby, I've been haunted by the ghosts of yesteryear. And unbeknownst to me at the time, Eve's own ghosts have become firmly implanted by the experience. For a few years hence she'll cringe and cry at the sight of anyone clothed in white.

By now, I've been forgiven the Christmas debacle, and am back on good terms with my parents. Mom calls one day in February quite upset.

"Your dad has suffered a work accident," she informs me. "He's lost a portion of his middle finger."

Two months later in April Dad injures a rib. Mom calls as soon as they arrive home from hospital to say his x-rays have revealed a growth on his right lung. She's terribly distraught.

"Can you hear me, Irene?" she whispers hoarsely. "I have to talk quietly. He's gone for his nap and I don't want to awaken him. I'm so upset I don't know whether I'm coming or going. Meanwhile, he's totally unconcerned. I can hear him snoring from here." She hesitates, carefully choosing her words. "I'm afraid it may be something serious, Irene." Mom would never utter the "C" word. It terrified her.

"Listen, Mom, you can't just jump to conclusions. Not every growth is serious." I, too, refrain from upsetting her with the actual word. I know she lost her best friend to cancer years ago, and Star's death didn't help to allay her fears regarding it. "Besides," I add, "suppose it *would* be the worst—which I seriously doubt—it would never have been discovered if Dad hadn't broken a rib. In that case, you might want to regard his injury as providential." Somewhat placated, she thanks me for my pep talk and promises she'll try to be more positive.

Unfortunately, it turns out Mom's fears are not without substance. Subsequent tests reveal the growth is malignant, and by early June, Dad undergoes a lobectomy. Two thirds of his right lung is surgically removed. We visit him in the ICU following his surgery. He's still quite groggy from the anesthetic.

"How do you feel?" I inquire gently.

"Not exactly like riding a bicycle yet." He raises the stub of his middle finger and murmurs sleepily, "It never rains—." As I mentally complete the sentence an icy finger of fear momentarily chills me in regard to the implications.

Prior to his discharge the doctor informs us the outlook is hopeful. "The growth was localized. I'd say he has a better than 75% chance of survival," he declares. Mom and I are encouraged.

Dad recuperates quickly at home. By the time our summer holidays approach, he's regained the weight he previously lost. He and Mom decide on a day's visit to our campsite on the lake. We now have a trailer, which we bought after being rained-out in our tent the previous year.

"I've never seen Dad looking better," I remark to my mother in an aside.

"Yes," she agrees happily. "He's been so well lately. I can't help but feel a sense of relief."

Her relief is temporary. Dad soon begins suffering severe digestive upsets. Mom pleads with him to remain home from work a little longer, but he insists he's fine and returns to the job he acquired upon retirement from the army.

"Your father's not well, Irene," she reflects sadly on one of her afternoon visits. "As you know, he's not a complainer; nor will he discuss his innermost feelings with me. He never has. Yet I'm not exactly blind. It's not like him to take pills, and I've caught him swallowing painkillers regularly now. I see him rubbing his stomach after each meal and I can tell he's in pain but he's always so evasive. *Just a bit of gas*, he says. He has no appetite and eats such bird-sized portions. He's losing weight again. I know he must be suffering at work and I wish the hell he'd quit his job. It's not as though we can't manage on his army pension. There's no way I can get through to him. He absolutely refuses to see a doctor. He claims they're just a bunch of ghouls. He's so damned obstinate."

"Let's look at this rationally," I suggest. "His follow-up lung x-ray was negative. I know what you're thinking, Mom, but this problem could be totally unrelated to the previous one. It could be any number of things, even an ulcer."

"If only I could convince him to see a doctor," she says morosely.

"Come on," I propose. "Let's not get morbid. How about a game of Shanghai Rummy? A dime says I'll beat you." True to form, she amicably agrees. She loves playing cards and I'm pleased to have distracted her. "I want you to stay for supper with us," I insist. "Dad's on the afternoon shift and there's no point in you going home to an empty house." I'm pleased to see she obliges, and Len drives her home later that evening.

In the days to follow, Mom becomes totally wrapped up in her worries over Dad and calls me daily with reports on his worsening health. It's becoming increasingly difficult to console her. I'm helpless to change the situation. I, too, have approached him in regard to seeing a doctor. In his usual no-nonsense manner, he's told me to mind my own business.

Mom's fears are playing havoc on my own nerves, and my intake of Valium increases in conjunction with my anxiety. I'm balancing on a tightrope, and the slightest gust of wind may blow me away. I suspect it's not normal to be this fearful and afraid, but as I recall Dr. Garret's unwillingness to do overtime, I somehow feel I'd be similarly stymied elsewhere and thereby have no choice but to get through this alone.

The following Friday Mom suggests Len and I join her for a night out at the Legion.

"We all need to change our minds a little. A few games of darts and a couple of beers with friends will be good for us, Irene. Dad insists he wants to watch some programs on TV. He's been urging me to get out for my own good. He's probably right."

Later, at the Legion, we're conversing with a married couple that are acquaintances of Mom's. The subject of marriage arises and Glenda says, "Harvey and I have been married over forty years now. I honestly don't know how people can get married a second time. If they do, it's surely a need for companionship; or, as in Len's case, probably the need for a woman to mother his children. It can't be possible to love a second spouse as much as a first."

I feel the blood drain from my head. Surely my face has whitened. I wait for Len to make some kind of reparation in regard to the damage he surely knows this statement has caused me. I can see him squirming as I sit quietly, fraught with anxiety.

In order to deflect the discomfort arising from this highly-charged moment, he chooses flight over fight. He gets up. "Would you like another drink, hon?" he offers.

"No thanks," I mutter. He nevertheless heads for the bar without another word.

The moment to remedy the situation has passed and my anxiety turns into seething anger. How can he do this to me? He could at least have told Glenda he married me for love as opposed to a surrogate parent.

Livid, I knock back my drink and feign a yawn. "I'm really tired and would like to go home now," I sigh. "I'll just use the restroom first."

Mom follows me. "I can tell by your face that you're put out by Glenda's remark. I know you. You're my daughter. You mustn't take any notice of her, Irene. It was not done maliciously. She hasn't a clue. She lacks both education and breeding and expresses her thoughts as she sees them. It was not meant as an attack against you. Only an ignorant person would cast such a stupid opinion–and especially in front of a man's new wife. Anyone with an ounce of brains knows that young marriages are often mistakes. Some of your own friends are prime examples."

"Believe me, dear Mother, I'm not at all offended with Glenda. I know exactly where she's coming from."

"Okay. I realize you're angry with Len, but try not to hold this against him. His problem is shyness, not lack of love. He's confided in me about his first marriage, and I believe him. Why don't you do the same and let sleeping dogs lie?"

"Sleeping dogs do not *lie*, Mother. They fucking *bite*. I have a whole pack of them inundating me with this kind of shit constantly. If Len would just speak up when it happens it would stop, but he's simply not man enough to defend me. Do you think Dad would put up with it if he were Len? He'd simply say, 'I've never heard such an asinine remark. You don't know what the hell you're talking about.' In *exactly* those words, and *you* know it!"

"You're right," she sighs, "but you must remember Dad has a totally different temperament. Len is more insecure. He's concerned he may make bad friends or, worse still, a fool of himself. Dad doesn't give a damn. He's too aggressive, and his obnoxious behaviour often embarrasses me."

"At least people respect him," I retort. "They vie for his attention and are pleased when he deigns to acknowledge them. Len's no coward. He's a trained fighter and pity the person who should ever accost him once his temper is aroused. Yet, the verbal shit he lets roll by is unreal!"

"Simply because it *evades* him. He's not a worldly person, Irene. He's naïve in a lot of ways."

"Why use fancy words? He's a fucking peasant!"

"You sure as hell aren't perfect! I can't understand anyone being jealous of the dead."

"The dead become very much alive when they're constantly thrown in your face. Half his damn family still call me Brenda and a few do it deliberately. You sympathize with his insecurities but don't give a rat's ass about mine!"

"Well, just don't plan to run to my place if you have another fight tonight, because I'll throw you right out," she admonishes.

"That's the last place I'd go. I know damn well I won't earn frequent flyer points by gracing your door after an argument with Len, no matter if I were bleeding to death," I snarl.

She slams out of the restroom. I'm grateful there's no one else in it.

There's an icy silence between Len and me on the short drive home. I pour myself a beer as he prepares for bed. Knowing full well what he's done, he decides to apologize. He approaches me in his underwear.

He was stunned when Glenda made her idiotic remark, he confides; he began to boil over inside and was sure he'd fly off if he opened his mouth. It was better to remain silent than respond like a savage, yada yada yada.

"Yeah, right! That's a flimsy fucking excuse," I lash out. "Now everyone figures I'm second-best. I can't stand it anymore. You're such a bastard. You probably did it on purpose!" A long stream of expletives flow from my mouth as I slam and debase him. Unable to compete with my tongue, he resorts to his only defense. He grasps my shoulder blades and shakes me violently.

"Shut up, for Christ's sake. *Shut the fuck up!*" His face is livid and his teeth are bared.

"*Let go!*" I shriek.

His grip slackens and, blinded by my inner pain, I impulsively toss my beer in his face.

The gates of Hades open. In a bellow of rage his hand flies out and strikes me. My head reels from the force of his blow and I fly back at him in demented fury. He's unprepared for my surprise attack and my long fingernails shoot out like claws, ripping through the sides of his cheeks and scourging the bare skin of his chest as he stands unprotected in his briefs.

He throws me violently to the floor. "You *fucking* bitch!" he explodes. His hands clasp his face as blood oozes between his fingers. I rise to my feet, still locked in my own well of fury. He begins whacking the hell out of me, yet I feel no pain. I'm temporarily deranged. It's lunacy to enter into combat with a man of superior strength; yet my intent is to injure, scar and maim in retaliation for the agony he has caused me. The pain of his blows pales in comparison to the blinding ache within my heart. I fight blindly . . . kicking, clawing, biting.

Until the bell clangs my defeat.

He storms into the bedroom and begins getting dressed. I spot my wallet in his hand as he passes the living room door. Seized by another great surge of fury from this final indignity, I rise to my feet. Limping to the kitchen, I grab an empty two-litre glass coke bottle I spy along the way. Opening the back door, I blindly pitch it at his car as he backs out of the driveway. Hearing a thunderous crash, my mind clears abruptly. *I've broken the front windshield! Oh my God, he'll kill me!* Shocked into sanity, my life suddenly holds great value again. As visions of motherless children arise, I only know I desperately want to preserve that life.

I flee down the street in panic, hoping I'll make it to the relative safely of the small convenience store before he catches me. Unable to outrun him in my debilitated condition, I've barely made it when a large hand grabs my hair from behind, arresting me in my tracks. I scream in terror as he strikes me on the head . . . over and over. Thankfully, the door of the store opens and he abruptly leaves.

I crawl into the shop in relief. "I see what he do, Missus," the proprieter says in her broken English. "You come in. You call cops on my phone. Sit down. I bring you water."

Sometime later the police bring me home. Len has vanished. If the teenagers are awake, they are wisely keeping out of sight. Keith is crying in the kitchen.

"He took Eve, Mommy! I tried to stop him and he hit me. I'm sorry, Mommy."

Oh God, what have I done? I console Keith as best I can as I freak out about Eve.

The officers are sympathetic. However, Eve is Len's child as well. There's nothing they can do before morning when they'll advise me where I can obtain a document of temporary custody; I must be certain, however, that I want to follow this recourse through with a separation. Meanwhile, do I want to press charges for assault? *No, not now,* I tell them. I know Eve is his ammunition. He's liable to phone me with some sort of ultimatum. I don't want anything to happen to my baby, and since he's extremely angry and upset, I'll do anything he asks of me. *Anything!* I can't bear to lose another child. And oh God, not my darling Eve!

The cops leave. I refuse to let them take me to Emergency to be checked over. Somehow, I get Keith settled back into bed. I sit dazed in the living-room, staring through the window and praying for Eve's safety. My beautiful plants have been smashed, but who cares? All that matters is my baby. I know he won't willfully hurt her. This is an attack against me. Yet, in his distraught frame of mind, he could have an accident and Eve could be killed.

An hour elapses. It may as well be a century. I will sit here forever and watch for my child. My thoughts run amok. *How could he do such a thing? She's only two years old and she must have been terrified and crying for me when he yanked her from her bed. Oh God, what a terrible mother I am? How can I have such little control of myself? I'll kill the bastard!*

The telephone rings shrilly, urgently. *Oh God, is it the police calling to report an accident?*

"Hel-lo," I quake falteringly.

"Are you still pissed off and are the cops still hanging around? If so, I won't bother coming home."

Relief washes over me. "Is Eve okay?"

"She's fine. Did you think I would kill her, maybe?"

Asshole! Maniac! I silently spew. My anger rekindles until I visualize Eve's frightened face.

"I'm not angry, just tired and upset. Please come home. The cops are gone and I promise I won't contact them. Nor do I want to fight with you anymore."

My thoughts reek with malice. *I'll get even for this!* Now, however, Eve's safety tops everything.

Much later, when Len has returned and slammed off to bed, I make Eve some warm milk and hold her in my arms as she drinks it. After soothing her, then tucking her back into bed, I lay in silence on the living-room couch while Len snores. I wonder what I can really do to avenge myself. The answer is: nothing at all. I'm a prisoner in my home, too afraid to go more than a few blocks on my own.

There's something drastically wrong with me and I know not what.

After a two or three day cold war, we make up. I can't stay angry for long and he's sincerely sorry for hurting me and upsetting Eve. He shows me his bruises and I recall the severity of my onslaught against him. I observe the ugly gashes that have formed scabs on his face and I know he's black and blue from the vehemence of my kicks. His inner and outer wounds are not lesser than mine.

Neither of us is blameless.

He gently kisses my wounds and entreats me to forgive him. Childlike, I do the same. Our insecurities have left us both with scars that will perhaps never heal.

"I want to prove beyond a fraction of a doubt that I only ever loved you," he declares tenderly. We're entwined in each other's arms and oblivious to our recent dispute; the making-up is always a tender renewal.

"The teenagers need to know the truth once and for all. I was never in love with their mother, and vice versa I'm sure. I know it's not been easy for you. They're quick to let you know they never heard arguments between their mother and me, and their false conclusions lead you to believe my first marriage was idyllic. It's time they're made aware of how things actually were. I know you hear about her a lot, and I can relate. If our positions were reversed, I'd not want to hear about Karl all the time."

I'm elated. I believe this will finally kill my demons forever.

Several weeks later, during which time Len has ignored his promise, my demons are outraged. They begin performing their usual cacophonous dance in my head as they gloatingly mock me. *He's a liar. You can't believe him. He's like all men. A bastard. He really doesn't love you.* They alternate between cackling harshly and tirelessly harping. Meanwhile, I'm being driven to distraction. Unable to abide the noise in my mind, I finally confront Len.

"Why the hell did you suggest what you did in the first place?" I accuse him hotly one evening. "It was your idea, not mine. Now you're too chicken to follow it through. Obviously you're happy the kids think as they do."

"I don't need your pressure."

Yes, Karl.

Suddenly, a strange look crosses his countenance and he hollers for the kids to come upstairs from the playroom. I'm gripped with an ominous feeling of impending disaster. I dart into our bedroom, unable to face what I fear may be coming. From behind the door, I hear him announce bluntly, "Irene wants me to let you know I hated your mother. That's all. Go back to whatever you were doing."

I wish I could shrivel up and die. I'm absolutely mortified. How can I ever face the kids again? He enters the bedroom. "Well, it's been done. Hope you're satisfied. Perhaps you'll get off my back now." Shocked and stunned, for once I am speechless.

Later, when he sleeps, I pack some belongings for Eve and myself. I quietly telephone Jane. Hearing how stricken I sound, she tells me to come to her place right away. I phone a cab.

I see Jane's face in the window when the taxi pulls up in front of her door. After helping me bed Eve down for the night, she says, "I want you to know that you and Eve are welcome to stay here as long as you want. I don't forget all the times you took Rory and me into your apartment under similar circumstances. Now tell me what's been happening. Get it off your chest. You'll feel better."

I rant, gulp, and weep, on an off, seemingly for hours. She listens sympathetically throughout.

Finally I can no longer keep my eyes, or my mouth, open. "I'm so sorry to have dumped on you like this," I apologize.

"What are friends for? If it's helped you any, I'm glad," she answers. "Try to get a good night's sleep and we'll talk again in the morning. You really need to think of leaving that asshole," she adds.

I sleep fitfully. Something inside me has surely died. I feel shattered and broken. I have given him my trust and he has betrayed me in the worst possible way. How can I forgive such treachery? No physical blows could produce such pain. I'd rather him flog my body than my soul. I fall asleep weeping . . . for the death of my trust.

The next day I inform my mother of my whereabouts. I don't want to upset her if she calls and finds me gone and Len starts in on her. As usual, I'm the bad guy and she gives me shit. Later, Jane and I go over my options. She's aware they are few in view of my fears. I know she's worried about me. I finally speak with Len on the third day. I've been refusing his previous calls. I consent to go home. Only because I've nowhere else to go.

I'm a prisoner of my fears.

I later find out that Jane's car has been vandalized. Her tires have been ripped, and her engine has been filled with sugar and has to be replaced. It will cost her a thousand dollars. She's in tears. As soon as I hang up, I check the spare bag of sugar in the cupboard. I know there was plenty in the sugar bowl to tide the family over during my absence. Sure enough, half the contents of the new bag are missing, and I know Len has done this to my friend. I call Jane back and insist on paying for the damages from my own savings. She accepts, but tells me it's best I don't return to her place. Much as she loves me and would never think of pressing charges against my husband for my sake, she fears what he may do to her on a similar occasion. "He's nuts," she says.

Well, that makes two of us, I think sadly.

There is no way out anymore. My last safe haven has been obliterated. He could do the same to any one of my friends. *Life is hell,* I decide. *It's the wolf gobbling up Red Riding Hood and her grandmother.* Later that evening I compose the words to *The Prisoner,* a poem which upgrades—or perhaps downgrades?—my previous status of a *puppet* to a *prisoner;* though in some ways the two interlock.

It's not easy to face the teenagers upon my return. Discreetly, they do not refer to the incident. I wonder what they are thinking. I have no way of explaining things. Guilt adds to guilt and I feel profoundly ashamed. Inwardly I blame Len and hate him for it.

He voluntarily tries to correct things when I return. He talks to the children and explains what he first set out to do. He tells them it comes from him, not me. I have doubts they believe him now. I wonder if they hate me. Most of all, I hate myself.

Things eventually take on a semblance of normalcy. Len wins me over again with little kindnesses; but I know my anger still roils beneath the surface, waiting to be ignited when the right moment presents itself. Meanwhile, I've become too concerned about my father's failing health to dwell too much on my own situation. Once again, Len and I mend fences and a period of harmony ensues.

It's around this time that Len implores me to take a partial hand in the discipline of the teenagers. Our frustrations are not just confined to the little ones. The big kids contribute their share in triplicate. Mark and Ken often come to physical blows. They're big boys now, both of average height and build, and extremely attractive like their dad. Mark has recently turned nineteen and Ken is three years younger, but just as strong and muscular. At times when they're fighting, one will swerve and the other's fist drives through the wall.

251

Len is often plastering the walls. Apart from our own particular brand of destruction to the home, the boys leave their earmark of havoc upon it. And Merry sometimes joins the fray. On one occasion, the downstairs toilet tank cracks in two "of its own volition". Another time, a large chunk of the cork which lines the foyer walls breaks away "all by itself". Whatever the breakage or mishap, "nobody did it".

Add to this, a few of my personal issues.

Len often says, "There are so many things I don't notice as a man. Instead of complaining to me if they walk over your freshly-washed floors in muddy boots, or whatever the case may be, tell *them*! I could do with your help. It's all on *my* back."

"I'm not their real mother," I protest.

"No matter. You're in charge of the house and should be running it as you see fit. I expect this of you. They should have no reason to dislike you for doing your job. You know I always back you up."

I can't argue there. In household issues, he always does. Unfailingly.

When they leave a mess in the home, I now speak to them candidly. Understanding they may not want to take orders from someone who is not their real mother I address my rights in another manner. *I'm the housekeeper here and I work hard to keep this place clean. I expect you to respect that. I just washed the floor and since it's your mud all over it, please clean it up.* Or: *You and your friends have left a sink full of dirty dishes and a mess. Please clean it up. I'm the housekeeper, not the maid. There's a distinct difference.*

I introduce other rules as well.

I'm scarcely more than a decade older than the teenagers and, until now, have been more a big sister than a mother. This changeover is not easy for them, least of all Merry who became mistress of the house by default after her mother died. However, I've been a silent homemaker too long. I couldn't have cared less during my breakdown. Now, it's time I have some say regarding the family as a whole. I work hard in the home. My personal say-so is overdue.

It seems to be around this time that my relationship with Merry begins to deteriorate. In the beginning, she was the little sister I never had. I still love her as such, and feel extremely close to her. I lend her clothing and I relish in sharing girl talk with her. I love applying her make-up and styling her long, raven hair. Blessed with classic features and thickly-lashed emerald eyes she's a stunning young woman. For her part, she has been a great help to me over the years; not only during my breakdown when she willingly took time off school to help in the home, but in countless other ways as well.

Now, she's no longer the same carefree girl. It's understandable she's not happy with the change. Nor would I be in her place. She's being usurped by an intruder. She says not a word; but–as I am to regretfully fathom only much later–she, too, lost her crown. And I am the person who stole it.

In the midst of introducing this new system, I'm increasingly concerned about my dad's failing health. Mom's daily feedback is not optimistic, and her upsetting tales–along with my father's refusal to see a doctor–are beginning to unnerve me.

"I wish your mother wouldn't keep on to you about your father," Len remarks. "There's nothing you can do. Your old man's too stubborn to accept any help. She's only making you sick with this. I really should talk to her."

"No, please don't!" I plead. "You must promise me you won't do that. She has no one else to fall back on. She's old and afraid. I don't want her to get sick, too. I have to try and be strong for her. She needs me."

He grudgingly promises. As usual, he will prove to be an invaluable source of help to both my mother and myself. Like Karl, he can always cope beautifully with my suffering–providing he is not the cause of it.

Years later, I'm to learn that we each choose our own suffering from which our souls learn and grow. The situations and people we encounter in our lifetime are merely the window dressings we have chosen–as they, in a similar manner, have chosen us . . . as a necessary part of the journey.

Merry is less friendly of late. She has finished school and is now a working girl, and I wonder if she's just more preoccupied with her friends and new lifestyle. I question myself on the way I've handled things and hope it has not caused a rift between us. Were there not so much else going on, I may have dug deeper, and I would later wish I had. Quite unexpectedly, she informs us that she and her friend have rented an apartment. She'll be moving out by the weekend. She has barely turned eighteen. Len and I are both very upset. In vain we try to convince her to stay. Her decision, however, is final.

My parents join us on Christmas Day a few months later. Dad puts on a good show as he laughs and jokes cheerfully with the kids. Apart from the sadness in my mother's eyes, the overall spirit remains outwardly festive. Dad insists upon serving himself when dinner is ready. Appalled at the tiny portion on his plate my eyes fleetingly link with my mother's and I acknowledge her silent entreaty: *Do you see what I mean?*

An inordinate sadness engulfs me as I perceive this Christmas as the last one we'll spend with my dad. Despite our differences, he's not been without his many good points. I'm suddenly stricken with the knowledge of how much I actually love him, and that I can't bear to see him die.

Later, as I lie awake in bed, time rolls back in my mind's eye. I see my dad, my protector and champion, once again young and strong as he removes my childhood splinters; extracts a plump, ugly leech from my flesh that has sent me screaming out of the lake; cheers me on in competitions; and is ever the proud onlooker at my school plays and Sunday school pageants. He was not an absent dad . . . though I may have wished that he were.

I was an absent daughter.

I again recall my delight in the gifts he brought home for me when he returned from postings: the books, the dolls, and the Disney Cinderella watch which I wore with such pride.

Time races onward in my recollections. I see myself as a young woman, privately opening up to him and revealing my doubts about getting married. I explain that I care for Len deeply, but I fear a part of me is not over Star's dad. Phlegmatic as always, his thoughts are quite simple. *Len will take good care of you and Star. He's a responsible man. You'll never go hungry. 'In love' is over-rated. That's my advice.*

A few days later–after setting up an appointment for me with Dave Marsh–Dad counsels me: *He's the new minister, a great guy . . . and young, not stuffy. It'll do you well to confide in him.*

He has always kept a protective eye on me. My big, strong dad. My unrecognized hero.

Now a pitiful shadow of what he once was.

The New Year of 1973 brings with it an increase in Dad's pain; yet he still struggles to work each day, stubbornly refusing to quit. Mom is more wretched than ever. I later learn that Dad was determined to stick with his job–at least until the new collective agreement at the plant was finalized. The latter would increase employee death benefits . . . his parting gift of love to my mother.

Mom calls me one day in January to say Dad has a raging fever. I assure her I'll be right over. It's a Sunday and Len accompanies me.

"Strip him down to his underwear, would you please Len?" I fill a large container with cool water and I proceed to bathe him, limb by limb, for over an hour. I succeed in decreasing his high fever to 101.5. "That's better," I sigh, "but still not good."

I address my father. "Dad, you can't afford to be stubborn any longer. You need medical attention. Len and I are bringing you to the hospital, okay?" His eyes are somewhat brighter and he seems less groggy, despite his deathly pallor. Thankfully, he nods his assent.

We sit in the ER of the same hospital where he underwent his lobectomy. Feeble and ill, the long wait is a tremendous strain on him. He sits patiently and speaks only once.

"The sun is shining on my head," he mutters. There's no hint of sunshine anywhere. I feel strangely chilled.

Finally, his name is called and Len and I help him into a cubicle. "I'll speak to the doctor alone," he indicates. We take the hint and join

Mom in the waiting room. Later, we're appalled to discover the doctor is shipping him back home in such a weakened, feverish condition. Dad claims he's had a chest x-ray and has been scheduled to see his lung surgeon a few weeks hence. That's it.

His lung surgeon shows no interest in his stomach complaint and he's sent home with a jar of antacid and some Vitamin B tablets. He's told to report back in two months. He's so feeble and frail it's doubtful he'll be around two months hence. It's obvious his surgeon knows the cancer has spread, yet he's callously washed his hands of my father. Dad says nothing; but he later reveals that it appears his surgeon has abandoned him as a lost cause. My heart aches for him.

My mother gets in touch with the family doctor who refers him to a stomach specialist at a different hospital. The new doctor takes his condition seriously and he's admitted to the Lornewood Hospital two days later. His distended abdomen resembles that of a nine-month pregnant woman.

Shortly before entering the hospital, he privately telephones me relaying his death wishes. The conversation deeply unsettles me but I promise to observe his requests which I realize are important to him.

"While we're on this subject, Dad, please tell me if there's something you've been concealing from us. You've been decidedly secretive concerning your visits to the various doctors and I know it's because you don't want to worry us, especially Mom. But I swear you can entrust me to not betray your confidence. It's important that at least one of knows what's happening with you. Have you been told you are going to die?" I ask him point blank.

"No, Brat, I haven't," he replies. "I do know I'm not in good health. Perhaps I can be fixed up. I just want to be prepared in the event something does happen."

I see no logical reason to doubt him.

Daily, Len, Mom and I, visit him in hospital. My mother's depth of horror and sadness is revealed in her hollow eyes. She bravely holds together for her man, determined to share the brief time he has left. By now, we've been told he's in the last stages of his illness: advanced cancer of the liver.

A few days later we're told by Dad's oncologist that he's to be discharged the following day. I can't believe it. He's at death's door. We can't possibly take care of him at home at this stage of his illness. The hospital refuses to give us time to find an appropriate facility. They want his bed.

"You'll have to collect him in the morning," the doctor decrees. "I've already signed his discharge papers."

My mother is in tears. I am in rage stage.

I look him squarely in the eyes. "Well, you'd just better *un-sign* the papers, because there'll be *nobody* here to collect him tomorrow. You'll have to put him out on the street, and *that*, I assure you, will attract the vultures. And I promise you *I'll* be there with the full story for the media."

"Surely, if you loved your father—"

"Don't you dare try to hand *me* a guilt trip. I can't believe the hospital would be so mercenary as to throw a dying man out on the street at a moment's notice! C'mon, Mom, we're getting out of here." I grab her hand and lead her away as she sobs pitifully.

"Perhaps he's right," Mom says. "Maybe your dad would rather be at home."

"That's exactly what he *wants* you to believe so he can throw Dad out on his ass in good conscience. How about we give Dad the choice? If he wants to come home, I'll help in any way I can; but I think we both know he's too independent to want any of us looking after him in such a helpless state. Now dry your eyes, and don't let that SOB get to you."

Shortly thereafter, we broach the subject to Dad.

"Of course I'd love to get out of here, but surely they don't intend to send me home in *this* condition?" Despite his weakened state, his words are succinct and to the point. "I'm *beyond* home care and these bastards know it. I'm a case for a fucking hospital."

My mind reels back to my breakdown when he uttered those

exact same words to Len regarding me. I'd despised him for it then, yet he's not presuming a fraction more for himself.

I stick to my guns and do not remove my father from the hospital. Neither his specialist nor the hospital administration approaches me about his discharge again. Perhaps they would rather not test the force of my ire. Whatever the case, it's a relief for my dad, my mother, and myself.

A few days before slipping into a coma, Dad inquires groggily, "How are things going between you and Len, Brat? Any better?" So close to death, yet he still has the foresight to care. Why don't I dissemble a little, align myself with the good things in my marriage rather than focusing on the quarrels? I know I should try, but I just can't.

"All right, I guess." My voice lacks enthusiasm. Len and I have had words. Again. Why must I always wear my heart on my sleeve? My dad deserves the peace of believing his daughter is content. And especially now.

"I know things have been tough, but you'll come through. Love is spelled t-r-u-s-t," he says. "So is marriage. I gave your mother trust. Our marriage was not so hot in the beginning either–a lot of arguments. It all worked out. The first years . . . are the hardest . . ." His voice trails off. He opens his eyes for a moment and says, "Take care of your mother." They are the last words I will ever hear him speak. I give him my promise, and he nods back off.

A day or so later the chief oncologist enters the room. I am alone. Mom and Len have gone for coffee.

"Mrs. Snow, your father will never wake up from the state he is in. Yet, he has a very strong heart and he could go on for days or even a few more weeks like this. Or—" He looks at me intently.

"Or—?" I question.

"Or, we could give him a stronger dosage of Demerol and hasten the process. It would be more merciful."

I regard him steadily for a few moments before asking, "How long will it take?"

"It should be over within forty-eight hours. I'm asking your permission. It needn't go further than these walls."

"Yes," I say. If there's one last gift I can give him, it is this.

I know they want his bed, but it is a question of what my father would want.

JUNE 30, 2012, SATURDAY

Dana is on her way to hospital. Her labour will be induced at 8:00 AM. About time! She's twelve days late and they're concerned her baby may be close to nine pounds. *Oh my God, Dana has such a small frame! I hope she doesn't need a C-section.*

What a week! Prior to completion of his third cycle of chemo, Gary came down with a raging fever and had to be rushed to hospital. Eve said he was neutropenic. I had no idea what that meant and she explained that neutropenia happens as a result of chemotherapy and is a term that's used when the immune system falls dramatically. I nearly freaked out until she assured me it's a normal happening under the circumstances and Gary's daily injections will help build up his white cells. Then, as the effects of the chemo wear off, the neutropenia will gradually resolve itself.

"He was put on IV with a heavy dose of antibiotics. Thankfully, whatever afflicted him was resolved and he went home that day," she went on to say. "But we have to be extremely cautious and wear a medical mask when we're in contact with him, and he has to remain indoors until his immune system improves. He'll see his oncologist again before his birthday and if he's back up to par he'll be able to dine out."

We'll know the verdict soon and if he's not allowed out, we'll put on facial masks and pay him a short visit at home on his special day, and bring along his gift.

Meanwhile, I've been anxiously waiting for news from Dana who lives in Ordala which is about a two-hour drive from Cassellman. An e-mail from her husband arrives just after our evening meal. It reads: *Please meet your new granddaughter—born this evening at 6:24 PM, weighing in at 8 lbs 6 oz."*

I download the picture. *Oh my God, she's so beautiful!* Len and I are enchanted. I can't wait to see her and I'm overjoyed to learn that both Mom and baby are doing just fine.

Chapter 15 – A Ray of Light

As you start to walk out on the way, the way appears."
—*Rumi*

I inform Mom about my talk with the doctor and she tearfully agrees it's what Dad would have wanted. I stay overnight with her in anticipation of the call that could come anytime. The phone rings just before midnight.

The waiting is over.

In accordance with Dad's wishes the viewing is private and the casket is closed. Dave, our minister, officiates for the final services. Later, on the journey home, I recall the precept Dad quoted shortly after his surgery almost a year earlier. Silently I complete the ending: "—but it pours."

It's to pour for a while. Mom maintains a brave front but she's having a difficult time adjusting to Dad's death. She wants to continue living in the apartment they shared together for so many years; she feels close to him there. Len good-naturedly includes her on most of our outings, even those of a more personal nature such as our anniversary celebration. He also assists her with odd jobs in her home.

Sometime after Dad's death, my dreams about Len and Karl appear less frequently. My "Brenda demons" seem to have quietened down as well. Possibly, my self-esteem has raised a few notches in regard to the way I've handled Dad's death. In taking care of the final arrangements, personally handling all the accounting to close his estate, helping my mother in every way I can, and perhaps more than anything avoiding the nervous set-back I dreaded, I've regained a sense of pride in myself.

Quarrels between Len and I are fewer, and in general life becomes more tranquil. We discuss our bad habit of taking sides against each other with the teenagers and agree it's a practice we must cease. We discuss other areas that need improving upon, and vow to work together to achieve more harmony in our union.

I choose this time to make it clear to him that I've never felt any personal animosity towards his first wife. How could I? I never knew her. Any cruel thing I ever said about her has been intended to wound *him*.

"I wish I were in your position," I divulge on one occasion. "You can run down Karl to the hilt. Simply because he's alive, you're not looked upon as the bad person that I am for speaking ill of the dead. Also, you never have to worry you may hurt or offend any stepchildren. Sometimes, I think it is hardly fair. I always look like the evil one. It sucks to be the wicked stepmother. That damn Cinderella story played hell with the stepmother image . . . which doesn't help me one iota if they complain about me outside of the home."

"I don't think the kids think of you as wicked, hon, c'mon. But I see your point. Kids complain about their parents all the time, but you rarely hear about the wicked mother or father, though there are many parents who can be a whole lot worse than step-parents."

It helps to discuss these things and clears the air.

The July following Dad's passing, we vacation again as a family at our campsite on the lake. We find a nearby rental cottage for Mom, which she shares with a close lady friend. We all get together daily and this little getaway is good for my mother. It helps keep her active and occupied. It's during this particular vacation that Len and I decide to have another child.

By December 1973, we're elated to discover I'm two months

pregnant. The due date is estimated for our anniversary next July which appears to be a good omen. Barring the occasional argument, the months ahead are more serene. I've always loved being pregnant, and especially when I feel the first stirrings of new life within me. Our main floor dining-room–where Eve slept prior to being moved upstairs with the others–has been converted to a nursery again. The cycle is renewing itself.

In early 1974 Eve, at age four, undergoes her second and final eye surgery. Her eyes are now perfectly straight and it makes a world of difference in her appearance. Her long blond hair covers her one remaining defect, outstanding ears, which will be next on the surgical list. She's a beautiful little girl–my chocolate-eyed princess, as I affectionately call her–who, for now, deserves a rest.

Spring emerges from beneath winter's heavy blanket of snow and our thoughts turn to summer and Len's two-week vacation at the end of July when the plant closes down. I suggest we sell the boat and trailer and apply the proceeds to a swimming pool.

"With the new baby coming, we can enjoy a backyard vacation this year. On subsequent holidays we can simply rent a cottage for two weeks if we prefer to get away, and then enjoy the pool for the balance of the summer. It's such a hassle camping with babies or toddlers. Besides, we've paid off the house and are in a better financial situation. What do you think? I expect you'd miss camping though?"

"Not really, hon. It was a cheap holiday, that's all. I look forward to a change of pace. Now that the house is paid off and we start getting some money behind us, all your efforts are going to pay off. I'm going to buy you everything your heart desires. I'll even cover you in jewels and furs," he says teasingly. "You'll see how very much I love you."

I kiss him affectionately. "You say the sweetest things sometimes."

"I mean every word."

"I know you do, and I also know you love me, despite my hang-ups. You make me happy in a million little ways and I'd rather have you than all the minks and diamonds in the world. Of course," I add jokingly, "I could *try* to be happy with both."

By early June, we are all enjoying our above-ground pool. Eve is too short to touch bottom, but swims about with water wings on. One afternoon, when family and friends are gathered around the pool, she jumps in and swims from one side to the other. She surfaces, hauls herself out of the water, and positions herself to jump back in. Len hollers, "Eve, where are your water wings?"

Suddenly, I hear a loud commotion from outside the kitchen where I'm peeling vegetables. I run to the window to see my daughter screaming in horror while everyone is laughing and cheering. The potato peeler drops from my hand as I race outside.

"She swam all by herself!" the group cries out.

"She just discovered she swam without her wings on, and I think she's in shock," Len says

"Eve, honey, that's wonderful! I'm so proud of you. Everyone is!" I begin clapping for her with the others and suddenly her small face lights up joyously as she becomes truly aware of her accomplishment.

"I can swim all by myself, Mommy! I can *SWIM!*" She howls in delight. "You didn't see me. I'll show you!"

She jumps in the pool and makes a brave repeat performance with full knowledge she's without her wings.

"Oh my, if only your grandpa could see you! He'd be so proud," I praise.

From that day forward, she discards her water wings for good.

My third child, another little girl whom we name Dana, is born in late July, almost two weeks overdue. Len is by my side in the delivery room, and I am able to observe the whole process by way of a mirror that is set up solely for that purpose. For what will likely be my last child, I've decided upon natural childbirth.

I've never felt so well following a birth. I begin trotting around immediately. On my first day home from hospital, as I clean and vacuum the house from top to bottom, I recall how edgy I felt prior to Dana's birth. Just the thought of being trapped in the hospital and the possibility of experiencing a severe panic attack while confined filled me with dread. I tried, with little conviction, to assure myself that if I flipped out I'd be in the right place. Thankfully, my concerns were unfounded, but I was never happier to be out of there. Now, as I go about my household tasks, I know I don't want to harbour these fears indefinitely.

Soon, I promise myself. I will find help . . . some way . . . somewhere.

Dana is a beautiful child. She's also healthy, robust and exceptionally alert. The other new mothers that joined me in the hospital nursery where we congregated daily to feed our young dubbed her the *nosy-parker*. While *their* babies could scarcely stay awake to be fed, Dana's eyes never closed. One could almost believe she was astutely sizing up her surroundings and carefully appraising them.

I'm soon to learn that Dana is not a daytime sleeper. She's prone to taking very brief cat-naps, and I can no longer count on the few quiet hours I gained in the day with Star and Eve. No more chatty telephone calls to friends or personal quiet time since Dana's arrival on the scene! She sleeps well during the night though. Within a relatively short time, I can count on her sleeping a five or six hour stretch.

Keith and Eve are delighted with their baby sister. Keith, at age seven, tends her like a regular little mother. One morning, much to my concern and astonishment, he asserts proudly, "Mommy, I was up real early, and I changed Dana's diaper while you slept." I'm momentarily in shock. It's a cloth diaper with two safety pins. *What if*—? *I didn't hear her scream, but . . . oh God, oh God!* I run to the nursery and am astonished at the excellent job he has done.

Keith is a marvellous source of help with the new baby. By now, the memory of the *Terrible Twins* has receded, and I remember Star as the whole person she was, prior to becoming conjoined with Keith in my mind. I likewise view Keith the same way. He's my special little man and my excellent helpmate. I've grown to love him dearly and it never fails to irk me when the odd person refers to him as my stepson. I've raised him from early childhood.

He is *my son*.

As things settle down and Dana begins to sleep through the night, I ruminate more frequently on the fear that keeps me a prisoner. I envy people who come and go as they please as I once did, without a hint of anxiety or panic. It's been so easy to learn to *fear* fear. It's become a conditioned response to the stimulation of facing new situations, and its underlying complication still lingers: avoidance behaviour. How much longer am I to suffer its residue? Surely, there's a way one can *unlearn* fear . . . minus the constant terror of walking through flames?

It's a degrading illness which I constantly contrive to hide. *Nobody* understands it, except maybe Jane who has a phobia of her own. But hers is confined solely to birds, and far simpler. She only has birds to avoid; whereas for me, it's the whole damn outdoors. People who've not suffered it cannot relate. They equate it with their own more rational fears–the latter a drop in a bucket as compared to being hit with a tsunami.*"Pull yourself up by your bootstraps,"* they say, failing to realize the straps have been broken.

I've finally realized I need professional help. I cannot manage this *thing* on my own.

On January 1, 1975, I welcome the New Year in with a firm resolution: I will once again be well and whole.

Chapter 16 – Search for a Cure

"Whenever you take a step forward,
you are bound to disturb something."
—Indira Gandhi

Len and I sit patiently in the small anteroom of an old, rather, dingy building. It appears to be a large, antiquated home that has since been converted into offices.

"For some reason, this place gives me the creeps," I whisper to my husband.

"What did you expect, Buckingham Palace?" he quips. "This is the only shrink you could find on such short notice."

"Mrs. Snow?" a voice inquires. I arise from my seat. "I'm Dr. Gregory Tolhurst. Would you care to come into my office?"

In those few moments I gather my first external impressions of my new shrink. He's a youngish man of approximately my height, rather slight of build with medium brown hair and mundane features. Not anyone you'd glance twice at in passing. A thick moustache almost conceals his upper lip.

"Please take a seat," he advises as he indicates a chair on the opposite side of his imposing wooden desk.

Seating himself directly across from me he inquires, "Please tell me what appears to be concerning you." His penetrating eyes bore into mine. Uncomfortably, I rummage through my purse before speaking. I nervously light a cigarette.

Momentarily, he goes ballistic. *"No! No! NO!* Put that out immediately! I do *NOT* permit smoking in my office. It pollutes my fresh, clean air. I'm convinced you won't perish without a cigarette for the next forty-five minutes."

I nervously extinguish it in the clean ashtray which I realize must be there for stubbing purposes only, whist wondering how many other nervous patients find it difficult to function when deprived of their pacifier. I think of making a joke, but he has such a humourless face. *Why are shrinks so dour?*

Tense and ill at ease, I begin my story. Every so often I notice him regarding his watch which increases my sense of malaise. I've hardly been there ten minutes and he's not even being surreptitious about the frequent glances at his wrist. I talk more rapidly. Every so often I pause in the hope of gaining some feedback. "Please continue," is his general response. Once or twice he asks some leading questions about my childhood and inquires about my relationship with my parents.

"Were you ever raped or assaulted?" he inquires at one point.

"No, to your first question. What do you consider to be an assault? I expect there are levels in that regard?"

"Any cruel beating," he clarifies. "In your case, originating from a member of the opposite sex."

I tell him I had the odd beating from my dad as a child, nothing severe enough to cause bodily harm. I refrain from mentioning Len's physical assaults. I'm more often than not the instigator and I expect that makes me a bad guy as well. I certainly don't want to go there this early in our acquaintanceship.

"What exactly would a beating represent in regard to my present condition?" I ask curiously.

"What do *you* think?"

"I haven't the foggiest."

"Think about it between now and our next session," he suggests.

"The general idea of this therapy is for you to form your own conclusions."

Yes, Dr. Freud, I think glumly.

"Medicare only pays me for forty-five minutes," he declares abruptly. "We've overshot the mark." He hands me a small card indicating my next appointment.

"Incidentally," he announces, somewhat to my surprise, "I don't accept every patient who walks into my office. I make that decision during our initial interview. I must have empathy for the person whom I treat. I have empathy for you. In order to achieve the most beneficial results from therapy, there should be a *mutual* empathy between the patient and the doctor." He regards me inquiringly.

Is he implying he's picked up bad vibes from me? If he asks me directly about *my* feelings, should I tell him to think about it and draw his own conclusions between now and our next session? I'm none too pleased with his tell-me-about-your-childhood approach which does not give me an ounce of input regarding the problems I'm facing *right now.* I wonder if I have to reside in my prison for several *more* years . . . until he's unravelled the early ones.

"I'm sure we can get along famously together," I prevaricate. Regardless, I'm determined to try my best.

The following months leave me no time to be slack. Between household duties, tending to youngsters and a new baby and jotting down thoughts to discuss with my new shrink, there are too few hours in a day. Our son, Mark, has recently married and his wedding has also kept us hopping.

Mom, as usual, disapproves of my visits to a psychiatrist. "What the hell has a shrink ever done for you in the past?" she reiterates time and again. "I could cure you of this thing if you'd only *listen,* and take my advice. You have to want to help *yourself. You* don't."

Since Dad's death, I'm more frequently in her company. Often, we clash. In her mind, I'm still her little girl. She is not less bossy than when I was a kid, and often she interferes in my disciplinary measures with the youngsters, undermining my authority directly in front of them by saying such things as: "Irene, I wouldn't get after Keith about ruining the backs of his shoes if I were you. God only knows how many shoes *you* ruined as a child;" or, "Irene, it's cruel to make the kids wait for the candy I brought them until after supper. A little bit won't hurt them right now;" and, perhaps the granddaddy of them all: "I know you like Eve with long hair, but I prefer it short, so I got her a haircut while we were out today."

Much as I love my mother, there are times she really pisses me off. Worse, there's nothing I can do to alter it. We have words, and I decide I won't call her until she agrees not to overstep my rights as a parent. Soon afterward, she calls to say I've made her sick. And, it seems she really *does* get ill. *Perhaps I am killing her,* I think dismally. Next thing I know, I'm placating her and back to square one again.

"You don't know how bossy you sound," I respond to her latest jab. "If I punish the children, I'm cruel or too hard on them. If I yell at them, I sound like a witch and I make you ill. If I decide to see a psychiatrist, it appears you have your own degree in psychiatry. A superior one. Damn it, Mom, you're exasperating."

"If that's how you feel, perhaps it's best I refrain from stepping into your house in the future," she retorts.

"Don't twist things. You know I love having you over. I just wish you wouldn't disapprove of every damn thing I do. I smoke too much, swear too much, and drink too much. Do I have any qualities incidentally? Or am I just bone-rotten?"

"Now *you're* the one who's twisting things. I just try to advise you for your own good. Of course you have qualities!"

"Gee Mom, I'm just south of 40, not 14 anymore. Nobody's perfect. *You* drink, smoke, and swear. I don't bother *you* about it."

"I'm not proud of myself for it. You're still young and have a chance to make a better life for yourself. I don't know why I try to talk to you anyway. You *never* listen, and besides, you're beginning to upset me now."

"Okay, let's settle down. I'm sorry if I upset you."

Let her have the last word, I decide. Her blood pressure rapidly fluctuates at times, and last month she scared the hell out of me when she passed out cold. We were engaged in verbal warfare and I thought I'd killed her. Thank heavens Len was there and able to assure me she'd only fainted. I couldn't live with the guilt if she died during an argument with me. Big deal if I lose a round. I just wish we could see eye-to-eye more often, and that she'd refrain from using her health to manipulate me. Although it may not be done on a conscious level, it nevertheless leaves me powerless; which she probably *is* aware of–*on a conscious level.*

Despite my irritations, Mom's good points are many. She arrives for Sunday dinner with a bag stuffed to the brim with home-baked goodies. She treats Mark and Ken to movies and bingo games; the youngsters to the circus and children's films, nice clothes and, yes . . . unsolicited haircuts. All the kids–big and small–adore her. She's an extremely generous person, and she's always ready to help. She grumbles about my fears but will always avail herself as my ready escort.

I can count on her.

Throughout the winter of 1975 I continue to see Dr. Tolhurst. By spring, I've learned very little. I've also made no progress. I travel the short distance from point A to point B as I did in the past. Point C, if unaccompanied, is still out of my reach. Nor has the doctor offered me any suggestions as to how I might arrive there without freaking out.

"We'll sort it all out eventually," he says. "But we need to go back in time to get to the root of your problem."

"Can you tell me exactly what type of illness I have?" I ask.

"In a nutshell, you fear *fear.* You anticipate panic when you surpass your designated safety radius. Any irrational, exaggerated fear is deemed as a phobia."

His method of treatment is limited to psychoanalytical therapy alone. As the doctor, I expect he knows best. Our sessions continue to centre on my childhood and early adulthood, and at times my dreams. He occasionally interrupts my revelations with an inquiry, but invariably responds to my questions with questions. The conclusions I personally derive about my life or my hang-ups remain unverified by him . . . and consequently by me as well.

"Do you have any other phobic patients that have achieved success through this type of therapy?' I ask on one occasion.

"Why yes, indeed. Presently, I have a young girl who I've been treating. She was unable to go anywhere alone. At the moment, she's doing very well, and moving about quite freely."

"Well, that's encouraging," I sigh. "So far, I'm as terrorized as ever to drive beyond my range of security. I still panic to enter a large store on my own. I'm wondering if I'm one of the *incurables*."

"You mustn't push a cure, Mrs. Snow. Your phobia did not originate overnight. The underlying cause lies somewhere within your past. In time, you'll interpret the answers through therapy," he assures me.

"Then what? Will I suddenly be able to move about unaccompanied, as freely as I wish?" I question.

"Your fear will greatly diminish once you understand it," he claims confidently.

Upon departing his office, I am not overly hopeful.

My next appointment is in early June. It's a sweltering day, and following the long, torrid journey by car with no a/c, my linen dress is deeply-creased and adhering to my flesh like glue. I'm thoroughly wilted by the time we reach his building.

"How are you today?" he asks both Len and I. We are sitting side by side in the vestibule.

"We feel as though we've died and arrived in hell," Len answers. "I missed my daily dip in our pool after work." *Wrong answer indeed.*

"You're very fortunate to own a swimming pool," he remarks

blandly. Sensing an ill-fated vibe, I surreptitiously cast my husband a look which clearly indicates he should shut up.

Later, in the doctor's office he inquires as usual. "So, how have you been keeping, Mrs. Snow?"

"Very well, apart from the phobia. And you?"

"Not that great, I'm afraid. Have you any idea what the government pays a psychiatrist on Medicare?"

"No, I don't."

"The pay is so paltry I can barely exist," he grumbles. "Sometimes, it takes months before I receive any remuneration. It's not easy to live in the interim."

"That's a shame," I acknowledge sympathetically. "It takes a great deal of education to become a psychiatrist. I can certainly relate to your resentment."

The balance of our session mainly reflects Dr. Tolhurst's woes. I'm inclined to feel genuinely sorry for him.

Later, I remark to my husband, "Please keep our pool under wraps in the future." I relay the gist of the conversation with Dr. Tolhurst. "I actually entertained the feeling that your remark might lead him to ask for more money. I'm happy to say I'm wrong. Perhaps it's because I made sure to clarify our pool is an above-ground one. Not one of those expensive in-ground models."

"Did he give you any time, or did he only talk about himself? I don't exactly relish paying the gas to transport you to his office in order for *you* to give *him* free therapy," he says sarcastically.

"Well, I have an assignment which may help me. Actually, it was *my* suggestion. Now it's my homework. I asked him if he thought it may be beneficial for me to compile a brief summary of my life from childhood onwards. By doing this I may uncover some recollections that evade me. You see, I'm looking for the *underlying causes* of my illness. He agreed this would be an excellent idea and that he'd be interested to read and evaluate my account upon its completion. He also asked for copies of the poems I wrote after Star died. He says there may possibly be some clues in my poetry."

That evening I optimistically commence my project after the

children are bathed and put to bed. I'm hoping to unearth the *Great Discovery* and annihilate my demons forever. It is, in a sense, a labour of love. My report is comprised of 30 pages and I enclose it in a manila envelope with at least a dozen of my poems.

"This is for you," I announce at my next get-together with Dr. Tolhurst. "I'm most interested in the evaluation you promised me."

He opens the large envelope and views the contents. "I certainly hope I'll find time to read all this, Mrs. Snow. I was not exactly expecting such a *lengthy* report." His tone suggests he's somewhat put out and I feel my cheeks burn with embarrassment.

"In regard to the Medicare problems I've spoken to you about, I've found it necessary to take on new patients, and I have work over my head," he grumbles.

I suddenly hear him loud and clear. He doesn't expect to do this extra work without decent remuneration and I'm far too proud to expect something for nothing.

"I've worked long and hard on this compilation, and your professional evaluation is of major importance to me. I'd be willing to offer you fifty dollars for the extra work involved if you consider that to be a fair amount. I've no idea of the length of time involved in such a task."

For the first time, I see him genuinely smile. "That will certainly be adequate, Mrs. Snow." He accepts the cheque I proffer and continues to smile copiously for several seconds. "I'll read the contents in their entirety between now and our next session," he promises. "Now, tell me what's been happening lately?"

We dig into my past once again, and he soon begins to yawn, fidget, and consult his watch. I perceive he is utterly bored and, as usual, I feel guilty and am glad when my time is up.

"You know," he interjects prior to ending our session. "I find you very well-adjusted. Your basic nature is quite sunny. I have some really sad cases. Compared to my patients in general, you don't seem ill at all."

Should I feel flattered, or worry that he thinks I'm crying wolf? "I *am* fairly happy in general. Nevertheless, I'm crippled by my fears, and while I don't wallow in this fact, I desperately wish to be able to move freely again and be released from my prison."

"All in due time, Mrs. Snow. All in due time."

The next few weeks drag on indefinitely due to my eagerness to receive my doctor's evaluation. I refrain from telling Len about the fifty dollar cheque as I know he'll have my head on a platter. At least I don't feel like a beggar. I'm being independent and paying for a service I believe is worth every penny.

On the date of my next appointment with Dr. Tolhurst, I sit in the lobby impatiently awaiting my turn. I eagerly bound out of my chair as I see his previous patient depart.

After our preliminary greetings, I inquire earnestly, "Have your read my notes and my poetry?"

He nods in assent. "I've perused the lot."

"And? Did you draw any conclusions, or form any opinions as to what may be causing my phobia?"

"Well, your poetry was most inspiring on a conscious level, but it depicted little in the way of covert emotions."

"How about my personal notes?"

"Very interesting," he replies dully.

"Have you made an evaluation?"

He pauses. "Well, um, I've actually formed several conclusions. However, I feel it may adversely affect your therapy if I discuss them with you at this time. I wish to reserve my comments and conclusions for a future session. Meanwhile, I'd like to hear what *you've* concluded from your writings, if anything."

I swallow my disappointment. I paid for a specific service which I expected to receive. I'm not a wealthy person and fifty dollars is a lot of money. I feel I've been robbed. Yet, what does one do in such a case? If Dr. Tolhurst was a salesman and denied me my merchandise I'd demand my money back, but this is not the case. I can only assume that, as my psychiatrist, he has my welfare at heart.

"Unfortunately, I've concluded very little," I answer half-heartedly. "I was so hoping to hear *your* comments. When might I expect to have your personal input?"

"In the near future. First, I want you to carefully probe into your notes *yourself*. I'm certain you'll uncover some clues. I'd like to hear *your* thoughts, even if you don't find them personally meaningful. Surely, even now, you have a thought or two."

I begin discussing a few points regarding past rejections and invalidations which may have led to an early loss of self-esteem. His questions, on certain aspects clearly outlined in my report, soon lead me to wonder if he's actually read it. I originally give him the benefit of the doubt by assuming he's either ascertaining the veracity of my narrative or has simply forgotten a few details. His further queries lead me to believe it's highly improbable he's even glanced at my work. Once this thought jells, I'm determined to unveil his duplicity and I begin artfully setting traps.

He invariably ensnares himself.

I do not reveal I've uncovered his subterfuge. Truly, I'm not angry. My feelings go much deeper. I'm absolutely crestfallen. One hardly expects to be duped by one's doctor.

I put on a good face during the drive home. My husband will remain in the dark regarding my painful discovery. I'm far too ashamed to openly acknowledge my naiveté; but beyond my shame is a distinct feeling of failure. My shrink did not read my report. He considered it worthless which equates with *me* being worthless.

I take an extended shower that evening for one reason only: I need to vent my anguish privately within the solitude of the pounding crescendo of water that cascades upon me in torrents. I sob and sob . . . until the surging spray runs cold.

I am totally let-down and rejected. I am four years old and Daddy has ejected me from Mommy's bedroom and the comfort of her arms. I am broken-hearted.

Mother has not defended me . . . equals I am worthless.

I awaken the next morning, furious with Dr. Tolhurst.

Despite my ire, I show up for my next appointment. If I quit now, I abandon all hope of a cure. I absolve him with a multitude of excuses: he was truly too busy to read my report and perhaps he's keenly perused it since; he's lied to me, yes, but have I never used a similar ploy? Am I lily-white? I vow I'll no longer deviously try to ambush the man. It hurts me far more than him. I've lost enough time in my prison. My cure may be just around the corner. A petty grievance is minor by comparison.

Dr. Tolhurst chooses this visit to reap the harvest of the crop he has planted. "You know, Mrs. Snow," he digresses from what we are discussing shortly before our time is up, "I dislike being placed in this position, but there is a matter that needs to be addressed. I'm barely surviving these days. Therefore, I must ask each of my patients if they're willing to subsidize my Medicare payments in some way. Only, of course, if they're financially able to do so." He regards me knowingly. His eyes are challenging as he waits for me to declare that I am broke.

Damn Len and his big mouth, I curse silently. "What would you consider a fair amount?" I enquire. I endeavour to keep my face and tone expressionless.

"I prefer to leave that to the discretion of my patients," he responds. "I expect it would depend upon their personal circumstances combined with their estimation of the value of my services." He pauses meaningfully. "Unfortunately, I may be forced to cancel the patients who are unable to offer this assistance. I don't wish to do this, but I foresee no other recourse at present."

I'm unprepared for the axe to fall so suddenly. I've not yet assessed the actual extent of my need of his services. I must examine this factor. I'm fully aware he's resorting to the emotional blackmail of a psychiatric patient . . . and perhaps more than one. Distasteful as this is, I need time to adjust to severing the bond.

Ten bucks, I decide, as I hand him a cheque. "This is the very best I can do, I'm afraid. I have a large family. I certainly hope it will suffice," I add mildly.

"That will be fine, and I thank you for your co-operation, Mrs. Snow." He hands me the card for my next rendezvous and leads me suavely to the door.

I discuss the new set of developments with Len, without revealing my fifty buck rip-off or the extra ten dollars I've just doled out.

"There's no way you're going to give one penny extra to that bastard!" he shouts. "If he can't manage his money, it's not our fault. We make do on a lot less. What he's doing is not even legal."

"I may be dropped as a patient if I don't go along with it."

"Good. You don't need him as a crutch. You're not in a breakdown now. There are other shrinks, even if it means you're on a waiting list. I'd like to know if any other patients are actually paying him. Maybe he's just hit on us."

"You're right," I agree. "However, I've come up with an idea." I reveal it, and he agrees.

Two weeks later in Dr. Tolhurst's office, I give him an insurance form at the end of our session. "Our insurance company pays for expenses over and above those not covered by Medicare," I explain. "If you care to fill this out with whatever additional fee you request, I'll submit it to the company directly."

Momentarily he's nonplussed. Then, he takes the form and says, "I really don't have time at the moment. You should have presented it to me earlier. I'll have it done the next time I see you." He hands me the appointment card he has already prepared for me.

Two weeks later, Len and I arrive at Dr. Tolhurst's office for my next visit. His door is locked. Although we wait twenty minutes in the lobby, we see neither hide nor hair of him.

We are not surprised. Dr. Tolhurst's feathers have been unpleasantly ruffled. We don't expect to see him . . . not ever again.

JULY 6, 2012, FRIDAY

We meet our new granddaughter for the first time today. She's five days old and absolutely enchanting with her pink and white skin, delicate features and big blue eyes. Enfolding her in my arms, I'm flooded with memories of my own babies lying quietly in repose upon my bosom in a similar fashion. Momentarily I yearn to turn back the clock.

We give Alex, Dana's little boy, the treats we've brought him, along with big hugs. He's a lively little guy and very loving.

"Have you any news regarding the gestational diabetes?" I ask Dana.

"Yes. I'm fine now. I've been checked since giving birth, and my blood sugar is back to normal."

"Excellent. And how about the baby? Has she been checked by a pediatrician?"

"Absolutely. I'm so glad I changed hospitals. There was a team of at least eight in the delivery room including my obstetrician, the resident doctor and a nurse, and even a neurologist and respirologist as well as a pediatrician who examined the baby at birth."

"Wow! I'm impressed."

Our visit goes by too quickly. Len wants to hit the road in order to avoid rush hour traffic. We hug Dana and her husband, Zack, and after one last kiss to the children we're on our way.

Homeward bound, I give thanks that Dana and baby are both well, and that Gary's immune system rallied for his birthday which we recently shared with him in a Chinese restaurant. Following lunch, he entertained us on the piano and the flute. All in all, it was a lovely day.

I now look ahead to Monday, July 16th, the start of Gary's fourth and hopefully last cycle of chemo. I pray that the end of his cancer is in sight. For now, he's doing well. Numerous friends and church groups are praying for him, and the vast amount of prayer energy surrounding him lifts our hearts in hopes of a good outcome.

Meanwhile, I'm thankful for my many blessings: my wonderful

family; my good friends, Leila and Colina that remain in the city and have been so supportive during Gary's illness; along with other dear friends such as Tish and Jane who have moved but remain in contact. Most of all, I'm grateful for Len, my constant companion and my very best friend.

At this moment, all is well in my world.

Chapter 17 – A Mother's Love

"When you look into your mother's eyes,
you know that is the purest love you can find on this earth."
—Mitch Albom

Since my disastrous experience with Dr. Tolhurst, I've had neither the incentive nor the fortitude to seek out a psychiatrist who may be another dud.

A few years pass by uneventfully until one day my eyes light upon a section about phobias in the local newspaper and for the first time I learn about agoraphobia, the Greek word for "fear of the market place", which describes my symptoms to a tee. My exhilaration is nothing short of remarkable. The article goes on to say that a prominent psychiatrist in one of our major hospitals has had a great deal of success in treating this particular phobia, amongst others.

"Len!" I cry. "I finally know exactly what I have! My phobia has a label. I *must* see this doctor!"

I call the next day and make an appointment with the physician in question.

A few weeks later, after a short interview with this new doctor, it is confirmed I have agoraphobia.

"With what you've been able to accomplish on your own, I believe you have a 75% chance or better of being cured," he informs me.

"I'm no longer taking phobic patients here at the hospital," he continues. "My wife Karen, a psychologist, is looking after that end of things. She has a clinic in town which I personally oversee. She has a well-trained, dedicated staff and they work solely with phobic patients. I believe you'd be an excellent candidate. I'm confident that her clinic is the answer to getting you moving again." He hands me her business card and suggests I contact her for an appointment.

Before leaving I explain what happened when I went to Dr. Tolhurst for help. He grins. "Poor Gregory, from what I understand he's having a lot of financial difficulties. You mustn't let that deter you in seeking a cure." Upon leaving his office, I can't help but question *his* scruples.

Psychologists, I learn, are not on Medicare; nor are their services compensated by most insurance companies in 1977. We'll have to absorb Karen's fee on our own.

Len knows how desperately I want to get better. "Go for it, hon. We'll find a way to manage it," he assures me. I make an appointment and climb on the phobic band wagon.

I'm soon to learn that the main method employed in the clinic is flooding, which parallels my mother's final ploy to get me moving during my breakdown. Combined with this, is something they call desensitization therapy. I'm asked to write an essay about one of the most fearful situations I can imagine encountering as a phobic, which I am later instructed to verbally record. I then listen to myself reading my narrative aloud while wired to a device which emits shocks into my thumbs at key intervals throughout the scariest parts of my story. I'm told that my aversion to the shocks will help desensitize me to the fear.

In regard to facing the fear head-on, it's suggested I begin travelling on the bus alone for short distances to be increased daily. Within a month, the treatment appears to have worked in reverse: I've become so highly sensitized to my fear that I never want to get on another bus for the rest of my life. Similarly, the shocks–which are obviously transmitted at a tolerable pain level–have made no significant dents in my desensitization progress.

This attempt brings me to another dead-end, and we're a few

hundred dollars poorer. It was not entirely a wasted effort, however. I have the comfort of knowing there's a name for my illness and there are others who share my plight.

It's around this time I become aware of no longer being mentally plagued about Brenda. I never bring her up and if her name arises, I could care less. It seems I've finally become secure in my skin and know beyond doubt that I've *never* wanted for first place in Len's affections. Consequently, the taunting of the demons and my need for proof has ceased.

In retrospect, I recognize this as a major stepping stone in moving beyond my age-old belief that I don't deserve first place.

Yet, what if life's circumstances placed me in another affair of the heart? Could my demons be incited once again? I'd like to think that by recognizing I'm role-playing again—and why—that I'd be able to nip things in the bud. Yet, I cannot truthfully predict such an outcome.

On a spiritual level, it's of far greater importance to reach an enlightened state where I'll no longer need first place, or even love. A place where I'll be content to just be what I am: Love itself. While I suspect that, for most of us, such a vision is light years away, it nevertheless awaits us . . . upon awakening.

The years pass quickly. In February 1978, we make a combined birthday party for both Keith and Eve whose birthdays are just over a week apart. Keith will be eleven and Eve, eight. Dana will be four this summer and starting kindergarten next year. I've been blessed with such good children. They are more malleable than I was as a child, less rebellious, and more eager to please.

I've often thought of bringing them to Sunday school, but I have not forgotten my early exposure to fire and brimstone and the damage it did to my mind. It also brought me to the conclusion that I don't need a church to have God in my life. For now, my aim is to teach them the important truths I've acquired in my ongoing spiritual search: that there *is* no hell, and most importantly–as my heart dictated all along–*no* duality in God, who is *only* Love.

Len and I go to the Legion regularly on weekends and bring Mom along. We belong to a Friday night dart league. We generally drop in on Saturday evenings as well, even if there's nothing special going on.

On one of those evenings, I strike up a conversation with one of the regulars named Tish, and from that moment forward we become friends. This is a first for me as, ever since my agoraphobia began, I've shied away from making new friends. There's just too much time, energy, and guilt absorbed in the process of hiding my illness, and I gravitate to the easiest path: retaining the few long-standing friendships I have–which are devoid of judgment or pressure– whilst steering clear of forming new ones.

I'm soon to learn that Tish is mildly agoraphobic herself and can well relate to my fears. This common ground becomes part of the glue that binds us. Apart from seeing each other weekends at the Legion, we soon begin calling each other regularly and our friendship becomes cemented. Before long–since we live in the same vicinity–we spend time at each other's homes as well.

We soon learn we have a lot in common. We're both avid readers of similar subjects. It is she who first introduces me to the works of Edgar Cayce in regard to reincarnation, a topic I have given little thought to in the past.

I think there is, in all of us, a part of our higher self that recognizes a personal truth when it appears. In reading Cayce's books, I knew I was glimpsing one of my own eternal truths and I have Tish to thank for her part in pioneering me along the spiritual journey that my daughter's death kept urging me to follow. I believe our meeting was one of the synchronous events life presents every one of us . . . each evoking the chain reaction that nudges us along our own particular pathway to Love.

Spring of May 1979 marks nine years since my nervous breakdown. While I still suffer from a chronic anxiety condition, a daily dose of tranquilizers generally keeps it at a tolerable level, provided I don't tempt fate by extending my boundaries. While the daily anxiety is a morbid thing beyond my control, I have not once been afflicted with an actual panic attack and dare to hope that particular horror is behind me.

Dare is the operative word.

One afternoon, I take the car alone to pick up my mother for Sunday dinner. I've been reading a number of self-help books for people with nervous disorders written by Dr. Claire Weekes who similarly upholds the flooding method. She advocates welcoming panic and accepting it in a relaxed way. *Yeah, right. Easily said. I wonder if the good doctor has ever personally suffered a panic attack.* Whatever. I want to get better with every fibre of my being. Ergo, I'm increasing my therapies.

I'm later to wonder whether my extensive reading somehow re-sensitized me to my fears and precipitated the whopper of an attack that followed.

While driving to my mother's, I find myself ruminating over Dr. Weekes' take on welcoming panic. *How can one possibly welcome it?* Antsy and ill at ease from merely entertaining such an unsettling thought, my nervous discomfort increases ... to a point where I'm later to wonder if I actually conjured the attack that seemed to suddenly strike from out of the blue with the force of a tsunami.

As wave after wave of panic floods over me, a small fraction of my logical mind dictates I must try to relax; but relaxation, in face of such terror, is virtually impossible. There's no way in hell I can simply pull over, stop the car, and placidly wait for this hideous attack to subside. *How ridiculous can this lady get?* Reaching the safe haven of my mother's home becomes my one coherent thought. My sole hope of salvation. Heart pounding furiously, I floor the accelerator and shoot by several cars along the way. I'm on auto-pilot and far too obsessed with panic to even consider the possibility of being stopped for a traffic violation.

Upon reaching my destination, the attack subsides almost immediately, and I'm able to transport my mother to my home with no qualms whatsoever, although I make sure Len drives her back after supper. There's no way I want to face the possibility of experiencing another such horror.

Back to square one, I put Dr. Weekes' books aside. My case does not respond well to her concepts.

Our home of ten years has been on the market for several months and has finally sold. Property taxes have almost doubled in our neighbourhood and we've decided to rent for a time. In early July, we move into an apartment. Once settled in, I feel nervous and estranged and extremely frightened of being on my own again. It's somewhat easier to cope over the summer because the kids are on holiday. Although Eve and Dana are only nine and five respectively, Keith is twelve and quite grown-up. Knowing the kids are nearby increases my confidence and I make sure that when they're playing outdoors they remain within my range of vision and calling distance as well. Otherwise, my anxiety becomes unbearable. I realize how unfair this is, especially to the older two, and I feel worse because they do not complain.

I explain my plight to the family doctor prior to the start of school. He increases my dosage of tranquilizers, but I remain acutely anxious. I'm also very depressed at this juncture, and the beginning of the school year is hell. Dana has started kindergarten for half-days and I anxiously await her comforting little presence at lunchtime which seems to take the edge off my dread. My apprehension has become severe and I sense I am walking on a narrow ledge.

This continues until November of the same year, when I am relieved to notice that my daily suffering has become less intense. My anxiety has reverted to a more moderate level and the improvement permits me to drive to my mother's on my own again; albeit not without the usual trepidation.

By early December 1979, Mom begins having frequent digestive upsets, quite similar to what Dad suffered previously. She has intense pain after each meal. She begins shedding pounds rapidly, and she experiences a distinct loss of appetite.

I'm beside myself with worry. Not unlike my dad, she refuses to see a doctor; but for a different reason: She's afraid of what will be uncovered. She's terrified it may be cancer and although the word is never mentioned, it hangs in the air between us. She seems to think that not knowing is better than knowing what she believes may be the worst, and although she hides behind a veil of ignorance, her actions reveal that a part of her believes her days are numbered.

By Christmas her pain has intensified. She nevertheless puts on a good face in front of the children. "It's probably just an ulcer or some other digestive problem," she says to me. "Don't worry, Irene. I'll get over it."

"Won't you please, please let us take you to a doctor, Mom?" I plead.

"There's no way I intend to subject myself to the horrors your father went through," she says adamantly. "If it is my time, God will take me; if not, I'll get better."

On New Year's Eve at the Legion, she sits at a table with Len and me and a few friends. As the strains of *Old Lang Syne* fill the air at midnight we embrace each other as we welcome in the year 1980. "I think this is my last New Year," she confides, quietly and sadly. My eyes fill with tears. I sense she speaks the truth.

Early in January, her condition has worsened and I'm truly frightened. Her failing health ignites a rerun of previous horror films and I'm overwhelmed with the dread of losing her. During my long fight with anxiety she has always represented a security blanket for me. Len has to go to work. My kids have to attend school. Mom is always there—a short drive away. This knowledge alone has helped keep me anchored. My fears begin escalating, and once again I become severely anxious when alone in the house, and plagued by the worry of what will happen to my children if I can no longer cope on my own.

I'm becoming frantic to find a way to get better.

It's around this time I read a book entitled, *Dianetics: The Modern Science of Mental Health,* written by the founder of The Church of Scientology, L. Ron Hubbard. His techniques seem to offer a whole new concept on mental health and I become convinced that they may be my saving grace. I want to have the strength to help my mom through her grim ordeal and to be a proper mother to my children. Both goals pre-empt a sojourn in the nuthouse.

I make an appointment at the closest branch of the Church of Scientology. Len accompanies me for my free technical estimate. I'm told I can be "mentally cleared" by being audited on the E-meter, whatever that is. I'm also informed I need to undergo a drug purification program prior to auditing. This requires my abstinence from all tranquilizers. "Your drug history is deplorable," I'm told. I find myself becoming increasingly distressed and my mornings at home without the help of a Valium are wretched. However, I will do *anything* to be cured at this stage.

My husband, deeply concerned about my nervous decline, removes six thousand dollars–their current price quote–from our retirement fund. They refuse it. They say my condition is worse than they anticipated and the revised price is a donation to their Church in the amount of ten thousand; the latter, in the year 1980, approximating one quarter the price of a three-bedroom bungalow! Desperate as Len and I are regarding a cure, reason prevails. Such an exorbitant fee is surely not geared to the average person's budget. Only the very wealthy can afford to take such a chance. We walk off in dismay . . . and disbelief.

Once home, I toss Mr. Hubbert's book in the trash.

By March, I sense I'm hanging on by a thread. My mother calls to say she can no longer stand the pain. It has intensified to the point of being all-encompassing. "I refuse to go to the same hospital your dad was in," she says. "He was treated worse than a dog in there. I will not go to his stomach specialist."

"Let me see if I can get you an appointment with a specialist at another hospital," I suggest. I'm aware that her agreement alone is a barometer revealing the intensity of her suffering. *Oh God, how terrible that it has come to this!* I manage to get the appointment without a referral but she has a three week waiting period, and scarcely two days later she's no longer able to abide the crushing agony.

"I can't go on like this, Irene. I've never known such pain. I need medical help. Now."

"There's only one doctor I can think of that might see you on such short notice, and that's Dad's former stomach specialist, the one you don't want to see. I know he's not Mr. Personality and that you'd rather not deal with him, but he *is* a good doctor, and it seems to be urgent you see *someone*. Perhaps he can help you with some pain killers to tide you over until you see the other doctor. I could call him."

"Go ahead. I have no choice. I've left it too late. I have to do something."

I call Dr. Walsh's receptionist explaining my mother's plight, and it appears we're in luck. There's been a cancellation and an opening is available the very next day.

Len drives us to his office. After a thorough examination of my mother he tells her it's imperative he admits her to hospital. She makes no objection. I'm not surprised as she's now living and breathing her torment. All she desires is relief–in whatever form it will come.

Thus begins my mother's eleven week stay in the Lornewood Hospital, on the exact same floor as my dad before her, a daily reminder of past horrors that will confirm her worst fears at the eleventh hour. Fortunately for me, a four-week strike at Len's plant coincides with her hospitalization and for the first four weeks we're able to spend a good part of the day with her while the children are in school. Later, we'll visit her every night for the remaining seven weeks of her confinement.

Test after test comes up negative, and one day runs into another, each as bleak and fear-filled as the last. As I bear daily witness to my mother's decline, the horrific fear that overtook me during Star's illness plagues me daily. Aware of the inseverable, symbiotic tie that bound Star to me as my child, I'm keenly cognizant of this selfsame bond that inviolably links me to my mother as her child. Star was a part of me; likewise I'm an adjunct of my mother and in some indefinable way, her loss also equates with losing a part of my self.

Tish entices me to drop into the Legion the following Friday after my visit with Mom. "Have a few beers with Charlie and me," she urges. "You need to get out, Renie."

She continues to nag me until I comply, and I will later be very glad I did. Len and I join Tish and her husband who are sitting with Martha, one of Tish's friends who recently confided in me that she's bipolar. Consequently, I open up to her for the first time regarding my agoraphobia. I tell her how concerned I am that my fears are getting so far out of hand I can no longer keep them at bay.

"I have some good news for you, Irene. My psychiatrist is now specializing solely in agoraphobia. While he's not dismissing any of his former patients, he's currently only taking agoraphobics as new ones. I've heard that curing agoraphobia is his passion. I strongly recommend him to you. I'll give you his number. Just tell him I referred you."

I leave a message for Dr. Richards the next day. When he gets back to me, I tell him I've been diagnosed with agoraphobia but have not responded well to previous treatments and that my panic is currently intensifying in view of my mother's health crisis. I relay truthfully that I'm unable to travel downtown alone, a situation he well understands. He offers to see me a few days hence on Good Friday. Amazed at how cheerful and friendly he sounds, I exclaim, "You don't know what a great gift this is to me, and in more ways than one: Good Friday is also my birthday!"

"Well, well, let's hope that makes our visit a special occasion for you, Mrs. Snow. I want you to keep the faith. I know I can help you." His voice is animated and upbeat. For once, I too know something: This doctor is definitely not dour and I'm going to like him.

My 39th birthday appointment with Dr. Richards goes well. I judge him to be in his mid-forties. He's of average build with dark hair, and warm brown eyes that literally sparkle when he smiles, and he regards me kindly from an unexpectedly pleasing and animated face. His winsome, engaging manner instantly puts me at ease and as I explain my case in detail, much to my amazement, he listens with empathy and genuine interest.

He's the first doctor to explicitly delineate the many symptoms that have beset me over the years. He explains that my agoraphobia originates from panic disorder–the latter, an illness that is generally preceded by panic attacks.

"Isolated panic attacks without consequence are generally not the norm," he continues. "In the majority of cases, the incredibly debilitating nature of a panic attack itself is often enough to precipitate an ongoing condition of panic disorder, closely followed by agoraphobia. You are exceedingly brave to have dealt with panic attacks during your working years for as long as you did without succumbing to full-blown agoraphobia."

"What is your opinion regarding flooding as a means of a cure?" I ask.

"Flooding definitely has its downside. Not too many of us are eager to greet such intense panic without a buffer. As a point of interest, the horror and anguish of a full-blown panic attack closely correlates with the intense fear experienced in a heart attack. Agoraphobics are *not* cowards, Mrs. Snow. The mental pain they suffer can only be withstood by the very brave of heart.

"The buffer I use to help my patients achieve an appreciable reduction of fear is an MAO Inhibitor called Phenelzene. Its brand name is Nardil. It's an anti-depressant medication that is very helpful in cases such as yours. Obviously, intense anxiety is related to depression, so it's important to raise you to a higher emotional tone if we don't want to thwart your efforts to get better. Are you with me?"

"Yes, I completely understand."

He goes on to say, "I'm currently involved with the relatively new methods of treatment being used in biological psychiatry. I believe in the necessity of using medication to treat your emotional pain in the same way your family doctor will give you something to alleviate your physical pain.

"I disagree with the psychoanalytical techniques employed by your previous doctor. The latter method could take years and is of no real value in regard to your particular problem which screams for help *now*. I personally prescribe a combination of behavioural therapy *along* with medication. You'll still need to take steps to conquer your fear on your own, but it will be nowhere near as difficult for you."

His explanations are simple and to the point. He's completely unhurried and shows empathy for me as a person, which is something I *feel*. His keen sense of humour puts me at ease, and I gravitate to his magnetic personality from the onset. It's evident he has an absolute passion for his work and a total belief in what he's doing. Despite being a little scared about starting anti-depressant medication for the very first time, he has inspired within me a faith heretofore lacking in regard to doctors in general.

I agree to try the new meds, and he informs me that I should notice a distinct mood lift within a few weeks. "If perchance your fear begins to worsen prematurely–before the meds take effect–I want you to know I'm here for you, and you can call me anytime."

I almost instantaneously bond with Dr. Richards. He has become Mother–my ticket to continued survival.

Dr. Richards also explains the dreaded symptoms I experienced during my panic attacks and subsequent breakdown. "Patients who suffer your particular illness are often plagued with a myriad of symptoms which are in *no way* psychotic in nature," he explains. "Your sensations of being detached from reality and disconnected from your *self*, along with the array of frightening symptoms that accompany these perceptions are, in psychiatric lingo, referred to as derealisation and depersonalization. They are not uncommon in cases of extreme anxiety and/or panic disorder and I assure you that, although alarming, they should not concern you regarding your sanity."

As I depart his office, I am feeling more anchored, and I have a renewed confidence that this caring doctor, in conjunction with the new meds, is the answer I've sought for years in regard to overcoming my illness.

Two weeks later, I'm surprised and ecstatic to realize my tone level has remarkably ascended from sad to glad. There's a distinct change in my equilibrium. I feel more balanced and calm and I've become more poised and self-confident in all situations. I relay the good news to Dr. Richards on my next appointment and he responds with pleasure.

Somewhere around the end of April, I'm approached by my mother's prospective surgeon. "To date, Mrs. Snow, all your mother's tests have been negative. Our only significant finding pertains to her gall bladder which is badly diseased. However, she has some suspicious symptoms which seem to indicate we may have overlooked something. Our only way of knowing whether or not we have anything more to contend with is to perform an exploratory operation. It's our last resort. I sincerely hope it *is* just the gall bladder, in which case I will extract it and she can recuperate and get on with her life."

On the day of Mom's surgery, Len takes the day off, knowing I want to be with her. *What would I do without his constant support?* I ponder. Standing beside her gurney before she's wheeled away, she says to me quietly for the first time, "If it's cancer, I hope I die on the operating table." As I bend down to kiss her cheek, I squeeze her hand and tell her I'm sure all will be well; but I, too, am crippled with uncertainty and fear.

Sometime later, when her surgery is over and she's too groggy to make any sense, I spy her surgeon coming towards me in the hallway. He takes me aside and says, "We found some tumours, Mrs. Snow.

They're *behind* the liver and that's the reason they were not picked up on her nuclear scan."

I feel the blood draining from my face. "Please," the doctor adds quickly, "we mustn't jump to conclusions at this early stage. There's always the possibility the tumours are benign. We'll have the results within the next few days."

I hang onto this hope; but whatever the outcome, I have to be strong for my mother. This becomes more difficult as I witness her gradual decline, and I'm only grateful the Nardil is keeping me more centred. I think back to one of our talks not long after my father died.

"I had the most horrible dream," she says. "I got on a bus and saw your father sitting alone on a seat by the window. I walked toward him, horrified by his gaunt, deathly appearance. He said, 'I realize you're cringing to see me this way, but you'd best get used to it. A few years from now you'll look in the mirror, and it will be *you* who looks exactly like this.' He would never be cruel enough to say this to me and I somehow think it's an omen, Irene. I'm so afraid it *will* be me going down the same road."

"Mom, you have to get that out of your mind and not dwell on it. It's your own deep fear showing its ugly face in your dream. Remember what the Bible said about Job: 'That which he feared came upon him'? Please, please get it out of your mind. It is *not* an omen, but it *could* become a self-fulfilling prophecy if you believe it strongly enough."

I, for one, know this to be true. By entertaining a myriad of negative, emotionalized thoughts prior to my breakdown, I unwittingly used faith in reverse and, not unlike Job, I obtained unholy results. My fear came upon me . . . to a point I was one with it.

Faith is extremely powerful, whether used positively or negatively. Dreading that something will happen is interpreted by subconscious mind as a prayer—albeit a negative one—and if the thought is emotionalized and sustained, it will in time become manifest in the flesh. I knew I had to warn my mother.

Mom is somewhat pacified by my explanation, but her dream has nevertheless led her to another thought. "I'm not as brave as your dad," she continues. "If I'm *ever* in the same boat, I would not want to know. It would be the beginning of the end for me. I would live in daily terror. You must promise me that you'd never tell me, and that you'd insist the doctors don't inform me either. Promise, Irene."

"Of course, I promise, if that's your wish. But you have to promise me not to dwell on something that in all likelihood will never happen. After all, Dad was a very heavy smoker, three packs a day. It's not surprising he got lung cancer. The liver thing merely resulted from metastases of the original growth. You don't smoke anywhere near as much as he did. Why start fearing you're going to be like him? That's nonsense Mom, and you have to stop it. *Now.*"

"Okay, okay, I promise. And incidentally, thanks for your pep talk."

Was it an omen, or had her deepest fear become a reality? I have no way of knowing. But I do know one thing: I have to talk to all of the doctors that are connected with her and alert them to her wishes. If it's cancer, she *doesn't* want to know.

I'm soon to discover this is not an easy task.

That night I type a letter to her surgeon, with several copies which I address to her specialist, and the chief oncologist, along with a general letter to "All staff", the latter to be left at the main desk. I inform them of my mother's deep-seated fear of cancer and her wishes to not be told, explaining that it will be the beginning of the end for her if cancer is revealed. I keep these letters in my handbag, to deliver if I'm apprised of a negative verdict. Her surgeon has already promised to contact me first with the biopsy results.

Mom is beside herself. When she fully awakens from surgery she tells me, "I know the results are not good, Irene. A strange thing happened. Directly after the operation I awakened and became completely lucid for a few moments. I asked about the findings. They've discovered some spots on my liver and have taken a biopsy."

"I'm sure they're benign, Mom. Remember how scared you were

when they found a growth on your bladder several years ago? It turned out fine. Most growths are benign."

"I'm still very worried. If it's serious, I want to die right now."

I take her hand in mine. "You're going to be okay, Mom. I just know it. Please keep positive."

A few days later I spot her surgeon in the corridor on my way to the restroom. "Have you had any results from the biopsy yet?" I ask fearfully.

He draws me aside and puts an arm around my shoulder. His eyes are sad. "I'm afraid so," he says gently. "The growths are malignant."

"*Oh, God.* What are her chances?"

"Not good, I'm afraid. The cancer is advanced."

"How long do you think she has?

"Six months. A year max."

"*Oh, my God, no!*" My eyes fill with tears.

He regards me with strangely sombre eyes.

"If it's any consolation, Mrs. Snow, I can fully empathize what you're going through. I've just learned my father has the exact same type of cancer. He's on this same floor."

I express my sympathies, then open my purse and give him my typewritten letter. "Please read this. I urge you to follow my wishes, which are my mother's own," I implore. "She must never know she has cancer. If it's revealed to her, whatever life she has left will be a living hell."

I enter the loo and lock myself in a cubicle and weep until my tears run dry. I wonder how I can ever bear up to the loss of my mother. Despite our occasional disagreements we're as close as two peas in a pod. I run the cold water over paper towels which I place over my eyes to reduce the puffiness, and then apply some extra make-up in an effort to conceal the red, blotchy reflection that regarded me dolefully in the mirror. I square my shoulders as I return to Mom's room to deliver the "good news" that the tumours are "benign".

I wonder how I can continue to walk down this road of horror without revealing my own pain and grief, the latter which is not dulled by the Nardil in this moment of truth. I pray God for strength.

I don't think my mother ever fully believes my story. She asks questions at times to trip me up but I see them coming and skillfully evade them. At one point she remarks sadly, "You wouldn't tell me if it *were* something serious, would you, Irene?"

I take this opportunity to meet her eyes truthfully, without guile. Perhaps she wants to know, in which case the kindest thing is to tell her and try to help her deal with it. "That would depend on whether or not it was something I thought *you* would truly want to know," I say. I keep my eyes locked with hers.

She lowers her eyes first. "I don't think I would want to know," she says dully.

"Well, at least I know how you feel if ever the occasion arises. For now, it is *not* a question. The tumours are benign."

"Why hasn't the doctor told *me* that?" she asks.

Her surgeon has already informed me he won't lie to her if she demands her results directly. Otherwise, he's promised—in deference to our wishes—he will not tell her anything of his own volition.

"Probably because he has already told *me*, and I promised him I'd let you know exactly what he said."

Under normal circumstances, the upsetting events in my life would leave me severely depressed and unglued. Regular chats with Dr. Richards, along with the help of the Nardil, have changed that. My mood has lifted to a point where I recognize a distinct transformation in myself. While, I still feel the strain of Mom's illness and the overwhelming sadness of her impending death, I'm more able to cope. For the first time in years, I've become a normal person who's able to contend with life's crises without falling completely to pieces and it's no longer necessary to flog and debase myself. My newly-improved outlook has given my lagging self-esteem a well-needed boost. Besides, Dr. Richards has assured me that panic disorder and agoraphobia are illnesses, no less valid than severe physical afflictions, and no more responsive to merely "pulling oneself up by one's bootstraps".

A few days later, the axe falls directly on my mother's head. Dr. Greer, the head oncologist, decides to pay her a bedside visit. He totally ignores my letter and addresses her. "Are you one of those people who prefer to remain oblivious to their medical condition?"

Alarm bells go off in her head; yet, too ashamed to admit the depth of her fear, she inquires, "What do you mean?"

"Well," he continues, "I'm wondering if you're interested in learning the results of your recent biopsy?"

Despite the incredible fear which has become a live entity within her, she says stoically, "Well, yes. I would like to know."

"You have advanced cancer of the liver," he says bluntly. "You need to put your life in order at this time. For our part, the hospital sponsors death therapy sessions which are a valuable aid in helping terminally ill patients cope with and adjust to death before it happens."

This is all Mom hears before she blanks out and slips into a well of horror. She calls me at home in tears. I can barely understand what she's saying as she tries to enlighten me on what has transpired. I finally get the gist of it and I'm absolutely livid. Surely this monster could have respected her wishes and left her with the flimsy thread of hope she yearned for. He would have been less cruel to kill her on the spot.

No matter how I deny his words by telling her he's mistaken, and that she must trust her surgeon who's the one person who knows for sure her tumours are benign, I believe she only pretends to agree with me from that moment on. Deep down, his words have destroyed her.

Her decline is rapid thereafter. Her nurse becomes angry that she's unable to get to the sink to wash herself and accuses her of being lazy. She's subjected to similar barrages of verbal cruelty in her final days in hospital.

I finally demand she be released in my care, and I bring her home to die.

Keith willingly gives up his bedroom and temporarily moves into a cot in the girls' room. Keith has a comfortable room with a pleasant decor. The open-weave, burnt-orange curtains on the window with matching bedside mats blend well with the pale blue walls, navy furniture and blue and white-striped duvet. I place a small TV on the dresser and a flowering plant on a small table. When Mom arrives,

I plan to assure her that her stay is only temporary, until her health improves. In accordance with her wishes, I'm continuing to pay her monthly rent at her former residence.

The next day, May 31, 1980, Mom is waiting patiently for us in her hospital room. "I'm so glad to be getting out of this place," she says. "It's been hell."

"I know. Things will only get better, Mom. I plan to help you get well."

"I don't believe that's possible, Irene. And I worry about you. I need trained professionals for this task. You have no idea of the scope of the burden you've taken on in regard to my care. It's not fair to you. You have your own family to look after." Her voice is infinitely sad.

"What's all this nonsense I'm hearing? I'm a lot stronger than you think—physically *and* mentally. I've finally found a good doctor and I'm doing fine. No trained nurse is going to give you the love and care that I will. You mustn't deprive me of this. I want you with me. We all do."

Her eyes fill. "You haven't had a taste of it yet. I'm more helpless than you think. You're only human and you'll get fed up with me."

"Don't pass judgment in advance," I admonish her gently. "Besides, it won't be this way forever. You're going to get better, you know."

Around the time my mother first became ill, my friend Jane lent me a book by Dr. Joseph Murphy entitled, *The Power of Your Subconscious Mind*. I'm hoping that by applying the power of positive thought and faith, as he advocates, I can help my mother overcome her illness. I know this is not an easy task, especially when it comes to disregarding exterior appearances, an extremely important factor in establishing the implicit belief necessary to manifest positive results. I'll nevertheless try my best to keep the faith . . . for my mother.

I am yet to learn of individual pre-birth choices, and to realize that my mother's soul's work was likely done and it was the choice of her higher self to depart from the world.

I nevertheless believe that Jane's book was not a coincidence. The eminent psychiatrist, Dr. Carl Jung, explains in his writings that synchronicity is a causal principle that links events (seemingly by coincidence), which have a similar or related meaning in one's life; thereby forming a unity between mind and matter.

In hindsight, as I review my own life, I'm aware of how one apparent "coincidence" such as Jane's book inexorably led to others . . . each a necessary adjunct to aid me along my own particular journey.

"How does it feel to be on the outside again?" I inquire. It's a beautiful, balmy day and a slightly floral breeze gently caresses us as Len and I walk to the car, supporting Mom's fragile, emaciated frame between us.

"A little strange," she replies. "I guess I've been in there too long. The seasons have changed."

I recall the raging blizzard on the day she was first admitted. Now winter has morphed into spring.

I become aware of Mom's distinct lack of strength as she hobbles into the car. Drained of all vitality, she's gasping for air by the time she's seated. I wonder how they can judge a woman in this condition as lazy. How utterly cruel!

She's aged dramatically, and refuses to look in a mirror because she no longer recognizes herself. Ravaged by the disease, she's haggard and gaunt. Loose folds of skin hang limply from her flaccid jowls. Her eyes and mouth appear to have inverted into her skull and her skin portrays a sallow, deathly pallor. Deeply-set wrinkles web her cheeks and I wonder how many can be contributed to the mental abuse she's been exposed to in the hospital. The last spark of light has gone from her eyes and her fine fighting spirit has been almost broken.

The journey home has left her prostrate with exhaustion. I remove her clothing and bathe her over-heated body before helping her into a clean nightgown and settling her down in her bed.

Len stays with her while I make some tea. Returning to the bedroom, I notice her crying softly. Len's arms enfold her. I slip quietly away and return later. "Tea's ready," I announce.

Mom's eyes are red and I pretend not to notice. "I was just having a little powwow with your husband," she explains, trying to keep her voice light.

"Shall I exit for a while?"

"No, we're through now. It's so good to be home, Irene. Thanks for giving me a few days in my own apartment before I come to yours. It means a lot to me. You're such a good daughter to volunteer to spend the weekend here with me. I love you such a lot, you know. Perhaps I should have told you more often. I'm not much for fancy words, but you know I have always loved you, don't you?"

"Of course, I do."

"I also know you n-need me in m-many ways and—"

Her voice chokes up and she impatiently wipes away some stray tears. "Well, if anything should happen to me I can take it, but I don't want t-that horrible thing to happen to you again. You have the k-kids. They need you. I-I worry so about you. I only pray you'll be strong enough to carry on for them."

She's so concerned I'll have another breakdown. I pray I can convince her.

"Mom, there's one thing you must believe. I'm a lot stronger now. I have a good doctor. He's very supportive and will be there for me. Look at me, and believe what I say: I'll carry on and be strong. I promise you."

"Thank God to hear you say that. I've been so worried. I keep praying for you. Perhaps God has heard me."

"Of course He has, and I pray for you as well. Please try to keep your faith in getting better."

"I try, I really do. I've always believed in God. I just wish my faith was as strong as my mother's."

Len leaves to go home soon after, and I prepare a light meal and bring it to my mother's bed. She eats very little, and her body rejects any form of solid food. I find it incredible she had no dietary restrictions in the hospital, but hopefully I have remedied that. I have bought her high caloric, nutritional beverages such as *Ensure*, along with yogurts and strained baby foods.

We chat aimlessly for awhile. Then, seemingly out of the blue, she says, "Irene, I hope you've forgiven me for some of the hurtful things I said to you over the years. There were times I felt I had to be cruel to be kind, but perhaps I was wrong. I also know it wasn't easy for you as a child with your father. Maybe I should have left him for your sake . . . I n-never meant to harm you in any way a-and . . ." Her voice chokes up and her eyes fill with tears.

This is not the first time she has brought this up, and I realize she's undoubtedly recalling the times I blatantly condemned her over the years for so much that was wrong in my life. I couldn't place any overt blame on my dad; he'd simply not accept it. Mom was the willing scapegoat. Yet, my own mistakes were countless compared to hers.

"Mom," I tell her now. "You did your very best, and I am okay with your choices. You've been a wonderful mother and one of my life's greatest blessings. I want you to know that, and to always know how much I love you."

As I take her in my arms and we weep together, I know I'll always be grateful that we've been graced with the opportunity to fully exonerate each other and experience a wondrous renewal of love in these, our final days together.

"Len will be coming with the children shortly, Mom," I remind her now. "I know how much you want to see them, so let's dry our eyes now, and I'll bring you to the living-room."

Just the act of getting her to the couch, where I prop her up on pillows, has physically sapped her and she's drenched with perspiration again. I am only glad that, for the first time in days, she retained the small amount of food she ingested. *Perhaps she will regain some of her strength,* I think optimistically.

Len and the kids arrive soon after.

"Hi Granny!" they cry in unison, and suddenly remain transfixed. They're appalled to see their grandmother so debilitated by illness that they no longer recognize her. *Surely, she's noticing their reticence,* I think sadly.

Eve is the first to break free, and she rushes to Mom's side. "I've missed you so much, Granny!" she cries, and rushes straight into Mom's open arms. They hug and kiss and regard each other with such love, it's almost painful to watch. Suddenly, they begin weeping copiously together. Nobody speaks during this poignant moment in which a little girl and her fatally ill grandmother speak of love from their tears and their hearts. It's as though Eve *knows*, and that she and her grandma are saying goodbye.

This is harder on Eve than the other children. Mom has always been her advocate. "Eve reminds me a lot of myself as a child," she's often said. "She's deeply sensitive and introverted. There's a world of feeling within her that she's too reserved to let surface. She'd like to, Irene. Try to be more patient with her. Your impatience blocks her. She's not being ornery, as you often think when she won't speak up." Mom had a special empathy for Eve, and in her grandmother's company, she unfolded like a cherished and beautiful flower.

Now, as I see my other two children still frozen in place, I break the moment by addressing them. "Well, aren't you going to say hello to your grandmother?"

Dana and Keith rise to the occasion and their grandmother hugs them fondly. All three children chat with her until she finally suggests Keith buy some treats at the nearby store. Later, noticing Mom bravely masking her pain, I signal Len to take the kids home.

Eve is hesitant to leave. She's spent the entire visit kneeling beside her grandmother, clasping her hand and stroking her arm. Mom regards her tenderly. "I'll be living at your house for a while you know, and I'll be able to see you every day." Only then is Eve appeased enough to tear herself away and leave with the others.

I give Mom a 15 mg. codeine pill before helping her back to bed. Her pain has intensified since the effects of her last dosage wore off. I sit with her awhile and hold her hand before tucking her in for the night. "Have a good sleep and just call if you need me," I remind her. "I'll be in the next room."

The following day we bring Mom to our apartment. Len is very good to her. He often sits by her bedside and holds her hand. When he comes home from work he prepares the evening meal, realizing her care is a full time job for me.

I formulate a basic schedule for my mother which I adhere to daily. She generally awakens somewhere around 2:00 AM in excruciating pain. Being far too weak to administer her own medication, I insist she call me. Her bed is against the same wall as Len's and mine which is in the room directly next door. "If I don't hear you, bang on the wall," I tell her; and I leave a baton on her end table which she often uses. Once up, I make myself a cup of cocoa and sit with her until her pain ebbs, often just massaging her back to help her relax. "Don't leave me," she whimpers. I promise I won't, and I stay with her until the pain subsides and she falls back asleep.

Her second bout of extreme agony usually occurs around 6:00 AM. I give her another codeine pill and stay with her until the pain abates. I then see the children off to school. Later I give Mom a little breakfast, either in bed, or at the kitchen table if she feels up to it. It's a terrible struggle for her to get out of bed, even with my help, and she really tries hard.

Following her light meal of baby cereal and strained fruit, I attend to her basic needs before she becomes too drowsy from her meds. I give her a complete sponge bath in bed, swab and disinfectant her drainage gap from the surgery, clean her dentures and change her sleepwear and bedding.

During her frequent naps I take care of her laundry along with our own, and tidy the apartment. Sometimes, I take a brief catnap until she invariably awakens in pain.

At some point I contact her surgeon regarding the agony she's experiencing.

"I expect the cancer is metastasizing," he says. "Just keep her as comfortable as possible; it's all you can do. You can increase her dosage of codeine from one tablet to two, every four to six hours."

I'll later cringe to think that was the strongest dosage of medication she would receive when the pain was literally unbearable during the end stages of her illness.

She alternates between showing the will to get better and giving up. Her ordeal, when she fights for life, is stupendous. "I don't want the bedpan," she argues. "I want to try to make it to the bathroom." I comply with her requests when she shows the will to fight. Lowering her onto the toilet frightens me as I fear my strength will give out and

I may drop her. When she shows concern I may wrench my back, I pretend to be Superwoman.

I pray constantly for strength and this God gives me. In abundance. My energy is boundless and I rarely weary; nor does my back give out despite my misgivings. Towards the end of the first week, Mom can no longer raise herself up from the bed. I tell her to clasp both her arms around my neck and distribute her weight there. I always find some way of lifting her.

Eve often sits by her grandmother's bed and holds her hand. I witness Mom's strain as she tries to smile and make conversation with the little girl she loves. I allow the children only a few moments with her which is the most I know she can handle. "I feel so sorry for the children," she says mournfully. "I'm in so much pain, I have trouble hiding it. I don't like them to see me like this. I don't want them to feel unhappy."

I soon come to realize Mom's experience in hospital has injured her very soul. Sometimes she asks me woefully, "Why were they so cruel to me, Irene?" Her eyes fill with tears. Mainly she refers to Dr. Greer who glibly disregarded my request, and callously informed her of her impending death . . . leaving me with her broken remains. I have no real answer to her entreaty.

"Try not to personalize, Mom. Some people should never be in a helping profession." That's all I can think of to say.

She now becomes terrified if I have to leave, even to run an errand. "No!" she cries. "Please, Irene, don't leave me! You're all I have. I don't want to be left with anyone else!" Her eyes reflect stark panic. She has finally been rendered phobic, and who can relate more to her fear? I promise her I won't leave.

In the interim I cancel an appointment with Dr. Richards, explaining how childlike and fearful my mother has become. He, too, completely understands.

My heart breaks for my mother. What did she ever do to deserve such misery? Sadness pierces my heart for the heavy cross she bears.

She's rapidly becoming less lucid. For brief intervals she's clear in her speech and fights bravely for her life. More often than not, she shows little interest in carrying on. In her clear moments, I occasionally ask if she'd like to talk about her illness, or concerns. I want her to know I'm not afraid to help her face whatever lies ahead. I know she's fully cognizant–at least on some level–that the end is near; yet she continues to pretend. For herself? For me? I have no way of knowing.

I only know she does not want to discuss death and I respect her wishes.

The first time she accidentally soils the bed she weeps bitter tears. "I'm so sorry, so sorry," she reiterates over and over. I'm unable to console her. She's completely mortified to have been reduced to a state where her daughter needs to change her like a baby. This terrible illness has stripped away her last shred of dignity.

From the depths of my soul, I try to find words to convince her of the truth: I don't mind in the slightest. "You don't know how much joy it gives me to help you, Mom," I assure her sincerely. "I feel I'm returning a tiny smidgeon of what you've given me. Please allow me this privilege. Let me give you a part of myself because I love you so much."

Her hand reaches up and gently touches my cheek. "My baby," she murmurs softly. Her tone is infinitely tender and I behold the most exquisite expression of naked love on her face. My heart constricts painfully, and from somewhere inside I hear a little girl's silent plea: *Please Mommy, don't leave me!* I place my head on her breast and her arms enfold me. In that brief moment, I feel completely secure and at peace.

"*Mommy,*" I whisper.

"*My baby,*" she murmurs softly.

For the most part, our roles have been reversed from her illness; she has become *my* child. But in that tender interlude, she's fully lucid and she's *my* mommy again. Disregarding the pain that consumes her, her soul hears my cry, and she reaches out to me in mother love.

The spell breaks and she says, "Oh, Irene, where would I be

without you? I'd have nobody to care for me. I've always thanked God to have you, you know."

She begins to decline more rapidly thereafter. The disease has abased her and mercilessly stolen her self-worth. She retreats more frequently into her inner kingdom, and gradually bars off all entrances. I intuitively know there remains but one–a small passageway she's left open, for me alone. As long as she's able to withstand the horror of her reality, her love will not lock me out. Over the days to follow, I'll crawl through that narrow opening and try to imbue her soul with the strength of my love.

The medication no longer eases her suffering and I'm at a loss. She's always had an exceptionally high level of tolerance to pain, and at times when she says, "Oh, Irene, the pain, it's awful," I wish I could administer something stronger than the maximum dosage allowed by her doctor. After witnessing her hell, I often hide myself in my room and silently cry. I've no idea the end is so near and that she should be on morphine. I'll forever retain my own personal sadness that she left this world suffering the agony of the damned . . . on not more than codeine tablets.

Because I didn't know any better.

One evening, I ask Len about his secret powwow with my mother. "She told me she's very worried about you," he says. "She asked me to promise, should anything happen to her that I would take care of her little girl. I told her how much I loved you, and vowed that I'd always look after you, that she must believe me and have a free mind."

Hearing this, I too begin sobbing, fearing my own heart will break. How much I will miss her love! Yet, how lucky I am that I have my husband. I have not been left comfortless.

A few days later, Mom experiences a new symptom. She's propped up on her pillows and I'm trying to feed her some yogurt. Her eyes are dull and expressionless and she's totally unresponsive to the spoon that I gently press to her lips.

Momentarily, she becomes lucid and says fretfully, "I've lost all feeling in my fingers." I rub her hands within my own in an attempt to stimulate her circulation. "I still feel nothing," she whimpers pitifully.

How horrible to realize you are slipping out of this world when you don't want to die! Her eyes close and she nods off again. I keep her hand in mine and my tears fall unbidden.

Unexpectedly, she opens her eyes. Her voice is distressed. "What's the matter, Irene? Are you okay?"

I search for a plausible answer. "It just hurts me to know you have pain and that you don't feel like eating. I want to help you get well."

"Don't cry," she pleads. "I'll do anything you say." Weak and debilitated and lost in a world of her own, she allows my sadness to draw her back into the horrific reality of *my* world, which greets her with non-stop pain.

"I'll try to eat," she promises me. "I'll do *anything!* Please don't cry." She points to the yogurt, opens her mouth, and she eats every last teaspoonful. Such a horror that must have been for her. And such a gift of love to me.

I'll never cry in front of her again, I promise myself.

On Sunday, her eighth day at home in my care, her face is gray. Her skin is damp with a cold sheen of sweat. Her temperature is too low to even register on the thermometer. Her pulse is faint and irregular and she's totally lifeless as I administer to her. I sense her condition is critical and she needs more help than I'm equipped to give her. She's trying to speak, and as I place my ear close to her lips I decipher the word *bedpan.*

Oh God, her urine is bright red!

I quietly slip out of the room. "Her only hope is the hospital," I inform Len. "If there's any chance they can do something for her, I have to take it. I hate to send her back there. I promised her I wouldn't, but I see no other choice. If she dies here, I'll always blame myself."

He agrees and I call an ambulance. I return to my mother's room absolutely dreading what I must tell her.

"Mom," I say gently. "You have some blood in the urine. You mustn't be frightened. It's probably just a bladder infection, but I don't know how to treat it. I wouldn't forgive myself if something happened to you because I didn't ensure you had the proper care. You'll need to go back in hospital–just for a short time until this thing clears up. Do you understand?" She doesn't respond, and my heart feels as though it's breaking. The doorbell rings. "I'll be right back," I promise.

I explain Mom's condition to the EMT's and tell them how badly she was treated at the previous hospital and ask if she can be taken elsewhere.

"Another hospital will refuse her," they explain. "They'll request she be sent back to where she's been originally treated. We'll be wasting our time to even try."

After examining her they assure me she needs immediate hospitalization. "Please give me a moment alone with her," I beseech them.

I take Mom's hand in my own. She's completely lucid and her pupils are wide with fear as I tell her she'll have to go back to the same hospital.

"It's because your files are there. Another hospital won't accept you. Oh, Mom, I know I promised not to send you back there, and I don't want it to be this way. I just don't know what else to do right now. It won't be for long, and you'll be home again soon. Remember how quickly a few days of antibiotics in your IV cured your last urinary infection? I love you and want you to get better. Please understand," I voice tearfully.

"I understand," she mutters indistinctly; yet her eyes mirror the horror within her heart.

Had I any idea she was so close to the end I would have let her die at home with the love and security of her family surrounding her. If I'd even suspected there was nothing more to be done other than to make her last few days comfortable, I would have honoured my promise to her with such a glad heart . . . and done *anything* to give her that final gift of my love.

Now, as the EMT's strap her on a gurney, I quickly explain to the children that their grandmother has an infection that needs to be treated in the hospital. Eve's mournful eyes belie my words as they follow her grandmother's passage from the bedroom to the front door. My mother's stricken gaze as she views the children contains a world of grief and sorrow and I wonder how much pain the human heart can stand.

I sit with Mom in the ambulance while Len follows by car. Neither of us speaks during the half-hour drive, but for once.

"You'll be okay," I say to the eyes that remain open and fearful.

"Will I?" she replies tonelessly.

"Of course you will. You'll soon be home with us again."

Her eyes betray her disbelief. *I'm going to die,* they tell me. *I don't want to, and I am afraid, but I have no choice. My body and spirit are too weak to fight any longer.*

I lapse into silence, not knowing what else I can say. She *knows.*

Once we arrive at the hospital Mom is placed on a bed in one of the small cubicles in the emergency room. Her eyes are closed. She appears to be in a stupor and I'm unable to arouse her. Her eyes flicker open every so often, but her gaze is vacuous and unresponsive. Occasionally, she mutters unintelligibly.

From time to time, she calls out, "Irene!" I take her hand or stroke her arm and speak gently, assuring her of my presence. She then drifts back into her trance-like state.

At some point, I have the strongest urge to sing the lullaby she composed for me as a child. Perhaps it will give her a sense of comfort and protection. Though she's snoring, the urge overtakes me and I begin to sing softly, lovingly.

"That was a waste," Len comments later. "She hasn't heard a word."

"I *know* she heard." I reply, believing it beyond a doubt.

He grins indulgently. Neither of us expects that the moment of silence which follows will suddenly be broken by Mom's voice raised in song. Her eyes still tightly closed, she begins to sing the words, although slightly garbled, of *Hush-a-bye.*

There's no longer any doubt in Len's mind that Mom's inner receiving station has picked up the lullaby. I'm moved to tears. He gapes at my mother incredulously. "She's singing it in her sleep," he says dumbfounded. "You really *did* know, didn't you?"

By the same token, I continue to believe she hears every word I say to her over the following days. Outwardly, she's impassive. She's finally become fully locked within her inner world from which she'll no longer emerge. Yet my narrow channel of entry has not been totally blocked. She *hears*. And she knows she is not alone.

She's admitted to a room in the terminal section by Dr. Greer. We've had prior words about his disregard of my written wishes, and I'm concerned he'll not forgive me for my angry spiel, and my mother may reap his venom. Conversely, he's inordinately kind. I tell him I don't want her to die alone, that I want to be with her. I ask him how long she has. He says he no longer makes predictions; that he's too often wrong.

"I can only tell you her condition is critical. I'll be keeping her under close surveillance, and I assure you if I notice a further decline I'll inform you immediately," he promises.

I sit by her bedside. Locked in her world, her supper tray remains untouched. Unwilling to leave her just yet, Len departs for the coffee shop to pick up some sandwiches. I use this time to whisper my own eternal truths in her ear. I tell her not to be afraid, that God loves her and is taking care of her; that God is only Love. I ask her to trust in Him; that He will not let her down. It's as though some force compels me to brainwash her with enough love to eradicate all the fear that resides in the depths of her soul.

I will do this every chance I get.

The following day, I check her body from head to toe. There are no signs of artificial attachments. I look beneath the covers and am appalled to see her toes are completely blue. I later notice that both her breasts are the same gruesome colour. She is losing her circulation and I'm aware this does not bode well.

Alarmed, I approach the nurse at the desk. She assures me she's aware of this and that the doctor has been apprised. I ask for an explanation but she's completely evasive and insists I speak with Dr. Greer.

It's only later that I would realize the hospital had left my mother in God's hands. In my own state of shock and incomprehension it did not occur to me that her lack of attachments–and the fact she could no longer eat or drink–signified as much.

"They won't tell me anything, Len," I say. "She's going to die very soon. I feel it. Please, would you take a few days off? I'd like you to be with me when it happens."

"The doctor said it could go on a month or more, he can't predict. I can't stay off indefinitely."

"He also said it can happen *any* time. Please," I beg, "Please, just *believe* me. I know it will happen very soon. Within the next few days. She's very close to death right now."

He regards me doubtfully, and I continue. "I'm so certain that I promise you one thing. Take two more days off. Until Wednesday latest. If she's still hanging in, I won't say a word. You can go back to work."

That night I call my mother's only sibling, her older brother who is now retired and living with my aunt in the Pacific Northwest. I also call her best friend, along with Dave, our minister. The latter two individuals promise to be at the hospital the next day and my uncle says he'll fly in as soon as possible.

On Tuesday, Len and I spend the day with Mom. Her fingers are now turning blue as well. The minister drops in for an hour. He sits near her, gently stroking her arm, and speaking softly to her the whole while. He says prayers for all of us and promises to return the following day. Her friend drops in later, and we become so emotional we have to leave her room for the lounge where we weep copiously together.

Through all this, I'm thankful for the Nardil which is keeping me together. I'm overcome with sadness, but I'm rational and not flipping out.

Before leaving, I whisper in my mother's ear. "I'll be back in the morning, Mom. I know you hear me. Please wait for me."

A sense of total peace engulfs me. I *know* she'll honour my request.

My uncle calls that night. "I've made my flight arrangements," he says. "I'll be arriving at 5:00 PM. your time Thursday evening. I wanted to come sooner but I have a doctor's appointment tomorrow which is quite important. I pray she'll last."

"Me, too. I'm just so glad you'll be coming in."

Early the next morning, Wednesday, I receive a call from the hospital. Mom's vital signs are declining and it's only a matter of hours. Dana has already left for school, and I call Tish.

"Don't worry about a thing, Renie. Charlie and I are on our way over. We'll be there for Dana when she comes home at lunch. Take as much time as you need. You're my twin after all," she says fondly, "and I love you."

I feel a sense of urgency to get to the hospital as quickly as possible. I'm waiting at the door with Len in a fever of impatience when my friends arrive. It seems to take forever to drive to the hospital and I tap my foot restively as I wait for the elevator to transport us to the sixth floor.

I zoom past the nurses' station and burst into Mom's room. I'm weak with relief to see her form beneath the covers, and I utter a prayer of thanks to have found her alive. Regaining my composure, I sit on the edge of her bed.

"It's me, Irene, your baby," I whisper softly in her ear. "I'll be staying with you now. I won't leave your side."

I place her hand in mine and kneed the blue fingers between my own as though this futile act will restore her circulation. I press my warm lips against her hand, momentarily overcome with the burning desire to heal her with my kiss.

A raw grief and compassion sears through me as I view the wasted creature that was once my strong, dauntless mother. Scalded by the multitude of emotions her defenceless form evokes, I yearn to give her comfort. She's lying on her side and I climb onto her bed and spoon my body against her pitiful shell, placing an arm tenderly around her in the hope she may draw succour from my warmth. I say a prayer that I may, in her final moments, find words to uplift her.

From somewhere beyond my ken, words of total love begin flowing freely from my lips to her ears as my very soul seeks to merge with her own. I speak continuously for several minutes. Finally, I ask God to help her cross over in peace.

At this self-same moment, I'm overcome with a sense of absolute Love–an unremitting joy and serenity I've never before encountered. As I open my eyes, the whole room seems to radiate with light and I know beyond doubt that I'm safe and loved. It's as though God's own hand holds mine. Surely I've united with the ecstasy of heaven.

The bliss gradually begins to fade, imbuing me with the awareness that my mother's soul is crossing over. My eyes fleetingly seek her face as I hold her hand and watch her draw her last breath.

Her painful journey is over.

JULY 25. 2012, WEDNESDAY

Gary has recently completed his fourth and final cycle of chemo, which hopefully marks the end of the poison. And poison it is. He's now had a total of sixteen doses of it but on the bright side, so has the cancer. It's not been easy on him. He's suffered vomiting, nausea, fatigue, lethargy, hair loss, and neutropenia. Throughout, he's maintained a great morale and, unusual for one so young, has not bemoaned his plight. We pray it will all be worth it. He'll now be free until his next scans in a few weeks, which will tell us whether or not he's in remission.

On a spiritual level, I've come to understand we must honour each soul's personal choice in regard to the time they choose to leave this world; which is when on a deeper level they intuitively know they've accomplished whatever they set out to do. Love, if it's to be egoless, must be all inclusive; not exclusive to our own wishes.

*Yet, who is actually cognitive of the true desires of the soul—either one's own, or another's? And what of the soul's choice **now**? Can that not override a pre-birth choice?*

I believe one's current desire, if sustained and emotionalized by faith, is the deciding factor. On a conscious level, Gary chooses to live.

So, Gary the Brave, may your choice—along with the help of the multitude of prayers surrounding you—grant you many more years of life!

Chapter 18 –
When the Bough Breaks...

"The children have to save themselves,
because the parents have no idea"...
—*<u>Donnie Darko</u>*

My mother is laid to rest on June 16th. As I stand by her gravesite with Len, Eve, my uncle, and three dear friends by my side–Leila, Jane, and Tish–I visualize my little girl, Star, running freely through these same grounds on that glorious day so many years ago, chasing squirrels and joyfully picking me wildflowers.

On that same day, Mom had stood in this exact spot, at her own parents' graves. Now, she and Star have both joined them.

I reflect upon the words of the poem I recently discovered in her night table drawer which she wrote prior to going into hospital last March: *Don't weep for me, I will be free, no worries and cares, just peacefully be; in one long sleep, never say die; my spirit will live, so it's not goodbye.*

Her soul knew all along.

How little we know of what the future holds, and surely that is well. Do we really wish to know the brevity of time we have left with our loved ones? Or the precise moment that fickle fortune will snatch away our joy and cast us into the valley of sorrow?

In these fleeting moments, as I bid my mother a final goodbye, I recall another poem, the first and last one I ever wrote for my mother. It was a Mother's Day poem I composed for her last year and I entitled it, "My Mother". The words of the last verse flow back to me now: *Her legacy of love I'll hold, in my heart's treasure chest; planted in forget-me-nots, for she who loved me best . . . my mother.*

Perhaps my *own* soul knew all along.

I will profoundly miss her presence on my journey.

The following morning, as I sit in bed sipping my first cup of coffee, Eve joins me. "I saw Granny again last night," she says. "Before I went to sleep. I know I wasn't dreaming."

"I believe you, sweetie. Will you tell me about it?" My personal quest since Star's death has taught me that all things are possible.

"Well, it happened like it did the previous night. I was thinking about her and she suddenly appeared and sat on top of my toy box again. I told her how much I loved and missed her, and asked her why she left us. She said, 'Granny was very sick, and I had to leave you, Eve. But I will always love you and watch over you.' I'm so sad to lose Granny, but it's starting to scare me when she appears like that."

"I understand your feelings, Eve. Much as I'd like to see her myself, I think it would unnerve me as well. If she comes back, tell her truthfully that her appearances are scaring you. Once she knows you're afraid, it won't happen again. She loves you too much to ever want to frighten you."

"Okay, Mommy. I just don't want to make her feel bad."

"Oh Eve, don't ever worry about that. You could *never* make your grandmother feel bad. She knows how much you love her. That's why she appears to you, to try and comfort you by letting you know that she's watching over you. She'll always love and be near you, even if you no longer see her."

Losing her beloved grandmother has been hardest for Eve. Dana is still too young to fully comprehend things, and Keith was not as close with Mom. My own grief has touched Eve as well. Recently, she heard me crying in my bedroom and came in.

"Please, Mommy," she implored me, "don't shut me out. I loved Granny, too. Let me share the sadness with you. We can cry together."

I'm truly guilty of shutting my little girl out. Today, I realize what a mature soul resided in her young body; yet I was afraid of upsetting her with my grief and preferred to force a smile and hide it from her. She was not fooled. I'm only sorry I was not equally evolved. For surely I would have thanked her for offering me such a precious gift. And willingly cried with her.

My predictions to Eve regarding her grandmother's appearances hold true. Eve sees her one final time, tells her how frightened she is, and Mom never appears again. Over the years, Eve loses all recall of this experience.

I've no doubt Mom is very close to us following her death. Occasionally, upon awakening from an afternoon nap, I become steeped in the knowledge that she is with me. I never see her, but I feel her presence so strongly that my soul feels comforted.

One afternoon when Keith awakens me from a nap, he exclaims: "Oh, my God, I feel as though someone's in the room with us, Mom! I'm really scared."

His intuition confirms my own. "I feel it as well, Keith, so please don't worry. It's a loving presence, and you've nothing to fear. It's your grandmother watching over us." He takes this in stride, and is even somewhat pleased that he's been able to intuit it.

Although this is the one and only time Keith admits to having this otherworldly experience, the sense of my mother's presence abides with me for six months or so. It, along with the Nardil, helps me cope with my grief.

On my next visit to Dr. Richards, I tell him how grateful I am to have finally found relief from my mental suffering.

"I had no idea how depressed I actually was prior to the Nardil which has significantly raised my mood. Having existed in such a low emotional state for so many years, it had become the norm. I actually forgot there was any other way of life."

"I'm happy to hear that, Mrs. Snow. Many of my patients have expressed similar sentiments. Mental pain is as grievous as physical pain, and often more so. It's important to find a way to relieve *all* forms of suffering."

He goes on to say how pleased he is that I've come through my mother's death relatively unscathed, mentally and emotionally, and he urges me to begin taking some constructive steps to overcome my agoraphobia. "Gradually," he advises, "as you feel ready."

Len's holidays roll around at the end of July. Our family has now dwindled down to five of us in the home: Len, me, and the three young children. Over the past four years, both Mark and Ken have left home to get married.

Len's brother offers us the use of his country home for a week. It's located about fifty miles away in a densely-treed, mountainous area which borders on a small lake with a sandy shore. His rustic cottage is nestled between magnificent firs and evergreens that infuse the air with the tangy scents of cedar, pine and spruce. Once happily ensconced within, we all express our delight at the peace and beauty in our midst. Spying the mountain trails that surround us, I promise myself that once we're unpacked, I'll begin my therapeutic walks again. Dr. Richards has made me aware that the only way to eliminate my dread is to face it. Again and again. Until its demise is certain.

The fear—when I recommence my walks alone—often skyrockets.

But I now understand this is a conditioned response that is limited to these particular occasions, and my elevated mood serves as a buffer to strengthen my resolve. Thanks to my meds, I know my preliminary dread will not spill over into panic attacks or a generalized anxiety condition. In order to subdue my initial apprehension, Dr. Richards permits me to take a tranquilizer. By the time the week is over I've significantly increased the distance of my solitary walks and, as my confidence increases, my dosage of Valium decreases.

By early fall, we trade in our car for a brand new half-ton pickup truck. Dr. Richards has reminded me of the importance of beginning to drive on my own again. The prolonged period of Mom's illness has brought me back to the starting gate in most areas. I know I must remain consistent and not deviate in my therapies if I ever hope to overcome my phobia. With this in mind, I decide to get back behind the wheel.

On my first drive alone, I surpass my previous record by at least two miles. The following day I manage a few more miles. On the third day, I absolutely astound myself by driving a full fifteen miles to the centre of the city where I'm forced to creep through a flow of heavy, slow-moving traffic. Rather than being possessed with the usual fear, I'm overcome with the elation that I've managed this great feat, and I feel my anxiety drain through my pores, thanks to the incredible feeling of control this accomplishment has given me. Within the knowledge that I'm beginning to master my own destiny again, I perceive a glorious sense of freedom and I silently utter my gratitude to Dr. Richards. And to God for leading me to him.

Aware that I could never have achieved such incredible progress on my own, I write Dr. Richards a note of thanks which I attach to a condensed version of my memoirs similar to the one I once compiled for Dr. Tolhurst. I conclude by highlighting the incredible gains I've made with the combined help of our talks and the antidepressant medication.

It's not without trepidation that I present him these notes on our next appointment. Unsettling memories of Dr. Tolhurst rush to the fore as I recall his total disregard for my previous efforts. But now, as Dr. Richards scans my journal, my original fears dissipate before his warm smile.

"What a joy it will be to read your memoirs!" he exclaims. "I can hardly wait. However, I don't want my reading to detract from our verbal dialogue at this particular moment. I want to know how you've been doing since our last visit."

I'm beside myself with pleasure as I elaborate on my recent achievements. "For the first time in over a decade, since my panic disorder first began, I've driven all the way downtown on my own," I relate proudly.

"That's absolutely wonderful news, Mrs. Snow," he beams.

So unlike my shrinks of the past, his genuine delight is heartwarming. And there is no time wasted in dwelling on my childhood. He is solely interested in the *now*. After a lengthy chat, he gives me an appointment for two weeks hence.

I'm totally unprepared for the proposal he presents me with at our next session.

"First, Mrs. Snow, I want you to know how much I've enjoyed your memoirs. They are extremely well-presented and I actually *lived* them with you. You mentioned in your journal that you have entertained the hope of writing a book one day, and I believe you should follow your dream.

"I'd like to propose you write your autobiography. I've recently read the published story of an agoraphobic, which in my opinion is in no way comparable to yours in either content or quality. Furthermore, your remarkable progress on Nardil to date lends great credence to my belief in treating such problems on a biological–as opposed to a purely psychological–level. Mind you, I'm not belittling the latter. The fact remains, however, that a patient cannot be expected to successfully fight a phobia when in a severely depressed state–no matter *how* that state came about."

He pauses. "So tell me, what do you think of my suggestion?"

"I don't know what to say. I'm amazed you would find me capable of such a feat. Amazed and delighted! I would *love* to try. Do you really think I would have a chance of publishing my work?"

"Absolutely. During the time I practiced psychiatry in New York City prior to re-locating here, I treated a few patients from the publishing world. We have kept in touch, and I know I could have your manuscript reviewed by one of them as based upon my personal recommendation. Your work is eminently readable."

"I can't believe I've been lucky enough to find you, Dr. Richards. Not only am I making great strides in my illness for the first time in years, but you've given me the confidence to take a stab at a lifelong dream. I'll start writing immediately!"

"Godspeed, Mrs. Snow."

The next day, after discussing Dr. Richards's proposal in detail with Len, we gather the children together to review it with them. They're now aged thirteen, ten and six respectively and, after filling them in, I conclude by saying honestly, "It won't be an easy time for any of us. The book will entail a lot of work over the next several months. I'll have to ask all of you to pitch in and help more often than before. Whether there'll be a reward at the end, I can't promise. I can only say that if my book gets published—and more importantly, *if* it becomes a hit—we'll have a lot more money than we have now, and we'll be able to do a lot more interesting things together. Bottom line though, kids . . . there's no guarantee."

What wonderful, supportive children! They all tell me to go for it and promise they'll help all they can. Even to my little Dana who, at barely age six, looks out for me daily by checking my pill vial and often reminding me to take my medication. Len is behind me all the way as well.

Thrilled with my green light, I sit before the electric typewriter Mom bought me last December—her final Christmas gift. And a very special one whereby she expressed the hope I'd one day use it to follow my dream of writing a book. *Wish me luck, Mom,* I whisper silently. *And, thank you!*

Before beginning, I reflect on how the relationship between Len and me has improved over the past year since we reached another important agreement. We solemnly vowed to never again destroy our personal property, or assault each another physically. I told him *irene snow*

I could no longer live like an animal and that if he were not in full agreement, I could no longer live with him. He readily complied. He, too, had reached his personal limits. That is not to say our arguments do not still blossom fully on occasion. Moreover, it's to signify that we've remained faithful to our promise, and have refrained from being physically abusive or destructive.

I slip a blank page into my typewriter and entitle my book, *Humpty Dumpty*. I believe the title describes me to a tee.

I apply myself to my book as I apply myself to everything else in life that captivates me: heart and soul. I observe no limits. Len and the children outdo themselves with their unfailing and uncomplaining help and support. I unwisely do the same by refusing to pace myself. My motto: the book should have been finished yesterday.

In between writing, I occasionally make time to indulge in my therapies. I know it's important to not become complacent and lose ground again. I'm now able to do just about anything on my own, and I know I'm close to being the person I was before the agoraphobia existed. The therapies are at a minimum, however. As are my household duties. I'm unaware of how deeply exhausted I'm becoming from the long hours I sit at my typewriter. One of the side effects of the Nardil is an incredible increase in energy. I now sleep very little without noticing any consequences. I believe my rest is adequate, because I do not feel particularly tired.

Within three months, I've written approximately four hundred pages. I estimate at least another fifty are needed to complete the first draft of my manuscript. I want to reduce the content to not more than three hundred pages in the final editing.

It's now December, and I wisely decide to take a break for Christmas.

The next week or so is spent in a flurry of last minute holiday shopping for the children. Often Tish and I shop together and she remarks on my energy.

"I can't keep up with you, Irene. I find the energy you have since you've been on Nardil is unnatural. It's manic in nature. Perhaps you

324

might want to discuss decreasing your dosage with your doctor. I'm worried about you."

That is the *last* thing I want to do. I've never known such a buzz. I feel absolutely euphoric and I'm relishing every moment of my high!

As the New Year of 1981 dawns, I become interested in learning more about certain elements of my formative years that may have led to certain predilections that motivated some of my self-defeating behaviour. I decide it would be interesting to do a self-analysis and perhaps incorporate some specific findings into my book. If I'm to do this, I'm not without the realization that I have a lot to learn.

And so begins an extensive search which will continue over the next several years.

I begin by purchasing an encyclopedia on human behaviour which I supplement with the purchase of similar texts, all related to the field of psychology. While not discounting the biological angle (the genes inherited from my mother that predisposed me to being more mentally fragile), my research leads me to a clearer understanding of the early psychological factors that were present as well, and that likely played a role in my own particular journey . . . and possibly my eventual downfall.

Aside from becoming aware of how we tend to role-play and frequently transform our earliest perceptions into self-fulfilling prophecies I recognize that ego, being geared to survive, perceives the two polarities of the survival pole as "control", and "loss of control"–the former representing "life" and the latter representing "death". From this, it becomes apparent that for the majority of us our greatest fear is loss of control. A fear that undoubtedly gave birth to ego's defense mechanisms.

In reviewing ego's desire for control, it also becomes obvious that anger is its most trusted henchman: by judging and blaming others, and thus winning points, ego maintains a simulation of control over its environment. However, when life deals blows that can no longer be manipulated or assuaged by anger (or faith), ego experiences a distinct loss of power. Anger is then forced to back down (turn inward), and one of the lower tone levels such as depression, anxiety, fear, or apathy may follow. The lowest levels can be associated with a "breakdown". A breakdown of ego, such as my own . . . each in its own way unique.

Years later when I delve into the spiritual aspect of life I will come to realize that, in moving away from Love (our higher self), it is truly our spirit that becomes shattered.

I show Dr. Richards my work which, at this juncture, deals solely with psychology. It is still unfinished, but he peruses it with interest. "I find your work evocative," he states. "However, research is extremely time-consuming. You might want to finish your memoirs first. Once your book sells, if you're still contemplating a theory of sorts, you'll be able to afford to hire people to do the grunge work for you. That alone will make the job a lot less strenuous and time-consuming."

I explain the importance of interspersing some snippets of my corollaries into the book itself. "Perhaps they may shed some light on the subjective tug that seems to unwittingly prompt us all. I really want to help others, if I can," I explain.

I know he believes my wisest choice is to complete my book, first and foremost; nevertheless, he accedes to my particular aspiration in view of its importance to me.

I become lost in my dream. I'm unaware that I'm neglecting the needs of my family. My children are growing older and I'm losing the best years of their lives, whilst they in turn are losing the mothering they need. I will live to regret my choices—choices I falsely believe will eventually benefit us all.

Meanwhile, I'm scarcely aware of the strain I'm under regarding the enormity of my project. The sky's the limit, but I will fail to reach it. Unaware of my limitations, I've set myself up for another fall.

Humpty Dumpty is far from together.

Tish calls me from the hospital one afternoon. Her adult son, a paraplegic, has uremia again. It's at a toxic level. "He has less than a one percent change to survive until morning," she sobs. I console her as best I can and promise to drop over as soon as she returns home.

Strangely unsettled, I rest on my bed and meditate. During this quiet time, the strangest thing happens. I'm suddenly infused with peace and love and the actual *knowing* that Tish's son will pull through and *live*. Aware I've received an actual prophecy for the first time, I later share the wonderful news with Tish. She longs to believe it but, understandably, fear holds her back.

The following morning she rings me early. "The doctor just called and says it's a miracle. There is now concrete hope that my boy will pull through. His chances have risen to 50%. I believe it now, wholeheartedly. He *is* going to live!"

I discuss this with Dr. Richards on my next appointment. "I can't believe this happened to me. I've never had any psychic ability in the past," I confide.

"It's the Nardil, Mrs. Snow," he discloses. "Several of my patients on this medication have mentioned becoming more attuned to such phenomena. I recall you telling me about the revelation you experienced when your mother crossed over—your feeling of uniting with *Absolute Love*. This is another example of paranormal experiences patients have experienced on Nardil."

I accept his explanation, but feel profoundly deflated. I had hoped it was a new facet of *me*; that *I* was becoming more intuitive. It is disappointing to attribute it to the mood lift I've attained from my meds.

Similar experiences would follow while on Nardil. Much as I'd like to connect more intuitively with my Source, none have recurred since ceasing the medication; but I'm no longer disheartened. The experience itself has lent full credibility to heretofore undreamt of possibilities. And who's to know? Perhaps one day I may experience a naturally-elevated state that leads to same . . . if the time should become right.

The months pass quickly and when Len's holidays arrive in July, we decide on a motor trip to visit my uncle and aunt in the Pacific Northwest. It's a long drive and we expect to be on the road for several days. We tell the kids to pack whatever clothes and games they want to bring with them in the rear of the truck which is completely enclosed. We fill our cooler with sandwiches and drinks before hitting the road. The kids are ecstatic.

By the time of this trip, I'm entirely off Nardil. I recently decided to see if I could manage without it by gradually decreasing my daily dosage of four 15 mg. tablets to zero. Over the past few weeks, I'm offsetting my edginess with the occasional Valium tablet. Extremely nervous about this long trip, I splurge on a bottle of cherry brandy for the road.

I'm decidedly hyper throughout the voyage, despite the several slugs of brandy I imbibe along the way. I'm inclined to turn back but don't want to disappoint Len and the children. Somehow, we finally arrive, and I'm still in one piece.

We find an affordable motel which borders on the Pacific Ocean. It also sports a large swimming pool, and the kids are in their glory. My uncle and aunt visit daily for the two weeks of our holiday. We have dinner together and play cards in the evenings. I adore both of them, and it is such a joy to spend this time in their company. I take a few Valium tablets to get through my day, and I have a few cocktails with our visitors in the evening which helps me through the night.

The holiday is enjoyable for all of us, and it goes by without a hitch insofar as I don't experience any outright panic, but I do know my anxiety has reached a higher level. On the drive home I rely solely on Valium which has a more calming effect than the booze.

Once home, I confess to Dr. Richards that I stopped the medication and am reverting back to a depressed state. He does not reproach me for not consulting him prior to my decision and renews my prescription for Nardil. I expect he realizes I've learned the lesson that I'm clinically depressed.

I'm unaware my Nardil high is not exactly normal. I *am* aware of how wonderful it is to finally be removed from the mental agony of chronic anxiety and depression again. It's such a relief to be in a more elevated state. The fact that I'm perhaps *too* happy is not something I care to question or discuss with my doctor.

I continue with my work and do not question my serious lack of sleep. I'm deeply involved in my research and there are not enough hours in the day as is.

While Nardil has been my mainstay to date, Dr. Richards has experimented with antidepressants that are not of the MAO Inhibitor variety to see how I'll fare. One, in particular, is Imipramine, which does not prevent me from having a severe panic attack during the time I'm taking it. This is to my detriment as it leads to another setback whereby I'm back at square one for a time. Consequently, Nardil becomes my drug of choice . . . and that of my doctor as well.

By summer of 1985, I've been on Nardil approximately five years. Len and I decide we've had enough of apartment living and I call my friend Jane, currently a real estate agent who is now living in the western suburbs of Cassellman. Enchanted with the tranquility of the pastoral area in which she resides, which is rife with a bountiful array of mature trees and green space, we decide to buy a house there. She patiently drives us around the vicinity until we fall upon the home of our choice: a three-bedroom bungalow on a large lot. The basement is partially-finished, containing a playroom; the larger, unfinished portion allows plenty of room for Len to incorporate a second bathroom, and a fourth bedroom.

It's during this property search that I become more aware of how tired I actually am. I no longer have the boundless energy I did in the past. I'm also slightly off balance and prone to falling. My legs just give out occasionally and I find myself on the ground. I've no idea why this does not ring a warning bell. Prior to taking the Nardil, I would have been exceedingly worried about what was happening to me. In my current euphoric state nothing much concerns me and such incidents more often than not fill me with mirth. I fail to recognize how out of character this is and I see no reason to mention

329

these occurrences to Dr. Richards. I'm just not aware that anything abnormal is happening to me.

"What's the matter, Irene?" my friend asks as she sees me stumbling. "You're walking about like a drunk."

"Well, I haven't been drinking. I think it's exhaustion. I'm too tired to stay on my feet lately."

"That's not good, my friend. I think you've been overdoing things in general, and now—in view of looking for a new house and a probable move—it's more important than ever that you think of pacing yourself. You need to get more rest or you'll be sick."

"Yes, Doctor Jane. Thanks for the diagnosis. How much do I owe you for the service?" I quip.

"I'm very serious, Irene," she rebukes me sternly.

"I know, I know. Sorry. I don't mean to undermine your concern."

Once settled in our new home in early July, I seriously contemplate my considerable lack of vitality, and decide it must be due to burnout. I've had little energy for my work, or anything much else for quite some time now, and my memoirs and research remain incomplete. Bank statements and other concerns are piling up on the back burner. There are still scores of boxes left to be unpacked from our move. Just getting out of bed is becoming a feat in itself, and I find I'm beginning to spend more and more time *in* bed. I've become chronically fatigued and my previous flow of energy has been sapped. Yet I'm still unable to sleep more than a few hours a night.

At this point in time, my writings, theory and research come to a standstill. I haven't the foggiest idea that this "temporary hiatus" in regard to the actual completion of my memoirs will span the next three decades.

Meanwhile, I try to spend some quality time with my children, yet I no longer have the energy to go back to the way things were before I started my writing and research. This is extremely sad because the years are flying by much too quickly. Keith—slender, dark-haired and attractive—is already quite grown-up, having celebrated his eighteenth birthday last February. Eve's fifteenth birthday followed shortly afterward in the same month. Her ears have long since been surgically corrected and she has bloomed into a lovely young woman. She's tall and slim with classic features, full lips, thickly-lashed chocolate eyes and long, blond hair. Even little Dana is quite grown-up . . . a beautiful, child-woman with her dark, shoulder-length silken locks and iridescent hazel eyes which sometimes morph to a shimmering, emerald green. Bubbly and effervescent, she embraces life head-on. Today, on her eleventh birthday, she's a picture to behold in her pink, frilly dress. It's to be solely a family party this year as the children have not yet met any new friends. We'll have a BBQ outdoors with cake and ice cream for dessert. Despite my lack of energy, these special occasions are always a priority.

Drained for the most part, I'm unable to spend much time with my children. Quality time wherein I can truly lend an ear and *hear* them. The best I'm able to do is prioritize regarding their physical needs: their medical and dental appointments; shopping with them for personal items; and chauffeuring them places when necessary. Len and I occasionally bring them to visit Mark and Ken who have children of their own now, and reside about an hour's drive away. It's important they continue to interact with their older siblings and their families. Merry, from what we've learned from the grapevine, now lives in a city several hundred miles away. Not that this is of consequence at this juncture as she's not been in contact since her departure many years ago.

When school starts in the fall, I enroll both Eve and Dana in evening Judo classes which they both enjoy. A year later when Eve turns sixteen she joins a driver's education program at her school in order to obtain the driver's license she covets. Once she achieves it, I let her drive my truck to and from school. My energy has declined to a point that I rarely drive during the day anymore, and the daily chores I previously managed have fallen to an all-time low.

During this time, my relationship with Len has become rockier. We don't see eye-to-eye regarding the discipline of the children. In my estimation, he's far too strict with them. A small misdemeanor can lead to him grounding them for a month.

There's no way I can reason with him in regard to his ridiculous punishments. In the end, I simply go against him and tell the kids they are no longer grounded and I allow them to go out. He, of course, is furious and another blitzkrieg ensues. Fortunately, our wars remain verbal in deference to our previous vows.

During these times I curse the fatigue and uncertainty that keeps me tied to my marriage, which I believe I'd leave if I were self-supporting and well. Len and I are at constant logger-heads over the children, especially when he occasionally strikes them, at which time I feel as enraged and trapped as when my own dad let loose on me so many years ago.

There is also Len's possessiveness to contend with, which has always been a source of unresolved conflict between us. He resents the time I spend on the phone with old friends—I've not had the energy or the will to make new ones—deeming it detracts from attention that should rightfully be his. If I could devote myself to him alone, he would be the happy, giving person he was during my breakdown.

But I need more.

We both do.

In hindsight we were angry with ourselves. We resented the unresolved hang-ups and needs that led to our dependence upon each other, and blame became a handy defense mechanism. Long ago, we'd sniffed out each other's insecurities and knew the buttons to push for war or peace.

Do I believe this man was a pre-birth choice? Absolutely. Like all of us, he was a mixture of both the good and the not-so-good. He was my teacher; as I was his. Our road was filled with love and pain alike. Both were a necessary part of our growth. The fact that we were two very controlling (i.e. insecure) individuals, led to many sparks. We did not handle things well.

Years later, we still have our angry moments, but they're far more trivial and superficial. Once over, there's neither blame, nor judgment. For the most part, we accept each other unconditionally.

Surely, if we'd possessed the coveted 20/20 vision of hindsight back then, it would have naught but hindered whatever worthwhile fragment of evolvement our souls were in need of attaining on their journey from darkness to light.

I discuss my sleep problems and lack of energy with Dr. Richards on our next appointment.

"The insomnia is undoubtedly a side-effect of the Nardil," he informs me. "However, you've not fared well on other forms of antidepressant medication we've tried in the past. I think it best to keep you on Nardil, and I'll prescribe Desyrel as a sleep aid."

One day runs into another. My sleep does not improve. I spend more time in bed in the hopes of gaining some extra shut-eye and increasing my lagging energy. I'm still unable to accomplish more than a minimum of duties. Research and writing remains at a halt. Avid reader that I've been all my life, I no longer have the wherewithal to even pick up a novel for light entertainment.

I now look forward to the rare good day.

As home chores drastically pile up, my concerns multiply and I'm beside myself over my inability to be on top of things. I implore the children to assist me, and offer them an increase in allowance as a reward. Except for the rare spurt of energy, I'm absolutely taxed to try and perform the most menial duties. Between the Nardil and the Desyrel, I wonder if I'm mixing uppers and downers, and if the Desyrel–being more of a relaxant–is responsible for taking the edge off my previous high. I have no idea. Nor does it occur to me to discuss this with my doctor. I just seem to accept things as they are.

Perhaps it's the sleep deprivation over such a long period that is subjecting me to more frequent mood swings and irritability of late. I have less patience with the children and I become irrationally angry at the slightest provocation. A molehill becomes a mountain. I have little control over my moods and consistently overreact. I'm blind to the effect this is having on my children. And I'm totally unaware that I'm not acting normally.

I can no longer see beyond the woes of daily living, and can barely drag myself through the day. My indiscretions are varied and plentiful. I act unwisely and rashly. Our move has uprooted me and removed me from the support system of close friends. Even Jane has disappeared from my life, having moved to the West Coast. I'm inclined to regard my children more as peers, and this sorely deprives them of the parental guidance they need. This, too, is beyond my ken. I have no idea how much some of my actions are hurting my kids.

By 1986, a year after our move, Keith tells us he's moving out. He is only nineteen. This appears to be totally out of the blue, but only because I've not foreseen it. Keith has had enough, from both his father and me.

I'm unaware of my part in his decision, or even his father's. I beg him to change his mind, but he's adamant in his resolve. I sob myself to sleep the night he leaves, reflecting upon some of the fun times we've shared "as friends", discussing some of our favourite subjects while he's been perched at the end of my bed, or–during my infrequent energy spurts–going on shopping excursions together which we both enjoyed. I can only remember the good times. They're forever behind me now. My son has left the nest and I only know I'm heartbroken.

The night of his departure I dream that someone has ruthlessly chopped down one of the two stately, pine trees on our front lawn–imposing, majestic trees that were part of my initial desire to purchase the house. Beautiful trees that I dearly love and are a part of me. I am devastated. Yowling in despair, I awaken in tears.

I know in an instant that the fallen tree is symbolic of Keith, and that I am mourning the loss of my son.

My initial writing and research had led to a working relationship with Dr. Richards which gradually blossomed into a friendship. He gave me carte blanche for Friday night meetings following the departure of his last patient. These get-togethers gradually fused into social occasions. Generally hungry, we would naturally gravitate to discussing work-related issues over dinner and wine. Despite the current fatigue which has brought my writing to a halt, our Friday night meetings have continued, although I now make certain to arrange a rendezvous on the rare Friday that my energy is at a more optimal level.

In retrospect, perhaps it's my pleasure in his friendship that prevents me from revealing the complete picture of my predicament and how truly debilitated I've become. I thoroughly enjoy his company and I know he finds me entertaining as well. Our evenings together–completely platonic in nature–have become the rare times I'm able to feel good about myself, and especially since I'm no longer able to tackle my dream of writing *The Great American Novel*. The idea that this brilliant doctor will avidly discuss his work and endeavours with me–and at times, actively seek my feedback–is, to me, not only of keen interest considering my own particular passion for psychiatry itself, but a badge of honour. *Nothing* must jeopardize these coveted social evenings.

On one of these get-togethers, he tells me he believes I have a fear of success.

"You have the classic symptoms. One of which is sabotaging yourself just prior to reaching the finish line. It seems to me you have done this with your book. It is something you might want to think about," he suggests.

"I'm absolutely intrigued," I say, and mean it. "You've likely hit the nail on the head. I could have been trained for swimming in the Olympics at one time. I assumed it was rebellion against my dad that made me desist. Yet, I do recall feeling acutely anxious when being confronted with the chance to possibly succeed."

I ruminate on this considerably following our talk, and I think Dr. Richards is probably right. It seems reasonable that he may be thinking my current fatigue can be attributed to my unconscious desire to sabotage myself. And so it may be. Yet, there remains a part of me that wonders if this is the full answer. And there remains another part of me that is too exhausted and downtrodden to truly care.

Several years later there is little change in the status quo. I remain on a cocktail of Nardil and Desyrel. I sleep very little and remain in a state of chronic fatigue which considerably lowers my spirits. During this time my daughters continue to be burdened with far too many responsibilities in the home, the brunt of which falls on Eve, the eldest.

I do not confront Dr. Richards about my lack of improvement. By now, I've accepted this state as my lot in life. I believe nothing more can be done for me. I cancel appointments, and call him on the odd Friday that I experience a mood lift. On these particular get-togethers, I manage to be outgoing and friendly. Above all, I do not want any change to occur regarding our occasional Friday night meetings . . . the one highlight of my life.

By 1991, there's a noticeable and unforeseen development in my condition. Although my medicinal cocktail has not altered, I gradually experience another mood lift. But this one's *extreme*. I'm absolutely exhilarated, and especially in view of the incredible energy I once again possess. I have no desire to sleep. It seems a waste of time in face of the intoxicating glee that's such a stimulating part of my waking hours. Some evenings find me doing a major clean-up at 3:00 AM. Len awakens at times and becomes extremely aggravated to see me scrubbing floors in the middle of the night. From the get-go, he accepted my neurotic behaviour without ever claiming to understand it. To him, it was part and package of the nutbar that I am. Perhaps this is why he finds my behaviour irritating, rather than abnormal.

After years of virtual burnout, this blessed high strikes me as nothing short of manna from heaven. I'm vital and alive, and that alone is a miracle. Unbeknownst to me however, I'm experiencing some distinct behavioural changes which I'll only recognize in hindsight. After diligently saving for years, I'm now revelling in spending sprees and my purchases are frivolous and stupid. I sometimes spend a few hundred dollars a month on Australian lotto tickets, presumably in the hopes of becoming rich and giving my husband and children the good life. Being the sole manager of our finances, I'm responsible for gradually depleting our savings over the next few years.

During this high, I abandon my medication. It's obvious I don't need Nardil or Desyrel. I'm far from despondent. However, I'm becoming increasingly manipulative and confrontational, often embarrassing the children on their social occasions such as judo contests and sports events. I become argumentative with other parents, and especially offended if another child is more favourably rated in a competition than one of my own. At such times, I become paranoid regarding the judge's decision. I believe he or she is playing favourites and I do not hesitate to voice my opinions. This does not sit well with my contemporaries, let alone my children who are upset and humiliated. My apologies–on the rare time I actually recognize my behavioural extremes–do very little to serve as balm for their wounds.

Perhaps fortuitously for those around me, my high is destined to be short-lived. Within a few weeks, the inevitable happens. My intense joy wears off and I plunge back to ground level. Determined to be strong enough to fight this without resuming antidepressant medication, I assure myself I *can* pull myself up by my proverbial bootstraps. Have I not been assured of this enough over the years?

Despite my valiant efforts, it's not long before the earth opens up and I begin to free-fall . . . further and further into the depths of a cavernous black hole. My life becomes reduced to mere existence: a ritual of daily agony that's almost too painful to bear. Daytime is especially excruciating. I look forward to the few hours in the evening before I turn in when the pain of the depression eases slightly–to the point where it becomes bearable enough that I feel able to live with it. My limbs ache constantly, and the mental suffering is so exquisitely painful that it seems to permeate my whole being on a physical level as well.

I rarely rise from my bed. Days go by wherein I neither wash nor dress. I'm afraid to live and afraid to die. Being on the cusp of both fears, I'm suspended in an unthinkable hell. I'm at my lowest ebb.

Len begins making the evening meals when he arrives home from work. The girls later clean up. They bring tea and food to my bed, and they mother me when they're home. I expect they worry about me as well. If so, I'm unaware. I'm too removed from the real world to ever want to rise up to greet it again. I've no idea what to do about myself and do not have enough interest in life to care. It is simply my cross to bear. Len, for the most part, retreats. We rarely speak. Possibly, he attributes my plight as being his cross to bear as well. I expect it is.

At some point, I become rationale enough to realize I have to start the Nardil again. Screw the unwieldy, allegoric bootstraps. There is no way I can function without it.

The following months on Nardil find me back where I was, prior to the short-lived euphoria that intervened. I'm in a virtual state of fatigue again, the latter which is doubtless a natural place to be if I factor in the years of impaired sleep. Despite this, I'm thankful that the Nardil continues to prevent me from becoming inordinately depressed.

The year 1992 brings with it another notable behavioural change. For the first time, one of my highs vastly eclipses its gleeful, hypomanic limits, and I gradually move into a psychotic state.

It begins with episodes of frantic, non-stop chatter that I'm unable to control. My actions also become frenzied and my behaviour gradually becomes markedly deranged. I'm personally unaware of becoming unhinged. For the most part, I feel powerful and euphoric, and very much in control of not only my world, but the planet as a whole.

And perhaps even the universe.

I develop a new daily pastime. Len has built a wooden platform linking the exterior wall of our garage to the top of the above-ground pool. Several stairs lead up to it. We now have a pool deck which also gives us easy access to the garage roof; the latter which we all tend to use has a sun spa. Aware I can now easily hoist myself onto the house roof from the summit of the garage, I do this regularly. I strut back and forth on my new perch whilst chanting, mumbling, or gleefully saluting the neighbours.

I see nothing strange about my actions, be it talking non-stop, trotting about on the roof (often in my nightgown), or waking the girls with little treats in the middle of the night in order to chit-chat. My behaviour jumps from loving to confrontational and aggressive. I'm becoming extremely paranoid as well.

On one occasion, when I believe Eve's boss at the store where she works part-time as a student has mistreated her, I call and give him a piece of my mind. Fortunately, this does not cost her the job. Another time, when I call her at work and the receptionist says she's unavailable, I don't believe it, and I call the lady a witch. I also ring one of Eve's teachers at his home in the wee hours to redress him for some imagined slight to her. My daughter now finds herself in the uncomfortable and mortifying position of frequently having to apologize for the untoward behaviour of her demented mother. Being well-liked, people are sympathetic to her, but obviously she wonders how long their good nature will last. My behaviour is far from appropriate, and often obnoxious.

Eve begs me to stop calling people on her behalf. I can only see that I'm trying to help out and that she's being a thankless ingrate.

Dana begins to suffer as well. When she misses a day from school due to illness, I write an actual tome to the teacher explaining her absence in minute detail. When my prose is received on a derisive note, Dana is humiliated and approaches me in tears, begging me to write brief notes only. I am beyond seeing the error of my ways. Dana, I'm to later learn, eventually resorted to getting her friend's older sister to forge her absentee notes. And trashed mine. (Bravo, Dana!)

My behaviour further deteriorates as I become more paranoid. The girls have to depend on themselves to survive the horrors they regularly encounter from having a mentally disturbed mother. Eve begins excluding me by no longer discussing her life with me–even at times when I appear more together. She denies me access to phone numbers of any of her new contacts. This increases my paranoia. I simply do not have the presence of mind to realize that both of my daughters are doing their utmost to protect themselves from the damage my illness is inflicting upon their lives.

I alienate a few close friends in the process. My telephone calls, be they cheery or full of woe, are not well-received in the wee hours. When I'm told point blank that I'm *not*, under any circumstances, to awaken them in the middle of the night again, I interpret this as a lack of caring, and I do not hesitate to insult them as well.

I soon begin conversing animatedly with God. He has a wonderful sense of humour and tells me the most hilarious jokes. I pass them on to Len and the girls. They do not find it at all funny that God and I are now on a friendly basis. Len and Eve approach me on one occasion. Eve does most of the talking.

"Mom," she begins, "We're very worried about you. You're not yourself anymore. You daily walk on the roof and say and do all sorts of weird things. You're even sharing jokes with God. Apart from being aggressive and confrontational, you've also become cunning and manipulative . . . and paranoid as well. You're really starting to scare us. I want to make an appointment for you with Dr. Richards. I'll take you myself. He's your doctor and he needs to know what's going on. You need help."

As opposed to *walking* on the roof, I now *hit* it. With a vengeance. "You're telling me I'm crazy, right? *LOT'S* of people talk to God, Eve. I know you don't believe that *I* do, but it's a fact. As to walking on the roof, what's the big deal? I have a great view from there. It's good exercise. As to your other accusations, I now realize I have good cause to be paranoid. I see that you think I'm crazy and you want Dr. Richards to have me locked up. Well, you better not call him on my behalf or I'll never forgive you. Just because you're studying psychology in university doesn't make you an expert on my condition. You're just jealous that God talks to *me*, not *you*. You and Dad are the ones with a problem!"

Things worsen. I often walk into a room and notice that Len and the girls suddenly fall silent. Aware they've been discussing me, I go ape over it. I begin calling the friends I still have and relaying my grievous tales regarding my family—how they hate me and want me locked up.

Finally, Eve gets in touch with Dr. Richards without my knowledge. That evening, she updates her father and me on what has transpired.

"I've been to see your doctor," she addresses me. "I want you to know I've done this *because* I love you, and *because* I don't want you locked up, and *because* I don't want anything bad to happen to you. Please try to understand that, Mom." She hands me a vial of pills she picked up at the drugstore.

"Dr. Richards wants you to stop the Nardil right away, and to begin taking these new meds to bring you down from your high immediately. He said this is imperative, or you'll only get worse. He stated in writing that if you don't agree to treatment we're to obtain a court order to have you psychiatrically evaluated."

"How could you *do* this to me?" I shriek. "How could my own daughter be such a bitch? I knew it, Eve! I knew you wanted me locked up forever. I will *never* take the damn pills or stop the Nardil! You and Dad and everyone else are against me—including Dr. Richards! I hate the lot of you!" I begin weeping and run off to my bedroom.

A few days later I find myself strapped in an ambulance and on my way to the hospital. My fault. Len starting arguing with me about taking the damn pills and I made an urgent 911 call to say I was being threatened by my husband and wanted him removed from the house. Either Len or Eve gave the paramedics the letter Dr. Richards had written regarding my condition.

As it turns out, *I* am the one being unceremoniously carted away, and I have never been more scared. I worry that I'll be locked up for the rest of my life. And I'm paranoid enough to believe that's exactly what my family wants. (In hindsight, I'm only thankful Eve had the foresight to seek out the help I needed.)

After being evaluated by a psychiatrist at the nearest hospital, I'm admitted without delay. Amongst other things, he is likewise unimpressed regarding my communication with God. I accuse him of being an atheist.

Sometime later, when I'm settled in the psych ward, I'm approached by a nurse with a small container of mixed pills which she insists I take. I understand they are to bring me back down to planet Earth. Perfectly happy with whatever planet I'm on, I absolutely refuse. I am then sternly admonished that I can either swallow them of my own accord, or a special team will be called in to subdue me; but I *will* be taking the medication. The easy way or the hard way. My choice. Albeit grudgingly, I swallow the pills.

Due to a law that psychiatric patients must be treated in the hospital within their jurisdiction, I'm unable to be admitted to the downtown hospital that Dr. Richards is affiliated with, which is definitely upping my fear quotient. I feel intimidated by the dour psychiatrist that has been assigned to my case and although nobody is actually unkind to me, I'm literally terrified I'll rot in here forever.

My actual hospitalization lasts only a week. Within several days of ingesting the new meds, I'm no longer on my happy planet. I've fallen to Earth with a mighty thud. I am anxious and depressed again and I only know I want *OUT OF HERE!* I call Dr. Richards from the pay phone in the ward and beg him to ask the hospital psychiatrist to release me. Aware that I'm no longer psychotic, he advises me to simply have Len drop over and request my discharge.

"They can't keep you as long as you are not a danger to yourself or anyone else, Mrs. Snow, but I want you to promise to see me as soon as you get home," he admonishes me.

"Absolutely," I agree.

Against the advice of the medical staff, Len collects me from hospital the next day. He drives me to see Dr. Richards a few days later. I only recall the gist of our conversation.

"I have no idea what happened to me prior to being hospitalized," I say. "I only know that I'm very depressed right now. They took me off Nardil and this is what I've been given in its stead." I show him the vial of pills. "All I've been told is that I had a psychotic episode.

I'm so afraid of ending up in a mental institution. Oh my God, what is wrong with me?"

"I personally think it was a reaction to the Nardil. In view of what's happened, it's perhaps not our best choice anymore. I want you to give your new antidepressant medication a chance. I know you're going through a difficult time just now, but I assure you there's no danger of you *ever* being institutionalized."

I have no success with my new meds, and before long I find myself plunging into the proverbial well of despair. I beg Dr. Richards to prescribe me the Nardil again. I remind him that I've been taking it for years, and prior to my recent episode I've never become psychotic. Sympathetic to my earnest plea, he finally agrees to give the Nardil one final shot.

"We must both hope this never happens again, Mrs. Snow," he states unequivocally.

It is not to be.

In late November 1992, six months after my first psychotic episode, I enter another manic state. Prior to this, the Nardil indeed lifts my mood to a more desirable level and I'm filled with gratitude to finally be relieved of the daily agony of depression.

All too soon however, I become euphoric again, and by early December I develop all of the classic symptoms of mania. My behaviour becomes increasingly more erratic, aggressive and abnormal. God is ever in the picture, always keeping me entertained with His great jokes, which no one else in the family appreciates. I tell myself it's not my fault they are not as close to God, and I can't help but feel superior to these less privileged beings. I'm unable to realize how grandiose my behaviour has become.

Len wants to take me to Dr. Richards for evaluation. At his suggestion, I go berserk. I begin ranting and raving, and telling him in no uncertain terms that he is the most rotten human being to walk the face of this earth. He, in turn, loses his cool and a screaming match ensues.

I'm suddenly hit by the brilliant idea that I can remove him from the house. I make the same faux pas I did the last time. I call

911 when he's momentarily indisposed. This time I say that my husband is beating me and I need help. Before long, an ambulance arrives along with the cops. Since I'm not bruised and bleeding, I cunningly explain that Len has slapped me practically senseless across the head in order to not leave marks, and I'm suffering from a violent headache. The cops believe me, likely because my actions have provoked Len to a point of fury and he begins ranting that I'm a lying bitch and that it is *me*, not *him*, who needs to be removed from the house. "My wife is absolutely mad!" he asserts.

Bottom line: I'm transported against my will–*once again!*–to the hospital via ambulance. Len is likewise conveyed–contrary to *his* will–to the police station via cop service. Later, in my bed in the psych ward, I'm approached by a police officer to sign a complaint against my husband for domestic violence. This, I do with aplomb. I'm aware that I'm lying; however, I remind myself of all the times he got away with hitting me in the distant past and I assure myself this is simply payback time.

The next day I find out from Dana that Eve has packed some clothes and moved out. Eve told her sister, "I love Mom, but I have to leave to survive. The fights, along with her behaviour, are getting worse and Dad is going off the deep-end as well. I'm gradually falling to pieces. I'm so sorry, Dana. I know you'll be alone in it, but I promise to keep tabs on you."

Dana is four and a half years Eve's junior, and Eve has been more of a mother than a sister to her during the years of my chronic mental illness. Eve has toughed it out until age twenty-two. Dana is still an insecure eighteen.

My initial reaction to Eve's move is surprise. I am also indignant. I simply can't believe she has done this to me. Clearly I'm thinking only of me. I dearly love my daughter, yet I have absolutely no conception of her personal suffering. Locked in my world of madness I cannot see beyond the murky, dark walls of my own inner prison.

Len, who retired last August at age sixty, is free to come and go as he chooses now. It's several days before he deigns to visit me. He's still nursing his own inner fury for the night he spent in jail following my bogus complaint. Consequently, he now has to appear in court in January. He's none too pleased with the whole situation and who can blame him?

On the day of his visit the glad-to-sad meds have again sent me crashing back down to planet Earth from my jubilant sojourn elsewhere . . . perhaps to the realm of my dear friend God, who tells me such hilarious jokes. I'm now at rock bottom–depressed, anxious and exceedingly distressed.

Len is tight-lipped with anger as he sits down beside me, and the first thing I do is apologize profusely.

"I'm so sorry, Len. I'll tell the truth to the judge, I promise you. I'll let the court know I've been suffering from mental illness, and that I lied about you assaulting me. I'll ask Dr. Richards for a letter specifying my condition which will be further proof to absolve you for what you didn't do. Can you please forgive me?"

He relaxes a little. "I know you're sick, honey, and I just want you to get better; but I'm beginning to lose hope. I don't know how long I can go on like this."

"Yeah," I sigh. "Me, too. Please, please bear with me."

I begin making noises about being discharged once the meds have removed me from my high, but they insist on keeping me under observation for a longer stretch. After being confined to the psych ward for two full weeks I have no intention of complying with their wishes any longer. I'm freaking out and I want to go home.

I phone Len and ask him to collect me. He refuses. "I did that the last time and look what happened. Six months later finds you right back in there again. Give it a little time, honey. Perhaps they'll find out *exactly* what's wrong with you."

"How can you be so mean? You know I'm scared to death in these places. It's not *you* that's in the loony bin surrounded by some people who are completely off their rocker. It's really frightening. Please, hon, I want to come home. I'm really a whole lot better now."

"Much as I want you home, I want you *completely* better. No, you won't convince me to get you out this time."

"Fine," I say, and hang up.

I ring home around supper knowing Dana will likely answer the phone. "I have something private to discuss with you," I tell her. "Please call me back when you're alone. For now, if Dad's within hearing distance, just let me know if you're able to visit me tonight."

"Sorry, Mom, I can't make it tonight, but I'll definitely be over to see you tomorrow."

Later, when Dana calls me surreptitiously, I beg her to come and get me the next day.

"I know I can leave on my own reconnaissance," I tell her, "but they'll do their best to try and stop me. I'm afraid I'll not be strong enough to split this joint if they gang up on me. Please sweetie, all you need to do is *appear*. If they ask you anything, just say you've come to collect your mother. Look firm. That's it. Name the time and I'll be ready and waiting to walk out with you." She reluctantly agrees, knowing full well her father will not be pleased.

And so it is that I once again fly over the cuckoo's nest. And just in time for the holidays . . . which could not be sadder.

I'm profoundly distressed Eve has left home and I'm constantly flogging myself for my part in it, which I now fully recognize. Worse still, she hasn't called since she left over two weeks ago. I've no idea what she's doing or where she's staying. None of her friends admit to having heard from her and I can hardly contain my fear for her safety. Finally, I hear from her friend, Jana.

"Eve is not staying with me, Mrs. Snow, but she's been in contact. She's okay, but she doesn't want to reveal her whereabouts at this time. I'm sorry. She wants you to know that if there's an emergency you can call me and I'll relay your message. She needs a little time, that's all. She says she promises to call home soon."

I'm in tears. My baby. My sweet baby. Will she ever forgive me? I've lost her. Will I ever feel whole again?

A few days before Christmas, Eve comes home to collect the remainder of her belongings. She's not alone. Jana and the new minister accompany her. Sadly, Dave–our former pastor and friend– died of a heart attack a few years back.

I have no chance to speak with my daughter alone, and I sense she has planned it this way. She wants neither my tears nor my histrionics to weaken her resolve. Despite the people surrounding her, I put my arms around her and hug her before she leaves. She stands as still as stone, and does not reciprocate my embrace.

"I'm so sorry, Eve," I say. "I never meant to hurt you."

"I know, Mom. But I have to survive. I'll be in touch from time to time, but I can't stay the way things are."

Once she leaves, I let my emotions spill over. I run to my room, sobs heaving from my chest, and I cry until I'm drained.

Christmas is just another day. There's no special dinner; no celebration; no presents. Even Len is too discouraged to make an effort. Deeply depressed, I mourn what I believe is the loss of another daughter.

Dana is away for most of the day. I'm only glad she seems to be holding together through it all. Thank God she can spend the holiday with her boyfriend, Zach. There's not an iota of joy in our home.

I'm only to learn much later that Eve gave Dana a number where she could be reached and made her promise not to divulge it to me. Entrenched in my illness and no longer able to love or care for myself, I failed to love Eve when she needed me most. Dana was left to her own devices as well. My beautiful girls, whose lives I would trade for my own in a heartbeat, were left to struggle on their own, minus the heritage of the abiding mother-love we all deserve; as was Keith before them.

I'm just beginning to accept myself for this part of my soul's journey that enveloped me in such darkness I failed to see beyond it . . . wherein lay the needs of those I loved most.

Now, as my blinded eyes begin to see, I pray it's not too late for them to know how much they are, and have always been, loved.

I recall very little of the Christmas of 1992. Bleak and forlorn within my valley of despair, I have no joy to give . . . even to my lovely Dana who means so much to me.

It's a season of darkness.

Eve calls today to let me know the results of the scans which followed Gary's final cycle of chemo. There are still no malignant cells to be found; however, a portion of the large tumour still exists, and although it has shrunk considerably, follow-up radiation is recommended as a precaution.

"We've spoken with the radiologist regarding the pros and cons. Without radiation, a stage three cancer has a greater chance of recurring. At this juncture, our only choice is to put our faith in someone more knowledgeable than we are. The radiologist also has a son, and he assured us he'd go that route as the lesser of two evils. We naturally gave Gary the final choice, and he agreed."

"Well, sweetie, I expect I'd make the same choice. It's ultimately in God's hands, and if Gary is meant to live, he will, but at least you'll know you tried everything possible."

"That's how I'm looking at it. Right or wrong, I'd blame myself if I forewent the radiation and the cancer returned. He'll be starting treatment on Monday, August 20th, and he'll be having a total of twenty-eight rounds of radiation. His sessions will run into October."

"Well, please try to get some rest in between. Let me know if we can help in any way. I worry about you. You never seem to stop!"

Such a long haul they've all been through! I pray all ends well, and that Gary will be cured.

PART III – love is all that is

Communion with God

Dear God, please help me find the way
My thirsting soul yearns to detect,
The means by which it can connect
To Your great Light, pure and Devine–
All of which you've blessed as mine;
How can I see your face this day?

Dear child, my face is everywhere!
'Tis mirrored in the silv'ry lake,
And waves on yonder shore that break;
'Tis in the floral-scented breeze;
The sun, the stars, the birds, the trees;
And all ye find that's good and fair.

Yet there is that which you malign
As lowliest of the low;
And of these things, you need to know:
The slugs, the bugs, the snakes, the mud–
They, too, are part of My Life's blood;
And in My Heart, ALL is benign . . .

As you, dear sons, are pure to Me-
Extending rays of God Itself-
You all are aspects of my wealth!
And once you see, the All is Me,
And know I'm LOVE, you'll have Life's key:
In loving All, it's LOVE you'll Be.
—<u>Irene Snow</u>

Chapter 19 – The Nest Is Almost Empty

"Dance when you are broken –
What you are seeking is you".
—<u>Rumi</u>

As usual, the hospital psychiatrist assigned to my case has given me a prescription for anti-depressants. He's aware I have my own doctor, and consequently I'm not given a referral for follow-up appointments. I'm still depressed but I'm not at my lowest ebb.

Not long after Christmas, Eve calls to say she's in hospital. She has suffered a pulmonary embolism. I tell her that her dad and I are on our way. She mentions she's in need of some decent underwear. I'm only too happy to oblige. I would bring her the moon on a platter if I thought it would help. Frightening as the circumstances are, I'm simply happy to be able to see her again and more so that she's including me in her life at this time.

Len and I sit by her bedside as she tells us she's over the worst of it. She'll be discharged soon and will be on blood thinner for the next while, the latter as a preventive measure to avoid further clots forming in her lungs. She thanks me for the bag full of undergarments which I absolutely refuse to let her pay for, though she insists.

When Len leaves for the cafeteria to buy a coffee, I ask her about her current whereabouts and if she has a telephone.

"I can't tell you that, Mom, and I'm sure you know why. I'm not trying to be cruel, but until such a time as I'm certain you're completely well, I have to protect myself. I know you haven't intentionally tried to hurt me or upset my life, but you have. Don't think it's easy for me to do this. It isn't. Please understand that it's the only way I can hope to survive."

"Do you not want any more contact with me at all, Eve?" I ask sadly.

"I'll call you from time to time," she promises. "But not on a regular basis. I need time to heal. If there's something urgent, and you need to reach me, you can call Jana, and she'll let me know. And of course, if it's important, I'll get back to you."

I silently agonize over the distance my illness has created between us—a span of many miles that words or apologies won't breech. She is not the Eve of old. She is more removed and aloof. And she has grown-up—way beyond her twenty-two years.

She has had no other choice.

The New Year of 1993 arrives with no more fanfare than the Christmas preceding it. Len's court date draws nigh, and I'm in possession of a document from Dr. Richards which clarifies my mental state at the time of my false accusations. This, along with my heartfelt personal explanation, is received with a depth of compassion and human warmth far exceeding my expectations, and I'm gladdened to realize Len is absolved of any wrong-doing.

I continue to take the medication provided by the hospital. While I don't hit rock-bottom again, I grieve for Eve with every passing day. I rarely see Dana, not that she has any reason to enjoy being home. She's eighteen and in love, and she spends most of her time at Zack's place. In hindsight, I realize how fortunate it is that this diversion was available to keep her sane. Nothing is very sane in her home.

For me, it's a time of heartache. I await Eve's monthly call and sob copiously when our conversation is over, knowing another month will elapse before I hear her voice again. How I'd love to call her from time to time, but I've lost that privilege. Be it my illness or my own particular stage of evolvement, I've not yet progressed to a level where I can fully understand why she's done this, or the role I have unwittingly played to make it happen.

I only know I want my daughter back, but it is not to be.

I continue to ruminate about the rift between us, and I become further distressed and despondent. I ask Len to take me to see Dr. Richards. For the past few years, I've no longer been able to drive myself downtown unless I'm accompanied; mainly due to lack of regular therapies, interspersed with bouts of mental trauma. Fortunately perhaps, our old truck has long since died and been sold for the price of scrap which has prevented me from even driving it locally, especially when I've become manic and deranged.

Again, I beg Dr. Richards for help. After much pleading, he finally relents, but not without admonitions.

"It seems you personally respond best to an MAO Inhibitor. However, Nardil is out of the question now. I'll try you on Parnate which is from the same family, so I'm positive it will relieve your symptoms. I only hope the side-effects will not be as drastic. I expect to monitor you closely while you're on this medication, Mrs. Snow. We must be circumspect about this. No calling to cancel appointments. Is that understood?"

Despite the friendship we share, Dr. Richards has never agreed to address me on a first-name basis, although I've suggested it. In fact, he's specified we continue to address each other formally, obviously to maintain the professional aspect of the doctor-patient relationship. In hindsight, I can relate to the significance of his thinking.

"I understand completely," I assure him.

My mood begins to elevate soon after taking the Parnate, and the winter passes uneventfully. Eve continues to call once a month and Dana is still very much involved with Zach who is a computer science student in his last year of college.

One warm day in June Len and I visit Mark, my eldest stepson, and I have a few beers at his home. The following morning I'm strung as tight as a drum, talking rapidly and unable to control my chatter. Fearing this could signify bad news, I call Dr. Richards.

"Is it possible that Parnate mixed with beer can cause hypomania?" I inquire.

I perceive a significant pause before he warily responds, "Why do you ask?"

"Well, I had a few beers at my son's last night and I'm extremely hyper today. Also, I can't seem to stop talking."

He asks a multitude of questions, likely as not assessing my responses carefully. In conclusion, he pronounces, "I can assure you this is *not* an effect of Parnate and beer. You are definitely in a hypomanic state, but at this point we can easily nip things in the bud. I want you to stop the Parnate right away, and I'll call in a prescription to your drugstore, the latter which will bring you back to a normal state. I hope you'll listen to me this time, Mrs. Snow. Things will only worsen if you don't, and surely you don't want to go back to hospital again?"

"No, I surely don't. I'll do whatever you say."

I stop the Parnate immediately. Len picks up the new meds at the drugstore later that evening after work. He currently has a job where he daily assists an acquaintance who owns a brasserie.

I decide I'll start the prescription the following morning; but I don't. When Dr. Richards calls a few days later to see how I'm doing I truthfully relay that I've only stopped the Parnate.

"You've told me in the past you believe it's the MAO Inhibitor that has caused my manic episodes. If that's the case, now that I've ceased the Parnate, the hypomania should clear up by itself," I argue. "I'd like to see what happens."

I no longer recall his exact response. He's pleased I've stopped the Parnate, but argues the other meds are important in bringing me down from my high as soon as possible. I remain resolute.

As the weeks go by, Len spends more time at the brasserie. He's gone from Monday to Saturday and rarely comes home before late evening. My hypomania has not lessened, but nor has it worsened. I'm enjoying a pleasant buzz, but I'm lonely. Dana is rarely home either.

Len finally purchases me a used car following my bitter complaints about how unfair it is that I'm alone all day with no vehicle while he practically lives at the brasserie.

Now that I'm no longer confined to the house–and at least up to driving locally–I often go to the shopping malls. One evening, while browsing through various boutiques, I stop in front of a nightclub. Momentarily rapt by the lively strains of music drifting through its doors, I'm beckoned inside by the beautiful voice of a female vocalist singing a retro song that is nostalgically reminiscent of my era. Spotting an empty table, I order a glass of wine. Before long, someone asks me to dance and, sometime later, I'm invited to join some regulars at one of the other tables. My new acquaintances consist of both sexes, mainly singles who are within my age range and good company.

Thus hails the start of my regular evenings out. The musicians and singers are there in the evenings from Thursday to Saturday which become my dancing nights. I stay fairly late, but make a point of leaving by myself and driving home alone. Len is so involved in his own thing that, for once, he shows no resentment to mine. From time to time he even gives me extra spending money from his earnings at the brasserie. Unbeknownst to him, every bit helps. I'm running up a bar bill on my Visa which is costing a few hundred dollars a month.

My generalized buzz is interspersed with the inner sadness that daily haunts me over losing Eve. I often pay the musicians and singer for the special request of a song that has been "hers" since childhood days. During these moments, I visualize the presence of my beautiful, lost child and imagine her ever close to my heart.

By late August, I once again slip into a psychotic state. My behaviour becomes increasing irrational and delusional. For the first time, I get caught up in weird, yet powerful, fantasies which I feel I am actually living.

One of these episodes involves me locking horns with God. I tell Him unequivocally that I am also all-powerful, and I warn Him that I'm vying for His position as head of the universe. He appears concerned about this, and in the hope of dissuading me from my stance, He offers me spectacular gifts to mollify me. *Total knowledge* is one of his many fine enticements. *Nay, not good enough,* I say. He ups the ante. Aware now, that *He* is insecure, I still refuse to settle. I want His position as ruler of *All That Is*, and nothing less will do. He finally loses His patience and zaps me to Satan. The next moment finds me in a grievous flight through space with the devil clasping my right arm, and guiding me . . . somewhere. Surely no place good. I realize, too late, the error of my ways for not settling with God. I should have jumped at one of His more favourable offers, but it's too late now. Petrified, I cry out for Jesus who appears instantaneously and grips my left arm. I'm now being literally torn between good and evil. My terror skyrockets, until suddenly I find myself back on planet Earth. The horrible fantasy is over almost as quickly as it began.

As usual, I have little awareness of the severity of my condition, beyond the fact that there are many crazies in the world but *I* am not one of them. Many weird occurrences come to pass. One relates to trying to reach Dr. Richards after hours. He forwards his calls to his home when he leaves the office and on this particular occasion I'm highly impatient for him to respond to my telephone message. I suddenly come up with the idea that he likely has an unlisted number, and I call information to retrieve it. I've no recall of how I actually accomplish this feat because the telephone company is not permitted to reveal private numbers under *any* circumstances, but I somehow obtain the number. I seem to be empowered to access all kinds of information–forbidden and otherwise–which I've never been privy to in a sane, normal state. Knowledge is conveyed to me in many ways–occasionally by simply hearing a disembodied voice that gives me the answer I seek.

By believing I am all-powerful, I become all-powerful–at least to a degree that is not possible in a normal state of consciousness. As the subconscious–or reactive mind–takes over, one becomes more attuned to the collective consciousness and the Universal mind.

This is akin to the methods taught in books such as "The Secret": that by consciously impressing the subjective mind with faith and belief regarding a specific desire, the latter will eventually be objectified on a conscious level. This, of course, is the long way around. A prolonged effort is no longer necessary when one is not quite sane. When the subjective mind is already at the fore, it is easily and quickly impressed with the conscious belief of receiving what one conceives of (such as an unlisted number), and consequently the desire is manifested almost instantaneously. I have noticed this in a number of instances, though admittedly not all . . . perhaps because some are simply not in keeping with the deeper needs of the soul.

Based upon a few of my own alien experiences when in this reactive state, I no longer have any doubt that, as it claims in the Bible, the faith of a grain of mustard seed can move a mountain.

One day, when Dana is home alone with me, she becomes exceedingly concerned about my well-being and calls 911. As to be expected, I'm shipped back to hospital and none too soon. Thank God for Dana's presence of mind, though I am thoroughly pissed with her to begin with.

This time, my visit will involve a much longer stint.

I retain only snippets of memory regarding the weeks of my hospitalization. One in particular depicts another experience that faith made happen. While waiting to be assessed upon arrival in an exceedingly busy ER, I jaunt up and down the corridor in high spirits humming the tune of *Blue Moon*. I'm wearing my alexandrite ring, a gift from my uncle, and feeling in total love and harmony with *All That Is*. Singing softly I smile, wave and beam immutable love to each patient I see being wheeled to and fro along the corridor. Ill as some of them appear, they reward me with a glowing smile of their own.

My eyes suddenly fall upon a lady who's being escorted into hospital by two adults who are supporting her on either side. She's limping severely and her face is contorted with pain. I glance at my ring and believe, for the first time, that the alexandrite is a healing stone. Catching her eye, I flash the gleaming reddish-violet gem directly at her, knowing beyond doubt she'll be healed. In that moment of eye contact I know that *she* knows this as well. And she's *miraculously and instantaneously healed*. She shrugs off the arms supporting her and begins to walk on her own without any hint of difficulty The pain has left her face and she looks as dumbfounded and awestruck as the two individuals who were formerly supporting her, the latter who are completely oblivious to what transpired. I quickly slip away unnoticed, not wanting to be discovered.

It seems, however, there *was* a witness—a man in a white garment, perhaps an orderly. He hands me a business card, beseeching me to call him when I get home. Once discharged, I'll dispose of his card. I know this is not something I'm capable of in a normal state. I can only put it down to a gift from beyond . . . which arose from *absolute* faith and love.

For the next six weeks, I'm confined to the psych ward. After the first seven days, the psychiatrist assigned to my case tells me I'm "too happy," and I'm deprived of the tranquilizers prescribed upon my arrival. I'm now without any meds at all.

My perky, racing thoughts soon vanish as I plunge into a solitary black void where terror reigns supreme. The anxiety is so intense and continuous I can no longer keep still. Restless and fidgety, I pace back and forth continuously. I'm literally climbing out of my tree as I twitch and writhe in an agony of mental torment. I begin pleading and begging my psychiatric day nurse to give me something for relief. Barring an emergency, one only gets to see one's shrink once a week. Thankfully, my nurse informs me she's spoken to my doctor and he's allowing me a few Benadryl daily. I fail to see how an antihistamine will slake such overwhelming anxiety and feel somewhat betrayed; however, she assures me it will produce a calming effect.

In fact, it does little to appease the acute anxiety. For the next few weeks, however, it's to be the extent of my meds, save for a maximum of two chloral hydrate capsules at bedtime which act as a healing agent in their own right. By helping me achieve a decent night's sleep, the mental anguish of the day is temporarily obliterated.

During the time I'm confined to the psych ward, I learn from Dana that Eve has moved to the city of Ordala, a two-hour drive from Cassellman, where she'll attend a university which is affiliated with a hospital in order to obtain her master's degree in pastoral care. She'll be gone for another two years. During this time, it's all I can do to get through each day. In my heart, I wish Eve well.

Finally, in the few weeks prior to my discharge, I'm given Librium to help me cope with the daily anxiety . . . which is another useless placebo.

Lithium follows.

I need not be told. The lithium itself announces the diagnosis. It's been determined I am bipolar.

Chapter 20 – Listen to the Children

"Children are the anchors of a mother's life."
—Sophocles

I t's early October when I finally arrive home. I'm still quite depressed, but as usual I've done my best to conceal it in order to be discharged. I've been told point blank that since the law prevents me from being hospitalized outside of my vicinity, it's high time I have a file with a community doctor, and I've been referred to a shrink in my area. I'm afraid if I fail to comply it may be to my detriment in the future. Add that to the fact that Len is no longer willing to drive me downtown to see Dr. Richards. He has resented our friendship from the outset, and now that I'm too depressed and phobic to get myself there on my own steam, he's wholeheartedly supportive of the hospital's stance.

My new psychiatrist, Dr. Sommers, is another dour shrink; yet despite his lack of external humour and stern facade, I recognize he's a kind person. "We'll definitely find an anti-depressant that will do the trick, Mrs. Snow, even if it's not in the MAO family. It may take a little patience on your part."

Make that a *lot* of patience.

Dana is also very distressed. Zach has been unable to obtain employment in Cassellman after finishing college and his funds have run out. Circumstances have necessitated his return home to Ordala which, interestingly enough, is the city in which Eve is currently pursuing her studies. Neither Dana nor Zack can afford to visit each other often in view of the high cost of provincial bus fare. Likewise, long distance calls have to be curtained. While Dana still has her close girlfriends, she misses both Zach and her older sister profoundly. During the worst of times, they kept her connected. She seems to be holding onto a narrow ledge herself these days.

Len is rarely home from the brasserie save for a few hours before bedtime and all day Sunday. Dana and I spend a lot of time indoors dealing with our own particular woes as best we can. Eve still calls once a month and she's rented a post box where I can contact her by mail. Obviously, she's as yet unable to place her trust in me, and nor can I blame her. In the past, she's suffered too many mother-related betrayals.

My relationship with Eve remains a source of heartache. I long to connect with her as we once did. I can only hope it may happen again someday in the future. Despite her monthly calls, I know we're still estranged and it hurts me profoundly.

Christmas is again a sad occasion and we merely strive to get through it as best we can. Dana and I are both depressed, and Eve has no intention of coming home for the holidays. Subsequently, we greet the New Year of 1994 with the hope of better things to come.

I continue to see Dr. Sommers and finally–after experimenting with several different brands of anti-depressants–one of them lifts my mood enough that I'm able to cope with my everyday life more successfully.

The first part of the New Year passes uneventfully until the month of July. On one of Dana's weekend visits to Zack's home, she does not return. He's now gainfully employed in Ordala and it's unlikely he'll ever come back to Cassellman on a permanent basis.

I call Dana and insist she stop being evasive about not coming home. She finally confesses, "Zach has suggested I stay, Mom. It's okay with his parents, providing I find employment. I can live with them. I'd like to give it a try, sort of like a trial to see if things can work out for Zach and me here."

I burst into tears. "Oh no, don't tell me I'm losing you too, Dana?" I sob. "You're only twenty. This is a life-altering decision. Please say you're not intent on pursuing this."

"I love Zack, Mom. I have to try this. Of course I don't know how it'll work out. I desperately need your blessing, and Dad's as well. I need to know I'm still welcome to come home if things don't go as I hope. It's not easy for me either, you know. I'm really scared and I'll miss you a lot. But I have to give it a try, and at least Eve is close by. Please, please, say you'll support me in this."

My heart is breaking and I feel shattered. Yet, I hear my daughter, and I assure her we'll always be there for her. Once off the phone, however, I'm hit with the horror that my children are all gone and my nest is empty. I wonder how the years have vanished so quickly without my awareness. And I have so many regrets. I've missed so much of their lives. The best I can do now is to be there for them with my love and support if they ever need it. Why could I have not been well enough *then*, when I was surrounded by my beautiful children? It seems so unfair . . . to all of us.

I only know I want to continue getting better. And to *stay* better. I owe it to myself, my husband and my children, and I will never stop trying. I will give it my very best effort . . . and hope it is not too little, too late. I want us to be a family again.

I write to Eve frequently at her post box, and I welcome Dana's occasional weekend visits home by provincial bus. I also happily embrace the fact that Len's job at the brasserie is over. His friend sold out to his business partner. I'm at least not totally alone. I think of what Jesus said, "I will not leave you comfortless," and as I look back over my own life, I know this to be the truth. When my cross was the heaviest, there was always a kind soul to help me carry it.

The months pass by quickly and Dana finds a job in Ordala. She and Zack seem to be happy together. Now that they are both employed they have decided to find their own place in the New Year and move out of Zack's parents' home.

Christmas 1994 is quiet. Dana and Zack drop in for a short visit.

Eve calls with good wishes but does not come home. I send her a cheque and a Christmas stocking full of goodies by Canada Post.

The beginning of the year 1995 marks fifteen months since I've been out of hospital. Len has noticed a marked change in my behaviour. It has remained stable to date. I continue to sleep through the night—every night. I'm no longer depressed. For all intents and purposes—apart from the idiosyncrasies that affect us all in one way or another—I'm a normal person again.

By September of the same year, I receive some welcome news. Eve is coming back to live in Cassellman and she's expecting. While neither she nor her fiancé planned to have a child prior to the completion of her master's degree, the baby had a mind of its own. After its birth, she'll return to Ordala for the remaining three months necessary to complete her degree. Meanwhile, she'll be moving in with her fiancé, Philip, who lives and works here in the city. I can hardly contain my delight. Not only am I about to have my first biological grandchild, but one of my daughters is coming back home as well! And she plans to live and work here permanently along with Philip.

Shortly after Eve arrives in town, she sets a date to introduce us to Phil. She schedules the meeting in a restaurant, and I immediately comprehend that she's still not ready to visit us at home—perhaps due to memories she does not care to relive. I take whatever she's willing to give with a glad heart.

The meeting, though brief, goes well. My daughter's fiancé is very protective and considerate of her and it's easy to see how much he loves her. Both are happy and aglow and, for this, both Len and I are well-pleased.

"With a baby on the way, we're looking for a bigger apartment," Eve says. "As soon as we move, I'll give you my telephone number."

I'm over the moon!

Before the year 1995 is out, Eve has arranged to have two telephone numbers on the same line, each with a distinguishing ring:

the family number, and a separate one solely for me. It's the only one I'll be given, but at least I can reach her again and I'm grateful. While I can't fault her continued need to protect herself, I nevertheless feel like an ogre, and I'm left with a deep sense of shame in regard to how low I fell during my illness.

She explains it to me kindly enough, "Mom, you've been doing well for the past few years, but I have to be honest. I still need time to feel sure that there'll be no change for the worse in your condition. I can't have you calling us at all hours, or doing some of the things you did when you were ill. It's going to take time for me to regain my trust in our relationship."

I know she's right, and I only hope time heals her personal wounds which are many. Most of all, I pray I'll never fall back to where I was. Even to contemplate such a thought scares the hell out of me. I couldn't bear anything to happen which could alter the glorious fact that my daughter still wants a relationship with me.

The year 1996 brings two major events: the birth of Eve's son, James, and her marriage. Len and I are delighted to share in both happy occasions. While, as yet, we have only a small role in their everyday lives, this is a vast improvement over the past. And I'm grateful to have my daughter back in my life, even though from here on in it is to be solely on her terms. She delineates these terms from the outset.

"In order that we maintain a healthy relationship, Mom, it's important for both of us to maintain boundaries that we don't mindlessly cross over," she explains. Eve has a well-rounded education with a BA in psychology and an MA in pastoral care. She's now qualified to be a hospital chaplain. She's also learned a great deal about dysfunctional families.

"We can't continue to perpetuate the dysfunctions of the past that go back to your mom and your grandmother. And likely your grandmother's grandmother. For example, your grandma used "a potential heart attack" as a source of manipulating your mom. Your mom, in turn, used *her* health to scare *you* into submission. You've tried variations of this with me. The time Dad called to say I'd upset you and you were sick, I told him I hoped you'd feel better soon and to give you my love. I was not trying to be mean by not rushing to your side as you would have done if it were Granny. I simply wanted to set a precedent. In order for us to maintain a healthy relationship there must not be any manipulations from either of us—unconscious or otherwise. This is what I mean by the need to establish boundaries."

She goes on to clarify these boundaries in detail. I cannot say I'm not offended, at least to a degree. After all, I'm the parent and it has always been *my* role to set the rules. Suddenly, I'm knocked off my high horse and, if nothing else, my pride is sorely wounded. Nevertheless, I know her motives are benign. I also know I have no choice. If I want to have a relationship with my daughter, I have to smarten up. If it includes being humble, so be it.

All things past have led to this moment of Now: a new beginning. Eve does not want a repeat of the past.

Despite my previous lapses into mental illness, I have a great deal of growing to do. Although I'm not cognizant of this on a conscious level, the unconscious part of me that wants to move ahead on my journey is very much aware of it, and it knows I have found a benevolent teacher and friend: my daughter, Eve.

It's amazing how synchronicity comes into play in our lives. Along our journey, our teachers appear as we become ready. Some pass briefly through our lives; others span longer periods. All of them—even the tough ones, such as my dad—prepare us for what we must learn, and we must welcome each and every one of them—both the lenient and the harsh—as guides from beyond.

And once our inner compass has set us in the right direction—and our hearts are oriented to the goal of actively seeking God—there is virtually no stopping us.

Sometime that same year, I decide to stop the lithium. On

occasion, I still speak with Dr. Richards on the telephone. Over the years, he has emphasized that he does not believe the lithium is necessary; that in my particular case, the antidepressant meds will suffice.

"While I don't discount the possibility of you suffering from a milder form of mood disorder such as cyclothymia," he explains, "I definitely rule out bipolar illness."

Nevertheless, I have continued the lithium for the past three years, despite the side effects, on the assumption the hospital diagnosis may have been the right one. More than anything, I've feared regressing and losing my gains. Especially in my most meaningful relationships. However, my limbs still jerk involuntarily, despite the lowered dosage.

I now fathom that perhaps, as Dr. Richards has always maintained, the antidepressants are enough.

I discuss my decision with Len. During the past months, the improvement in my condition has had a notable effect on our relationship. Things are more peaceful between us and we are doing things together again. This includes the occasional holiday trip. Len is all for me reducing prescription drugs if I can manage without them.

"Try it," he says. "I promise to keep an eye on you."

I vow, in turn, I'll go right back on the lithium if he notices the slightest hint of change in my behaviour. I know, deep within myself, that I'll hold to this promise. I'll do anything in my power to avoid hurting my family as I have in the past. It's enough that Keith has deliberately removed himself from our lives, and that we have no idea where he's located. Since leaving home a decade ago, he's absconded into oblivion.

In July of the following year, 1997, Len and I sell our home. With the children gone, there are more rooms to clean than necessary, and a pool to maintain that we seldom use. Len is sixty-five now and although I'm nine years younger, neither of us relishes the upkeep of a home that has become too big for us. Far less hassle to simply move into a two-bedroom apartment with janitor service. We choose an apartment that is not far from our previous residence. We have come to love the suburban area which has been our home for the past twelve years.

Within days of moving, Eve's second son, Gary, is born. Between Eve's two children, and those of the older siblings, we now have a total of six grandchildren.

We take a short holiday that summer with Mark and his wife Marge in Niagara Falls during the month of August. In September Len and I spend some time visiting a few of my old friends in Karlstown, the town where I first met the beloved kindred spirit of my teens, Lou. She has since moved to another city in the same province and we make a point of visiting her. The reunion is joyous, and we sense time dissolving as we become part of yesteryear's love.

We return in time for Gary's baptism.

It's now been over a year since I've stopped lithium and, as per Dr. Richard's original assessment, it was likely unnecessary. There's been absolutely no change in my behaviour.

One can't help but wonder how many unnecessary drugs we ingest over the course of a lifetime. Diagnoses are not always correct, and much of preventative medicine is still trial and error.

Somewhere around this time, Eve says to me, "You know, Mom, I hope you are grateful. I believe you finally have your life back."

"You have no idea how truly grateful I am," I assure her, and mean every word of it. Without the continuous highs and lows of the past, the sun truly shines again.

I'm also regaining my daughter's faith in our relationship. I'm no longer relegated to using the "Mom-only" number to get in touch with her. She has since cancelled it.

Four years have elapsed since I was last hospitalized and I

continue to move ahead and improve. I read a great deal. It's a time of inquiry and learning, and I have much to absorb.

I know I'm emotionally stronger; yet, always there's the small voice within that cruelly whispers that a severe life crisis could send me back to that dark place again. A place where I could lose all my gains, perhaps for all time.

Eve has briefly enlightened me of the horrors she personally went through during my long illness. A highly sensitive person, the emotional consequences were severe. She began seeing a therapist at the university—one of the reasons she had to keep her distance in order to heal. I am immensely proud that she had the strength to take this stand and get on with her life and her aspirations as well as she did.

In June of the following year, 1998, Eve is chosen for the position of chaplain and pastoral director at a large city hospital. It's quite an honour for one so young. At twenty-eight, she's striven long and hard to attain her goals, beginning with working her way through university. This position, though well-deserved, is a dream come true. As is the lovely new home she and her husband purchase several months later. I am delighted for her.

The following month, Len and I make the long motor journey to the Pacific Northwest for the second time in our marriage, this time sans children. We spend the month of July with my friend Jane in her new home. It's the first time we've seen each other since her move a decade earlier and our arrival is heralded by a big welcome sign in full view on her front lawn. Several colourful balloons are attached to it, all swaying gaily in the breeze. Although we've kept in touch by phone, Canada Post, and more recently e-mail, it's a joy to see her in person again. We spend the month sightseeing in her adopted hometown, and catching up on the news we've missed over the past decade. The distinct change in my marriage does not escape her. "At long last, you two have become *true friends,*" she beams.

Shortly after arriving back home, Dr. Sommers informs me he's retiring.

"I'm extremely pleased with your progress and happy to note that you've continued to improve, even after ceasing the lithium," he says. "I see no need to refer you to another psychiatrist. Your family physician can prescribe your antidepressant meds which is the only professional service you require."

By fall of the same year, however, it seems I am overdue in experiencing another of life's lessons . . . this time from my daughter, Dana. I've become accustomed to the boundaries Eve has set up in our relationship; but to date, my youngest daughter has not erected any of her own. Consequently, I still smother her to an extent that, unbeknownst to me, is abhorrent to her. I call her often and if she does not quickly respond to my messages, I become concerned something is wrong, that perhaps she's not well. I then become more persistent with my calls and messages. On one occasion, I wonder if she is just not returning my calls. Aware she has call display I impulsively dial star 67 in order to conceal my home number. Aha! This time she answers.

"Dana," I say, "I've been so worried. You have not responded to my messages. Are you all right?"

"I don't appreciate what you've just done," she says coldly.

"I'm really sorry," I apologize, immediately contrite and aware I should never have done what I did. "I've been worried about you. I should not have concealed my number. Please forgive me."

"Mom, you're suffocating me. I need to breathe, and you're making it impossible. I can't go on like this. I honestly need a break from you. I've been realizing this for some time now."

Oh, shit. I've done it again. I beg and cajole, to no avail. I'm very much aware that if I don't lay low now, I'll perhaps lose her for good, if it's not too late already. My heart is breaking. Somehow, my life's lessons don't come easy; but I am finally "getting it". If I want to keep my children in my life I must try to be the mother they want, not the controlling person I am.

I still have a lot to learn . . . a long way to go on my journey in order to become the person, and the mother, that I truly wish to be.

I respect Dana's request. I do not try to contact her. Nor does she try to contact me; or her father. Len is able to accept this more easily than I am. He understands she needs her space and that I have to give it to her. He believes she'll come back when she's ready. I send her a card on her birthday and another at Christmas, each containing a simple little message to let her know she's in my heart and thoughts. I do not enclose a monetary gift which may be construed as a form of manipulation. For the balance of the time, I honour her wishes and pray for the day she'll accept me again.

In retrospect, it's a period of learning, with both daughters as my teachers. They are capable and independent, qualities I'm grateful they possess. I learn there are facets of my behaviour they find unacceptable: I must not control; I must not manipulate or smother; I must respect their boundaries.

I could say "screw them" but having a happy relationship with my daughters comes before my pride. I choose to learn.

Christmas 1998 takes precedence as the highlight of my year. For the first time, Eve invites both Len and me to spend Christmas day with her family which will set a precedent for several years to come. It's our first really happy Christmas in a long time and we enjoy every moment of sharing it with Eve, her husband, and our adorable grandsons.

The millennium arrives and, with it, an early e-mail from Dana. She's getting married this coming June and she and Zack have planned on a large wedding. She'd appreciate the names and addresses of all the relatives on the Snow side. I'm more than happy to oblige, and I spend the next hour or so looking up the addresses of all the relations. I e-mail the information back to her, with a short note: *"Delighted to hear you and Zack are tying the knot, sweetie. Our congratulations. Hope this info helps. Love you, Mom."*

Later that day, she calls me. "Thank you, Mom. I have missed you," she states simply. "I think of you often, believe it or not. I hope you understand that I needed the space. I do hope that you and Dad will attend my wedding and that Dad will give me away."

I'm elated. It seems I've been waiting forever for this moment, and I assure her we'll be honoured to be part of her wedding, and her life . . . in whatever capacity she's prepared to receive us.

It is a time of learning, and I am a willing student. Dana, like Eve, is one of my teachers.

Dana is married that June. I'm proud to see Len walking her down the aisle. It's a lovely wedding. Dana honours me by wearing my pearls, which I later give her. She's a beautiful bride.

What's even more beautiful is to be part of my youngest daughter's life again.

Life still has much to teach me. Over the ensuing years, Eve occasionally retreats, though fortunately not for long. She, too, finds my behaviour smothering–or controlling–at times; and occasionally I resort to anger as a form of defense. Old habits die hard, and when I dig in tenaciously and refuse to let go, she retreats into her own space which no longer welcomes me in my current train of thought.

During these times, I nurse my personal wounds, all the while being unknowingly honed of my rough spots by a daughter I know is worthy and, that above all, I do not want to lose. There is no regret. These lessons in life from my children are amongst the most valuable Life has to offer me.

The more I learn, the more my life improves in general. The whole experience is benign. They teach. I learn. By finding the wherewithal to let go, they return to me of their own free will. The end result: I progress on my journey. By no longer having unrealistic expectations of my children, I have discovered the value of the words "live and let live".

I am learning to love myself and be happy . . . and for this, I can largely thank my children.

The millennium heralds many changes for the better in my life. Apart from honouring my resolution to give up smoking, I have gradually left other bad habits behind me. I no longer have the need to use alcohol to blot out my problems. While I still enjoy an occasional drink, it is solely for the pleasure of savouring a glass of red wine before dinner, or of having a beer or a cocktail on a social occasion. I'm caring about myself considerably more than I did in the past and behaving more constructively. It's been a long, slow process but I've finally come to the conclusion I've suffered enough and there must be a better way of doing things.

As I conceive of a "better way", life suddenly becomes more co-operative in the form of "teachers" that appear, some simply books that appear to fall from the shelf, begging to be read. Although the progress continues to be painstakingly slow at times and I occasionally fall back a few paces, especially with my children, my lapses begin to happen less frequently as I grow more aware. The more I learn, the happier I become. The less I expect, the more I receive. Being the parent, I always expected my children to hear *me*. I realize I am finally hearing *them*, and by complying with their needs I am not losing pride. Rather, I am gaining a true sense of self. There is no longer a need for any of us to covertly manipulate each other in order to be heard. The relationship between us is no longer about pushing buttons.

By choosing love over ego, I am finally content.

DECEMBER 21, 2012, FRIDAY

I'm surprised to see Gary's older brother at home when Len and I drop in this morning.

"Hey, Jim," I greet him, "how come you're not in college?"

He gives me a big hug and, as usual, I feel dwarfed by his height of 6'5" at only sixteen. "I have a bad cold," he rasps hoarsely.

"Oh, no! Give me back my hug," I wail, as I step aside in mock horror. We both grin.

Gary trots down the stairs to greet us. He has now completed chemo and radiation, the latter which ended on October 19th. He now sports a full crop of dark brown hair, which he is wearing slightly on the long side. His new growth of eyelashes pleasingly shadows and enhances his sea-green eyes and his cheeks are suffused with a healthy glow. He and Jim are such fine-looking boys, and both loving kids with big hearts. I pray they go far in life.

Gary's in remission now and we remain positive and hopeful regarding a cure. Despite his increased fatigue and appetite loss–a foreseeable consequence of the months of aggressive treatment–he's gradually recuperating. Currently in the tenth grade, he'll continue to be tutored at home until he regains his former state of well-being.

He occasionally plays floor hockey in the church basement on Friday nights when energy permits, though this is the extent of his athletic endeavours for now. He has also begun composing some classical pieces on the piano which are dreamy and romantic and stir the soul. He has grown through this experience and it shows in his music.

In many ways, we have all grown.

Gary's illness has played a major role in motivating his parents to immortalize his musical gift, and he is currently perfecting some of his favourite classical pieces to incorporate on a CD. He will include a few of his own compositions, particularly the one that inspired him a few days after his last treatment when, sitting at the piano, he was overcome with the wistful, yet compelling thought: *I hope I live tomorrow.*

Today, as he plays this special piece for us and we become engulfed in a realm of glorious, melodious sound, we are unaware of the concept that led to its birth. As the brilliant clarity of the soulful chords penetrate my very depths, I am virtually mesmerized by the poignant almost prayerful notes that bespeak something deeply profound . . . which I'll later learn from Eve is Gary's divine supplication–*for life*.

Yet, within my heart I already perceive the piece is sacred.

"Surely, I've been listening to the angels. I have never heard anything more beautiful," I affirm through my tears. Len agrees.

"Have you a name for it?" I query.

"Yes," he says modestly. I am calling it, *"L'Espoir."*

The French word for *Hope*.

I think with gladness of the children in the oncology ward who may one day listen and be uplifted by the riveting voice of Gary's heart.

There are times we all need hope.

Eve and I leave shortly afterwards for the hairdresser. We then treat ourselves to lunch in a restaurant before doing some Christmas shopping.

Much later, on a routine visit to my naturopathic doctor, she mentions how pleased she is that I've been holding up so well.

"I only wish I were not such a late bloomer," I reply. "It has taken me years to regard all people and events in my life–both positive *and* negative–as a necessary part of my growth, my own sacred choice as aligned with God's own. That doesn't mean it's always easy to accept "what is", but I know that's because only God sees the whole picture, which I unquestioningly believe unfolds for the greater good."

"We both know your knowledge has arrived at exactly the right time for you personally, and that it will become a part of your future lives. You've often mentioned you would like to have been in a healing profession. It's very likely that this lifetime has been a preparation for you–a so-called bridge to your next life–and that you may well return as a healer."

Jen's words touch my heart with whimsy, and as I leave her office I perceive Life sprinkling me with the remembered fairy dust of bygone years when Miss Steel, my high school English teacher, assured me I would write a book one day.

Worthy plans for future lifetimes?

Who knows? I muse with a smile.

Chapter 21 – Beyond the Dream

*I cannot imagine a God
who punishes the objects of his creation
and is but a reflection of human frailty.*
—<u>Albert Einstein</u>

By the millennium, my life is perhaps more normal than it's ever been. Mentally and emotionally, I continue to thrive. Even my dosage of anti-depressant medication is relatively low.

I'm hoping that Len and I can eventually establish a closer relationship with our youngest son, Keith. He's done well in the intervening years, having attained a master's degree in religious studies. He's finally been back in touch but he rarely communicates with us. In many ways, it appears we're still estranged. I sometimes wonder if he has perhaps not fully forgiven us the wrongs of the past.

Even with forgiveness, the pain body—the accumulation of one's pain over the years, so aptly described by Eckhart Tolle in his book, *The Power of Now*—is probably one of the last things to dissolve on our journey. Ego gleefully hugs it to its bosom with no desire to let go. To this day when someone equates anxiety or depression with weakness and the need to pull up one's bootstraps, I'm apt to find myself momentarily in attack mode. On the positive side, I'm generally able to see my anger is misdirected and that the source of my pain lays with my father and to a degree my mother as well, when they made similar comments to me. This tells me there's yet an unhealed part of me which can be stimulated on occasion. Aware of this, I'm more able to apologize for lashing out when such comments are made in my presence.

People know not what they say.

We've also been reunited with our daughter, Merry. It's a joy to know that all of the children are back in our lives. We are perhaps not the perfect family, but surely there is no such thing. And despite the fact that the "sins of the fathers" may not have been forgiven in their entirety by the children, we are at least a family again.

Ken, my older son, is involved in his own spiritual search, and we've become very close, each encouraging the other on our respective journeys which have closely paralleled. He presents an interesting point when he concedes, "It's the rare parents who would *deliberately* hurt their children." The wisdom of this has helped me deal with my own forgiveness issues. It has also given me a clearer understanding of how it is love, not time, that heals *all* wounds. In forgiving others, we release the pain and anger which corrodes our own souls and this becomes the greatest gift we can give to our *selves.*

We learn in ACIM that once we stop judging one another, forgiveness itself will be obsolete; for we will know God's ultimate truth: There is nothing to forgive. We have chosen each and every one of our life's teachers, and those who seemingly hurt us are merely acting out our own choice to learn through unhappiness. So how can we deign to forgive them for the wrong they have done us when we should be applauding them for the gift they have given us out of love?

Meanwhile, I find that forgiveness of self and others, and even God, is a most effective way of beginning to let go of guilt, blame and judgment, the latter three which are the root of all evil (error).

In 2004, Eve becomes ill. She has a multitude of strange yet critical symptoms, and due to the rarity of her affliction it takes a few years before she's properly diagnosed with a mitochondrial disease.

"Mitochondria," she explains, "are the cell's power producers. They convert energy into forms which generate fuel for the cell's activities. So when they are not functioning properly it can affect the individual in various ways. In my particular case, it has affected me with seizures, mini-strokes, muscle weakness, digestive problems and a movement disorder, amongst other things. There's no actual cure to date. Consequently, each symptom is treated separately."

"What is the prognosis?" I inquire with trepidation.

"A lot depends on the severity and genetic mutation of the mitochondrial disease. Not enough headway has been made in the illness itself to make a definite prognosis in individual cases. Each person differs. Some patients can live a normal lifespan and others can have their lives seriously shortened. I'm suspected of having MELAS which has a poor prognosis."

Oh my God, I think silently, *my poor Eve! I pray they our wrong in their suspicions.*

Her symptoms are severe enough that she's forced to resign her position as hospital chaplain and director of pastoral care, the career of her dreams. She has to give up her driver's license as well. Who's to know the extent of the grief this has caused her? It's a personal thing she does not share. Eve, being Eve, remains stalwart, resolute, and uncomplaining as she counts her blessings and continues to make the best of the hand life has dealt her.

Her trials are not over. In the fall of 2007, shortly after Len and I return from a long-awaited holiday to visit our relatives in the UK, Eve's youngest son Gary and her husband become ill simultaneously. Phil's surgery for prostate cancer coincides with Gary's hospitalization for a myriad of strange symptoms which include ptosis (drooping eyelids).

It's discovered that Gary has inherited his mother's illness. He loves playing hockey but is often too fatigued to show up for a game. Fortunately, he's an extremely good stick-handler, and the coach makes allowances for his absences.

Despite their adversity, they're thankful to learn Phil's cancer is localized and his survival predictions are excellent. It's also welcome news when Gary is discharged from hospital and, despite his illness, they can move forward with their lives. Gary, who has been playing piano since age four and is a gifted musician, continues with his musical studies. He enters competitions yearly and wins many awards.

It's around this time that I immerse myself even more deeply in my spiritual studies. I seek answers to life's tragedies and especially the hardships and pain that beset so many of us. I begin amassing scores of books from various spiritual leaders, from the West and the East alike, all of which I avidly study. The bottom line of each rarely differs: Our world is illusory; only God is real.

I continue searching, until I find the book that literally turns my life around: *A Course in Miracles.* Each and every paragraph virtually *enwraps* me in *Absolute Love,* awakening my soul with distant memories of some long-forgotten time when I *knew* this Love and was *one* with it. In totality.

My heart knows beyond doubt that it is the voice of Jesus who speaks, and this book becomes my personal Bible. But unlike the Bible of my youth, it is egoless. Jesus speaks of the *only* reality there is: *Love.*

Jesus teaches us what our souls have always known: God is Absolute Love. He is not the vengeful, punishing God who advocates an eye for an eye; or visits sorrow upon us. The Bible, though divinely inspired, was interpreted by man who mistakenly conceived his own mentality (in the flesh), was that of the Father's; whereas "being made in God's image" pertains to the egoless love we are in "spirit."

We learn there are only two emotions: Fear and Love. In the Absolute, only Love exists. There are no opposites. Hell, like evil, is one of the many dualities within our dream of separateness. It is relative, not absolute—a part of the illusory darkness we sometimes encounter as we journey through the many lives—and spiritual stopovers in between incarnations—on our journey back to Love. It is solely within life's illusion that we experience the action and reaction of karma and reap what we've sown. Each soul knows what it needs to learn in order to awaken, and over the course of many lifetimes will experience both sides of the coin of good and evil.

By walking through the darkness where error leads us, we actively seek the Light which guides us to our sole purpose: returning to the Love that we are. That is our quest . . . in life after life. And God has ordained that no soul shall be left behind. The time will come when we'll all comprehend the ultimate truth of "loving God with all our hearts and our neighbour as our self"; at which time—in the knowledge we are all One—we will cease to judge or condemn. A simple lesson of itself, but one that is taking us eons to learn.

By moving toward Love, we draw ever closer to awakening from the dream.

By 2009, Len and I spend our first of four winters in Florida. While there, a few of our children manage to join us for a short holiday which is most welcome. In my quiet times, I continue to read and study. The most important thing in my life now is to emotionally connect with my Source.

My studies in Psychology reveal that separation anxiety begins with separating from one's parents. Yet, as Jesus explains in ACIM, this angst has existed within all of us at a much deeper level for eons. Somewhere, beyond our conscious awareness, lays the greatest anxiety of all: the perception that we've been separated from our Source. Our inner yearnings often leave us fearful, anxious and disconnected as we search for that perfect love in a multitude of ways—most often in ego attachments that leave us bereft of the genuine love we actually seek. It is usually our darkest hours that lead us to seek out the only Love that can truly complete us.

In June 2010 I attempt, not for the first time, to stop my antidepressants. As usual, after a few short months, I become exceedingly anxious and depressed. My daughter Dana suggests that a naturopathic doctor may help. She has now obtained her BSc degree, and a position in the government of Canada. She is also the mother of an adorable two-year-old son, Alex. She extols the mental and physical benefits of a natural lifestyle which sparks my interest and leads me to Jen and a whole new way of life.

It's now two and one-half years since I've taken an anti-depressant, or any other prescription drug. There has been no need. A healthier diet and lifestyle, along with vitamins and supplements, have made a big change in my life, and apart from the concern I've had over Gary I'm feeling better than I have in years, both mentally and physically.

Len, observing my state of well-being, decides to see Jen as well. He, too, is taking no prescription drugs and enjoying improved health, which at almost eighty-one years of age attests to the value of observing a healthier life style.

It seems that as we grow older the years accelerate. Len and I have grown considerably mellower. Winning a point no longer has the importance it did in the past. As *ACIM* reminds us: *What is more important—to be right, or to be happy?*

Although Len is not a reader and we don't share our journey in books, we are supportive of each other. He is my rock and his steady love has helped to keep me grounded. I know this applies in reverse. There is no doubt in my mind that Life's plan was for us to share these many years of our journey together.

My harrowing experience with mental illness was surely no accident either. Apart from being one of my greatest teachers, it played its own part in steadfastly anchoring me to exactly where Life intended me to be.

I do not regret it.

My very old and dear friend Leila remains in my life as a spiritual helpmate as well. Her own journey has been personally rewarding. She's able to contact her spirit guide and her angels at will, the latter which have been a source of help and solace to her during rough times in her life.

While a part of me sometimes yearns to be as spiritually in touch as my friend, I know we are all in different aspects of our journey and must trust that we are exactly where we are supposed to be within the grand scheme of things.

As I complete this memoir it is 2012, and the old year is fast drawing to an end. At this time, Len and I have a combined total of eight grandchildren and two great-grandchildren. We savour the joy of having shared a beautiful Christmas season with our family, and the most precious blessing of all: having Gary among us . . . in remission from his illness.

I know I have yet a long road to travel. Surely too long for my remaining years to encompass, or to fully annihilate the sleeping monster who, in my occasional dark moments, mockingly whispers that I'm a fragile, broken thing, a mental misfit who must never become too complacent lest the ground become fertile enough for *It* to one day pounce and overtake me again.

At such times I remind myself that *Humpty Dumpty* exists only in the dream and, that no matter what the future holds, I am God's beloved and invulnerable child. Perhaps destined to appear in subsequent dreams in future lifetimes; but eventually ordained to awaken from the illusion of the world itself.

And so the title of my memoirs is transformed from the pre-conceived *Humpty Dumpty* to *Beyond the Dream* by way of joyously heralding the magnificence that awaits us all.

I still have much work to do regarding ego, my dark side, often deemed as "the shadow". As yet, it is very much alive and well, but I've come to realize that the only hope of ever transcending it is by honouring it with love rather than guilt and shame. It is there for a purpose, and will remain as long as necessary. It too is a teacher, albeit of fear, and the only emotion that will overcome fear is love. For way too long I've treated it as an unwelcome guest, but I have finally understood the spiritual importance of welcoming *every* "guest" as a special guide.

I'm now more aware of ego when it kicks in. When I respond to a situation in an unloving way, Life itself seems to nudge me a cue that I've misstepped. The correction is often felt as a simple loss of joy which reminds me I've erred and to make amends, if able.

There are yet many hurdles to surmount before I can hope to speak solely from Love, and to achieve the true sense of connectedness with my Source I desire. But life is a work in progress; it is ongoing. Knowing that this illusion called life is not my true reality, but rather a dream we share collectively, I'll not lose sight of my goal.

Meanwhile, I'm in a better and more loving place. In a way, Life has come full circle . . . from Star's cancer, to Gary's; from the family's splitting to its knitting together. I seem to perceive more of the picture, or perhaps I merely see it differently because my vision is less clouded.

I'm especially grateful for the love and kindness of all the caring people that have touched and continue to touch my life. And, yes, even former foes; for I've no doubt the latter also came to me with valuable and loving lessons to impart.

And then there is Star . . . from whose fine noble spirit I've learned that the rain brings the flowers, and God did not desert me, not ever. I deserted Him. She was by far my greatest and most agonizing loss, but I now know her love will never leave me; that it is not *she*, but *Time*, that is ephemeral. And when Time ends, as it must, we will all come to know that the *only* emotion we *can* internalize is Love. For *Love is All That Is*—the *only* reality we will eventually return to . . . at which time we, like God, need only "imagine" our most beautiful moments to instantaneously relive them.

And finally, there is Jesus, my greatest guide of all, speaking to me with love, through *A Course in Miracles*.

In retrospect, I don't doubt that, on a psychological level, a fear of success held me back in many aspects of my life. My earliest beliefs had firmly established the fact that I was not a good person and I did not deserve to succeed.

So, why do I believe in myself enough to finish my book now—at seventy-one years of age? Perhaps the truth lies at a deeper level, and we must implicitly trust that all things happen when the time is right. Years ago, I had simply not reached this point in my path.

Life is so much more a journey of the soul than the ego. It is, nevertheless, the invalid suppositions of the latter that become our impetus to seek out the deeper truths of the former. Thus, we need both as teachers in order to complete us.

And, eventually, as our beliefs begin to change, we come to know that each and every one of us is part of God's heart, beloved and deserving.

We are the ageless, timeless, sons and daughters of Life, engaged in an eternal dance of Love.